The Complete Watercolorist's Essential Notebook

Gordon MacKenzie

NORTH LIGHT BOOKS
CINCINNATI, OHIO
www.artistsnetwork.com

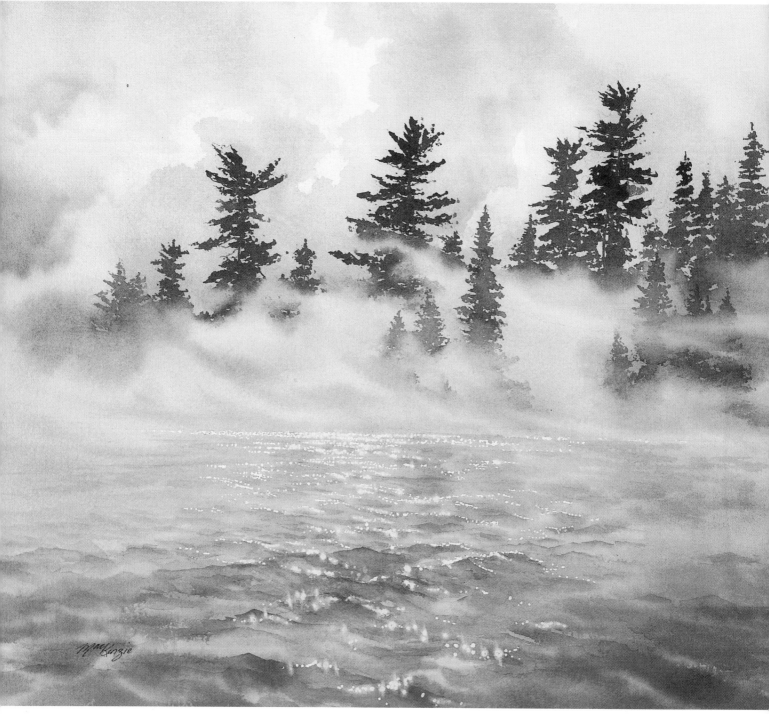

MORNING DIAMONDS
Watercolor on 300 lb. Arches medium cold-press paper,
19" x 22" (48cm x 56cm)
Collection of the artist
Photographer: Kevin Dobie, Kevanna Studios

The Watercolorist's Essential Notebook

Gordon MacKenzie

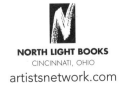

NORTH LIGHT BOOKS
CINCINNATI, OHIO
artistsnetwork.com

DEDICATION

This book is dedicated to the members of my family who gave up so much over the years so that I could pursue a painting career. I thank Jane, for her patience and understanding; Sandra, whose creative light fills my world; Michael, our oldest soul showing us the way; Barry, who keeps me in touch with nature; Cathie, who stabilizes her young family with love; and Rianne and Nicholas, our hope for the future. Also Don, an artist in wood; Pam, an artist in fabric; and Vera, who started it all by giving me my first paints.

ABOUT THE AUTHOR

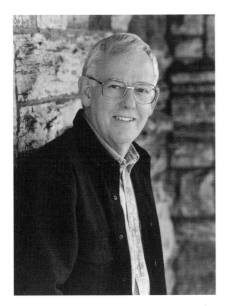

Gordon MacKenzie is a native of New Liskeard in northern Ontario. He now lives in Sault Ste. Marie, Ontario, where he maintains his painting and closeness to the outdoors. Even though the remoteness of northern Ontario precluded any formal art instruction, that same remoteness became the inspiration and driving force behind his work. His paintings reflect the emotional bond he has made with the natural world.

"An artist's work is a reflection of…the most significant aspects of their environment. Those perceptions are usually set at an early age, and for me it was the spirit of remote northern lakes and forests speaking in breathtaking images for the eye and timeless silence for the soul."

Gordon received his first formal art training at the Ontario College of Art while certifying as a visual arts specialist in education. Work in a variety of media followed, but none captured the transient and ethereal nature of the land as he saw it until the early 1970s when he switched to watercolors.

"The lively atmospherics and delicate transparencies of watercolors combined to present a whole new vision for me. Although my source was nature, I have always been more interested in capturing the essence of an experience than simply making a literal reproduction of a specific scene. Close contact with children and their art over the years has taught me much about the picture-making process. I've learned to use nature as a setting or stage on which to recreate and play out my memories and visions, much as children do in their work. It is these impressions from the heart that are hidden in my paint for those with kindred spirit and eye to experience."

Gordon has now retired after thirty-three years as a teacher and art consultant for the Sault Ste. Marie Board of Education. As a graduate of Laurentian University and specialist in art education, he has taught ministry of education and university-level art education courses for teachers for many years. With over twenty years of teaching private adult watercolor workshops as well, Gordon has earned a reputation as a first-class artist and instructor.

Gordon has had twenty-five solo watercolor shows in Canada and the U.S. and his work hangs in many private and corporate collections throughout Canada, the U.S., Europe, Africa and the Far East. He has found honors in several American shows, including that of the Detroit Institute of Art and the American Artist annual competition. He has been a successful participant in the last nineteen Buckhorn Art Festivals and his work has made the cover of *Readers Digest* in Canada, Switzerland, Finland, Australia and the U.S.

ACKNOWLEDGMENTS

The best way to learn something is to teach it, and the best way to teach is to learn from your students. With this in mind, I acknowledge all that I have learned over the years, both directly and indirectly, from my students. I also wish to recognize the many dear friends and colleagues whose support and direction has been invaluable to the production of this book.

And a special thanks to Jack Reid who first directed me to North Light Fine Art Books; Rachel Wolf, acquisitions editor, who made the opportunity happen; and Pam Wissman, editor, who always offered words of encouragement and sound advice all along the way.

TABLE OF CONTENTS

INTRODUCTION . . .9

 Tools of the Trade...10

WATERCOLORS . . . 11
  Transparent, Semitransparent or Opaque
  Staining, Low-Staining or Nonstaining
  Saturated or Unsaturated
  Permanent or Fugitive
  Flow
  Paint Characteristic Groups
  Differences Between Paints
  Check the Label
  Pigments by the Numbers
  Colors to Watch Out For

BRUSHES . . . 18
  Recommended Brush Types and Sizes
  Natural Bristle or Hair Brushes
  Kolinsky Red Sable
  Red and Pure Sable
  Hog or Boar Bristle
  Ox Hair
  Sabeline
  Camel Hair
  Badger
  Goat Hair
  Synthetic Bristles

PAPER . . . 21
  The Best Paper
  Handmade Paper
  Mouldmade Paper
  Machine-Made Paper
  Paper Texture
  Paper Weight
  Common Paper Weights
  Step by Step: Stretching Paper

PALETTES . . . 24
  Arranging Your Colors
  Your Palette's Physical Characteristics
  Step by Step: Do-it-Yourself Palette

PALETTE KNIVES . . . 28
  Step by Step: Cleaning Your Palette Knife

PAINTING SPONGES . . . 29
  Step by Step: Making Painting Sponges

MASKING MATERIALS . . . 30
  Liquid Latex
  Some Dos and Don'ts When Using Masking Fluid
  Masking With Tapes

 Painting Techniques...32

PAINTING WITH BRUSHES . . . 33
  Round Brush Techniques
  Flat Brush Techniques

PAINTING WITH A PALETTE KNIFE . . . 38

PAINTING WITH STICKS . . . 39

PAINTING WITH A SPONGE . . . 40
  Getting Paint on the Sponge
  Building Shapes With a Sponge
  The Big Payoff
  Examples of Sponge Painting

HOW PAINTS INTERACT WITH WATER . . . 43
  The Law You Cannot Ignore

MASTERING WASHES AND GLAZES . . . 44
  Laying on a Graded Wash
  Glazing

FADING OUT A COLOR . . . 46
  Brushes for Fading Out
  An Alternative Method of Fading Out Color

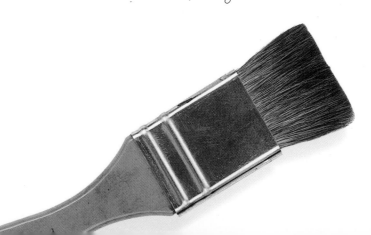

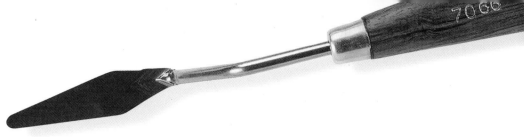

WORKING WET-IN-WET . . . 48
    Options for Wetting the Paper
    Options for Adding Paint
    Sustaining the Wet-in-Wet Process

MASKING . . . 54
    Using Liquid Latex
    Step by Step: Multiple Masking
    Masking Tape
    Packing Tape
    Step by Step: Masking With Tape

A MIX OF TECHNIQUES . . . 62

3 Putting Together Your Composition...64

FACTORS TO CONSIDER . . . 65
    Subject
    Center of Interest
    Picture Format
    Closure
    Shapes
    Negative Painting
    Step by Step: Flowers With Negative Painting
    Step by Step: Rocks With Negative Painting
    Step by Step: Hills With Negative Painting
    Lines and Edges of Shapes
    Classifying Shapes
    Shapes Often Suggest a Direction
    Repetition, Pattern and Rhythm of Shapes
    Leading the Eye With Shapes and Edges
    Movement
    Values
    Step by Step: Seeing and Recording Values
    Step by Step: Painting Light and Shadow on Foliage
    Color and the Color Wheel
    Setting Up Your Palette
    Color Harmony and Contrast
    Color Schemes
    Triads
    A Simple Principle for Clean, Brilliant Results
    Gradation

WAYS TO APPROACH COMPOSITION . . . 106
    Approach One: Working From Real to "Abstract"
    Keep Options Open When Using References
    What Grabs Your Attention?
    How Are Visual Elements Arranged?
    Sketch Various Ideas for Compositions
    Hold Your Horses
    Approach Two: Working From "Abstract" to Real
    Develop Arrangements in Thumbnail Sketches
    What Could it Be?
    Experiment With Re-Drawing Your Sketches
    Work Sketches Into Real Subjects
    Research for Detail and Accuracy
    Approach Three: Working From Memory and Imagination
    Quickly Make a Thumbnail Sketch
    Sketch Compositional Variations and Details

DEVELOPING A SERIES OF PAINTINGS . . . 124

INTUITION VS. PLANNING . . . 128
    Intuition
    Pursuing the Voice From Within
    Physical and Mental Blocks to Spontaneity
    The Smell of Fear
    Where Are You Going?
    Planning Keeps You in Control
    Stay Open to Possibilities
    Realism
    Developing a Style

TO SAVE OR NOT TO SAVE . . . 134
    Analyzing the Problem
    Making Changes—First, the Bad News...
    ...Now the Good News
    Problem: Run Backs and Hard Edges
    Problem: Incorrect or Ineffective Values
    Problem: No Particular Mood is Evident
    Problem: Focal Point Hard to Find
    Problem: Highlight or Dark Detailing Missing
    Problem: Misplaced Looseness
    Problem: Paint Splatters
    Problem: Small Paint Dots

GALLERY . . . 138

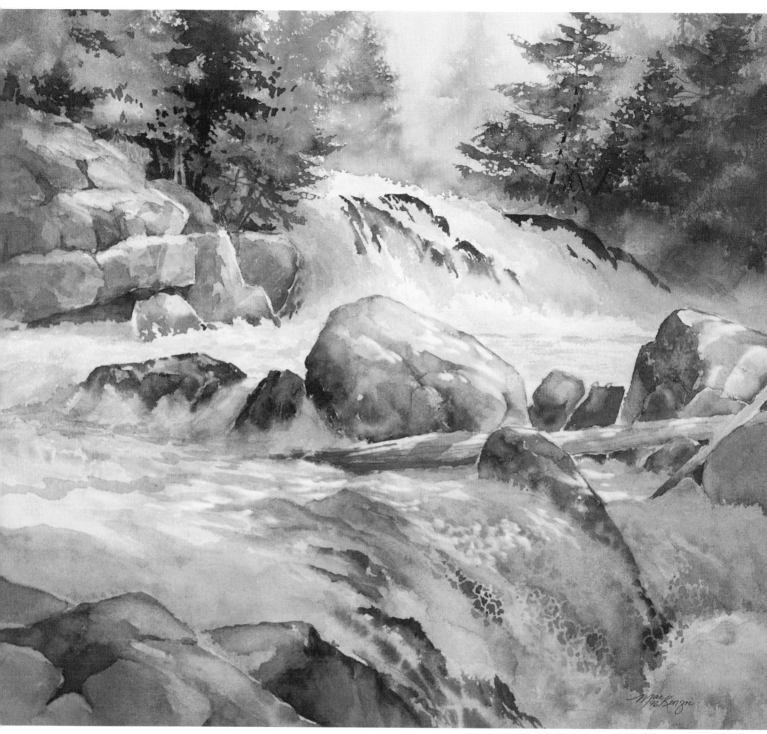

RENEWAL
Watercolor on 300 lb. Arches medium cold-press paper,
19" x 22" (48cm x 56cm)
Collection of the artist
Photographer: Kevin Dobie, Kevanna Studios

INTRODUCTION

Who you are and what you treasure most are found within you. As an artist your work is a visible means of reflecting those personal values and feelings through images of a particular place, experience or vision. No matter what level of technical virtuosity is applied, the primary objective of a true artist is always to go beyond a literal translation of the subject and communicate something that speaks of his or her unique inner self. Watercolors are an excellent vehicle for that expression.

However, a word of caution: Watercolors are not for the faint-of-heart but for those willing to explore and experiment, knowing that they risk failure, knowing that each piece of paper will not end as a "masterpiece." Nor are they recommended for those who are unwilling to relinquish the role of "master" so that they can become, instead, a "partner" in the process.

In this medium you must be willing to play the role of both patient director and alert stagehand, while the pigment and water are free to perform their magic. Try to push this medium around, and it quickly loses it charm, its transparent radiance and its life. If you already paint with watercolor then you probably know how important it is to remain open to its whimsical nature and the momentary opportunities that it offers along the way. Watercolor is a medium of countless options but few second chances.

Having said this, I should also mention the rewards of working with watercolor, chief among them being its depth. So long as you remain open to its nature, this medium will entertain you for a lifetime. There seems no end to what you can learn from and about watercolors. Those who have spent decades with it can testify how they are continually charmed and amazed by new discoveries every time they put paint to paper.

This is a medium designed to push you to your limits. So long as you keep rising to its challenges, it will keep opening doors on others. In time watercolor will become a reflection of you and your personality. Not only are your physical skills displayed, but also the style and vitality of your inner growth.

This book is based on the handouts I've produced over the years to meet the needs of students in numerous watercolor workshops. These materials were developed to clarify and simplify various aspects of the painting process, while at the same time challenging students with new possibilities. However, unlike a book of rules that tend to close our minds, this is a collection of principles, concepts and general information designed to expand the creative process. As you will see, much of this material is based on common sense, visual perception and your own innate sense of design. You will find here the basic information on tools, techniques and composition that will serve you well as either a reference or a basic foundation for your watercolor painting process.

One last thought before you begin your journey through this book: In my workshops it never fails to amaze me how people will travel great distances, pay out hard-earned cash for materials and instruction, and put up with crowded conditions just so they can study the effects of drying water. Along with a little pigment and manipulation, that's about all that's happening with watercolor. Think about it. This, the simplest of nature's processes, has been the catalyst that has filled us with wonder and challenged our imagination and ingenuity for many years. The results have been some of the most stunning expressions of mankind's creativity ever. This book is your invitation to join the magic world of watercolor.

1 Tools of the Trade

Selecting proper tools and materials for watercolors has a profound effect on the results you get. Notice that I said "proper," not "most expensive." There is a difference between buying the most expensive supplies and purchasing appropriate supplies that perform to the highest level, suit your needs and fit your budget. For example, not all paint brands cost the same. However, some colors can be of equal quality—see pages 14–17. On the other hand, buying cheap paper is only false economy. These are the kinds of things I will discuss in this part of the book, to prepare you for the next time you head for the art store. By the way, while you are out, you may want to stop at the hardware store. You will need some utility sponges and packing tape as well. What you will need for watercolors is often found in unusual places.

Watercolors

Watercolors come in tubes, cakes (pans), liquid and pencils. I discuss tube paints in this book.

Watercolors consist of finely ground pigments mixed with gum arabic, glycerin and a wetting agent. The gum arabic and glycerin allow the pigments to adhere smoothly to the paper when being thinned with water, while the wetting agent makes the paint flow evenly when diluted.

It's easy to become confused with terminology when buying watercolors. One hears about staining and nonstaining colors and wonders what the importance is. We wonder why so-called "transparent watercolors" are actually opaque. Are unsaturated colors better for a painting than saturated? From where did those fugitive colors escape, and who is chasing them anyway? Add to this the exotic manufacturer names used for colors, and it's no wonder there is confusion.

Following are the terms used in describing any watercolor paint. Understanding these characteristics is important to the results you will get.

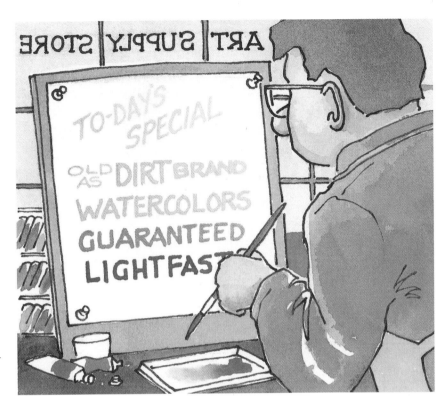

CHOOSE COLORS WISELY

Buy new colors based on their characteristics. You will be building a palette of better quality paints that have come from a variety of manufacturers. Since mixing is the name of the game, you do not have to buy every color offered. You can mix most of what you need from surprisingly few basic primary colors. Warm and cool versions of each of the primaries—red, yellow and blue—plus a few unsaturated colors are all you need. See "Setting Up Your Palette" on page 96.

TRANSPARENT, SEMITRANSPARENT OR OPAQUE

The amount of light that passes through a color, bounces off the white paper below and reflects back to the viewer's eye determines the color's luminosity (appearance of a glow under its surface). You can see the white of the paper through transparent colors. The more nearly opaque a color is, the less luminous the results, because opaque colors do not allow light to pass through them. Thinning an opaque color with water can make it more transparent, but then it loses its intensity. If you plan to build layers of paint to achieve a desired color effect, it may be best to use transparent and semitransparent colors.

STAINING, LOW-STAINING OR NONSTAINING

This characteristic has a bearing on some techniques you may wish to perform. For example, if you wish to lift paint by scrubbing, it would be wise to use a nonstaining color.

On the other hand, if you wish to have color show through when you push paint back with a knife, lift it with a brush or use salt; then use a stainer.

SATURATED OR UNSATURATED

The term *saturated* refers to the degree of vividness of a hue. Saturated colors are those closest to the pure colors in the spectrum (see the color wheel on page 95), for example, Cobalt Blue, Cadmium Red and Lemon Yellow.

Unsaturated colors are those not found on the color wheel but that are nevertheless useful—for example, Burnt Sienna, Raw Umber and Indigo. If a color is not seen in a rainbow, it is unsaturated.

PERMANENT OR FUGITIVE

The durability of a pigment is irrelevant if you are producing something with a short life span, such as a poster, newspaper advertisement or magazine. However, in watercolors we want pigments that will survive beyond our own life span. Stable colors will not deteriorate over time under normal conditions of light and humidity. Fugitive colors will deteriorate (fade, darken or shift color) because their pigments are not chemically stable. There is no need to use fugitive colors when permanent alternatives exist. Since there are still unreliable colors on the market, you have to be on guard when you select colors. The chart "Summary of Paint Characteristics and Quality" on pages 14–15 indicates reliable colors.

FLOW

Flow is the degree to which a pigment moves on a wet surface. Flow depends on the type of pigment used (organic, mineral, chemical or dye), how finely it is ground (manufacturing process) and whether or not the paint contains fillers or neutrals (e.g., white and black). White, as an additive, will slow a pigment to a crawl. Generally the more transparent a pigment, the better it flows. Only experimentation will tell you what your paints will do.

Flow is important when you want colors to "explode" on your paper or you wish to fade out an edge of a painted area (see page 46)—for example, painting fog.

PAINT CHARACTERISTIC GROUPS

A color's staining ability and degree of transparency most greatly influence the results you get. Please remember that the characteristics of the colors shown here may vary by manufacturer. Note that groups 1 to 4 contain saturated colors.

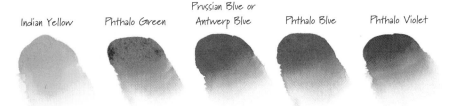

Indian Yellow · Phthalo Green · Prussian Blue or Antwerp Blue · Phthalo Blue · Phthalo Violet

GROUP 1—STAINING, TRANSPARENT COLORS

Pigments are bold and intense. They can easily overpower other nonstaining colors when mixed. They have maximum flow but are hard to move once set. They are good for layering and glazing (laying down a transparent layer of paint over an underpainting). Because they are transparent, they will not produce mud when mixed with other transparent colors. Mixed full strength, they produce rich colorful darks. Salt and water blossoms leave a stained mark.

GROUP 2—NONSTAINING, TRANSPARENT COLORS

Pigments are delicate and wipe back easily. Their transparency makes them excellent for glazing, layering and mixing of transparent grays from the primaries. Salt and water blossoms leave white marks. Flow is good.

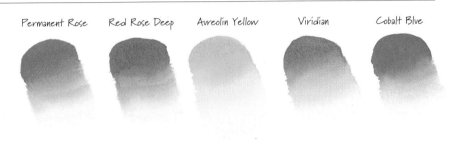

Permanent Rose · Red Rose Deep · Aureolin Yellow · Viridian · Cobalt Blue

GROUP 3—LOW-STAINING, TRANSPARENT TO SEMITRANSPARENT COLORS

Pigment intensity is average. Wiping back, scraping, salt and water blossoms work well but leave a slightly stained mark. Flow is average.

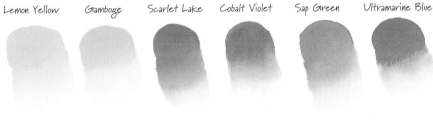

Lemon Yellow · Gamboge · Scarlet Lake · Cobalt Violet · Sap Green · Ultramarine Blue

GROUP 4—LOW-STAINING, SEMIOPAQUE COLORS

Pigment intensity is average. These colors are most luminous in washed or diluted form. However, opaque colors can create mud if they are overmixed with too many other colors. Wiping back, scraping, salt and water blossoms work well but may leave slight color. These colors have the lowest rate of flow.

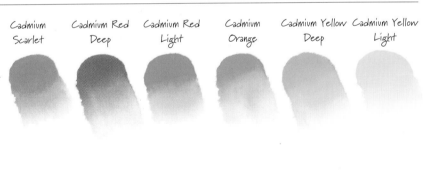

Cadmium Scarlet · Cadmium Red Deep · Cadmium Red Light · Cadmium Orange · Cadmium Yellow Deep · Cadmium Yellow Light

GROUP 5—UNSATURATED COLORS, MOSTLY LOW-STAINING, TRANSPARENT TO OPAQUE COLORS

Pigments have low intensity. Warm colors are usually earth oxide based. Low-Staining of most colors allows for easy wipe back, water blossoms and scraping. Blackened colors often stain. Opaque and semiopaque colors always have the danger of adding muddiness to a mixture. Flow varies.

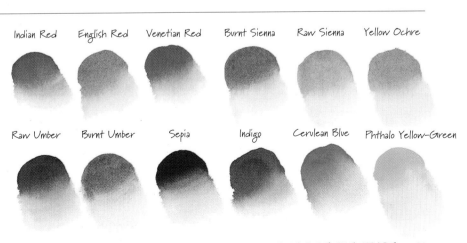

Indian Red · English Red · Venetian Red · Burnt Sienna · Raw Sienna · Yellow Ochre

Raw Umber · Burnt Umber · Sepia · Indigo · Cerulean Blue · Phthalo Yellow-Green

DIFFERENCES BETWEEN PAINTS

Those paint manufacturers with vested interests like to tell artists that one brand of paint will not mix well with another, or, for best results, you should stick to only one brand, preferably theirs. This is nothing but hogwash. This is like saying that we should eat only one brand of food because if we mix brands it might make us sick. The pigments are the same no matter who uses them to make paint. Differences arise in how much pigment a manufacturer uses, how well it's processed, and the type of binders and fillers added. These factors will influence individual performance but not compatibility between brands.

SUMMARY OF PAINT CHARACTERISTICS AND QUALITY
according to ASTM standards

CHARACTERISTICS

HUE	TEMP	TRADE NAME	transparent	semitransparent	opaque	staining	low-staining
yellow	COOL	Cadmium Yellow Light (Pale, Lemon)			•		•
yellow	COOL	Yellow (Hansa)		•			•
yellow	MED	Aureolin	•				•
yellow	MED	Indian Yellow	•			•	
orange	WARM	Cadmium Yellow Deep			•		•
orange	WARM	Gamboge		•			•
orange	VARIES	Cadmium Orange			•		•
red	WARM	Cadmium Red Light (Pale)			•		varies
red	WARM	Cadmium Red			•		•
red	WARM	Cadmium Red Deep			•		•
red	MED	Cadmium Scarlet, Scarlet Lake		•			•
red	COOL	PV 19- (Phthalo Crimson, Phthalo Red, Ruby Red, Red Rose Deep, Quinacridone, Permanent Rose)	•				•
violet	COOL	Cobalt Violet			•		•
violet	WARM	Phthalo Violet, Permanent Magenta, Bayeaux Violet	•			•	
blue	WARM	Ultramarine Blue	•				•
blue	MED	Cobalt Blue	•				•
blue	COOL	Phthalo Blue PB15 (Winsor, Intense, Helio, Hoggar, Monestial, Rembrandt, Cyanine, Hortensia, Primary)	•			•	
blue	COOL	Cerulean Blue			•		•
blue	COOL	Prussian (Antwerp, Paris)	•			•	
green	COOL	Viridian	•				•
green	COOL	Phthalo Green PG7 (Winsor, Intense, Armor, Helio, Cyanine, Genuine Deep, Holbein Viridian, Monestial)	•			•	
green	MED	Hooker's Green		•			•
green	WARM	Sap Green		•			varies
green	COOL	Indigo (Burnt Sienna + Ultramarine Blue)		•			varies
unsaturated oxides, low-intensity colors	WARM	Burnt Sienna (Dark Orange)	•				•
unsaturated oxides, low-intensity colors	WARM	Burnt Umber (Dark Yellow Brown)		•		•	
unsaturated oxides, low-intensity colors	WARM	Yellow Ochre (Light Yellow Brown)			•		•
unsaturated oxides, low-intensity colors	WARM	Raw Sienna (Light Yellow Brown)		•			•
unsaturated oxides, low-intensity colors	COOL	Raw Umber (Medium Yellow Brown)		•			•
unsaturated oxides, low-intensity colors	WARM	English Red (Yellow to Violet Brown)			•		•
unsaturated oxides, low-intensity colors	WARM	Light Red (Light Reddish Brown)			•		•
unsaturated oxides, low-intensity colors	WARM	Indian Red (Reddish Brown)			•		•
unsaturated oxides, low-intensity colors	WARM	Venetian Red (Dark Reddish Brown)			•		•
unsaturated oxides, low-intensity colors	VARIES	Sepia (Black + Brown)			•		varies

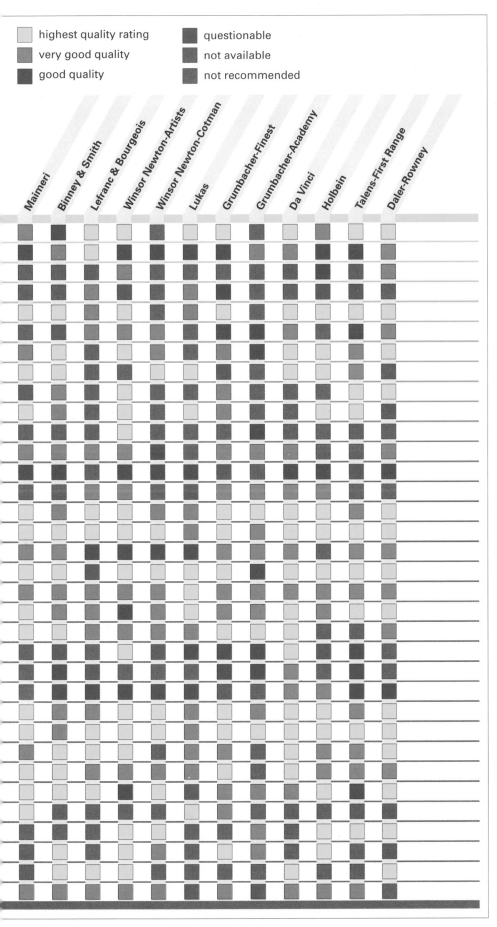

For your assistance, the following chart offers the characteristics and quality ratings of a range of commonly used colors. I have omitted many colors because they are unique to one manufacturer. On these pages you will also find pigment number charts that can be of value to you in finding the best quality paints.

Legend:
- highest quality rating
- very good quality
- good quality
- questionable
- not available
- not recommended

CHECK THE LABEL

More and more people are buying their food according to the ingredients on the package and not just the brand name. We must also start looking at the ingredients or pigments used to make our paints.

Trade names for tube colors (such as Winsor Blue, Red Rose Deep or Sahara Yellow) do not tell us much about what ingredients or pigments make up the paint. Winsor Blue, Hoggar Blue, Helio Blue, Brilliant Blue and Speedball Blue all contain exactly the same pigment—Phthalocyanine Blue, or Phthalo Blue for short. Since more and more manufacturers are indicating the pigments on their labels, we should be buying our colors according to those pigments and not just the trade names.

Studies—such as *The Wilcox Guide to the Best Watercolor Paints* (Artways, 1991) and Hilary Page's *Guide to Watercolor Paints* (Watson-Guptill, 1991)—have prompted manufacturers to offer more reliable paints. By listing the pigments on their labels, either by name or number, they are trying to show that quality is also one of the ingredients.

Research shows that there are many excellent quality paints. There is no need to use inferior types. The good news is that there is usually no price difference. Look for an American Society of Testing and Materials (ASTM) rating on the label. Get to know reliable pigment names and numbers. I would go so far as to suggest using only those brands that do tell what is in the tube.

PIGMENTS BY THE NUMBERS

Each of the pigments used in the manufacture of paint has an assigned number, and it's a good thing. It's a lot easier to remember and to say "PY154" than "Benzimidazolone Yellow H3G." You don't have to remember a lot of chemical names, just the numbers that represent them. Since pigments are not all created equal, in that some are more durable or lightfast than others, we need to know which are the good guys and which are the bad. We can do this by the numbers because many manufacturers are now putting them on their labels. The chart here contains the most common pigments (by number) used in watercolor paints. If paint contains a bad pigment and a good one, the bad pigment will always reduce the quality of the paint.

HUE	PIGMENTS TO AVOID	RELIABLE PIGMENTS
yellow	PY1, PY1:1, PY24, PY34, and NY55 are the most common offenders.	PY3, PY35, PY37, PY40, PY42, PY43, PY53, PY97, PY153
orange	PO1, PO13, PO34	All other Pigment Orange numbers (i.e., PO20, PO20:1, PO36, PO43, PO49, PO62)
red	Every Pigment Red number below 100, except PR5, PR6, PR7, PR9, PR48:4 and PR88MRS	Every Pigment Red number above 100, except PR105, PR106, PR112, PR122, PR146, PR173, PR177, PR181
violet	PV1, PV2, PV3, PV4, PV5:1 PV23BS, PV23RS, PV39	All other Pigment Violet numbers (i.e., PV14, PV15, PV16, PV19, PV46, PV49)
blue	PB1, PB24, PB66	All other Pigment Blue numbers (i.e., PB15, PB15:1, PG17, PB27, PB28, PB29, PB33, PB35, PB36, PB60)
green	PG1, PG2, PG8, PG12	All other Pigment Green numbers (i.e., PG7, PG10, PG17, PG18, PG19, PG23, PG36, PG50)
brown	NBr8, PBr8, PBr24	All other Pigment Brown numbers (i.e., PBr6, PBr7)

RELIABLE OR UNRELIABLE?
Unfortunately some watercolors still contain unreliable pigments. Fortunately more and more manufacturers are putting pigment numbers on their labels.

TRADE NAME	OFFENDING PIGMENTS That Would Compromise Paint Quality			
Alizarin Crimson, **Alizarin Madder,** **Madder Lake,** **Rose Madder,** **Brown Madder,** **Carmine or any other** **combination of these names**	NR4- NR9- PR83- PR83:1- PR181-	Carmine Natural Red Rose Madder Natural Red Rose Madder Alizarin Alizarin Crimson Thioindigoid Magenta	PR83:1- PR106- PO34- PY1-	Alizarin Crimson Vermilion Dairylide Orange Arylide Yellow
Crimson Lake, **Scarlet,** **Vermilion or any other** **combination of these names**	PR4- PR23- PR48:1- PR48:2- PR48:4-	Chlorinated Para Red Naphthol Red Permanent Red 2B (barium) Permanent Red 2B (calcium) Permanent Red 2B (manganese)		
Van Dyke Brown	NBr8-	Van Dyke Brown		
Chrome Yellow	PY34-	Chrome Yellow Lemon		
Gamboge	PY1- NY24-	Arylide Yellow Gamboge	PO1-	Hansa Orange
Hooker's Green or Sap Green	PG8- PG12-	Hooker's Green Green	PY1- PY100-	Arylide Yellow Tartrazine Lake

UNRELIABLE PIGMENTS
Do your favorite colors contain unreliable pigments? Here are the pigments that could jeopardize the quality of some common colors.

COLORS TO WATCH OUT FOR

The popular colors above have earned red flags beside their names because they often contain fugitive pigments. This is not to say that all makes of paint that carry these names are undesirable. Because of the popularity of many of these colors and the desire to produce a quality product, some manufacturers now produce them with more durable pigments. Only the ones containing the indicated pigments have questionable durability. Read the labels.

Brushes

Whether made from natural fibers, synthetic fibers or a blend, your brush is a major factor in the success you have with watercolors.

However, if you are like most people, you might find the array of brushes available in art supply stores a bit baffling. Many artists have purchased brushes that they have not yet figured out uses for, and many have bought brushes that did not meet expectations.

As a rule, the performance of a brush matches the price you pay for it, but remember that the price range varies with the type of bristle used. A cheap sable is still far more expensive than a top-of-the-line hog hair. The purpose of this section is to explain the basic characteristics of brushes so you can make a more informed choice the next time you are in the market for one.

RECOMMENDED BRUSH TYPES AND SIZES

As with any tool, you select your brushes according to the jobs you want them to perform. For a particular painting, we select our brushes according to how we want to handle each area or phase of the work. Each function requires a different brush, and the right brush, if you hope to achieve the desired results. Every artist has his or her own selection of favorite brushes, and you will undoubtedly develop your own. Here are some basic types that will allow you to perform a wide range of painting functions.

NATURAL BRISTLE OR HAIR BRUSHES

Down through history, humans have made brushes from all types of plant and animal fiber. Fur or hair has won the popularity contest (unfortunately for the animals). Each type of

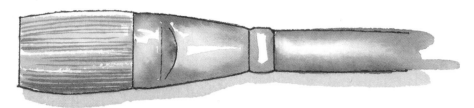

¾-INCH FLAT STROKE BRUSH
In a synthetic or synthetic mix, this brush has extra-long bristles that add great flexibility and range of use.

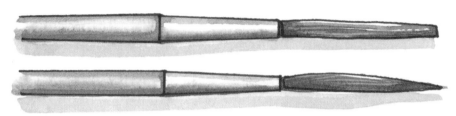

RIGGER OR SCRIPT BRUSHES
These have long, thin bristles, synthetic or blend, that come to a point. They come in various sizes. Similar small stroke brushes have a squared end. They produce fine lines of consistent width.

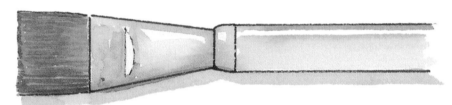

1-INCH SYNTHETIC FLAT
Look for brushes with bristles that have snap. Though the brush shown here does not carry much paint, the beveled clear acrylic handle makes sharp-edged strokes. When your paint is still damp, you can use the edge of the handle to remove paint and make fine lines. This brush is also good for drybrushing, wood grain, fabric, etc.

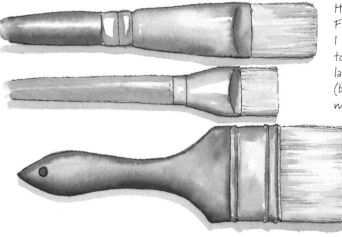

HOG HAIR FLATS
I recommend ¾- to 2-inch, or larger, hog hair (bristle) flat, stiff wash brushes.

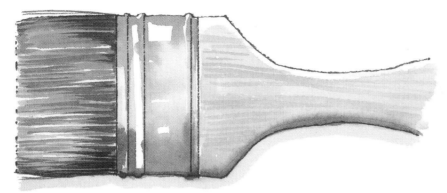

1½– TO 2-INCH OX HAIR WASH BRUSH
Very springy, this brush carries a great load of paint. It is not as rough as a hog hair brush.

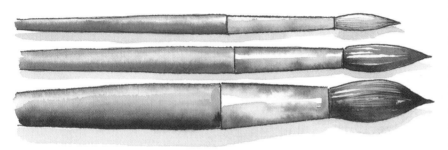

ROUNDS
I recommend nos. 4, 6, 8, 10 and 14 rounds made from sable, synthetic or a synthetic and natural blend. It is wise to have a selection of these all-purpose brushes.

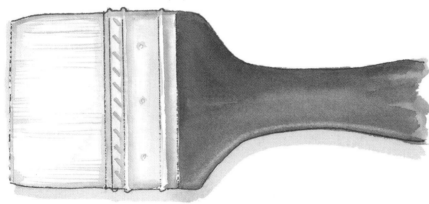

1½-INCH TO 2-INCH SYNTHETIC WASH BRUSH
Bristles may be white to red-brown, depending on the type of fiber used. They have excellent handling qualities. They make a very precise, hard-edged stroke that is great for positive and negative painting.

fiber produces a brush with a unique feel and handling characteristics.

The factors setting natural brushes apart from synthetic brushes are their overall durability, their ability to hold a lot of liquid, and their ability to release that liquid slowly and evenly. These features are due, in no small part, to the tapered ends of natural hairs. In some cases, natural hairs are also "flagged" (split ends).

Natural bristles vary greatly in their stiffness, particularly when wet. *Snap* is a brush's ability to spring back to its original shape when wet. Most painters favor brushes with snap, because they give far better control than brushes that bend and remain bent. However, it is not a matter of finding the stiffest brush. What most artists want is a brush with a combination of snap and flexibility, a blend of smoothness and sensitivity that makes the application of paint an effortless process.

KOLINSKY RED SABLE
Kolinsky red sable is the most valuable soft-brush hair, characterized by its strength, thickness, spring and fine point. The hair comes from the tails of Siberian martens (mammals related to the weasel).

RED AND PURE SABLE
Red and pure *sable* brushes are not as fine or springy as *kolinsky*, nor as expensive, but they make fine watercolor brushes. Hair comes from Asian (and probably North American) red martens.

OX HAIR
Often used in blends, *ox hair* bristles have strength and springiness and hold a fine point, but they cannot compare with red sable. Ox hair brushes range in color from white to black.

SABELINE
Made from the finest ox hairs dyed to resemble red sable, *sabeline* brushes are less expensive than sable, but sabeline produces only a mediocre brush.

CAMEL HAIR
Camel hair is a trade term that refers to a whole range of hairs that vary greatly in softness and performance. It could be squirrel, goat, pony, bear, sheep, monkey, etc., or a blend of these—whatever happens to be lying around, which is a good reason to avoid these brushes.

BADGER
Often used in blends, particularly in flat brushes, *badger hair* strikes a

good balance between the softness of red sable and the resilience of China bristle.

GOAT HAIR

Goat hair bristle is common in oriental brushes called hakes. They are very soft and hold a lot of liquid but lack the snap and control of a China (Hog) bristle, which it is often mistaken for.

HOG (CHINA) BRISTLE

The bristles of these brushes range in color from pure white to tan. They are stiff, have the capacity to carry a good amount of paint and water, and are relatively low cost. The white to platinum blonde bristles—called China bristles—are the best.

Hog bristle brushes are real workhorses that can scrub up color, and yet, by using the side of the brush, you can produce wonderfully loose, irregular marks that other brushes cannot imitate. The bristles are stiff when dry but develop a suppleness when wet. Be aware, however, that there is a tremendous range in the quality (and price) of hog hair brushes

The word *bristle* is a broad reference to any type of fiber used to make the hairy end of your brush—for example, "My brush has synthetic bristles." However, *bristle* can also refer to brushes made from hog or boar hair. Do not buy the black ones that some dealers call "bristle brushes." They are invariably coarse synthetic types that do not work well. See "Painting With Brushes" on page 33.

Unfortunately, good flat hog hair *wash* brushes are not always that easy to find. Art stores do not usually put them with watercolor brushes, but either by themselves, as gesso or mural brushes, or acrylic brushes (large flat acrylic brushes with hog bristles are excellent for watercolor).

You can tell if you are buying a good hog hair brush by spreading the bristles apart and looking

between them. If you can see the wood of the handle, do not buy the brush. On the other hand, if you see solid bristles, chances are you have a good one. The diagram here illustrates how the construction of hog hair brushes (and some cheaper synthetic wash brushes) influences their performance.

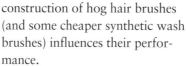

If you cannot find hog hair brushes in your art supply store, try your craft, hardware, building supply and cookware stores as well. These brushes show up in the oddest places and as many things, such as student tempera paint brushes, disposable paint and varnish brushes, basting brushes, etc.

Do not confuse hog or boar bristle brushes with *hake* brushes. Hake brushes are also flat blonde-colored brushes. The hake is a fine natural-fiber (goat) brush but lacks the snap of a hog hair. Beware of the cheap disposable types with inferior construction and poorly assembled bristles that look like a witch's broom when wet.

SYNTHETIC BRISTLES

Synthetic brushes have become very popular because of their price and handling ability, but we must remember that these also can vary in performance, depending on the construction and quality of filament used. Synthetic brushes usually have good snap and fine points, which give the artist a fair amount of satisfaction and control. However, the major drawback to pure synthetic brushes has always been their inability to hold as much liquid and release it as consistently as the natural fibers. The smoothness of the bristle surface

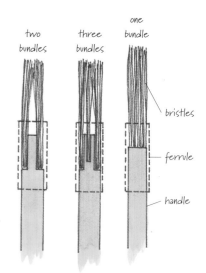

If you can see the wooden handle when you spread the bristles, it's a sign of inferior construction. Do not buy it.

Side view of handle

CONSTRUCTION OF HOG HAIR WASH BRUSHES
The cheaper, most inferior types have two and sometimes three separate bundles of bristles fastened to the side and middle of the handle. These brushes look fine until wet, when individual bundles of hairs separate, making painting almost impossible. A single bundle of bristles at the butt end of the handle makes the best brush, with all bristles held with glue and a ferrule (the part of a brush holding the hairs or bristles).

and the lack of taper in the fiber allow the liquid to slide off synthetics more readily than natural fibers. Manufacturers have developed finer, more tapered or flagged fibers.

Synthetic fibers also tend to break more easily than natural types. The result is that your synthetic brushes, particularly rounds, may lose their point faster than an equivalent natural brush, particularly if you do a lot of rough brush work. You can also lose the tip on your synthetic brush by jamming it onto the bottom of your water container when cleaning it. It's best to clean one of these brushes by rolling it on the inside of the water container.

Paper

Choosing cheap paper is a big mistake. Many students try new techniques with the best brushes and most expensive paint, only to fail because they are working on cheap paper. Unfortunately, they think it's their fault that they cannot carry off the procedure, when it's the paper that will not let them. You need all the help you can get, and your paper is one material that will give you that help.

You can buy watercolor paper by the sheet, roll or block (not to be confused with the pad). The cheapest and most versatile way to buy paper is in sheets since you can cut them to whatever size you wish and mount them on a board for painting. A watercolor block is similar to a pad, but it is bound on all four sides, except for a few unbound inches where you can slip a knife under the paper to remove the top sheet. A watercolor block may be more expensive than sheets, but it does not require mounting, because it has a sturdy backing board. However, a painting done on a block must be dry before you can expose the next sheet for another painting. This might be a problem if you do not finish with the first painting before you want to start a second.

THE BEST PAPER

The best watercolor papers contain 100% rag (cotton) fiber with a neutral pH of 7 (acid free) and are handmade or mouldmade. Paper containing 100% rag does not guarantee a neutral pH. Make sure your paper is acid free, because acid-free papers resist yellowing and deterioration over time. Some papers made in an acid environment are buffered with alkaline salts to obtain a neutral pH.

HANDMADE PAPER

Handmade paper is made with a mould (a screen that filters fibers through it) and deckle (a frame resting on or hinged to the edges of the mould that defines the edges of the sheet). A deckled edge is the natural, fuzzy edge of handmade papers. Handmade papers have four deckled edges.

MOULDMADE PAPER

Made by a slowly rotating machine called a cylinder mould, mouldmade paper looks like handmade, but usually has only two deckled edges. Mouldmade paper gets its strength from a beating process that interlocks the fibers from front to back into a single layer.

MACHINE-MADE PAPER

Machine-made paper has a uniform surface texture and size. Watercolor pads are most often machine made. Machine-made papers may contain the same quality fibers and neutral pH as handmade or mouldmade papers, but the fibers end up in layers. Try separating the edge of a piece of handmade or mouldmade paper and then a machine-made paper, and you will see what I mean. No matter how heavy it is, machine-made paper will not take the scrubbing, scraping, taping, masking and general abuse that a mouldmade piece will.

LIFE'S TOO SHORT TO PAINT ON CHEAP PAPER

When purchasing supplies, do not buy the cheap stuff just because you are a beginner.

PAPER TEXTURE

Watercolor paper comes in hot-press, cold-press and rough textures. Hot-press paper has a very smooth surface that is good for detail, but paint tends to slide around the surface for a unique effect. Cold-press paper has a medium-textured finish. It is the most popular choice because paint spreads evenly, and the surface allows reasonable detail. Rough paper has a heavily textured surface that is good for loose textural effects, but not for fine detail. All are well worth trying.

DIFFERENT SURFACES
The same subject painted on hot press (top), cold press (center) and rough (bottom) illustrates the effect that paper texture has on the end product.

PAPER WEIGHT

Paper also comes in different weights, which refers to how much a ream (500 sheets) of 22" x 30" (56cm x 76cm) paper weighs. Heavier paper absorbs more water, stays wet longer and buckles less when wet than lighter papers do. If you are pragmatic, you will also realize that the heavier paper will allow you to paint on both sides (in case you fluff the first side). The weight of a paper has nothing to do with its quality, though it does affect how much water it absorbs.

Some light papers stand up against extensive reworking and paint removal, while some heavy weights tolerate very little. If durability under scrubbing, masking, taping or scraping is your priority, try papers made by Arches, Waterford or T.H. Saunders. If it is your style to work only with brush techniques, try softer papers made by Strathmore, Winsor & Newton or Bockingford. Bockingford, made from cellulose fibers, has exceptional wiping back strength. It is ultimately up to you to find the paper type and weight that best suits your needs.

WHAT YOU NEED

Watercolor paper
Container of water large
  enough to immerse your paper
Rigid, waterproof board
Sponge
One of the following to hold
  your paper in place:
- Brown gummed paper
- tape, ½-inch wide or wider
- Thumbtacks
- Staples

COMMON PAPER WEIGHTS

Inexpensive to work on, 90-lb. (190gm) paper's drawback is a tendency to buckle. When anything larger than an eighth of a sheet is used, the paper should be stretched first or wet on both sides.

A popular weight for many is 140-lb. (300gm) paper. You can work on anything less than a quarter sheet without stretching. Just tape it to a board and go.

The easiest and most versatile to work with is 300-lb. (640gm) paper. Minimum buckling means it rarely needs stretching.

STEP BY STEP: STRETCHING PAPER

Stretching large pieces of light- and medium-weight papers before use prevents the annoyance of buckling. The other advantage is that you can use lighter weight paper, which is much cheaper, for large paintings. It takes about two hours for a stretched piece of paper to dry, so do it well in advance of your painting session and do several at a time.

The stretching process is quite simple, but it takes time. Soak your paper so it expands, then fasten it to a board. As it dries and shrinks, it will become taut and flat. The stretched paper will not buckle when you re-wet it for painting.

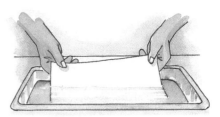

1. IMMERSE PAPER COMPLETELY IN WATER.
Let soak from thirty minutes to two hours, depending on its weight.

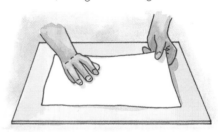

2. REMOVE PAPER FROM THE WATER.
Shake off excess water and place on a rigid, waterproofed board such as plywood or Masonite.

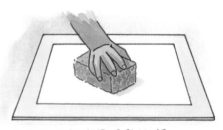

3. SMOOTH AND REMOVE EXCESS WATER WITH A DAMP SPONGE.
Slightly dry the edges with a folded paper towel.

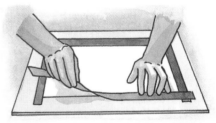

4. MOUNT YOUR PAPER.
Cut four lengths of brown gummed paper tape, and dampen each with the sponge just before applying. Do not over-wet the tape. A ½-inch (1cm) width should do for most applications. Use heavier and wider tape for large, heavy papers. Overlap the edges of the paper by about ½ inch (1cm) and press down firmly. Cut off excess tape and stand the board upright to dry slowly.

Palettes

Few beginning painters realize the subtle influence that their choice of palette has on the way they paint. A palette is more than just a place to store and mix paint. Your palette is where you coordinate your color strategy. A complicated arrangement of colors on your palette is not necessary. You only need a logical arrangement that allows you to find and mix colors with ease. A disorganized palette also can influence your spontaneity and confidence as you paint.

ARRANGING YOUR COLORS

Some artists like to lay out their colors in the order of the color wheel, with the primary colors occupying three sides and unsaturated colors the fourth. Some artists like a progression of warm colors on one side and cool colors on the other. Others like to separate staining colors from nonstaining colors, transparent colors from opaque. Like every other artist, you must find an arrangement that has a logic that works for you. It is worth noting that the fewer the colors, the simpler the logic required.

Regardless of your layout, remember color juxtaposition. The best way to arrange your colors on your palette is in spectrum (or color wheel—see page 95) order. That way, if one color accidentally spills into the next, the result is less damaging than if the colors were greatly different or complementary (opposite each other on the color wheel). Keep this in mind when devising your layout. See "Selecting and Setting Up Your Palette" on page 97.

YOUR PALETTE'S PHYSICAL CHARACTERISTICS

The way you lay out colors on your palette influences how quickly you can find what you need. The physical characteristics of the palette determine how easily you access your colors.

Many commercial palettes have tiny, deep color wells that are completely incompatible with large brushes. It's hard to be spontaneous with your big brushes if you cannot reach the paint. A large white platter would serve you better. I have even used clean Styrofoam meat trays. White enameled steel meat trays are ideal. I have made divisions for colors and mixing in mine with white silicone bathtub caulking (see page 25). The tray slips into a plastic bag for transporting. In my studio I use a similar palette made from a large piece of white arborite (e.g., Formica and melamine) originally cut out for the sink hole in my countertop. I squared it up on a saw, added an edge and made similar divisions with caulking.

A major advantage these palettes have over most commercial types is that the color wells are flat. This may seem insignificant, but the slanted wells on most palettes allow dirty pigment to run back over your clean paint. With a flat well, the dirty paint remains well below the lump of clean pigment, allowing you to access pure color from the top at any time. There are flat palettes on the market, but you have to look hard to find one with large wells. I have seen people make their palettes from white enamel trays from stoves and refrigerators that they picked up at garage sales. I have even seen artists use plastic serving trays bought in the housewares department of a store. You will find information on making your own custom palette on the next pages.

PALETTES YOU FILE AWAY

Use clean Styrofoam meat trays to mix up large batches of a particular color that you may need later. Simply let the paint dry in the tray until you need it again. Example: The blue-gray that I mix for the shadows on snow is unique to each picture. When working on more than one painting at a time, it is important that when I return to my snow picture I have the exact blue-gray for that piece. If I have saved some in a meat tray, I will.

PALETTE WELL SHAPES

The shape of the color wells on your palette seriously influences the cleanliness of your colors. Sloped color wells allow foreign colors, carried there during mixing, to flow back and contaminate the clean resident color. Flat wells, on the other hand, allow the dirty pigments to disperse away from your lump of clean pigment.

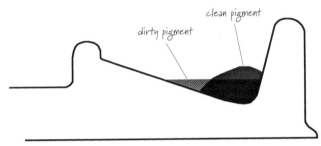

PALETTE WITH SLANTED COLOR WELLS

MUFFIN TIN DESIGN

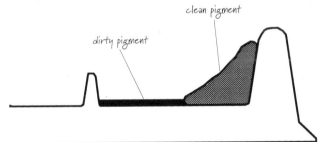

PALETTE WITH FLAT WELLS

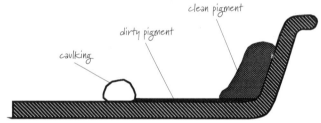

MEAT TRAY PALETTE WITH CAULKING WELL DIVIDERS

STEP BY STEP: DO-IT-YOURSELF PALETTE

One of the charms of working in watercolors is the opportunity it provides to be resourceful and inventive. If you cannot find what you need in an art supply store (or the price is too high), look else-where—other types of stores, your attic, garage sales, etc. I have obtained materials from drug or hardware stores, kitchen/housewares boutiques, and office product, photography, auto or building suppliers. You just never know where you are going to find watercolor supplies.

What you need may even be in that art supply store, but sometimes you just cannot find exactly what you need. The only answer is to take up the challenge and make it yourself. Such is the case of the palette described below. With minimal carpentry skills and tools, or a friend who has both, you can construct a studio palette that has the large wells and mixing areas you need.

The base of the palette is a piece of finished shelving found in building supply stores. This is a particleboard that has a white plastic sur-face on each side. It comes in 8-inch (20cm) and 12-inch (30cm) widths. Choose the width you desire, and cut off the length needed. The supplier can probably do this for you. There will be enough in one shelf to make several palettes, so why not make it a group project with some friends? You will need some material to make the edging on your palette. I have made some suggestions here.

The dimensions you need depend on the number of wells that you wish to have. They should be at least 2" x 2" (5cm x 5cm), so cut the board an even number of inches in length. I have shown some sample sizes here. Just because you make twenty wells does not mean that you have to put out twenty colors. It's best to allow a few empty ones for those new colors that always come along. See "Setting Up Your Palette" on page 97.

Remember that this new palette with its big wells will be for naught if you continue to put only a smidgen of paint in each well. Big brushes require a good lump of paint.

WHAT YOU NEED

8-inch or 12-inch-wide white particleboard shelving (palette base) in the length you want, depending on the number of 2" x 2" wells you wish to have

Edge molding that extends ¾ inch above the top of the base

Varnish for wood molding

Something to attach molding to the edge of your palette base, such as wood glue and nails or drill and screws

Well-ventilated working area

Tube of caulking

Scissors to cut the end of the caulking tube

Ruler

Pencil

Popsicle stick

10" — 16 wells — 12"

24 wells — 14"

20 wells — 18"

1. CUT BASE TO DESIRED SIZE.
Here are some size options for palettes with 2" x 2" wells.

12" — 26 wells

22 wells

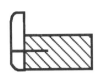 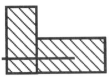 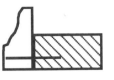

doorstop molding   a strip of the   custom cut   fancy molding   metal angle   metal stair nosing
                          shelving material

2. CHOOSE EDGE MOLDING.

The edging you choose is up to you. I have suggested some types of edging here. The only criterion is that it must extend about ³/₄ inch (2cm) above the top of the base.

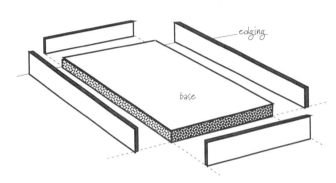

edging

base

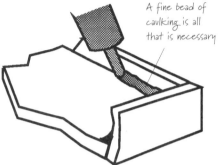

A fine bead of caulking is all that is necessary

3. ATTACH MOLDING TO BASE.

When cutting edging to length, don't forget to allow for overlapping or mitering of the corners. You may wish to varnish any wooden edging before attaching it so it won't absorb moisture and paint. Attach the molding to the edge of your palette. If the molding is wood, use glue and nails to attach it. If you choose metal, drill and attach with screws.

4. CAULK INSIDE JOINTS.

After the edging is on, run a small bead of caulking along the inside joints to keep your paint from getting away on you.

Apply caulking in a well-ventilated area. Cut the end of the tube of caulking straight across. Do not cut it at an angle as you would for most caulking jobs. Let the caulking dry.

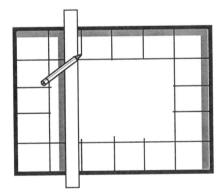

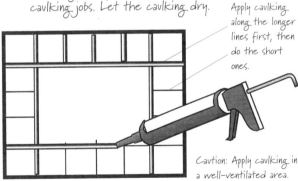

Apply caulking along the longer lines first, then do the short ones.

Caution: Apply caulking in a well-ventilated area.

5. LAY OUT WELLS WITH RULER AND PENCIL.

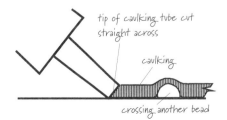

tip of caulking tube cut straight across

caulking

crossing another bead

6. APPLY CAULKING ALONG WELL LINES.

Try to keep the tip of the nozzle touching the palette as you maintain a steady flow. Lift it only to cross over other beads. For the short beads, start at the edging and move toward the center. Let the caulking dry at least twenty-four hours before adding paint.

Don't expect perfection! This is tricky stuff. This could be one of the biggest messes you ever get yourself into if you start touching the caulking with your fingers. You will more than likely get less than perfect beads and tails at the end of each run. You can smooth these out a bit with a very wet Popsicle stick. Don't worry about appearances. When you start painting with your new palette, you won't even notice.

Palette Knives

Many artists scrape back damp paint with a palette knife to leave light marks, but you can also use a palette knife to apply paint if the knife is clean and of sufficient stiffness (see "Painting With a Palette Knife," page 38). The most common palette knife is made of metal, but there are nylon types on the market that also work well. Regardless, choose one that is very stiff. A knife with an offset handle will make it easier to access the paint.

STEP BY STEP: CLEANING YOUR PALETTE KNIFE

The knife must be absolutely clean before it will hold paint. To clean it, use a small piece of 240- to 400-grit wet-or-dry sandpaper (sometimes called waterproof sandpaper). This superfine sandpaper can be found in most hardware stores. It is usually a dark gray color on a green paper backing. Use it with water, which acts as a lubricant when cleaning the knife.

WHAT YOU NEED

Palette knife
Superfine (240- to 400-grit) wet-or-dry sandpaper for sanding
Water
Edge of table

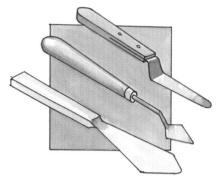

PALETTE KNIVES SHOULD BE STIFF
You can paint with almost any type of palette knife so long as it's stiff.

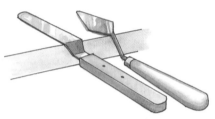

1. HOLD BLADE BOTTOM-SIDE UP ON EDGE OF TABLE.
Because it is more efficient to rub the paper on the knife than the knife on the paper, start by holding the blade bottom-side up on the edge of a table. It is not necessary to clean the top side of the blade.

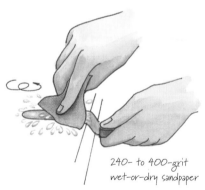

240- to 400-grit wet-or-dry sandpaper

2. SCRUB BLADE WITH 240- TO 400-GRIT WET-OR-DRY SANDPAPER.
Dip a small piece of sandpaper in water, and immediately start scrubbing the surface of the blade in a gentle, circular motion. You may have to keep re-wetting the paper and scrubbing harder to remove any dried oil paint. New knives have a clear coating of varnish that you must remove. Once you have cleaned your knife, it doesn't take much to freshen the surface when needed.

You can tell if the knife is clean by dipping it in water. If the water clings smoothly to the blade, then it is clean. If the water beads up, then the knife is still dirty and needs more cleaning. Make sure your palette knife is clean every time you wish to paint with it.

PAINTING STICKS

When you think of it, this was probably the first painting tool (after the finger). Any type of small stick or twig that you can shape with a small utility knife will do—a dowel, tongue depressor, Popsicle stick, etc. I use tongue depressors because they split easily into long tapers. I can then sharpen the tip with a utility knife to the size I want.

Apply paint to the stick with a loaded brush. The initial charging of the stick with color may take time, because the paint must soak into the stick. After that, it is easy to apply the paint to it. The more paint that covers the stick, the longer you can make marks with it. You need to experiment with various tips until you find sizes that work for you. You can make lines of varying width with great precision with a stick. See page 39. Sticks are also great for applying masking fluid. See page 54.

Painting Sponges

This is not what you did in kinder-garten, and it's not the type of paint-ing done with a natural sea Sponge. For this you will need the synthetic cellulose type sold in hardware stores and housewares departments. These sponges come as blocks, often in bags of five or six, but do not confuse them with the synthetic foam plastic ones. The way to tell the difference is by squeezing them. The cellulose sponge, unless it has been premoistened, is firm and bare-ly springs back when squeezed, whereas the plastic sponge is soft and springs back readily. The plastic sponge also has a shiny or translu-cent appearance, while the cellulose sponge is opaque.

STEP BY STEP: MAKING PAINTING SPONGES

For this type of sponge painting you work with a small piece of synthetic sponge that you have carefully shaped by tearing. The marks that the sponge makes are unlike those from any other tool, and yet to do it right the results should not look as if you used a sponge. It should keep the viewer guessing as to how you really did it. However, the unique footprints of the sponge are sec-ondary to the main reason for using it—speed.

As we know, timing is all-important to many of the techniques we use in watercolors. Using a sponge gives us an edge because it allows us to apply a lot of paint to a big area quickly. We are therefore able to perform techniques we can-not do with a brush. Once you have made your sponge as illustrated, turn to "Painting With a Sponge" on pages 40–41 for ways to use it.

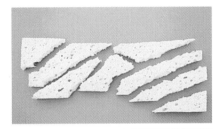

WHAT YOU NEED

Synthetic cellulose sponge
  block
Utility knife
Water

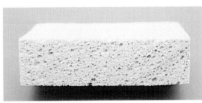

1. IDENTIFY YOUR SPONGE'S WORKING SURFACE.
Examine your sponge block. Two sides will have more deep holes in them than the others. Use one of these faces as the working surface of the sponge you tear.

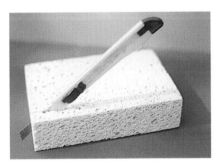

2. CUT A SLICE OF SPONGE.
Using a fully extended utility knife, carefully cut off a ½- (1cm) to ¾-inch (2cm) slice of one of the sides with deep holes. Do this when the sponge is dry.

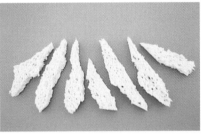

3. TEAR YOUR SPONGE TO AN OPTIMUM "LEAF" SHAPE.
The objective now is to tear out a number of smaller sponges from this slice. This is the hard part, but wet-ting the sponge makes it easier to tear into smaller pieces. You will also need some fairly strong fingernails. Ideally you want to tear off little sponges pointed on each end and irreg-ular along the sides—a rough willow leaf shape.

Start by wetting the sponge slice, then subdivide it into several smaller pieces. One slice will make several pieces, since each finished sponge will be only 2 (5cm) to 2½ inches (6cm) long. It may help if you start at one end and tear the slice lengthwise. Most sponges have a grain, and, if you are fortunate, yours will have one that runs diagonally across the slice.

Tearing diagonally produces long, tapered wedges that require only a small amount of additional tearing to achieve the desired shape. If you do not tear a tapered piece, then you will have to pick away at it until you have points on both ends.

You may have to repeatedly tear away little bits in order to achieve the shape you want. Believe me, there is a lot of room for variation, and no two sponges will come out the same.

Masking Materials

Masking is, in effect, the lazy man's way around negative painting. See pages 73-75. Instead of carefully painting around the light shapes, you cover them with some sort of masking material that protects them while you paint over the whole area. When the paint is dry, the masking material is removed to reveal the light shapes. There are several materials you can use to mask out an area in your painting, including candle wax, rubber cement, liquid latex and tape. These last two are the most common and the ones I wish to examine here.

LIQUID LATEX

This material has several names — Miskit, Frisket, White Mask, Liquid Resist, Drawing Gum, Maskoid, Grafigum, etc., depending on who makes it. It is essentially all the same material—an emulsion of natural latex, water and ammonia (preservative) and, in most cases, color. Quality varies, so you must search for one that suits your needs. Personally, I prefer Drawing Gum made by Pebeo. It covers well and its gray-blue color allows me to see clearly where I am putting it on the white paper, which white types do not.

SOME DOS AND DON'TS WHEN USING MASKING FLUID

Do test the masking material on your paper beforehand. *Don't* assume that it will work on all types of watercolor papers.

Do stir. *Don't* shake. Shaking a bottle of masking fluid puts air bubbles into the emulsion that will later break, producing pinholes where paint can leak through to your paper.

Do let masking fluid dry natural-

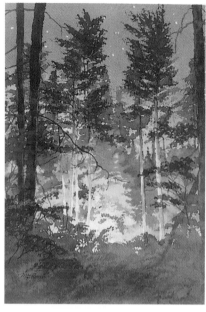

LIGHT IN THE FOREST
11" x 15" (28cm x 38cm)
Private collection

SHAPES PAINTED WITH A SPONGE

Light in the Forest makes use of both positive and negative shapes painted with a sponge. The dark, positive shapes of the background trees gradually lighten as they move downward, but they are kept dark enough to define negative space around the lightest trees near the ground. The lightest trees, in turn, contrast with the dark shrubbery in the foreground.

ly in the shade. *Don't* dry masking fluid in direct sunlight or with a hair dryer, unless you want it permanently bonded to your painting.

Do apply masking fluid to dry paper. *Don't* apply masking fluid when the surface is even slightly damp, because the paper will absorb it, making it impossible to remove.

Do wait until it is thoroughly dry before applying paint over it. *Don't* paint for at least twenty to thirty minutes.

Do remove when the paint is

OTHER MATERIALS AND TOOLS

As you experiment with watercolor, the following will also come in handy:
- Salt
- Spray bottle
- Rubber cement pickup
- Brayer (hand roller)

thoroughly dry. *Don't* rush things, or you will smear pigment into the masked-out area.

There are many tools you can use to apply liquid masking fluid. Among these are brushes, sticks, sponges, toothbrushes for spattering, calligraphy pens, atomizers, etc. See "Masking," page 54.

MASKING WITH TAPES

Always test the tape first on the paper you intend to use. Some very expensive papers won't stand up to taping. Masking tape is not always reliable on rough-textured papers. Its thickness will not allow it to follow the undulating surface, so paint can sometimes creep in under it.

PACKING TAPE

Packing tape is a thin plastic tape that comes in big, wide rolls. It's found in hardware, department and office supply stores. Packing tape can drive you crazy because it has a mind to stick to itself and everything in sight, but it is a wonderful, inexpensive way to mask large areas and produce sharp-edged shapes. Because of its thinness, it can follow the textural surface of the paper and not let any paint get underneath it.

Buy the gray or brown-colored types of packing tape. The clear version is like white masking fluid—it's hard to see. This tape will not harm harder papers, such as Arches, if lifted gently. Test beforehand on the paper you intend to use. Warming it with a hair dryer will also ease its removal.

To mask objects with this tape, cover the shape completely with the tape and then use a very sharp single-edged razor or knife to cut around the object. So how do you keep from cutting the paper? With practice you will get a feel for how little pressure you need to put on the knife to do the job, particularly if the knife is sharp. See "Packing Tape" on page 60 for ways to use packing tape.

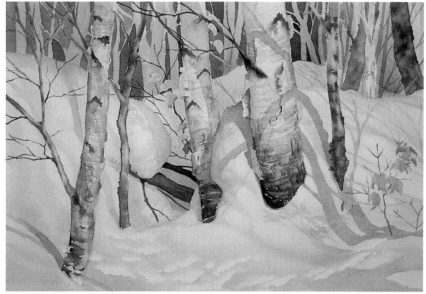

MASKING FLUID FOR TRUNKS, LEAVES AND SINKHOLES

In Afternoon Birches, I used masking fluid to save the foreground tree trunks and leaves, even though I knew that in places they would end up being darker than the snow around them. By masking, I was able to deal freely with the snow and its dark cast shadows as a unit and then turn my attention to the trunks. Notice how the masking fluid easily produces an irregular edge on a shape.

I also used masking fluid to create the sinkholes in the snow. I softened the saved white shapes on the back side of the holes to give the appearance of direct sunlight hitting them.

AFTERNOON
BIRCHES
15" x 22"
(38cm x 56cm)
Private collection

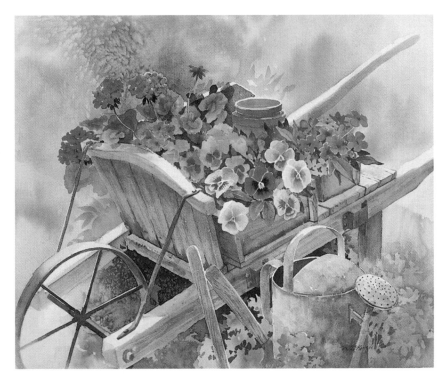

PROMISES OF SPRING
19" x 22" (48cm x 56cm)
Private collection

MASKING FLUID AND PACKING TAPE

I used the tape for the larger, straighter-edged shapes of the wheelbarrow and watering can. It was easier to handle the irregular shapes of the flowers with masking fluid. I completed the background and let it dry, then removed the tape for the wheelbarrow. I then applied liquid masking again to save the plants that were to hang over the edge of the wheelbarrow before I painted it. I removed the masking on the plants last.

2 Painting Techniques

It is wonderful to see something and then create a way to express it with watercolor. We call those ways techniques. Mastering techniques frees you to be more creative, but techniques do not make a painting. They will not give you sight. Techniques are only means by which you express your vision.

Become a master of applying and inventing techniques.

More often than not, the discovery of a technique involves new ways of letting the water and the pigments do the work. The techniques and procedures on the next few pages are only examples of ways to handle the medium—you may develop your own solutions.

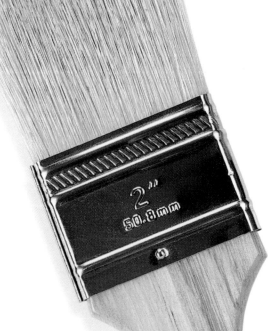

Painting With Brushes

Each brush performs a specific range of tasks. The following exercises will help you explore the potential of each type. Regardless of the type of brush, using a no. 8 or larger increases the range of marks you can make.

TIP FOR PRACTICING BRUSHSTROKES

If you practice your brush-strokes with clear water on any absorbent colored paper, such as brown wrapping paper, you will see your brush marks without having to waste paint and good watercolor paper.

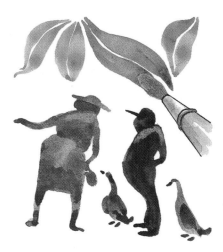

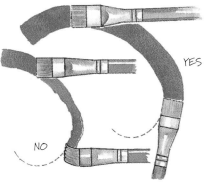

CONSTRUCT SHAPES WITH YOUR BRUSHSTROKES

Avoid outlining a shape with your brush and then filling in the hole with paint like a coloring book. Instead, build up your strokes for the shape until you achieve the size you want.

FOLLOW THE CONTOUR

When painting around the edge of a shape (negative painting), turn the brush so your stroke follows the shape's edge. This is particularly important if you are using a flat brush.

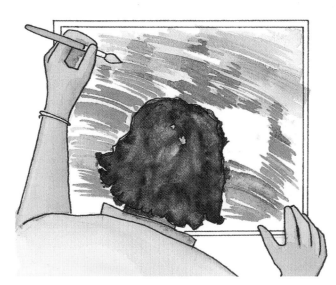

YOUR ARM IS NOT A WINDSHIELD WIPER

Vary the direction of your brushstrokes.

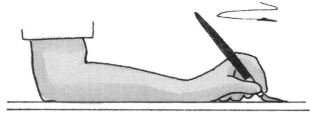

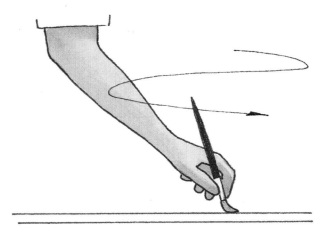

STAND UP

When you sit down, you have a tendency to paint from the wrist or elbow. That can lead to the windshield-wiper syndrome, which causes you not to vary your brushstrokes. Standing up allows for far greater movement of the whole body. That translates into greater variety and expression in your strokes. Save the sitting down for when you want more control for small areas and detail.

ROUND BRUSH TECHNIQUES

Whether synthetic or natural, a round brush is the basic watercolor brush that most watercolor artists feel comfortable using. However, remember that even this brush can produce a wide range of marks depending on how it's held and the direction in which you move it.

GAINING CONTROL OF THE ROUND BRUSH

It's hard to gain control of line width when your hand is off the paper. This is why people sit down to paint—so they can steady their hand on their elbow or wrist. The way around this is to use your little finger as a depth control while holding the brush vertically. This allows you to control the stroke weight while you remain standing. This technique also makes it possible for you to twist your brush to produce a fine point at the end of a stroke.

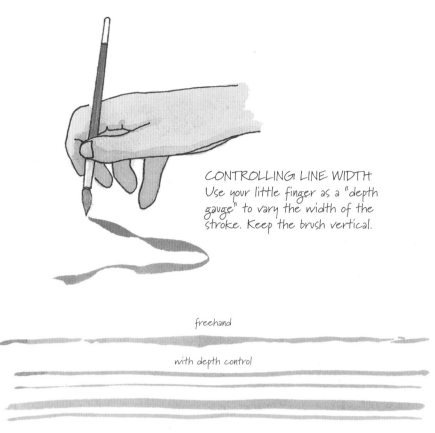

CONTROLLING LINE WIDTH
Use your little finger as a "depth gauge" to vary the width of the stroke. Keep the brush vertical.

freehand

with depth control

EXERCISE 1: GET CONTROL OF YOUR BRUSH
Stand up and try making a long, fine, continuous line of uniform width while touching the paper with the brush only (not with your fingers, hand or arm). Now, support your hand on your little finger, lower the tip of the brush to the paper and repeat the line. Now you should sense control. Practice making these lines of consistent width until this hand position feels natural.

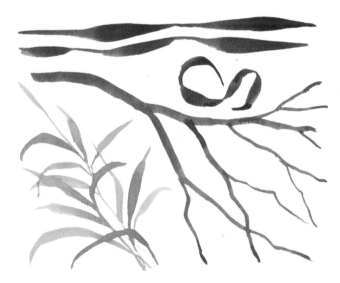

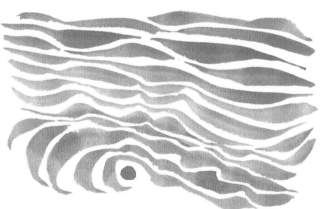

EXERCISE 2: PRACTICE VARYING LINE WIDTHS
Practice making lines that go from wide to thin, then thin to wide, using your little finger as a guide. Practice this on tree branches that change direction and weight. Try large blades of grass, curving lines and zigzags.

EXERCISE 3: PRACTICE PAINTING CLOSE LINES
Paint a line of varying width across your paper. Now paint a second, roughly parallel, line that is close to but not touching the first. To paint this line, you will need to vary the weight precisely with your little finger. Keep adding lines until you feel you are gaining control over the width of the lines you make.

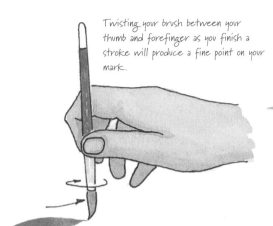

Twisting your brush between your thumb and forefinger as you finish a stroke will produce a fine point on your mark.

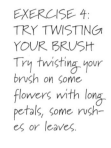

EXERCISE 4:
TRY TWISTING
YOUR BRUSH
Try twisting your brush on some flowers with long petals, some rushes or leaves.

SCRIPT AND RIGGER BRUSHES

Script brushes have fuller bodies and more pointed tips than riggers. Therefore, they carry more paint and produce a wider range of marks when you apply pressure to them. Both scripts and riggers make marks that are fairly consistent in width, but the length of their bristles can make them hard to control. Script brushes are best for free-flowing lines and shapes that suggest spontaneity. The large rigger is handy when you want a mark that is consistent in width and squared at the ends, like bricks, boards, stems, windows, etc.

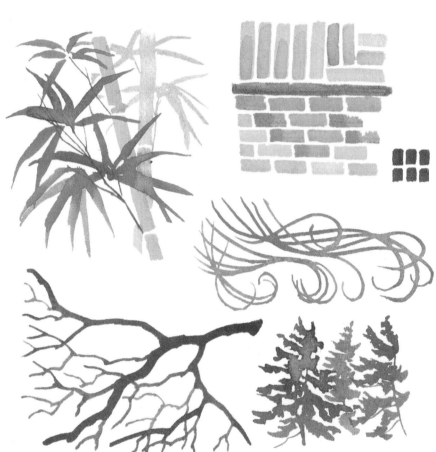

EXERCISE 5: SCRIPT AND RIGGER BRUSHES
Suggest growth or movement—for example, grasses, tree branches, hair, wood grain, etc. Experiment with stopping, starting and changing direction with your brushstrokes. Try building complex shapes by applying more pressure to the brush or drawing the brush sideways. Experiment with the rigger's ability to make squared lines.

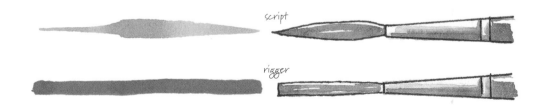

script

rigger

FLAT BRUSH TECHNIQUES

Flat synthetic brushes include wash and stroke-type brushes. These flat brushes are some of the most versatile to own.

Flat hog hair brushes, though not generally given recognition as watercolor brushes, are stiff, coarse workhorses that can produce some truly unique marks. Having several widths from one to two inches will prove invaluable. For these exercises, it is best to use paint and real watercolor paper.

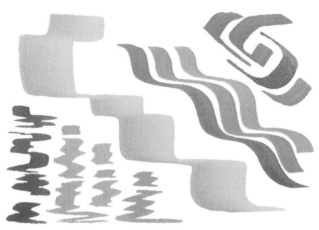

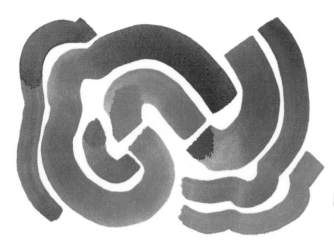

EXERCISE 6: KEEP STROKE WIDTH THE SAME

Now make circular marks of the same width by turning your synthetic flat brush and your arm as you make the marks.

EXERCISE 7: MAKE SINGLE "LEAF" STROKES

Start off narrow, pushing down on your synthetic flat, twisting 90° and then letting up on the pressure while turning 90° again. Try varying the length of these leaf marks. Try grouping and arranging to make more complex shapes.

EXERCISE 8: VARY WIDTH WITH BRUSH MOVEMENT

With a flat synthetic brush, make a variety of marks that vary in width depending on the direction you move. Keep the brush oriented in the same position—for example, horizontal—for each stroke. Move your whole arm with each stroke.

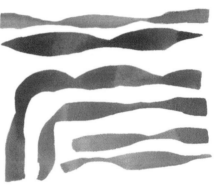

EXERCISE 9: TWIST BRUSH TO VARY WIDTH

With a synthetic flat, make marks that vary in size by twisting the brush 90° as you make a straight stroke.

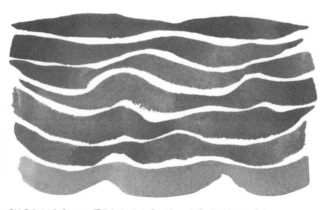

EXERCISE 10: PRACTICE CLOSE STROKES

With a synthetic flat brush, make a single stroke across the top of your paper. Vary the width of this stroke by turning the brush as you go. Now paint a second parallel stroke that also varies in width but follows the curves of the first without touching it. In order to maintain a consistent distance between the strokes, carefully control the amount of turn on the brush. (Focus on the gap between the lines and not on the strokes themselves.) Continue to add strokes, with each fitting into the curves of the previous one.

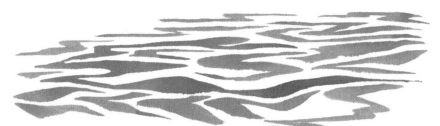

EXERCISE 11: REPRESENT WAVE MOVEMENT

Repeat the previous exercise, making the marks shorter and adding in zigzagging. You are now making marks that you can use to represent wave movement.

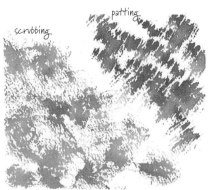

EXERCISE 14: PAT AND SCRUB FOR TEXTURE

With your hog hair flat, discover what marks you can make by gently patting the side of a well-loaded brush on your paper. Discover what textures you can make by scrubbing the side of a loaded brush on your paper. The more textured the paper, the better the effect.

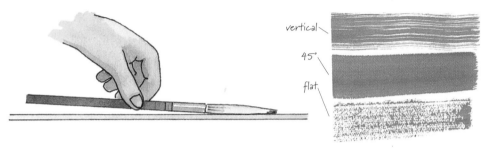

EXERCISE 12: DRAG FOR REALISTIC EFFECTS

By holding and dragging a well-loaded hog hair flat at various angles, you can get everything from lines (held vertically) to a solid mark (held at 45°) to broken lines (held flat). To get the brush low enough you will have to change your grip, because you want just the side of the bristles to touch the paper. These marks are useful for wood grain, sparkle on water, grass, fabric, rust and old paint, but I am sure you will find lots of uses of your own.

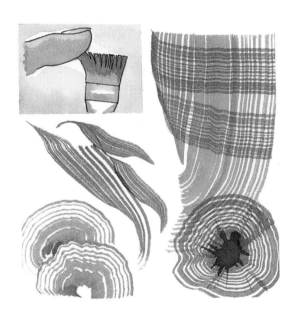

EXERCISE 13: DRYBRUSH FOR REALISTIC EFFECTS

Load a flat, short-bristled synthetic brush with concentrated paint. Wipe off excess moisture, then fan the bristles with your fingertip. The brush should be dry enough to allow the bristles to remain spread apart. Now you can make precise dry-brush marks with a flat synthetic brush. Great for wood grain, fabric, veining in leaves, hair, etc.

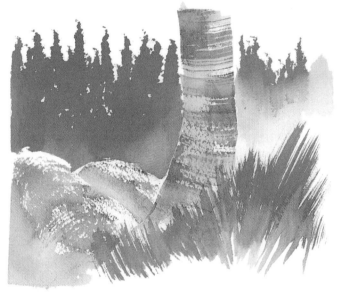

EXERCISE 15: PUT VARIOUS TECHNIQUES TOGETHER

Holding your hog hair flat vertically, make marks by dabbing the edge on your paper or by making short, sweeping marks. By varying the angle of the brush, repeating the mark over and over, you will soon discover textures and marks that can serve for grass, hills, bark, fur, rocks, clouds, etc.

Painting With a Palette Knife

Although palette knives have long been used for applying oil and acrylic paint, not everyone knows that you can also use knives for applying watercolors. Once you have cleaned your knife as described on page 28, the next step is to get the paint onto the knife blade.

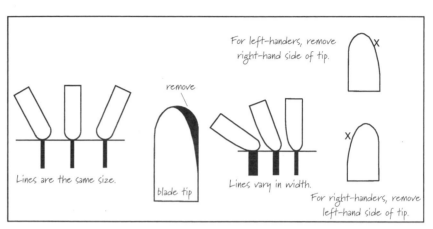

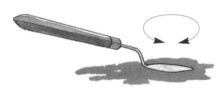

LOADING THE KNIFE
Mix a pool of concentrated pigment in an open area of the palette (not too thick, as it has to flow off the blade). Place the knife's blade face down in this paint and slide it around. The paint should adhere to the entire face of the blade. You are now ready to paint with your knife.

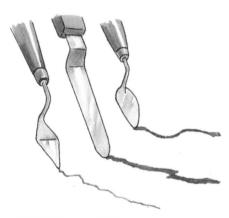

MAKING MARKS
The easiest things to paint with a knife are lines, but these lines have a character unlike any lines made with a brush. Hold the knife at a steep angle, and drag the tip across the paper.

RESHAPE TIP TO VARY STROKES
A regular mixing knife blade will make the same width mark no matter what angle it's held at because of the consistent curve of the tip. By reshaping the tip so the curve changes as it rounds the end, you can produce marks that vary in width as you change the angle of the knife. To modify the tip, grind it down and then smooth the edges with extrafine sandpaper or emery cloth so there are no burrs.

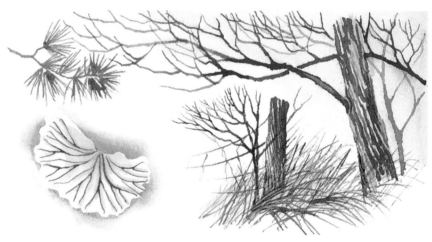

GIVE IT A TRY
Knives are great for making branches, twigs, grass, cracks in wood, fence wires, etc.—wherever you want a free-flowing fine line with a constant width. The size of the line obviously depends on the size of the tip on the knife.

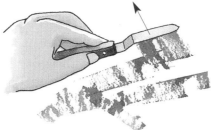

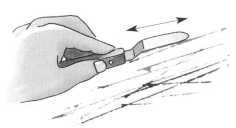

USING THE KNIFE'S EDGE TO APPLY PAINT
By pushing and pulling it you get fine lines.

DRAGGING THE KNIFE SIDEWAYS
You produce marks that suggest tree bark or texture on rocks.

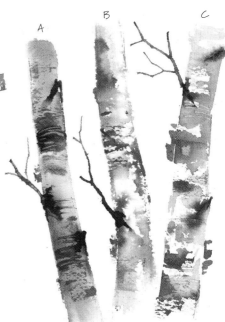

Painting With Sticks

Once you have cut your stick to the desired size and shape, all that remains is to add paint and start drawing.

THREE WAYS TO PAINT TREE TRUNKS WITH A PALETTE KNIFE
A. Paint applied to a tree shape that was completely wet beforehand.
B. Paint applied to a tree shape that was first made partially wet with a small hog hair brush.
C. Paint applied to a tree shape that was dry, then faded out in places with a wet brush.

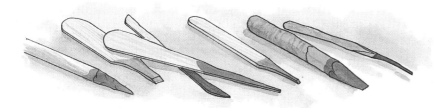

SHARPEN STICKS FOR PAINTING LINES
You can sharpen any type of small stick in a variety of ways for painting precise lines. Use a brush to load dowels, tongue depressors, Popsicle sticks or twigs with paint.

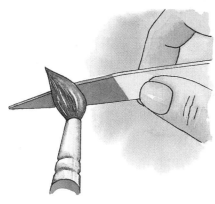

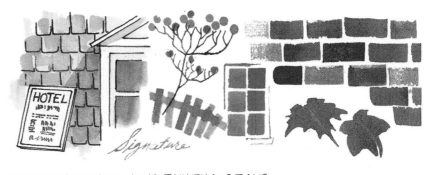

LOADING THE STICK
Mix the desired color with a brush, then apply it to the end of your stick. It may take a moment for the stick to absorb the first charge of paint.

EXPERIMENT WITH YOUR PAINTING STICKS
You will find that sticks can produce very precise, consistent lines, useful for detail work.

Painting With a Sponge

See page 29 for the preparation of your sponge. Wear a rubber glove, since many paints still contain pigments that are toxic. Besides preventing your own demise, you will also avoid the embarrassment of going into public with multicolored fingers.

GETTING PAINT ON THE SPONGE

You need a large puddle of paint in the mixing area of your palette, as well as a sponge fully saturated with paint. To do this, rub a wet sponge in your desired color, then squeeze out this mixture where you want it in your mixing area. Keep repeating this until you have a large puddle from which you can fully charge the sponge. I cannot overemphasize the need to fully saturate the sponge for this process. It doesn't matter how concentrated the pigment is, as long as the sponge becomes fully wet with paint.

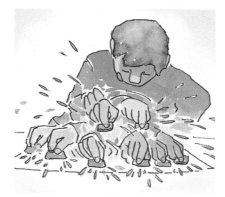

TOO MUCH ENTHUSIASM
TOO MUCH ENTHUSIASM
Practice on scrap paper, and try to curb your enthusiasm. Don't slam the sponge onto the paper as if you were killing ants at a picnic! This procedure demands a sensitive touch, and you'll need a sharp eye to keep a watch on each mark formed.

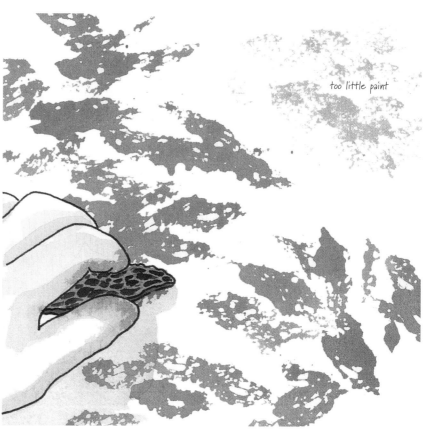

too little paint

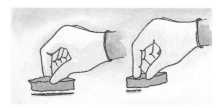

HOLDING THE SPONGE
Hold your sponge on its side so the sides with the holes face up toward you and down toward the paper. You will be painting with these faces and not the sides of the sponge. Most people find that working with the tip of the sponge gives them more control when building shapes. If you wish, use your forefinger to add support to the tip of the sponge. I recommend that you use a rubber glove.

EXPERIMENT
Experiment to find out what kinds of marks your sponge will make. Load it with paint, then gently touch it to the paper so that it leaves an irregular mark. If you load the sponge properly, it will take very little pressure to leave an impression. Practice until you can make clearly defined marks that still leave white areas within the marks. Try tilting the sponge from side to side to alter the marks. Flip the sponge over. Try both ends.

Too little paint on the sponge will produce a soft, lacy shape that lacks definition. If you wish to paint a pale shape, then add water to the paint mixture as you would if you were painting with a brush. If you wish to add more paint, just squeeze the sponge.

BUILDING SHAPES WITH A SPONGE

When painting large masses with a sponge, avoid making sporadic, isolated marks all over your paper. Most of the shapes you make with a sponge are made by building up marks. Make hills, trees, foliage and ground cover by starting with one mark and then adding to it until you form your desired shape. For example, for deciduous trees, start in the middle and work out from the center. For coniferous trees, start at the top and work down to the bottom. Work along a line for hills and ground cover.

THE BIG PAYOFF

Once you gain some mastery with a sponge, you will find that you can paint hills, trees, forests and foliage at astounding speeds. You can finish a whole forest and still have it wet for additional techniques in the time it takes to paint one tree with a brush. This opens the door for all sorts of wet-in-wet procedures (see page 48). An example is the forest. After sponging, I faded out the bottom edge with clean water and a brush, lightly spattered the forest with a spray bottle and then dropped in salt.

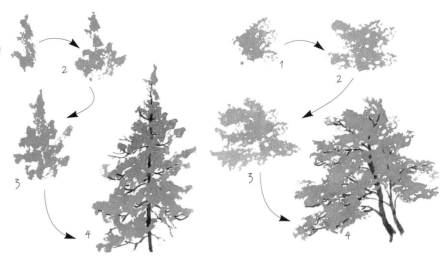

HAVE FAITH
Paint in trunks, branches and stems with a brush after painting the leaves. It takes a wee bit of faith that this meaningless mass of shapes will actually turn into something.
  Start coniferous trees at the top and work down to the lower branches. Start deciduous trees in the middle and work out to the outer leaves.

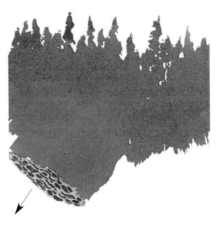

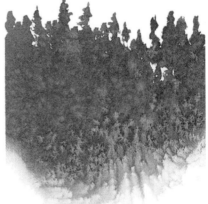

CREATING TEXTURE WITH SALT

Sprinkle grains of coarse salt into semi-wet paint. When the paint is dry, brush off the salt to reveal a pale, delicate texture where the salt granules have soaked up the pigment. You can use salt to create texture in ground, tree and background areas.

SPREAD PAINT
Spread paint by dragging the sponge.

USE SPONGES WITH OTHER TECHNIQUES
Because the whole shape is wet, you can use additional techniques, such as adding salt, which will bleach some of the color to produce a mottled pattern.

EXAMPLES OF SPONGE PAINTING

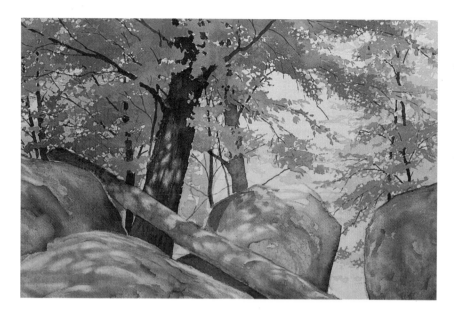

ON THE ROCKS
15" x 22" (38cm x 56cm)
Private collection

A RANGE OF SPONGED COLORS
I sponged in the blue-gray trees in the background of this picture first. When that was dry, I added the orange foreground trees. This is a good example of how you can sponge a range of colors on a shape. I did this by preparing a selection of oranges on the palette beforehand, then picking up different variations on the sponge, without washing it out, as I went along. I used Cadmium Orange, Cadmium Red Light and Cobalt Blue to produce my selection. Most importantly, I painted the tree trunks in after the leaves were in place.

This painting is also a good example of sun spots created by lifting color with water and a small "scrubber" brush.

HEADWATERS
11" x 19" (28cm x 48cm)
Private collection

ILLUSION OF LIGHT
WITH SPONGING
In Headwaters, I achieved the appearance of light coming through the forest by sponging lighter, warmer greens at the light source and gradually applying cooler, darker greens as I moved away from it. After the foliage was dry, I painted in the tree trunks. By making them darker than the leaves, I created the appearance of atmospheric clarity.

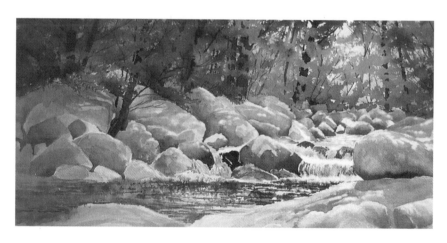

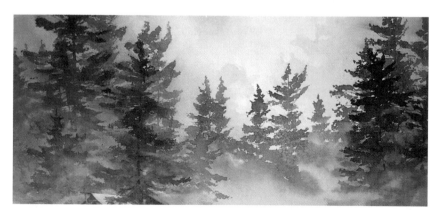

THE NARROWS
Detail
22" x 30" (56cm x 76cm)
Private collection

ATMOSPHERICS
I created the appearance of fog in this detail by fading out (see page 46) the base of the sponged trees. I could do this because the trees were a consistent wetness. This process of painting trees and then fading them out was repeated several times to create a sense of depth.

How Paints Interact With Water

The term *watercolor* would seem to suggest that the end result of a painting should look as if water had something to do with its creation. If your work looks like a paint-by-number because you have worked entirely in a wet-on-dry fashion, then you have missed the whole point of the medium. How will viewers know that it's a watercolor? There are endless ways of working so that water has an active role in the process and the effects you get.

THE LAW YOU CANNOT IGNORE

Basically, greater wetness will always flow into lesser wetness. The wetness could be either water or paint, and it does not matter where it is. The greater will always flow into the lesser in an attempt to balance the system out. You can see the effects that wetness has on the painting process.

GREATER WETNESS FLOWS INTO LESSER WETNESS

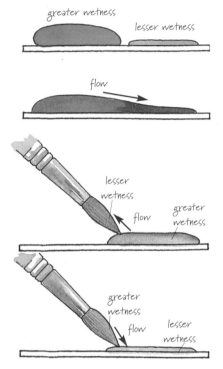

greater wetness · lesser wetness

flow

lesser wetness · flow · greater wetness

greater wetness · flow · lesser wetness

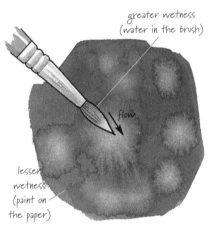

greater wetness (water in the brush) · flow

lesser wetness (paint on the paper)

If the greater wetness is water and the lesser is paint, then the water will flow into the paint, pushing the pigment aside. We call this a water spot, water blossom or run-back. Knowing how to create or avoid a blossom is of great importance in the painting process.

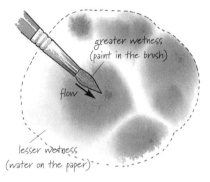

greater wetness (paint in the brush) · flow

lesser wetness (water on the paper)

If the greater wetness is paint and the lesser is water, then the paint pigments disperse smoothly into the water.

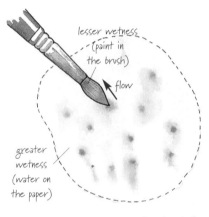

lesser wetness (paint in the brush) · flow

greater wetness (water on the paper)

Little happens here when the brush is less wet than the surface because the brush is trying to pick up water.

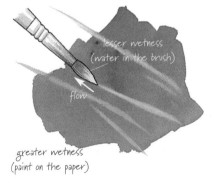

lesser wetness (water in the brush) · flow

greater wetness (paint on the paper)

Now you can lift off color as the paint attempts to climb into the brush.

Mastering Washes and Glazes

Washes are large, thin layers of color that cover the whole or partial areas of your paper. A wash that is usually applied to white paper can be uniform (flat) or graded in color or value. A glaze is a wash applied to an already-dry painted surface. Washes and glazes play an important mood-setting and unifying role in your painting.

GLAZING

This is the process of laying on a colored wash over paint that is already dry. You can use it to "adjust" a painting that may lack mood, unity or focus. While a single color helps to establish a more dominant mood within a work, it also adds to unity by giving all the colors a common overcoat. Darkening a selected part of a painting with a glaze helps the eye focus on more important lighter areas.

Glazing can be a tricky process because you are placing a very wet layer of paint over paint that is already in place. It is important to apply the paint quickly with a large brush and to avoid overworking any part of the surface, so as not to disturb the paint that is already there. When you glaze only part of the work, it is important that there not be any hard edges left from the glaze. Use water to fade out any edges.

One way to glaze is to wet the surface of the picture first with a spray bottle, then, while this is wet, drop or pour liquid watercolor into it. Tilt the painting to help direct the flow, and use additional spray to fade the edges. Even though there is no direct contact with the paper, there is still the danger that some colors, particularly dark opaque colors applied heavily, will blur. You will see this happening when the paper is first wet with the spray. Use the spray to wash away the blurring paint before you apply the glaze color. When the painting is dry, reapply the darks, if necessary.

LAYING ON A GRADED WASH

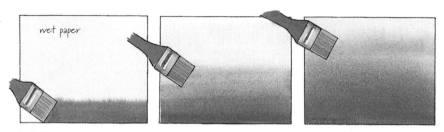

METHOD 1
Wet the desired area completely. Immediately paint concentrated pigment along one edge. Fade out that paint into the wet area with long strokes. To intensify the color, repeat this process, each time starting at the beginning. With each application the color deepens and extends into the wetted area.

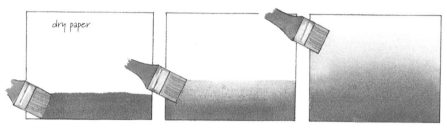

METHOD 2
With the paper dry, paint concentrated pigment along one edge of the wash area. Dip your brush (which still has paint in it) into clean water, and wipe off excess water on the side of the container. Apply this now-diluted color next to the first stroke. Keep repeating this fading-out process until you have achieved the look you want and there is no pigment left on the brush.

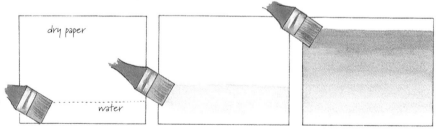

METHOD 3
Prepare your desired pigment in a concentrated puddle. With the paper dry, start by painting the edge of the wash area with a stroke of water. Charge your brush with water and a touch of the desired pigment. Apply this in long strokes along the edge of the wet area. Pick up more pigment only and apply it along the new edge. Repeat this process of adding more pigment (not water) with each stroke until you reach the other side of the wash area.

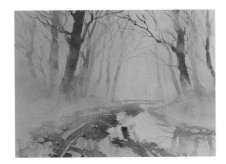

before

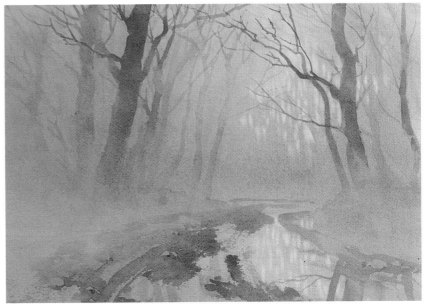

after

MOOD ADDED WITH A GLAZE

I painted a thin wash of Cobalt Blue through the center of this foggy road picture when it was dry. It provided the perfect opportunity to remove "sun spots" in the tree and puddles with a smaller scrubber brush.

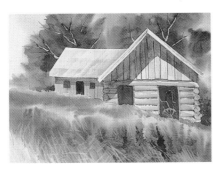

before

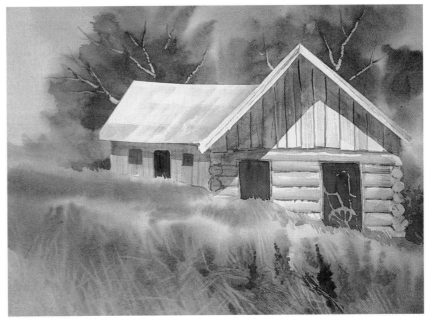

after

GLAZING HELPS FOCUS VIEWERS' EYES

Darkening some part of the picture, in this case the corners, with a thin glaze of Ultramarine Blue causes the eye to go to the remaining light area.

SECRETS TO ACHIEVING SUCCESSFUL WASHES

Stand so you can use your whole arm, work with large flat brushes, prepare lots of pigment in a large mixing area beforehand and tilt your board slightly to help the paint flow.

Fading Out a Color

Also called *pulling out* color, *pulling off* color or *softening an edge*, this technique is useful for achieving various effects in watercolor because of how the human eye perceives the edges of shapes. If an edge is sharp or well defined, we say that it is a *hard* edge—it attracts the eye, which will follow along its length. If an edge is fuzzy or indistinct, we say that it is a *soft* edge. The process of fading out gets viewers to see the hard edges you want them to see by softening the edges you do not want them to notice.

The terms pulling out or pulling off colors are misnomers because they indicate that you are physically moving the paint. To produce the effects you want, you must allow the water to move the paint in its own way. Your job is to place just the right amount of wetness in just the right spot at just the right time so the medium can do what it does best.

First, the direction in which you apply the water that will pull out the color is important. Do not reach into the paint and move it out with your brush. You will indeed spread the paint around, but you will not produce the smooth, graded effects that you want. What you are trying to do is to make a path of water movement that will attract the paint. This, of course, works best if the paint area is very wet and the brush is less wet or just damp.

BRUSHES FOR FADING OUT
For fading out small areas in a painting, either natural or synthetic brushes will work fine. However, synthetics have two drawbacks: They are unable to hold a large charge of paint for fading out large areas compared to natural bristles, and they have a habit of releasing their load all at once. Both of these features can make them frustrating when you wish to pull off a large body of color smoothly. Natural fiber brushes (squirrel, sable, goat, badger, ox, hog), on the other hand, hold a greater charge and release it more consistently, which makes them far better suited to this job.

To fade out color, you must apply water to the edge of the paint with a brush that is drier than the paint. A natural fiber brush, such as the hog bristle, will lay down a long path of water that is consistent from one end to the other. Synthetics tend to dump too much moisture at first, leaving about the right amount halfway and running out before getting to the end of a large area (see pages 18–19). The result is a run-back at the beginning, proper fading in the center and nothing at the end.

However, if the paper is wet first and you wish to add paint for fading out, you want a brush that releases its load quickly. In that case, a synthetic is the best choice for the job.

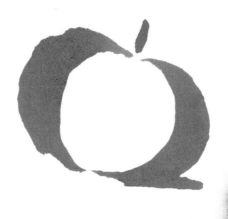

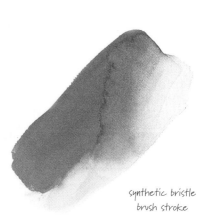

SOFTENING EDGES
Until one side of each mark above is softened, you are not quite sure what the subject is.

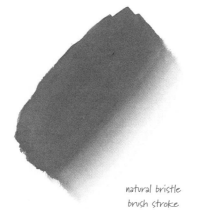

natural bristle
brush stroke

synthetic bristle
brush stroke

AN ALTERNATIVE METHOD OF FADING OUT COLOR

The reverse process for fading out color is to wet the paper first and then add color to it. Use this technique for large passages, such as skies, and for small areas, such as negative shapes. Negative shapes are the areas in an artwork not occupied by subject matter but utilized by the artist as part of the design (see pages 72–77). The only thing to remember is that the brush must be wetter than the surface moisture if you wish to achieve maximum flow for fading, because of "The Law You Cannot Ignore" (page 43).

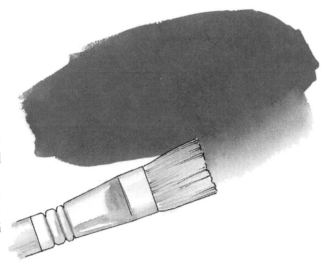

FOLLOW THE EDGE
In all cases, the brush is just damp and the paint is very wet. Make your stroke with the water, following the edge of the painted area. Be careful to just touch the color.

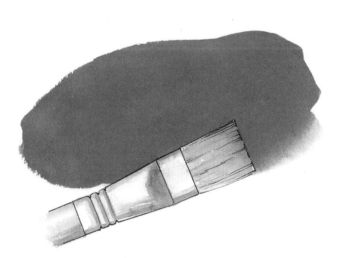

DON'T GO TOO FAR IN
If you go into the paint too far, your damp brush will act like a sponge and soak up the paint instead of causing it to spread.

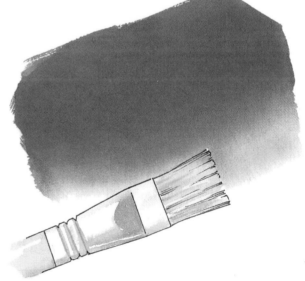

MAKE SUBSEQUENT STROKES OUT FARTHER
It may take several strokes to get the paint to move, but when it does, make the subsequent strokes at a greater and greater distance out. The paint will follow.

Working Wet-in-Wet

Working wet-in-wet means painting on a wet surface—any wet surface, whether it's wet with clear water or a mixture of paint and water. It is important to understand the role that the wet-in-wet process plays in the unique appearance of watercolors.

Nothing utilizes the potential of watercolors like the process of working wet-in-wet. To help you find techniques of your own, I have organized the painting process into three steps, each with options for you to explore. Basically, you start by wetting the paper in some way, then add color in some way to this wetted area, then extend the process. The unique results you get depend on the options you choose in each of these three steps.

COVERAGE

all over

OPTIONS FOR WETTING THE PAPER

METHOD

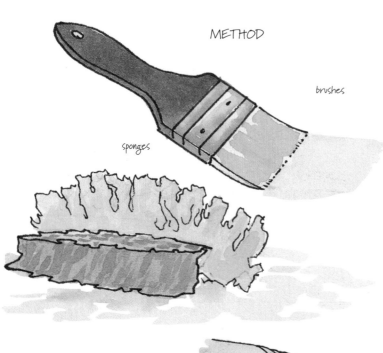

brushes

sponges

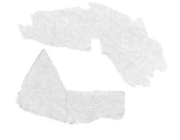

in an irregular pattern

defines specific shapes

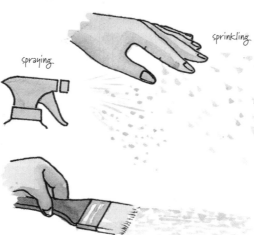

spraying

sprinkling

hog hair brush drawn lightly
across the surface

partially cover the surface

OPTIONS FOR ADDING PAINT

Now you have choices in the way you apply paint to the wet paper, but remember that at any time you could tilt your paper to help colors move. Also realize that a damp surface will not react to paint in the same way a wet one will, so experiment with the degree of wetness on your paper. There are many different combinations of wetting the paper and adding color for you to explore.

WET BY SPRAYING, PAINT BY POURING
If you wet the paper by spraying and add paint by pouring, you get something like this.

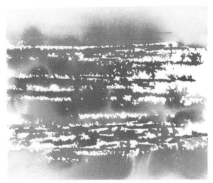

WET PARTIALLY, PAINT WITH A FLAT
You get this effect if you partially wet the paper with a hog hair brush and add paint with a loaded flat synthetic brush. You can get a similar effect by partially wetting the paper and adding paint with a sponge.

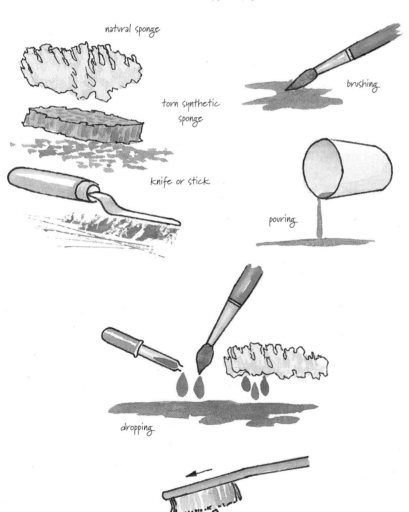

natural sponge

torn synthetic sponge

knife or stick

brushing

pouring

dropping

spattering

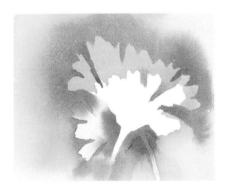

WET IN SHAPES, PAINT WHEN DAMP
If you wet the paper in specific shapes and add paint with a loaded brush when the paper is just damp, you get this.

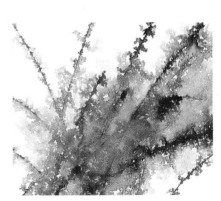

WET BY SPRAYING, PAINT WITH A PALETTE KNIFE
If you wet the paper by spraying and add paint with the edge of a palette knife, you get this effect.

SUSTAINING THE
WET-IN-WET PROCESS

Once the paint in the wet-in-wet process begins to dry, that is, to lose its shine, you enter a "magic time" in watercolors—a time when the medium comes to life. It is in these few moments, when the paint takes on a dull sheen, that you can perform many unusual techniques. You will not have much success if you try too soon or wait too long. It's at this damp stage that adding more color or water or removing paint can give the most dramatic results.

Every time you add paint or water, you add moisture to the paper—in effect, you sustain the "magic time." It is best that you use only nonstaining, transparent to semitransparent colors for this wet-in-wet process, because they are delicate, have good flow, and have the capability of leaving lighter areas when blossoms occur.

Options A and B are ways to add more water. Option C suggests ways to lift or move color. For adding color, use the methods suggested previously.

DROPPING SALT
INTO WET PAINT

This is also a way to remove paint, since the salt bleaches the color away, leaving irregular stars. The drier the paint, the smaller the stars are.

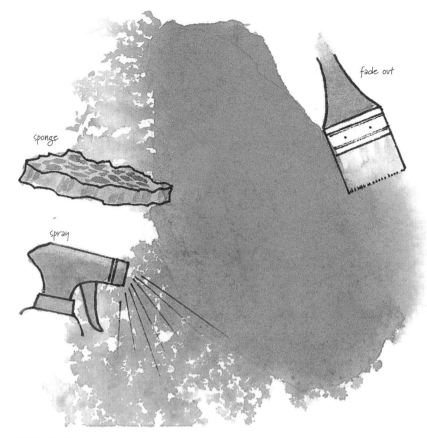

OPTION A
Add more water when the paint is wet.

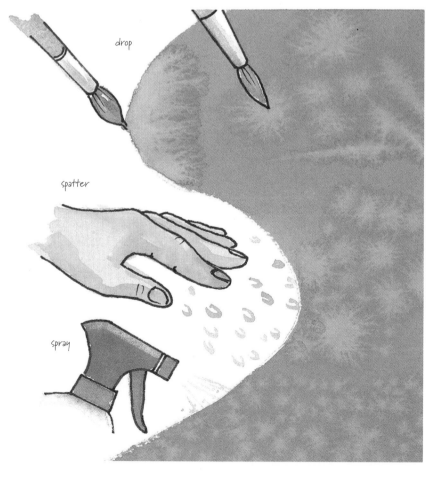

OPTION B
Add more water when the paint is damp.

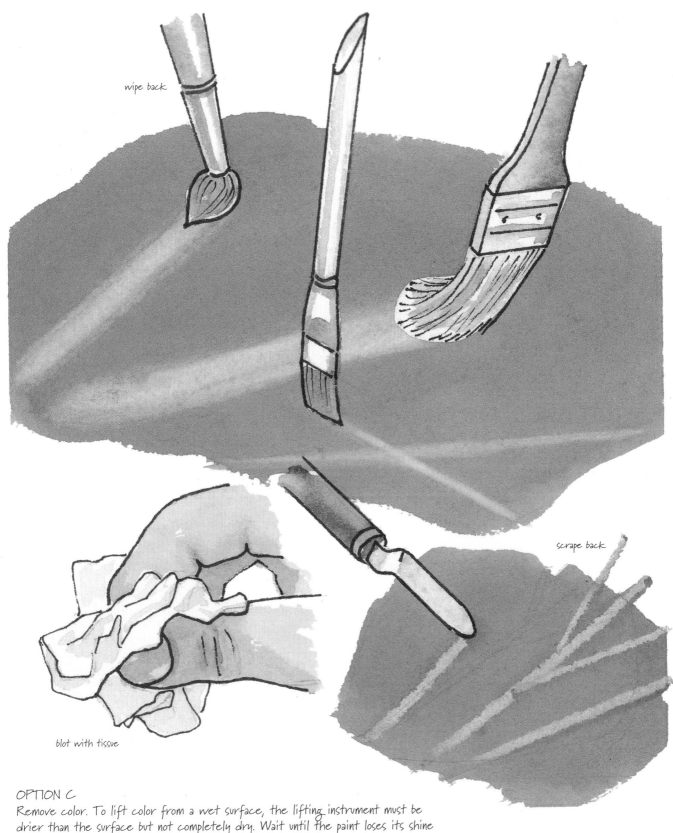

wipe back

blot with tissue

scrape back

OPTION C

Remove color. To lift color from a wet surface, the lifting instrument must be drier than the surface but not completely dry. Wait until the paint loses its shine and then use a stiff, damp brush to lift paint or a palette knife to push it back. You can also remove paint by wetting an area as in option A, wait a few moments, and then blot with a clean dry tissue.

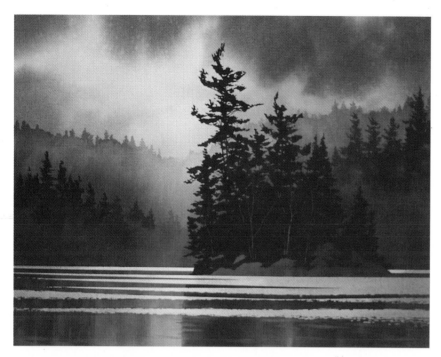

LAKE SPIRIT
19" x 22" (48cm x 56cm)
Private collection

MOOD AND TEMPERATURE
Wet-in-wet painting is a means of covering areas of your painting with soft, nebulous passages of color that help set the mood and temperature of the work. In Lake Spirit, the soft, cool atmospherics also encourage our eyes to move to the hard edges of the island trees and the light patches on the water.

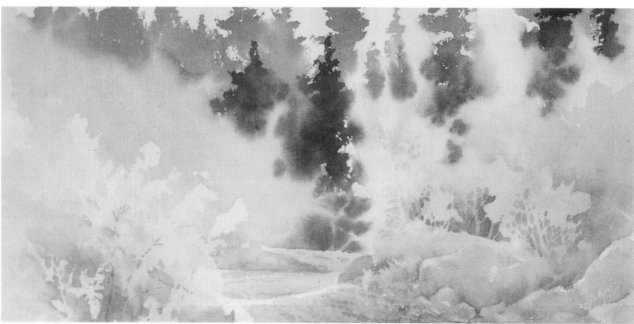

ELEMENT OF MYSTERY AND INTRIGUE
The ethereal effects created by the wet-in-wet approach can add that all-important element of mystery and intrigue to your work. With it you provide only the suggestion of reality—an area for the viewer's imagination to complete its own images. Here I intentionally left wet-in-wet areas for the viewer to ponder.

AUTUMN WALK
Detail
15" x 22" (38cm x 56cm)
Private collection

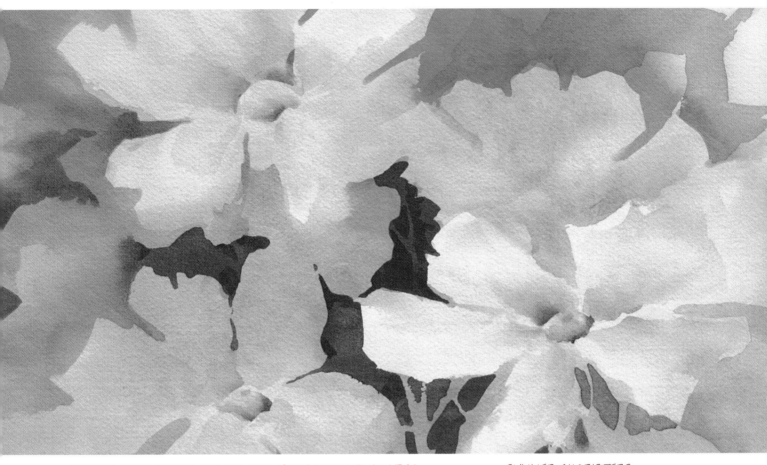

WET-IN-WET BACKGROUND AND FOREGROUND SHAPES

Sometimes wet-in-wet background shapes can evolve, with negative painting, into major foreground shapes and even the center of interest. Summer Choristers started as a loose wash of Cobalt Blue, Permanent Rose and Raw Sienna. After the wash dried, I used these same colors to carve out and model flowers from this background by painting around them.

SUMMER CHORISTERS
Detail
11" x 15" (28cm x 38cm)
Private collection

Masking

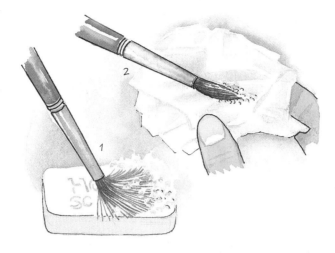

Masking is a technique used to cover an area temporarily in order to prevent it from being painted. It allows you to preserve delicate white areas or to develop special background effects that would otherwise be impossible. Masking should not be used as a crutch. Before using any masking material, ask yourself if you could just as easily save the area by painting around it (negative painting—see pages 72–77). If you do decide to use masking, test it on your paper first.

USING LIQUID LATEX

It is important that you use a decent brush to apply your liquid latex (also called masking fluid). If you use an old brush that you would not even paint with, as other books will state, you will end up with inferior brush marks and, therefore, less than desired shapes in the end. However, do not use a natural-fiber brush for applying liquid latex. The latex can damage the resilience of the fibers. Instead use a synthetic brush and protect it from the gum by first applying soap to it. When finished, immediately rinse, soap again, rinse, soap again and rinse. Your brush will last indefinitely. If you dedicate a couple of inexpensive synthetic brushes for masking, you won't have to risk your more expensive ones.

PROTECTING YOUR BRUSH
Before dipping your brush into liquid masking material, make sure you have soaped the brush well. Wipe excess soap from the brush with a tissue before use. Use a synthetic brush.

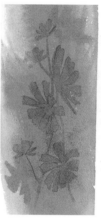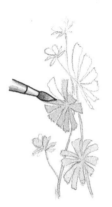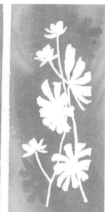

BASIC PROCEDURE
Apply masking fluid and let it dry. Always double-check for small spots that you may have missed. When the masking has dried thoroughly, apply background colors and techniques. When the paint is dry, remove the masking fluid with a rubber cement pickup.

OTHER WAYS TO APPLY LIQUID LATEX

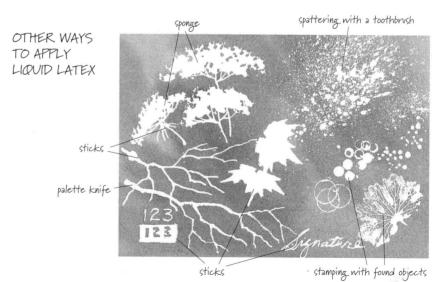

sponge

spattering with a toothbrush

sticks

palette knife

sticks

stamping with found objects

TIP FOR REMOVING LIQUID LATEX

If all else fails, lighter fluid will remove masking fluid that has dried on your brush.

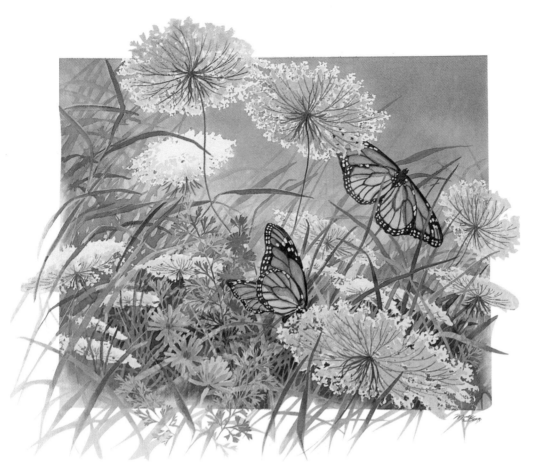

ROYAL VISIT
19" x 22"
(48cm x 56cm)
Collection of the
artist
Photographer:
Kevin Dobie,
Kevanna Studios

USING BOTH ENDS OF YOUR BRUSH

In Royal Visit, I applied the masking fluid for the Queen Anne's lace with a sponge and the butt end of a paintbrush (for individual florets). For the stems, I applied it with a sharp stick, and for the butterflies, grass and chicory flowers I used a brush. Once the background was dry, I removed the masking. Before I painted the butterflies, I saved the white spots on their wings by reapplying masking fluid, again with the butt end of a paintbrush.

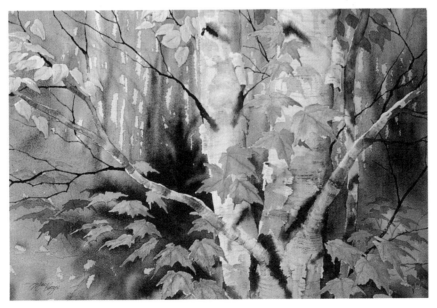

AUTUMN BIRCH
15" x 22" (38cm x 56cm)
Private collection

SOMETIMES YOU HAVE TO MASK OUT TWICE

Here, masking fluid for the trunks of the birches and their leaves was painted on with a brush. For the branches, I used a palette knife. I masked out the maple leaves using a flat, chisel-ended stick. I painted the background and let it dry. I removed the masking fluid, but before I could paint the birch trunk, I had to mask the leaves in front of it, again with a flat, chisel-ended stick.

STEP BY STEP: MULTIPLE MASKING

This is a technique of repeated masking over previously painted areas in order to preserve colors and shapes. It has a very unusual visual effect. Multiple masking requires a paper with great endurance, such as 140-lb. (300gm) or 300-lb. (640gm) watercolor paper. This process takes a while to complete because of the drying time needed between steps. Don't try to rush things by drying masking fluid with a hair dryer or in the sun. You will adhere the masking fluid to the paper.

Transparent to semitransparent colors are best for multiple masking because they are delicate and their transparency makes them excellent for layering. I use Cobalt Blue, Burnt Sienna, Red Rose Deep and Indian Yellow in the following demonstration. I did the masking with a brush and a palette knife.

WHAT YOU NEED

140-lb. (300gm) or 300-lb. (640gm) watercolor paper
masking fluid
masking brush
transparent to semitransparent watercolors of your choice
palette knife
watercolor brushes of your choice
salt

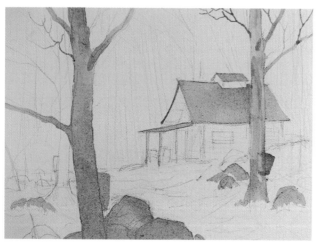

1. MASK OUT MAJOR FOREGROUND SHAPES.
With masking fluid (liquid latex), mask out major foreground shapes that you wish to remain white. Let the masking fluid dry.

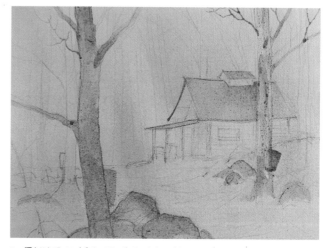

2. PAINT OVER THE MASKED AREA.
Apply a thin wash over the masked area — a mixture of Cobalt Blue, Burnt Sienna and Red Rose Deep. Let the wash dry.

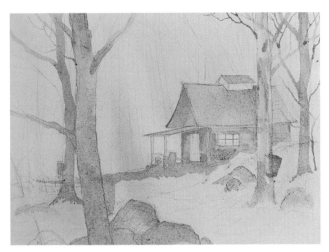

3. MASK OUT MORE SHAPES.
Shapes can overlap previous ones. Let the shapes dry.

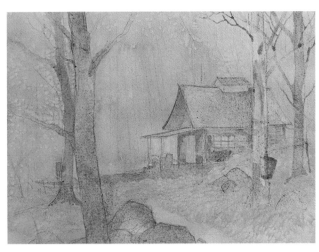

4. PAINT OVER THE MASKED SHAPES.
Apply a mixture of Cobalt Blue and Burnt Sienna over the masked area. Add salt in ground and tree areas. Let the paint dry.

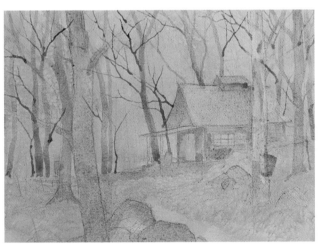

5. MASK OUT EVEN MORE SHAPES.
Again, shapes can overlap previous ones. Let the shapes dry.

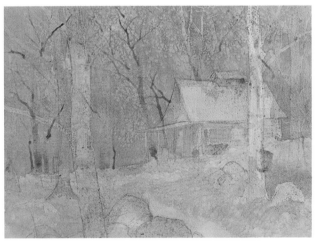

6. PAINT OVER THOSE MASKED SHAPES.
Apply a mixture of Cobalt Blue and Burnt Sienna over the masked area. Add more salt in the background. Let the paint dry.

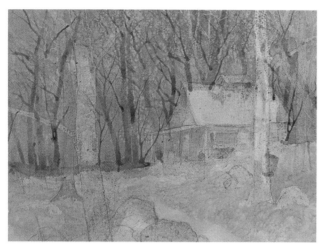

7. MASK OUT STILL MORE SHAPES.
Shapes can overlap previous ones. Let the shapes dry.

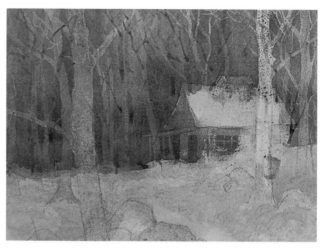

8. PAINT OVER MASKED SHAPES AGAIN.
Apply mixtures of Cobalt Blue, Burnt Sienna and Red Rose Deep over the masked area. Let the paint dry.

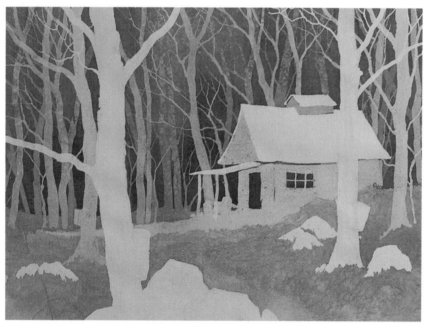

9. REMOVE ALL THE MASKING FLUID.
Remove all the masking fluid with a rubber cement pickup.

IT'S LIKE OPENING A PRESENT

When the painting is so dark that you can't see what you are doing, you should probably stop. Wait until the painting is perfectly dry, then remove all the masking gum with a rubber cement pickup (used to pick up excess dried rubber cement from paper or other surfaces). This is like opening a present. Bit by bit it reveals colored shapes overlapping into the darkness. The gum has a tendency to remove some color from the page, so you may want to go back in with more concentrated colors. You also may want to suggest shading and cast shadows on major shapes.

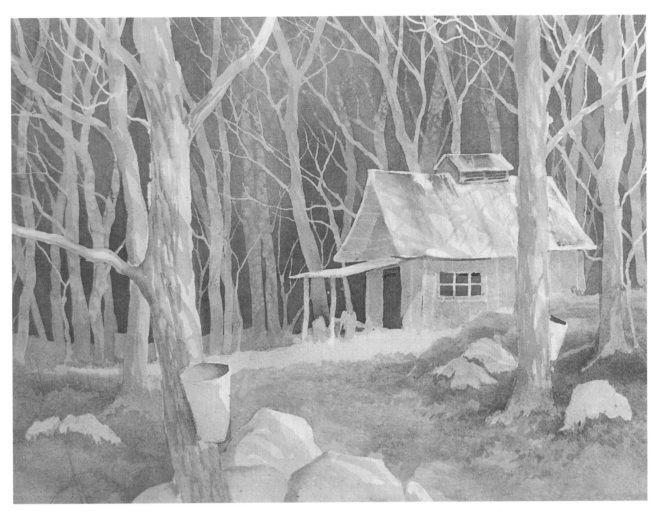

10. PAINT FOREGROUND SHAPES.
Touch up colors, then add shadows.

MASKING TAPE

You can put down masking tape in overlapping pieces to cover a large area, then cut it with a sharp craft knife to the desired shape. You can tear it lengthwise and then put it down to produce an irregular edge around an object. You can use it with a piece of paper in order to save tape. You can cut it into strips and then apply it to the painting.

DISADVANTAGE OF MASKING TAPE

Because of the thickness of some masking tape and the roughness of watercolor paper, paint sometimes seeps in underneath the tape, even when you think you have pressed it down firmly.

PACKING TAPE

This is the thin, 2-inch-wide plastic tape used to wrap parcels and boxes. It comes in clear, but buy the brown or gray so you can see it on the paper. It is transparent enough for you to see a preliminary sketch right through it. Do not buy the "heavy weight" grade. The cheap economy grade is thinner and does a better job of following the texture of the paper.

You can quickly cover large areas with this tape. You can cut shapes from it more easily than from masking tape, using a very sharp (fresh blade) craft knife and applying just the *slightest* pressure to cut the *tape* and not the paper. You will learn through practice how much pressure to put on the craft knife. Try it on a test paper or old painting first.

Lay the tape down with just enough pressure all over to hold it in place. Cut the desired shapes, then carefully lift the corner of the tape and remove the tape from the areas you do not need to mask. With only the desired shapes on the paper, press the tape down firmly. A clean rubber brayer (a hand roller) is excellent for this job.

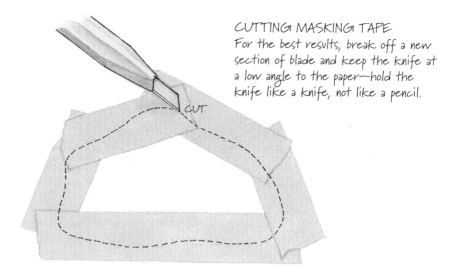

CUTTING MASKING TAPE
For the best results, break off a new section of blade and keep the knife at a low angle to the paper—hold the knife like a knife, not like a pencil.

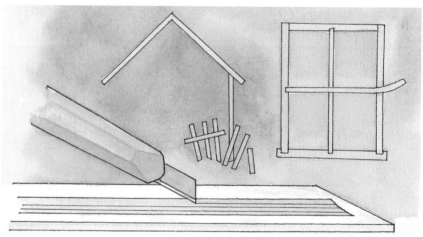

CUTTING TAPE OUTSIDE THE PICTURE
By placing a piece of tape on a smooth, hard surface, you can cut it into fine strips using a knife and ruler. Use these fine strips to define architectural detail. Press down well before painting.

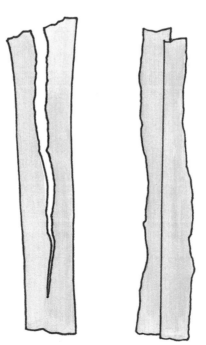

REARRANGING TORN TAPE
Tear the tape lengthwise. Rearrange the pieces to produce a shape with rough edges. Good for tree trunks and rocks.

TIP FOR LIFTING TAPE

You can lessen the tape's grip on the paper by gently warming it with a hair dryer.

ADVANTAGE OF PACKING TAPE

As mentioned above, because packing tape is so thin, it tends to follow the contours of the paper surface better than masking tape. When the tape is firmly pressed down, there is no leakage, even on small pieces.

Unlike masking fluids, which you can remove only when the painting is completely dry, you can remove tape (very carefully) while the painting is still wet. You might want to do this so you can fade out a few edges of the masked shape(s) with a damp brush to blend them into the background. This helps eliminate a cut-and-paste look while adding flow and unity to the work.

DISADVANTAGE OF PACKING TAPE

Tape may split when you lift it, making it troublesome to get off the paper.

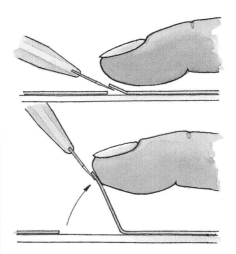

WHAT YOU NEED

watercolor paper
pencil
masking or packing tape
very sharp craft knife
watercolors of your choice

HOW TO REMOVE PACKING TAPE
Use the tip of a knife blade to carefully lift a corner. Press the tape against the side of the knife tip with your index finger and together lift the tape gently.

STEP BY STEP: MASKING WITH TAPE

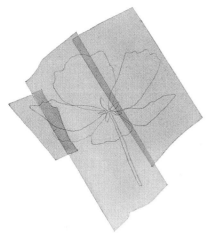

1. Cover your sketch with pieces of overlapping tape. Press down lightly.

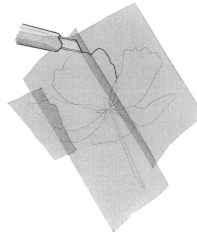

2. Cut around the shape with a very sharp craft knife, using just enough pressure to cut the tape.

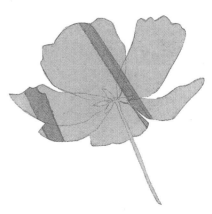

3. Remove unwanted tape, and rub down remaining tape firmly.

4. Paint on the desired background color.

5. When paint is dry, remove tape.

A Mix of Techniques

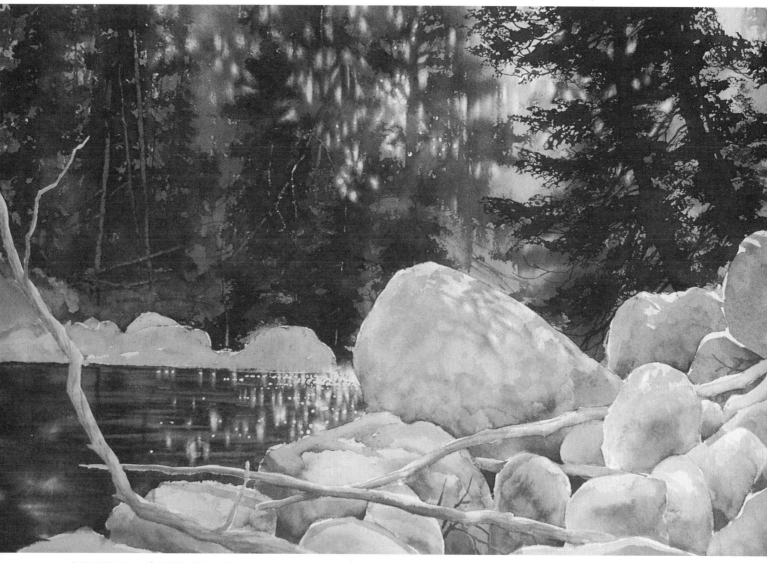

SUMMARY OF TECHNIQUES
Mottled rocks: drops of water dropped into damp paint. Background trees: partial wetting area with vertical strokes using a hog hair brush. I then painted the trees with a sponge. Foreground trees: sponged on when paper was dry. Water sparkles: masking fluid applied with the butt end of a brush for each sun spot. Smaller scrubber brush used to soften sun spots in trees, on water (when masking removed) and on rocks.

TROUT STREAM
15" x 22" (38cm x 56cm)
Private collection

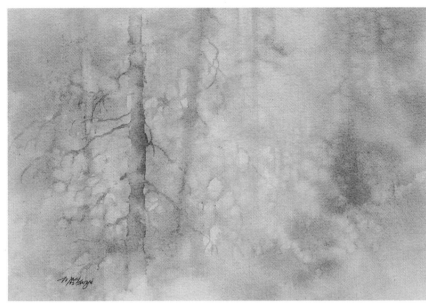

DREAM LIGHTS
11" x 15" (28cm x 38cm)
Private collection

SUMMARY OF TECHNIQUES
This is an example of a sustained wet-in-wet process. I laid down an initial wash of Cobalt Blue, Permanent Rose and Raw Sienna. I continued to move between adding more water by dropping and spraying, adding more paint by brushing and dropping, and removing paint with a damp brush or tissue. When it had evolved into what I found pleasing, I stopped.

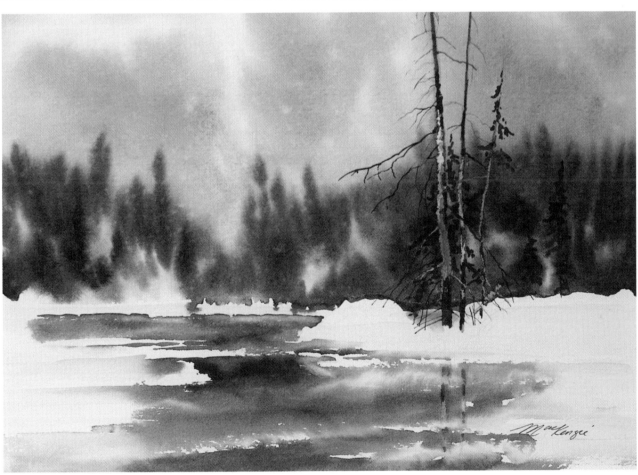

SUMMARY OF TECHNIQUES
Sky: a loose wet-in-wet wash of grays and blue carried halfway down the page. Shoreline: concentrated color added with hog hair brush while sky area was damp. Water: area partially wetted horizontally with large hog hair brush. I dropped in pigment with a large flat synthetic brush, then faded out around the edges with a damp hog hair brush. Tree: painted with a palette knife.

NOVEMBER BLUES
15" x 22" (38cm x 56cm)
Private collection

3 Putting Together Your Composition

You rarely find the perfect composition or design for a painting in real life. What you find instead are the seeds for a composition—the parts and pieces of ideas that you can combine or expand into a pleasing arrangement. You must manipulate and refine visual stimuli until they take on a whole new life of their own. The real magic behind the arts is the creation of new ways to express the ordinary.

You can learn much about composing pictures by studying works of more experienced painters, reading art books or taking workshops. In the process, you will encounter a conglomeration of rules, procedures and techniques, some of which will prove of value in composing your own pictures. However, the real source to rely on is within you. You already know how to compose. You did it once as a child, and now all you have to do is reawaken that instinctive ability by having the courage to believe in it and use it as you make compositional decisions.

Factors to Consider

Things to think about in your composition include subject, point of view and center of interest; picture format; closure; shapes, lines and edges; movement, repetition, pattern and rhythm; value, color, contrast and gradation. These are the elements and principles of your composition, or design.

Composing is the process of planning out your arrangement of shapes, lines, values, colors, etc., so you make the best visual statement possible. This process combines art, logic, skill, intuition and imagination. Alas, techniques alone do not compensate for a poor arrangement. On the other hand, a well-planned picture will survive some fairly sloppy techniques. Think of yourself as a "visual author." You have the right to manipulate the components of your picture in whatever way necessary to tell the most exciting story possible. Composing is just the process of thinking out the options and arrangements for your story.

SOME FUNDAMENTAL TRUTHS

1. It's our basic nature to create.
2. We all embrace an individual sense of what "feels right" that also seems to reflect an unconscious universal consensus.
3. We all go about creating what "feels right" differently.

SUBJECT

This is what your picture is about, e.g., the sea, flowers, buildings, people, etc. It's like the theme for a story and should emphasize those things that you find most appealing about the subject, i.e., color combinations, contrasts, shapes, lighting, mood, message, etc.

CENTER OF INTEREST

A picture needs a leading character. This most important object, area or aspect of your picture is called the focal point or center of interest. If you use strong contrast, unique color combinations and a pathway for the eye, the viewer will find it no matter where you put it.

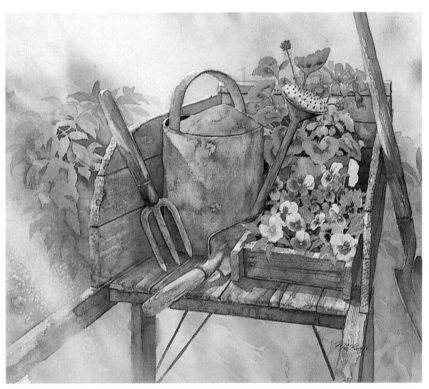

LOCATION LEADS THE EYE FIRST
A center of interest does not have to be the biggest thing in your picture, but it does need to have the greatest attracting power. It's an object's location, first and foremost, that leads the eye toward it—as well as value contrast, lines (edges), series of lesser shapes or unusual color.

In Planting Time, the convergence of the edges and handles of the wheelbarrow and the position of the garden fork and trowel lead your eye to the box of flowers. It is kept in this pocket by the leaning shovel and the spout of the watering can. The purity, uniqueness and light value of the flower colors contrast with the darker, dulled colors of other shapes in the composition.

PLANTING TIME
19" x 22"
(48cm x 56cm)
Collection of the artist

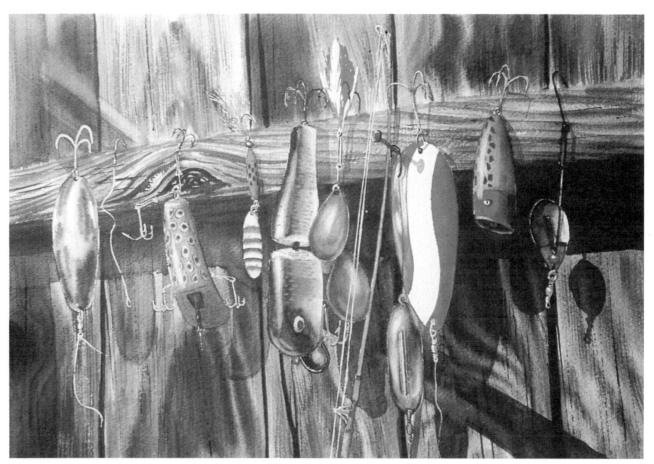

SEVERAL MINOR CENTERS OF INTEREST

It is possible to have several minor centers of interest to help lead the viewer around the picture. Take a look at Summer's Arsenal. The major object is the red-and-white lure. However, the other lures act as minor centers of interest, adding variety of shape, color and pattern that leads the eye back and forth along the wall.

SUMMER'S ARSENAL
15" x 22" (38cm x 56cm)
Collection of the artist

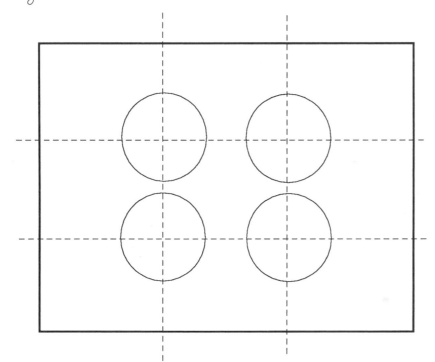

GOOD LOCATIONS FOR FOCAL POINTS
Divide your picture space into thirds vertically and horizontally. The intersections of these lines are good locations for a center of interest.

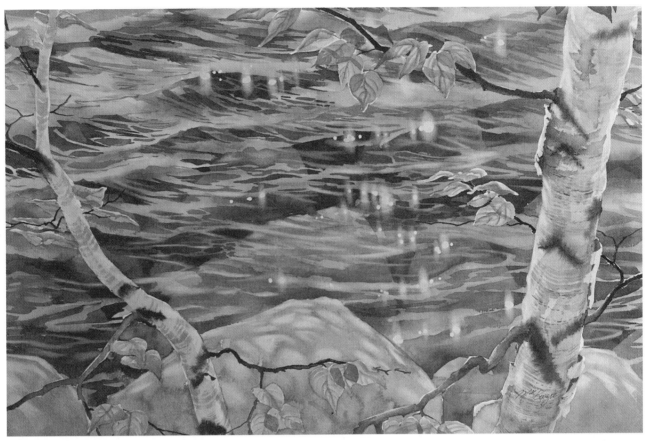

DRAW ATTENTION TO AN AREA

Sometimes, particularly in landscape painting, it is not a single object but an area to which you want to draw attention, such as sparkles on water, a sunset or a tree on a hill. In Liquid Diamonds, the sparkles on the transparent water are my focal point. I framed them with the trees and rocks.

LIQUID DIAMONDS
15" x 22" (38cm x 56cm)
Collection of the artist

TAKE ADVANTAGE OF HOW WE READ

Another way to view the picture space is in terms of quadrants, with each quadrant being a possible location for the center of interest. This method allows you to take advantage of how we read, that is, left to right, top to bottom, which influences the way we view a picture. We assume the beginning to be upper left and the conclusion to be lower right.

We see this bird immediately because of the way we read, leading the eye into seeing more in the picture.

We see this bird quickly, but its location suggests flight or suspension in space.

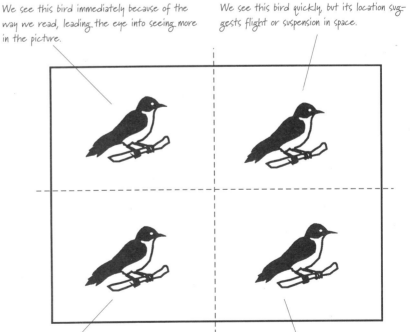

Our eyes delay moving to this quadrant. Locating the bird here suggests there is more to the story.

In this quadrant we feel as if we have come to the end of the story.

PICTURE FORMAT

This is probably the most forgotten aspect of composition, yet one that is fundamental to your treatment of the subject and its resulting impact. Format refers to the proportions (the lengths of the sides) of your picture and whether you use a horizontal rectangle or vertical rectangle. A vertical format causes the eye to move up and down and enhances feelings of growth, dignity and soaring. An exaggerated horizontal format improves the sense of distance and space. In this format, predominant horizontal lines emphasize calm or, if curving, rhythm and flow. Some artists believe the square format is boring; others see it as a challenge. Make up your own mind.

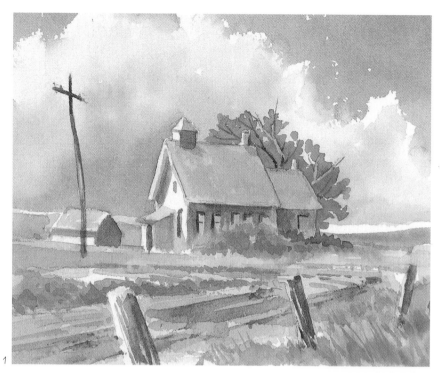

1

EXPRESSION CHANGES WITH DIFFERENT FORMATS

These pictures illustrate how a subject's expression changes simply by choosing a different format. By taking the subject of Figure 1 and expressing it in a tall format (Figure 2), I created a vertical movement between the foreground and middle ground, that is, between the flowers and the building. The vertical shape also allowed me to say more about this old country schoolhouse, for it, too, is pushing up daisies. In Figure 4, the greater horizontal expanse allowed me to better express the flow and movement of the stream than in Figure 3.

2

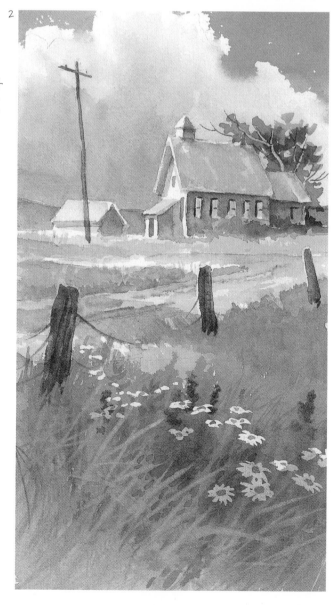

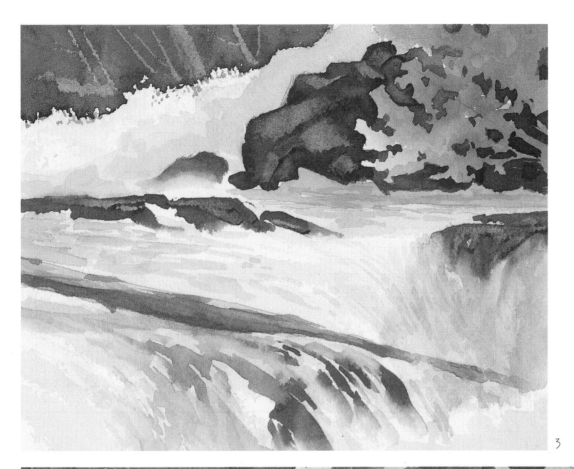

3

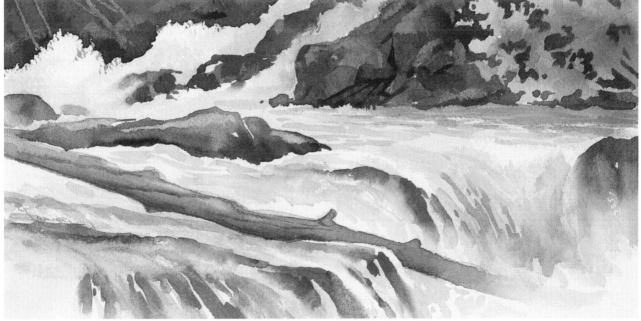

4

CLOSURE

Closure is the mental (usually subconscious) process of "finishing"—making connections between random bits of information to produce relevant meaning. The brain relies heavily on memory to identify things. For example, as you proceed through your daily life, you don't have to stop and examine every little detail that you encounter. You know from memory what your environment contains. You only slow down when your brain detects something unknown or different from the norm. At this point it switches from subconscious processing to conscious awareness until it can identify, process and file the new data for future reference.

With only a minimum number of clues (and memory), the brain jumps to conclusions. You only need to smell baking bread to know that it is there. When you see only part of an object, you take for granted the rest is there. The brain will make every effort to find some sort of meaning.

As humans, we take great pleasure in finding closure. Think of all the games, mystery stories, quizzes and puzzles there are. They entertain us by testing our abilities to find some hidden closure. It seems that the harder the problem, the greater the sense of accomplishment we experience in finding closure.

PLAYING MIND GAMES

Closure can work to your benefit when the viewer's mind completes an image. Strangely enough, with minimum clues the viewer's mind tends to complete the best image it can. The viewer, in turn, thinks that you are a wonderful artist. In other words, by painting less you paint better. An example of this is painting only part of a flower, leaving the rest to the imagination.

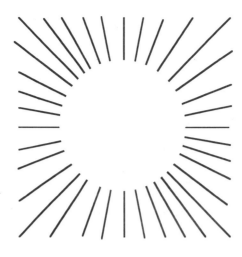

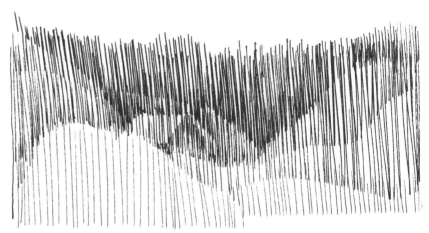

CLOSURE IS JUMPING TO CONCLUSIONS
What do you see in these two illustrations? If you see something other than the straight lines I have drawn, it is because your brain is jumping to conclusions in order to reach closure.

LACK OF CLOSURE IS FRUSTRATING
In this maze of lines there is a perfect five-pointed star. Can you find it? If you can, you are going to feel pretty good about yourself, because this is a tough one. You might feel frustrated and eventually want to look at the answer on page 72. Now if the answer was not there, you just might get a little more than cranky, because you might not have reached closure.

HOORAY FOR WATERCOLORS!

The soft subtleties of watercolors can create and suggest images that make use of closure. The fact that we can merely suggest images by using wet-in-wet or damp techniques is of immeasurable advantage when playing the closure game.

HOLDING THEIR ATTENTION

Billboards and road signs depend on instant closure in order to be functional. In fine art, however, we want delayed or multiple closures in order to hold the viewer's eye and interest as long as possible. The longer the eye lingers over a work, the more rewarding the closure feels. Viewers feel more a part of the work when there are more levels of meaning the mind can discover. If you have ever had someone say about one of your paintings, "Every time I look at it I see something different," then you are on the right track. If there is no room in your picture for viewers to reflect, contemplate or delve into what is before them, then they very quickly lose interest and stop seeing it.

Paintings rendered super-realistically run the risk of not leaving room for the viewer's imagination. A painting should speak of more than the artist's technical virtuosity. It should provide the viewer with essential information about the subject, in whatever detail the artist desires, but also leave room for the viewer's imagination.

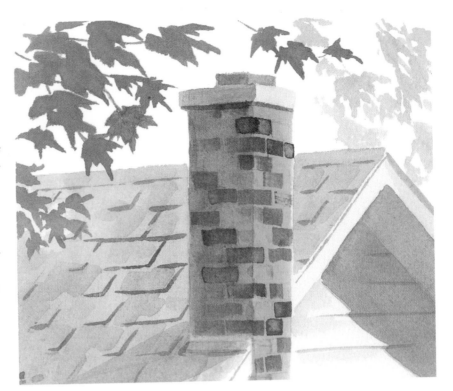

SAY MORE BY PAINTING LESS

Closure allows you to say more by painting less. For example, you may need to paint a great number of the same objects in your picture, such as leaves on a tree or bricks on a wall. If you paint a few realistically, viewers can identify them and come to closure, assuming the rest are also realistic.

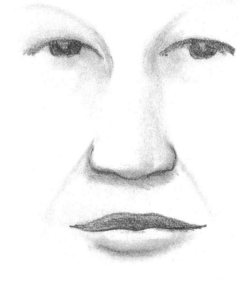

THE BRAIN GENERATES AN OUTLINE

Take a moment to stare at this face. The brain is so eager to see the complete face that it will generate a ghostly outline on its own.

SHAPES

Shapes are the building blocks of compositions. As such, their position, arrangement and characteristics play a vital role in our pictures. You may hear the subject, or positive shape, referred to as the *figure*. You may hear the background, or negative shapes, referred to as the *ground*. The term shape refers to both positive and negative areas. You may hear a large negative shape called a *passage* or *space*.

POSITIVE AND NEGATIVE SHAPES IN ACTION

In a picture, the ground (negative) is as important as the figure (positive). The role they play in relation to each other varies when a composition involves overlapping shapes. For example, the ferns (at right) are the positive figure against the negative background. In Figure b, the dark positive ferns now act also as the negative shape for the new positive foreground ferns. You can use this process of having one positive shape become the negative for another throughout your painting, primarily through value differences.

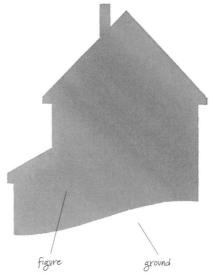
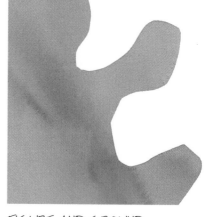

figure   ground

FIGURE AND GROUND
Depending on how the viewer perceives them, sometimes the roles of the figure and ground change. Which is the figure? Which is the ground?

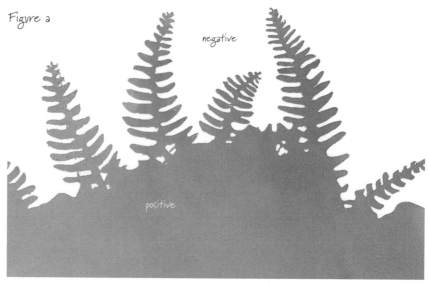

Figure a

negative

positive

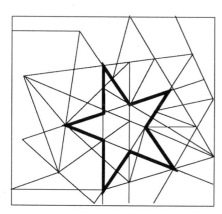

tah-dah

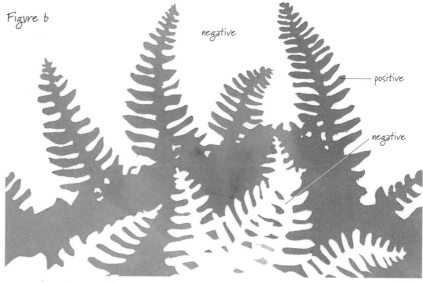

Figure b

negative

positive

negative

NEGATIVE PAINTING

This is the process of painting around an object to make it stand out in your composition. Because you do not use white or opaque colors to paint light-valued objects, you must learn to save them by painting the negative space next to them. Mind you, what might be the negative space for one shape may be a positive shape on its own.

Negative painting depends heavily upon closure (see page 77) for its effect. When you create objects by painting around them, you expect the viewer to identify those objects not by the paint you put down, but by the paint you do not. Not all negative painting uses the same rate of closure. By painting the complete contour (outline) of a flower you have immediate closure. By painting only parts of its contour you have delayed closure. By painting overlapping negative shapes you create multiple closure.

You, like many others, may find this process difficult to understand. You may believe that it requires some sort of optical gymnastics of which you are not capable, but you probably do it all the time and don't realize it. Every time you paint something dark behind something lighter, you are negative painting. For example, when you define the bricks in a wall by painting the lines between them, you are negative painting bricks. When you create fluffy white clouds in the sky by painting the darker blue sky areas, you are, in effect, painting the clouds in the negative. Once you understand how simple this process is, it will open doors to better and easier expression.

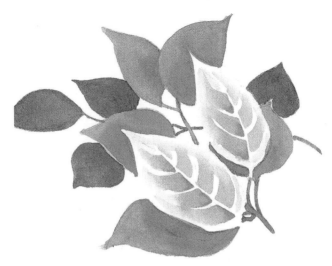

IS IT NEGATIVE OR POSITIVE? The negative space for one object may be a positive shape on its own.

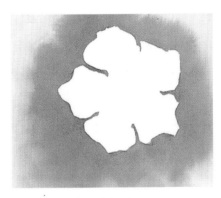
immediate closure

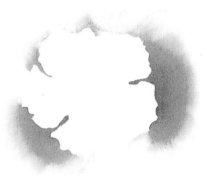
delayed closure

WATCH OUT

Because of the layering usually involved with negative painting, it is advisable to use transparent or semi-transparent colors. If you wish to show numerous shapes that are to be farther and farther back in the picture, then:

• Use light to medium colors for each layer. If you go dark too quickly, it becomes difficult to show much depth in the work.

• Save only one or two shapes with each layer. If you start by saving all the shapes in the first layer, the spaces in between are so small that it becomes difficult to paint any other shapes of significance farther back.

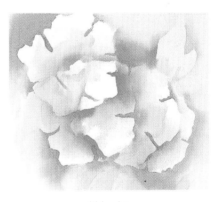
multiple closure

GENERALITIES WITH NEGATIVE PAINTING

- There are many variations in negative painting.
- Apply negative painting in stages, allowing the paint to dry in between stages. With each successive layer, you add new shapes and values to the work.
- The color you use to paint around a shape will be the underlying color of the next shape you define in the background.
- You can lightly pencil in shapes so you do not become lost in the process.
- You may proceed with the painting at your own speed. There is no need to rush except when you might want to pull off (fade out) an edge before it dries.
- You can use negative painting at any stage of a work. You may wish to begin your painting by saving (painting around) important white areas, or you can use negative painting later on top of a previously painted passage.
- How far you extend the paint beyond the shape you are saving is your choice. It could go a small distance or fill the remainder of the paper.
- As shown on page 73, you can vary the amount of contour you paint.
- Negative painting will give your work a fresh, spontaneous look that is hard to achieve with masking.

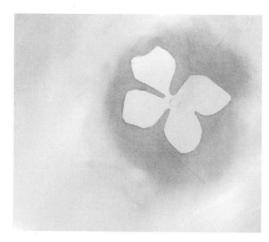

1. WASH, SKETCH AND NEGATIVE PAINTING.
Here I started with a wash of Raw Sienna and Permanent Rose for my background. When this was dry, I sketched my flower and painted around it with a mix of the same colors. I faded this into the background with a damp brush.

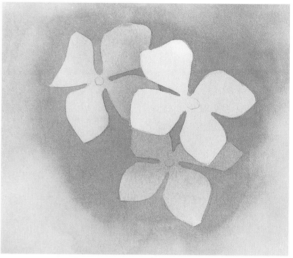

2. MORE FLOWERS AND NEGATIVE PAINTING.
When the paint was dry, I sketched in two more flowers, then painted around them and the first flower with the same Permanent Rose and Raw Sienna mixture.

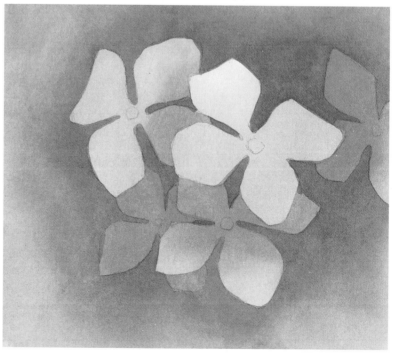

3. ALTER THE WASH MIX.
I repeated Step 2, but I began to alter the color by adding in a touch of Sap Green.

STEP BY STEP: FLOWERS WITH NEGATIVE PAINTING

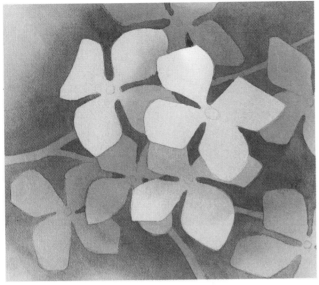

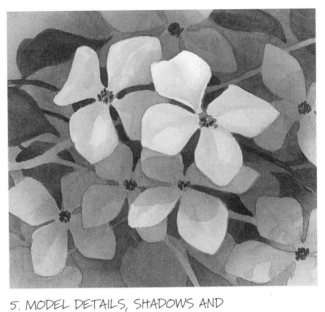

4. ADD MORE SHAPES, AND PAINT AROUND THEM.
When this was dry, I drew in some more flowers and limbs, then painted around all the shapes, adding more Sap Green.

5. MODEL DETAILS, SHADOWS AND BACKGROUND SHAPES.
I modeled the interior of the flowers with a pale Permanent Rose slightly dulled with Sap Green and the cast shadows with Permanent Rose cooled with Cobalt Blue. I also added some darker positive shapes in the background to balance the light shapes and suggest greater depth. Notice that these positive shapes are still the negative shapes for the flowers.

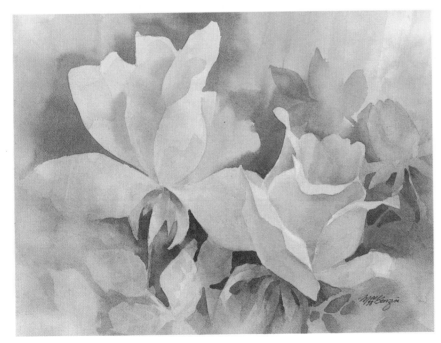

WHAT YOU NEED

watercolor paper
watercolor paints of your choice
- Raw Sienna
- Permanent Rose
- Sap Green
- Cobalt Blue
water
brushes of your choice

ROSE BUDS
11" x 14" (28cm x 36cm)
Collection of the artist

IMPRESSION AND MOOD OF BLOSSOMS
I used the same palette except with more Raw Sienna. Notice how you can create the appearance of flowers by only painting parts of the contours. Using this approach, it is so much easier to capture the impression and mood of blossoms. Notice also how the resulting hard and soft edges keep the eye moving and wondering what it's perceiving.

STEP BY STEP: ROCKS WITH NEGATIVE PAINTING

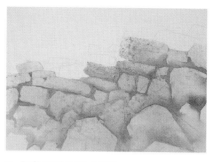

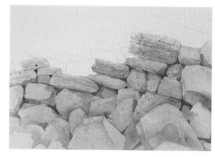

1. PAINT THE SHAPE OF THE AREA TO BE ROCKS.
After making a light sketch, I washed and spattered this area using a toothbrush, first with water, then with a variety of colors. To protect the part that was not rocks, I covered it with a cut paper stencil.

2. DELINEATE THE INDIVIDUAL ROCKS.
After the paint was dry, I laid out the individual rocks with pencil. I then painted the cracks between the rocks with a mixture of Cobalt Blue and Burnt Sienna. When I did this, I was, in effect, painting the negative space for each rock. In some places I faded the paint upward to produce shadow on the rocks. I faded the paint that defines the foreground rocks outward into the rocks behind. Then I let the paint dry.

3. REPEAT STEP 2 WITH A DARKER MIXTURE.
I used Cobalt Blue and Burnt Sienna, defining only the deeper parts of the cracks. Do some modeling on the foreground rocks.

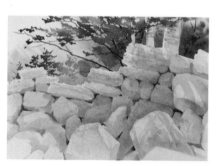

4. DEFINE THE TOP EDGE AND CAST SHADOWS.
You can't see the effect of sunlight until a dark background defines the top edge and cast shadows are added. I also glazed the rocks in the middle ground to unify and separate them from those in the foreground.

WHAT YOU NEED

watercolor paper

pencil

watercolors of your choice
- Cobalt Blue
- Burnt Sienna

water

brushes of your choice

toothbrush

paper and scissors for making stencil

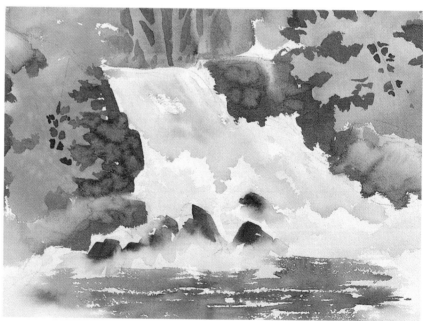

MANY TYPES OF NEGATIVE PAINTING
I used negative painting in many parts of this field sketch of a waterfall. The dark rocks define the white foam of the falls and the trees to either side. The dark water at the bottom indicates the limit of the foam. Within the water itself, pale blue and green shapes define the white surging foam. In the background, a medium value area is the negative shape that defines the top of the falls. When this dried, darker negative shapes were painted in it to suggest tree trunks.

STEP BY STEP: HILLS WITH NEGATIVE PAINTING

1. PAINT GRADED HILL SHAPES.
I first painted a passage grading from blue to green to yellow-green in the shape of the hills I wanted. I let this dry.

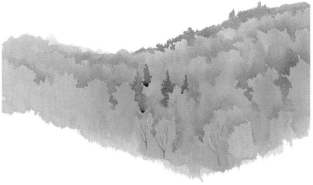

2. PAINT THE NEGATIVE SPACES WITH A SPONGE.
Using a dark middle green and a torn sponge (see page 29), I painted in the negative spaces between the clumps of trees. I painted only small areas at a time, then faded these upward. I worked from the top of the hill to the bottom.

WHAT YOU NEED

watercolor paper

watercolors of your choice

water

brushes of your choice

torn sponge

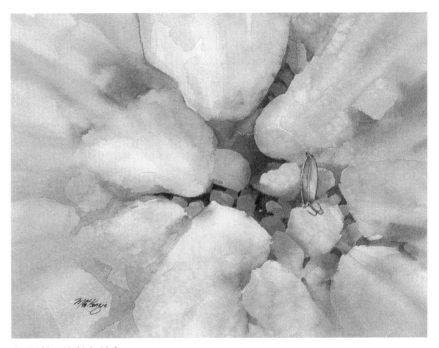

BURIED TREASURE
11" x 14" (28cm x 36cm)
Collection of the artist

NEGATIVE PAINTING AND CLOSURE
This underwater scene started with a loose, all-over wash of Red Rose, Raw Sienna and Sap Green. When this was dry, I created the rocks by painting in the negative spaces between them. Then, while it was still wet, I wiped back areas with a damp hog hair brush. Successive layers focused on darkening the area near the center of interest by defining more small rocks within negative spaces painted earlier. Even though I did not completely define each rock, viewers will mentally "complete" rocks and understand what they see.

LINES AND EDGES OF SHAPES

A line is a continuous mark that leads the viewer's eye through a work of art. The edge of a shape or boundary between two areas is also considered a line.

Try to make the edges of objects as interesting as the detail you put inside them. In fact, the edge is an extension of the surface treatment and should tell the viewer how the surface feels.

Our eye follows lines and edges and is attracted to anything that interrupts the flow, i.e., intersections, branching, breaks, sharp corners, etc. Since the eye is drawn to these places pay close attention when painting them, e.g. If you are painting tree branches and fail to connect them all it is very noticeable because there are breaks in the flow of the branches. If you are painting flowers pay attention to the valleys between petals and their tips because this is where the eye goes.

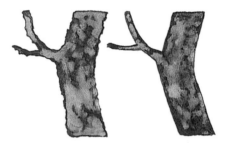

Which tree has rough bark?

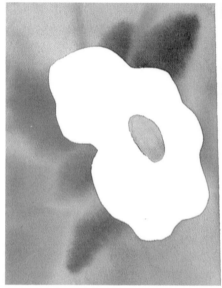
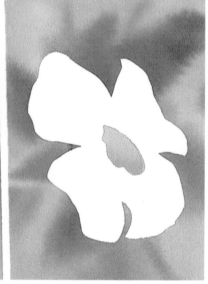

Tips of petals and valleys between them are the most important parts of their contours.

POINT OF VIEW AND SHAPES

An object can be viewed from many directions. Try to pick an angle that tells the viewer as much as possible about the object by the edge detail.

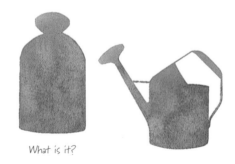

What is it?

SHAPES CAN IMPLY FEELINGS

From the contour (outline) of a shape alone, you can suggest feeling. We read sharp, pointy shapes as hard and dangerous (probably from experience) and smooth, rounded shapes as safe and soft.

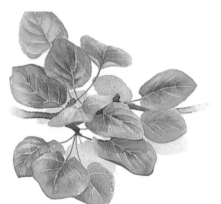
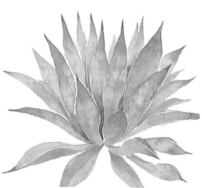

Which plant appears more dangerous to touch?

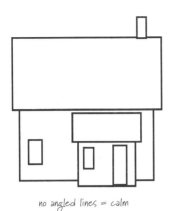

no angled lines = calm

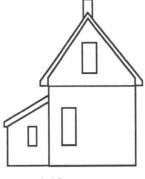

some angled lines = some energy

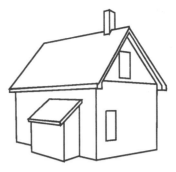

many angled lines = much energy

SHAPES CAN SUGGEST ENERGY

Edges that are parallel to the frame (horizontal or vertical) suggest calm and stability, while those positioned at an angle suggest drama, energy and movement. Use diagonal lines (edges) to add life to your work. One way to do this is to choose a dynamic point of view for your subject.

CLASSIFYING SHAPES

You can classify shapes as geometric or free-form. Geometric shapes suggest a sense of order, precision and predictability, while free-form shapes suggest informality, relaxation and freedom. You also can classify shapes as either natural (sometimes called organic) or human made. Natural geometric shapes include honeycombs, crystals and grapes. Natural free-form shapes include clouds, trees, puddles, fruits, vegetables and people. Human-made geometric shapes include buildings, railroad cars, towers and bridges. Human-made free-form shapes include pop bottles, autos, clothes, shoes and hand tools.

IMPLICATIONS FOR PICTURE MAKING

The type of shapes you select for your work is important. Selecting shapes that are all of the same type—for example, natural free-forms (such as certain types of flowers)—will add to the sense of unity in your work. You can achieve contrast in this type of work primarily through value, color or pattern. However, if you mix two types of shapes, you can create more interest and contrast for a focal point. Let's say your composition consists primarily of natural free-forms (e.g., flowers). You can create contrast by introducing natural geometric shapes (e.g., circular flower centers, berries), human-made free-forms (e.g., vase, basket) or a human-made structure (e.g., the bench in *Harold's Bench*).

WHAT DOES YOUR COMPOSITION NEED?

Inject creativity into your plan by making changes to strengthen the composition. Change things from what they appear to be to what they need to be for a good composition. You may need to enlarge or emphasize elements. You may need to change your colors, point of view, time of day, etc., to create the effect you want. Translation of the subject makes you part of the work.

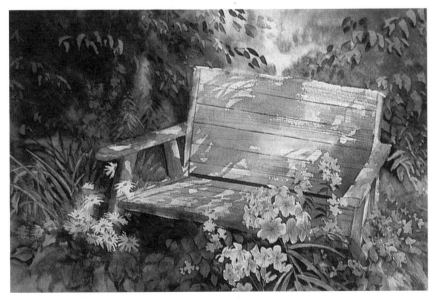

HAROLD'S BENCH
15" x 22" (38cm x 56cm)
Private collection

SHAPES OFTEN SUGGEST A DIRECTION

Shapes have a directional aspect that helps generate movement and point the way for the viewer's eye. Triangular shapes, such as the shapes of the boats shown, can lead the viewer's eye in a particular direction. A picture containing figures or faces causes the viewer to look in the direction that bodies, heads, faces or eyes are looking. Objects that have a "face" or "front" side direct the viewer's gaze in a particular direction.

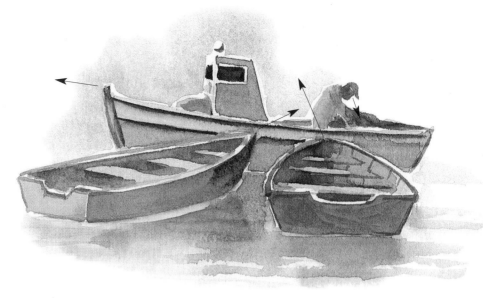

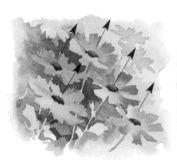

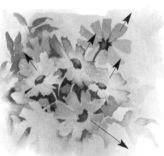

one direction = uniformity, monotony

multiple directions = variety, chaos

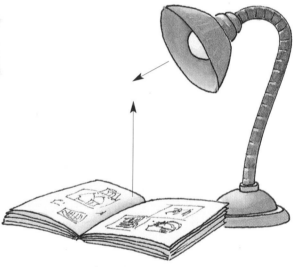

Eyes follow implied direction.

INTERPRETING DIRECTION OF PEOPLE

How we read the direction of the human figure depends on the distance we are away from it. When a figure is far away, we read the shape of the whole body. As it comes closer, we read the direction of the head (particularly the nose), then the whole face and eventually the eyes.

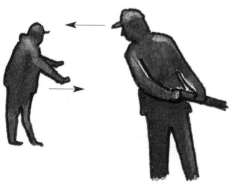

body

head

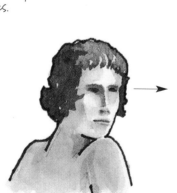

face

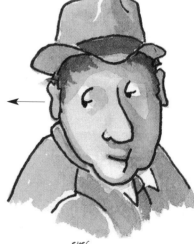

eyes

REPETITION, PATTERN AND RHYTHM OF SHAPES

Repetition and pattern strongly attract the eye, particularly if there are strong contrasts. Rhythm is the regular repetition of any of the elements of a design, with or without periodic alteration. However, the viewer can lose interest quickly if there is no variety. For example, repeated similar shapes can create unity and rhythm in a composition, but you should avoid monotony by introducing variety within the shapes. The eye stops seeing repeated shapes that are too similar.

GROUPING SHAPES

By grouping shapes together you can create a compound shape that is more interesting to look at. This also creates a sense of cohesion in the composition.

monotony

variety

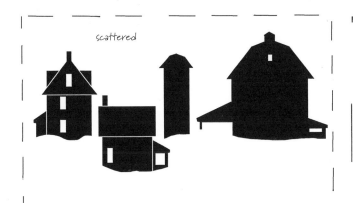

scattered

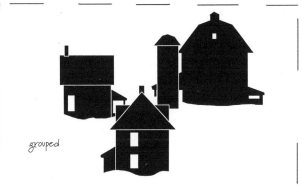

grouped

LEADING THE EYE WITH SHAPES AND EDGES

The arrangement of shapes can lead the eye like stepping-stones. Light-colored shapes attract the eye more than darks, so, if possible, make the stepping-stones light for the best results.

Clearly defined edges of shapes are called *hard edges*. Edges that fade out are *soft edges*. Hard edges take visual priority over soft edges because they provide something on which the eye can focus. Soft edges allow the eye to move freely.

In watercolors, soft edges are extremely easy to make, and they offer visual mystery and excitement to a work. Think of hard edges as a trap for the eye. Hard edges attract the eye as it moves over a work and lead it wherever the edge goes. A soft edge, however, is like a gate that allows the eye to move freely between shapes as well as in and out of the picture space.

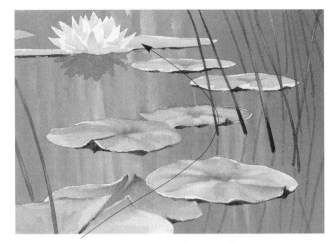

a path for the eye

Edges are critical to visual flow.

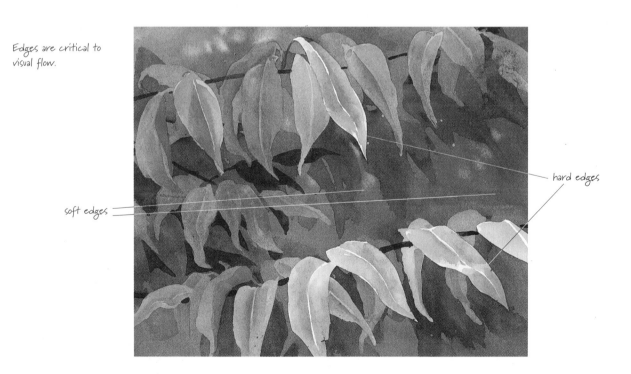

soft edges

hard edges

MOVEMENT

Movement attracts our attention. Visual response to movement is a primary defense mechanism: Our eyes go to anything that moves so we can determine its significance.

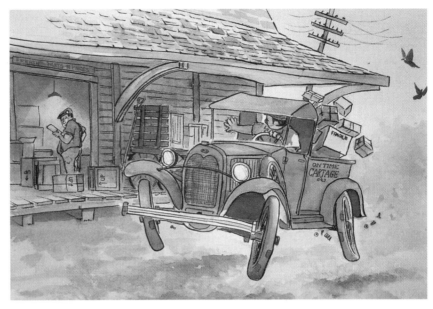

ON TIME CARTAGE
11" x 14" (28cm x 36cm)
Collection of the artist

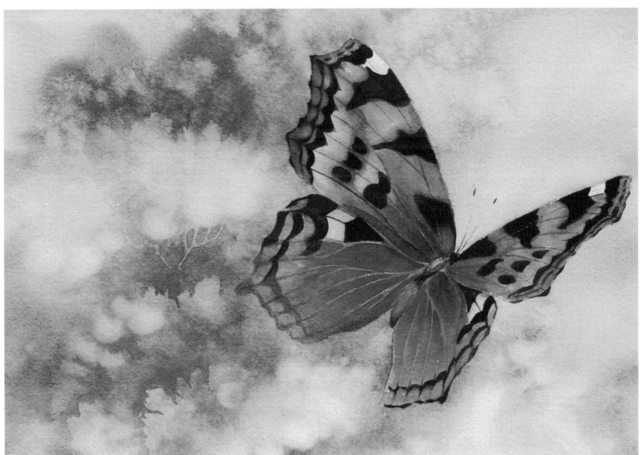

MOVEMENT WITH LINES AND SHAPES

On Time Cartage and Flight suggest movement, which attracts attention, with lines and shapes. Diagonals (wheels, roofline, butterfly wings) suggest movement and energy. Lines and shapes that are parallel to the frame are static. Suspended objects (trucks, parcels and butterfly) also suggest movement. In On Time Cartage, black outlines emphasize the edges of shapes more than usual. In Flight, lines and patterns on the butterfly wings attract attention. The hard edges of the butterfly take priority over the soft background where the eye is free to roam. The hard edges of the tiny twig area cause the eye to stop before it returns to the butterfly.

FLIGHT
11" x 14" (28cm x 36cm)
Collection of the artist

VALUES

Values are lights and darks. Light values, sometimes called tints, are high key. Dark values, sometimes called shades, are low key. Middle values are middle key. These key levels measure the amount of light falling on the subject.

In transparent watercolors, you make light values, or tints, by adding water. Light values have a quiet, ethereal effect, lacking eye-grabbing appeal unless they are next to something darker.

You can make dark values, or shades, by adding black. You can add Indigo, Sepia or Payne's Gray to darken a color. However, you must be careful that the blues and browns contained within these colors do not muddy or shift your color too dramatically. Dark values suggest strength, weight, solidity, mystery and dignity. However, a composition with too many dark values can be oppressive unless it is balanced with lighter values.

USE CONTRAST FOR YOUR FOCAL POINT

Through contrasting values we are best able to interpret our world—color differences alone do not do it. Therefore, objects and areas that you want the viewer to notice must have different values. The eye goes to the strongest value contrast, so save it for the focal point.

Nature uses a lack of value contrast to hide many of its creatures. We call it camouflage. Even though a creature may be a different color than its surroundings, if its value is about the same it will go unnoticed. Unless you plan to paint camouflage, you must use contrast. If you want the viewer to read your picture easily you must give adjoining shapes contrasting values.

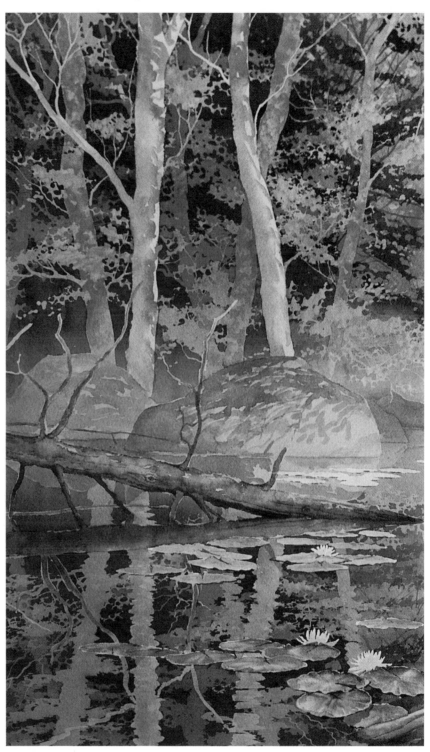

MUTED COLORS FOR SUBDUED LIGHTING
River Diamonds portrays a hazy, subdued lighting that is reflected in the muted colors used. The colors appear natural but are actually the product of Red Rose Deep and Sap Green (complements), with only the slightest help from some Cobalt Blue. Note the maroon shadows on the trees.

RIVER DIAMONDS, DETAIL
11" x 14" (28cm x 36cm)
Collection of the artist

DEVELOP MOOD WITH VALUE DOMINANCE

Allowing one value (light, middle or dark) to dominate your painting can play a role in developing mood and visual impact. Low-key paintings dominated by darks have a dramatic, mood-setting effect, conveying things we sense about darkness, such as mystery, intrigue, fear or sanctuary. However, a low-key painting also can appear overworked and oppressive, depending on the colors.

High-key paintings dominated by pale colors give the appearance of being bathed in light, setting a more ethereal mood. They can suggest optimism, clarity and life, but there is the danger of appearing weak, vague, washed out and trivial.

Most paintings are middle value because they offer the widest range of possibilities. You can have ominous drama contrasted with light cheerfulness in the same painting.

VALUE VARIATIONS SHOWING VALUE DOMINANCE

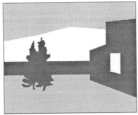
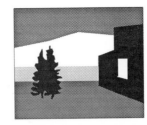
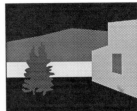
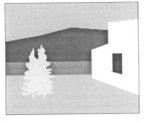
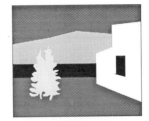
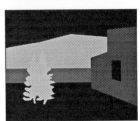
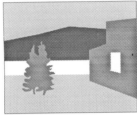
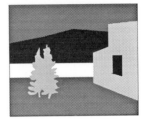
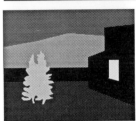
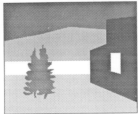
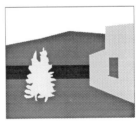
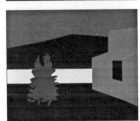

HIGH KEY
Lights dominate, with no extreme darks. Only white, light and two mediums used.

MIDDLE KEY
Middle values are dominant. White, light, medium and dark used.

LOW KEY
Darks dominate, with all values, including extreme dark, used.

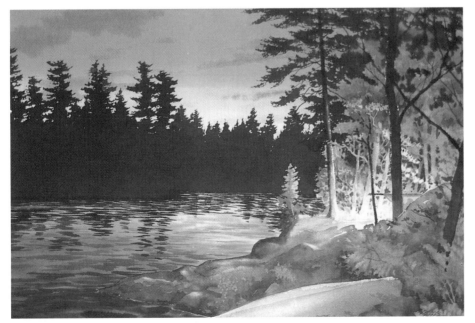

STAR LIGHT, STAR BRIGHT
11" x 14" (28cm x 36cm)
Collection of the artist

CENTER OF INTEREST AND CONTRASTS
In Star Light, Star Bright, the primary center of interest is the campfire light; the second is the light in the sky and the third is the reflected light in the lake. The clear northern air produces stark contrasts as night approaches, and we experience the last light of the day.

SUNLIGHT AND SKY LIGHT

On a clear day we see sunlight as white. Sky light is sunlight diffused by the atmosphere. It changes as the sky and atmosphere change due to such things as clouds, pollution and time of day.

TRANSLUCENT LIGHT

This is the light that passes through a semitransparent object, such as a leaf, flower petal, wave or thin ridge of snow. Translucent light tends to lighten and warm whatever it passes through.

REFLECTED LIGHT

This is light that bounces off one surface and back onto another. Like sky light, you only see this soft light when it strikes in a darker, shadowed area. Reflected light also picks up some of the color of the surface from which it reflects. In landscapes, this light is usually warm because of the earth colors of the natural surfaces and objects that reflect it.

LOCAL SHADOWS

This is the shading on the object itself that gives form to a flat shape. You can produce a shadow color by mixing the local color with blue (sky light) and a touch of its complement or gray. Each produces a darker, cool, slightly dulled local color. Warm reflected light also influences local shadows.

CAST SHADOWS

Mix cast shadows the same as local shadows, but be aware that because sky light influences them more than reflected light, they tend to be cooler. On a clear day, cast shadows on snow are bluish, like the sky. The darker you make cast shadows, the brighter the sun appears to shine. As atmospheric conditions change and sky light shifts color, so do the color, value and sharpness of cast shadows. They are darkest in areas where they are closest to the object casting the shadow.

EFFECT OF SKY LIGHT IN SHADOWS

For sunny days, add clean blue to your shadows. On dull days, add cool gray. On curved surfaces I also use a hint of cool sky color as a transition between the sunlight area and the darkest shaded side of the object.

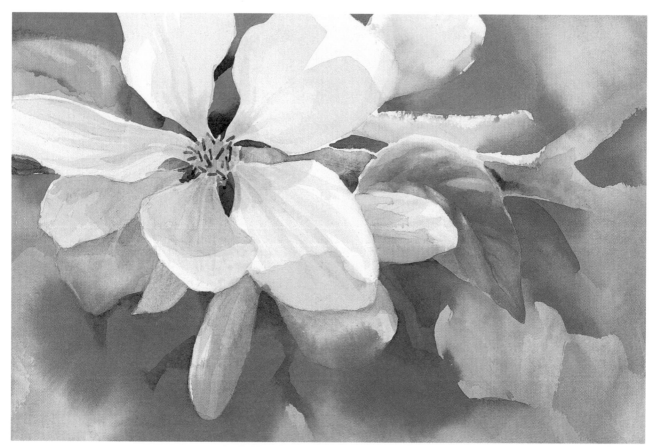

WARM AND COOL SHADOWS
These apple blossoms illustrate the role of warm and cool shadows in creating the appearance of light.

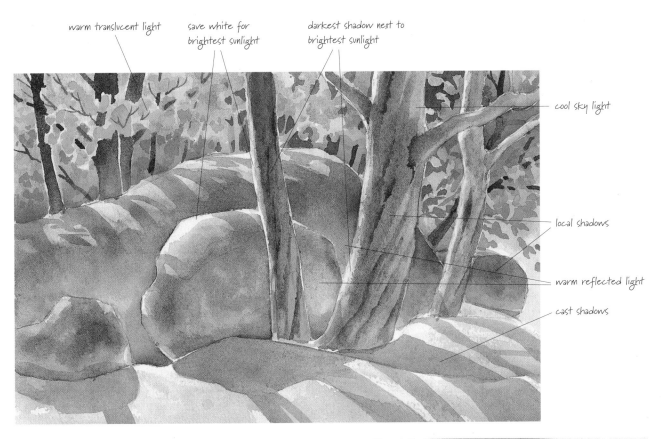

warm translucent light

save white for brightest sunlight

darkest shadow next to brightest sunlight

cool sky light

local shadows

warm reflected light

cast shadows

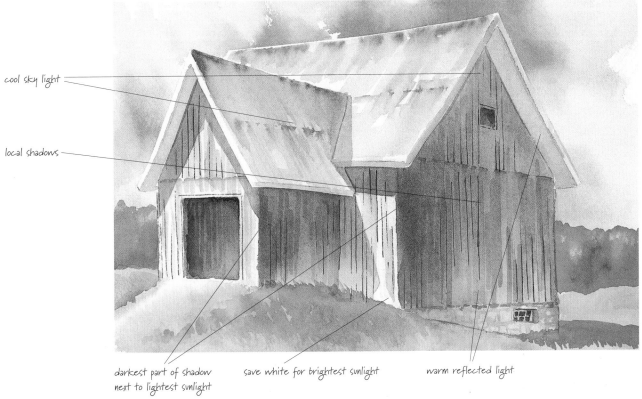

cool sky light

local shadows

darkest part of shadow next to lightest sunlight

save white for brightest sunlight

warm reflected light

DETERMINE DIRECTION OF CAST SHADOWS

The direction of a light source determines the direction of cast shadows. With one or two objects, determining the direction of shadows is not usually a problem. With multiple objects—such as tree trunks, fence posts, people, etc.—painting individual shadows properly can be a problem. You can solve this problem by using one-point perspective, with the sun or light source as the vanishing point. Base the location of cast shadows on lines drawn between the sun (the vanishing point placed well outside the picture space) and the base of the object. Undulations in the ground and tilted objects cause variations in shadows. Converging lines also lead viewers' eyes into the picture by creating the appearance of distance.

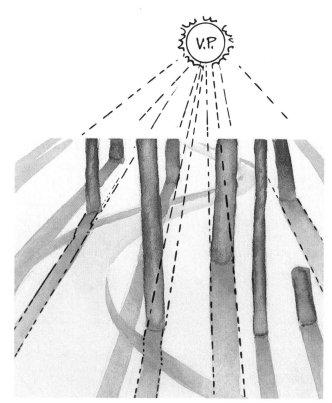

BACKLIT TREES

Draw two lines between the sun (vanishing point) and the outer points at the base of each tree. Extend those lines past the tree and off the page. If the sun is anywhere in front of you and the trees, or to your front left or right, the shadows will be between those lines on "this" side of the trees.

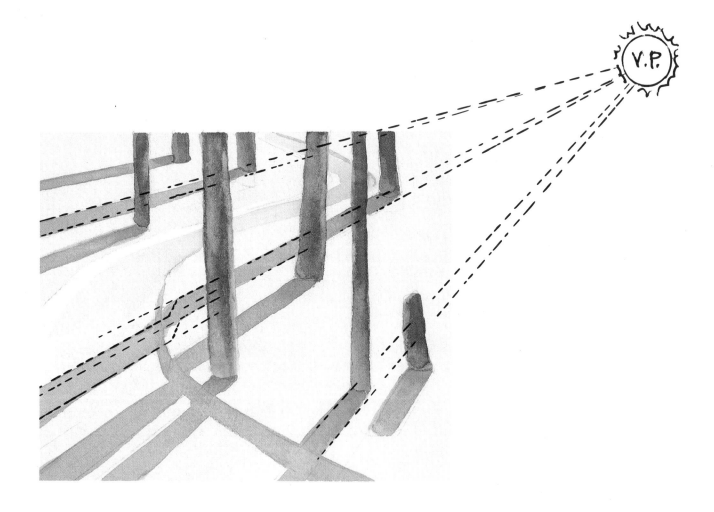

A DIFFERENT TIME OF DAY

These illustrations show the sun behind you or to your back left or right. In this case, you want the shadows to point toward the vanishing point. Again, draw in lines between the vanishing point and the outer points of the tree bases. Now the shadows are between these lines on the far side of the trees.

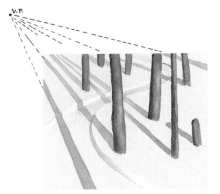
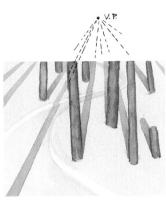

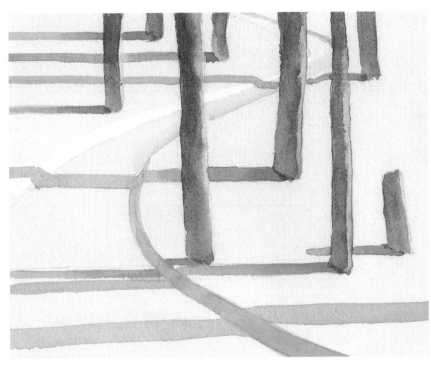

THERE IS ALWAYS AN EXCEPTION

When the sun is directly to the side and the shadows run across in front of you, they sometimes appear to be parallel.

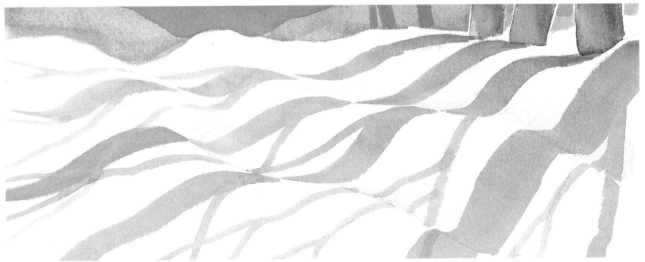

SHADOWS DEFINE AND MODEL LAND

A flat brush is easier to use than a round brush for varying the width of these shadow lines as they follow the surface.

STEP BY STEP: SEEING AND RECORDING VALUES

In the process of recording and manipulating values in thumbnail sketches (small, rough sketches), you are really working on two problems. The first is determining value dominance for the whole scene. This will influence the mood and impact of your final picture. Second, you want to identify and manipulate the value contrasts between specific areas and objects in your scene so your final picture is easy to read.

By squinting at your sketch and your scene you can see where value difference is not enough to make one shape distinguishable from another. Darkening or lightening one or the other where they interface will solve the problem. By working out these value contrasts in a thumbnail you will save a lot of "adjustments" to your painting later.

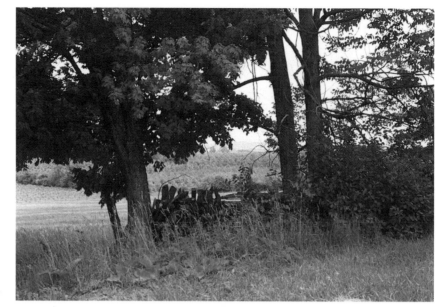

1. IDENTIFY LIGHT, MEDIUM AND DARK VALUES.
Keep it simple. Squint at your subject. In this case, my subject is a view on St. Joseph Island. Identify only the light (including white), middle and dark (including black) value masses.

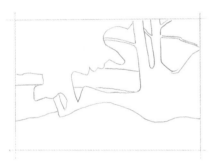

2. LIGHTLY DRAW CONTOURS.
Record only the general outline of these shapes with light pencil. Later you will make value variations within each of these as you refine the shape. Indicate the direction of the sun.

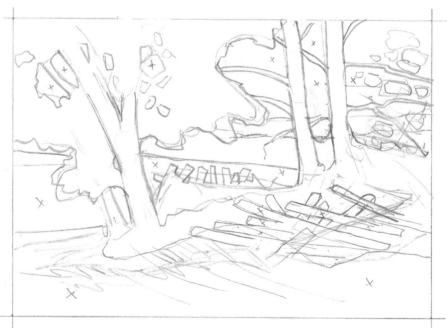

WHAT YOU NEED

white paper
pencil

3. LOCATE AND RECORD VALUE SHAPES.
Next, study and record the shape and location of contrasting values that intrude upon these large masses. This is the time to pay attention to the edges of these shapes, because they are most important in creating interest and dynamics within the work. Make any changes to the edges that you feel will help. Shapes do not exist in isolation. Like a jigsaw puzzle, each piece interlocks and interacts with its counterpart to create a whole. At any given time, a positive shape can become the negative shape for another (see page 72). Indicate with an X where the strongest light will be.

4. ADD THE LIGHT, MIDDLE AND DARK VALUES.

Consider the location of the strongest value contrast. This will have the greatest attraction for the viewer's eye and be a focal point. Save the lightest light (white paper) and the darkest dark for this contrast. As is often the case, the values of a mass will vary slightly across its surfaces (gradation), or it will have edges that vary—from hard to soft, light to dark. In your sketch you will invariably have to make value adjustments to some masses in order to achieve sufficient contrast, even though this may be contrary to the reality of the subject being viewed. You have a license to do this.

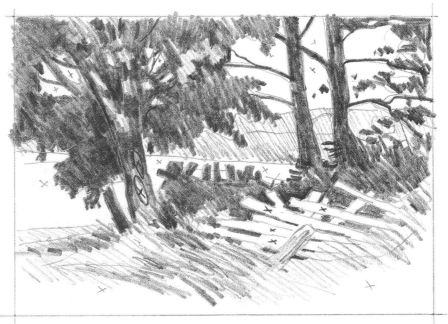

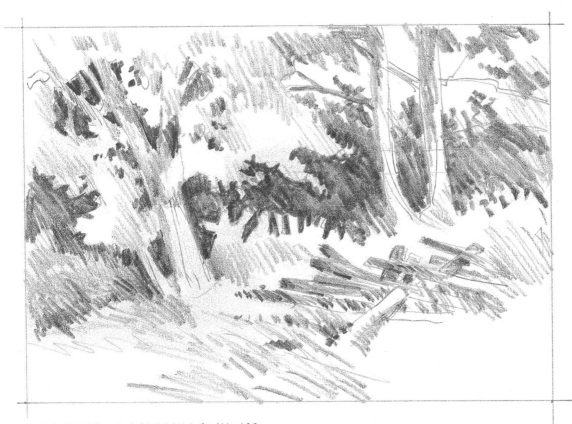

5. REVERSE OR REARRANGE VALUES.

At some point you will need to choose the dominant value for your picture. You can either make adjustments to your present sketch or redraw it. I strongly suggest that you redo your sketch anyway, so you can at least see the effects of reversing or rearranging the values. This can have a dramatic effect on an otherwise mediocre composition.

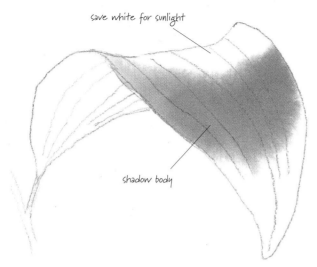

save white for sunlight

shadow body

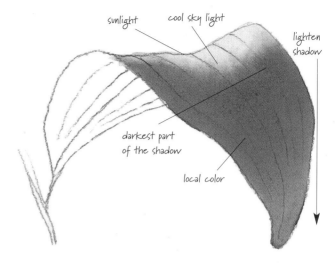

sunlight

cool sky light

lighten shadow

darkest part of the shadow

local color

1. APPLY SHADOW WET-IN-WET.

Wet the front face of the leaf. While still wet, apply the shadow body across the upper part of the face. This will diffuse in the water, so make sure you are far enough back from the top edge so it can remain white for the sunlit area. I used a concentrated mixture of Sap Green (local color) and Phthalo Blue (sky light), in addition to a touch of Permanent Rose to dull it.

2. APPLY BOTTOM PART OF SHADOW.

Immediately apply a second stroke of concentrated Sap Green to the bottom part of the shadow body, and fade this out toward the leaf tip. Warm the Sap Green near the tip with Raw Sienna, being careful to keep this area lighter than the shadow body above it.

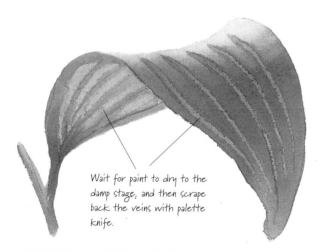

Wait for paint to dry to the damp stage, and then scrape back the veins with palette knife.

3. SCRAPE IN VEINS, AND PAINT UNDERSIDE.

When the paint gets to the damp stage, scrape in veins with a stiff palette knife. Now paint in the translucent light of the underside of the leaf with concentrated yellow-green (Sap Green plus Indian Yellow or Phthalo Yellow-Green). Grade this so it is darkest near the stem. When damp, scrape in the underside veins with a palette knife.

WHAT YOU NEED

pencil
watercolor paper
water
brushes of your choice
watercolors
- Sap Green
- Phthalo Blue
- Permanent Rose
- Raw Sienna
- Indian Yellow or Phthalo Yellow-Green
stiff palette knife
craft knife

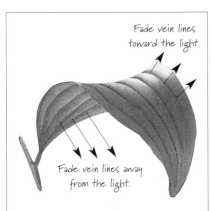

Fade vein lines toward the light.

Fade vein lines away from the light.

VARIATION ON STEP 3: ALTERNATIVE VEINING

Let the paint dry on the face of the leaf from Step 2. To paint the veins on the top face of the leaf (direct sunlight or sky light), use some of the concentrated mixture from Step 1. Paint the individual vein lines with a small (no. 4) brush, and as you paint each line, immediately fade it out to one side using another small damp brush. Fade the lines upward or toward the light. For the translucent light (light passing through the leaf), repeat this process but use concentrated Sap Green as the color, and fade each line downward or away from the light.

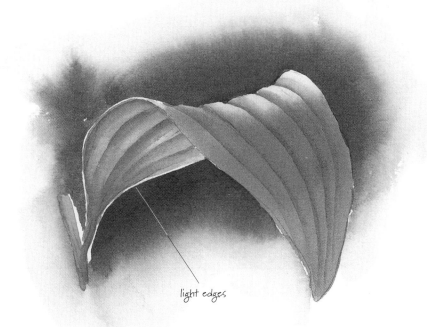

light edges

4. COMPLETE WITH A DARK BACKGROUND.

A dark background is essential to complete the appearance of sunlight and back-lighting. Notice how the light edges around the translucent light area can help suggest strong sunlight hitting the back side of the leaf. You can either leave them white or scrape them in with the tip of a craft knife.

VARIATION

On a white petal, use cool gray on the upper part of the face shadow. Blend to warm gray in the middle, then fade out near the tip, using Raw Sienna to warm the translucent light. Paint the veins with concentrated blue-gray on top and warm gray underneath.

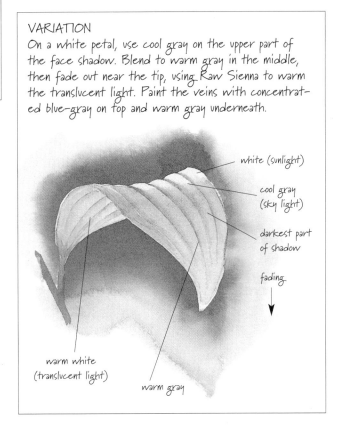

white (sunlight)

cool gray (sky light)

darkest part of shadow

fading

warm white (translucent light)

warm gray

COLOR AND THE COLOR WHEEL

Color is the element that best expresses the emotional aspect of a subject and the mood of the artist. A color's *hue* is the name of the color in its purest and simplest form—red, blue, green, yellow, etc. These are the colors of the spectrum and best describe their location on the color wheel.

Purity or *intensity* is the brilliance or chroma saturation of a hue. Colors are at their purest as found in the color spectrum (the color wheel). You can lessen a color's purity, or dull it, by adding varying amounts of its complementary color. The right amount will produce a form of gray. You will not find unsaturated colors—such as browns (oxides), Indigo, Sepia, Yellow Ochre or Phthalo Yellow-Green—on the chromatic color wheel.

Vivid hues have a powerful, full-volume personality. Reserve these for your center of interest. Be careful. The eye tires of these quickly, and too many vivid hues can cause confusion in your work. Dulled hues are less attractive to the eye but tend to reduce tension in a work. Their quiet, dreamlike quality sets a meditative mood. However, too many vague, dulled colors can make a

work appear uninteresting unless they are countered by samples of pure color.

Temperature is the psychological suggestion of warmth or coolness inherent to the color. On the color wheel (page 95), the side containing red, red-orange, orange, yellow-orange and yellow is the warm family. The other side—violet, blue-violet, blue, blue-green and green—is the cool family. Red-orange and blue-green are the warmest and coolest.

Almost any color can be relatively warm or cool compared to another color. For example, if red-violet is next to blue-violet, it will appear warm. But red-violet next to a red-orange appears cool.

Colors have warmer and cooler versions. Red becomes warmer by adding a small amount of orange or yellow and cooler by adding a small amount of violet or blue. Therefore, it is possible to have warm blues and cool reds. Warm hues attract our attention, excite our emotions and give the feeling of action. Their brash, cheerful exuberance jumps out of the picture at us. Cool hues are refreshing, relaxing and clean. Violets can be moody, but too much of any of them can be depressive or gloomy.

VALUES AND PAINT SELECTION

To maintain clarity and freshness in dark color mixtures, make sure you use only transparent and semitransparent colors (see page 13). In watercolor, the term mud refers to colors that have lost their vibrancy due to mixing the wrong colors together, overmixing colors or overworking paints on your paper. In a dark mixture, any opaque or semiopaque color will invariably produce mud. Be particularly careful with Burnt Umber and Sepia. They readily muddy up and flatten any mixture. Reserve opaque and semiopaque colors for high- and middle-key pictures, where you can thin them and make them more luminous.

cool red

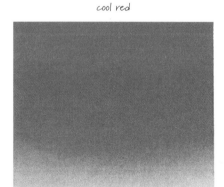

red

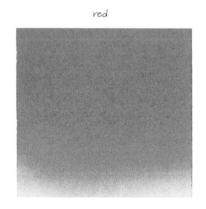

warm red

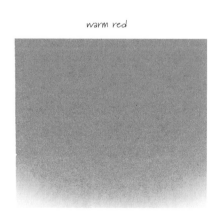

COLOR WHEEL

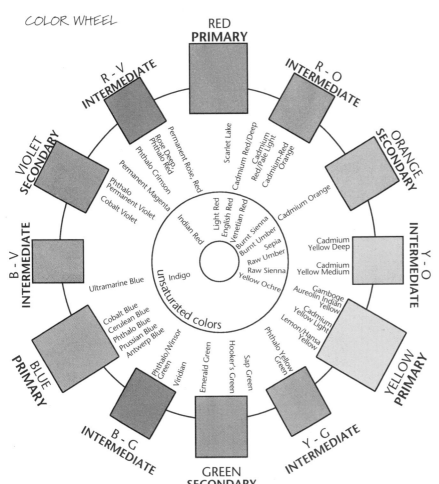

TIP FOR EMPHASIZING A COLOR

You can emphasize a color by placing it next to a color with opposite characteristics, such as opposite hue, value, temperature and purity.

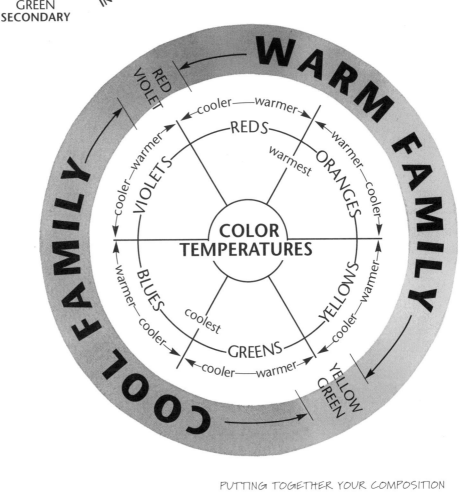

SETTING UP YOUR PALETTE

The pigments you decide to work with are an individual choice. However, you should realize that setting up your palette is not simply a matter of putting out every pretty color you own. By limiting your palette, you will find that you will not only learn more about the nature of the pigments through mixing but you will save money as well. In addition, by limiting your color selection you are better able to achieve the unified results you want.

Pure colors attract more than dull ones, but color combinations have greater emotional appeal than individual colors. Use the following guidelines, as well your imagination and intuition, to choose color combinations that reflect your preferences and feelings—not necessarily what nature provides.

TRADITIONAL PALETTE
Cadmium Red or Scarlet Lake; Hansa, Lemon Yellow or Gamboge; Ultramarine Blue. Used by many artists. Pros: Low-staining; brilliant oranges. Cons: Dull greens and violets. Opacity of colors can produce muddy results if overmixed. It is best to dilute colors to avoid flatness.

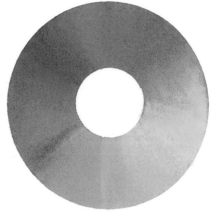

INTENSE PALETTE
Permanent Rose, Red Rose Deep or Phthalo Red; Phthalo Blue; Indian Yellow. Pros: Brilliant, transparent mixtures. Bold exciting results. Cons: Staining colors are hard to wipe back. Many may be too intense for your subject.

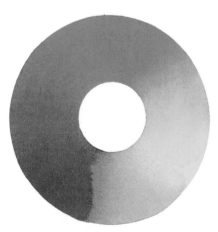

BLACKENED PALETTE
Indigo; Indian Yellow; Red Rose Deep or Permanent Rose. Pros: Extreme, luminous darks; transparent, bright lights. Cons: Indigo can overpower other colors. For best results, choose one that has a blue cast to it (for example, Winsor & Newton).

DELICATE OR HIGH-KEY PALETTE
Permanent Rose or Red Rose; Aureolin; Cobalt Blue. Pros: Transparent, nonstaining colors produce a great range of luminous mixes and grays. Cons: Extreme darks hard to produce. Viridian is a transparent, nonstaining green often used with this triad.

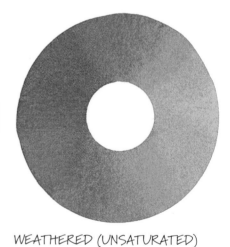

WEATHERED (UNSATURATED) PALETTE
Indigo; Raw Sienna; Burnt Sienna, Light Red, English Red, Venetian Red or Indian Red; muted mixtures. Caution: If you use either Light, English, Venetian or Indian Red, take great care to dilute them in order to avoid muddy mixtures. You can mix strong darks. Cons: Greens are very dull. For best results, choose an Indigo that has a blue cast to it (for example, Winsor & Newton).

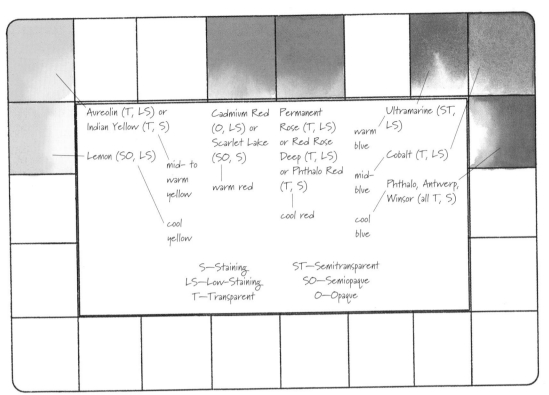

SETTING UP YOUR PALETTE
Start with warm and cool versions of each of the primary colors.

Aureolin (T, LS) or Indian Yellow (T, S)

Lemon (SO, LS)

mid- to warm yellow

cool yellow

Cadmium Red (O, LS) or Scarlet Lake (SO, S)

warm red

Permanent Rose (T, LS) or Red Rose Deep (T, LS) or Phthalo Red (T, S)

cool red

Ultramarine (ST, LS)

warm blue

Cobalt (T, LS)

mid-blue

Phthalo, Antwerp, Winsor (all T, S)

cool blue

S—Staining
LS—Low-Staining
T—Transparent

ST—Semitransparent
SO—Semiopaque
O—Opaque

Start with warm and cool versions of each primary color.

CONVENIENCE COLORS IMPROVE YOUR SELECTION
Now add some convenience colors (colors you don't have to mix) to improve your selection.

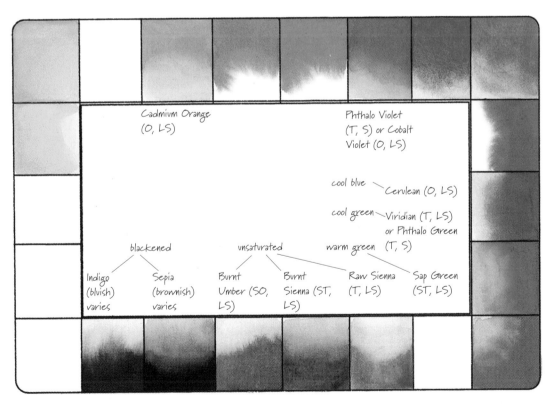

Cadmium Orange (O, LS)

Phthalo Violet (T, S) or Cobalt Violet (O, LS)

cool blue — Cerulean (O, LS)

cool green — Viridian (T, LS) or Phthalo Green

warm green (T, S)

blackened

Indigo (bluish) varies

Sepia (brownish) varies

unsaturated

Burnt Umber (SO, LS)

Burnt Sienna (ST, LS)

Raw Sienna (T, LS)

Sap Green (ST, LS)

Now add a few convenience colors to improve your mixing range and triad selection.

COLOR HARMONY AND CONTRAST

Color harmony is the joint effect of two or more colors, or variations on a color, that appeals to our inner sense of rightness. It is something you can see and feel. Colors that are neighbors on the color wheel (analogous) have the potential to produce harmonious schemes. Analogous color schemes are expressive because they produce a particular mood or atmosphere in a picture.

You also can suggest harmony by balancing contrasting forces. That means using complements (colors opposite each other on the color wheel) and the resulting dulled colors they produce when mixed. Choosing a complementary scheme automatically gives the viewer a one-two punch. Not only are the hues in contrast, so are their temperatures.

TIPS FOR INCREASING COLOR HARMONY

You will increase the chance of color harmony if you limit the number of colors in your color scheme. Two or three colors are more than enough to produce a wide range of mixed colors. Stick with these selected colors. Many color schemes fall apart because the artist, for whatever reason, slowly starts introducing colors that were not in the original plan.

Choose one color to dominate the scheme and set the mood. We are talking here about one color that is used in varying forms in many areas of the work, and that is found in many of the color mixtures employed. We are not talking about a color you may choose for sharp contrast at the focal point.

Glazing a wash of transparent color over part or all of your painting has a unifying effect because it gives all existing colors something in common. The same is true if you tone your paper all over first with a wash of a particular color or temperature. This color will influence and harmonize all others placed on top of it.

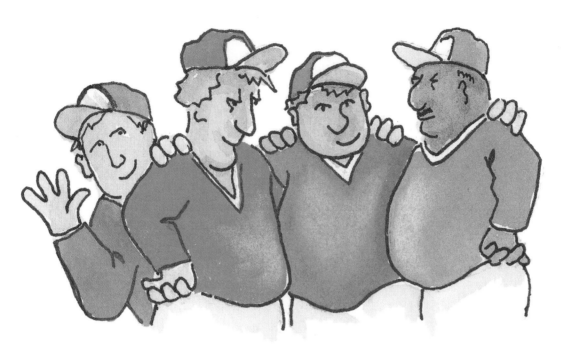

harmony through similarity

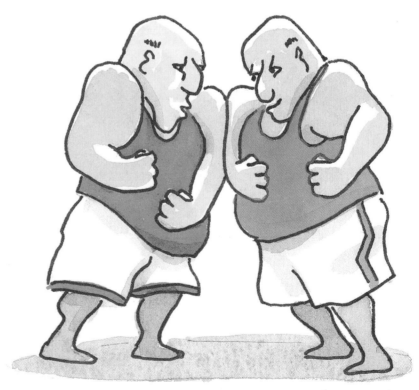

harmony by balancing opposites

MAKE CHOICES THAT EXPRESS YOUR INTERPRETATION

Reproduction of what you see before you is often important to an artist, yet what you should really be after is an interpretation of what you see. Make choices about what to include, what to eliminate and what to modify to express the quality or message you see in the subject.

For example, if I were studying a butterfly, I would want to capture the essence of flight. If I were painting a tractor, I would concentrate on the feeling of strength. If I were painting an old tree, I would want to capture the rigors of time. If I were painting water, I would concentrate on fluidity. First impressions are the seeds for what is important.

COLOR SCHEMES

When you choose colors for your work, your plan or strategy is your color scheme. Harmonious color schemes contribute greatly to the sense of unity within a painting. I show some standard color schemes on pages 100–105, with these words of caution—do not take rules of color selection too seriously. Although beauty reflects order in many instances, you cannot reduce the creative process entirely to pure analytical formulas. Allow your intuition and personal preferences to lead you to your own personal color schemes.

A question rarely considered when developing a color scheme is, "When do I choose my colors?" In many cases, artists choose a subject, develop a sketch or composition and then decide what colors to use. Invariably, the colors chosen will represent the real-life, local colors of the objects in the plan and show few imaginative variations. Take the time to experiment on a separate piece of paper. Find out how different color schemes work for you. Try all possible mixtures and proportions, and find out how these appear when you dilute them with water.

Develop a color scheme that represents a particular mood or captures an intriguing combination of pigments, then apply it to your subject of choice. You will invariably produce a work that is far more expressive of your feelings. In other words, use of local colors tends to block the imaginative use of color. This is one way around it.

You can find harmony in color relationships that emphasize both similarities and differences. Except for the monochromatic, the colors in each scheme have a logical, orderly relationship. See the color wheel on page 95 for specific colors for your scheme. Treat the unsaturated browns that are not on the color wheel as "dark oranges."

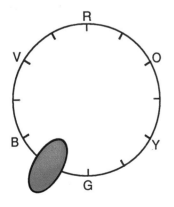

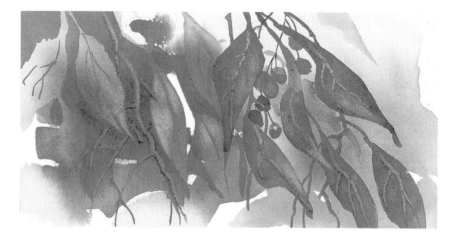

Phthalo Green

MONOCHROMATIC
You guarantee harmony with variations on one color, because it is impossible to have color conflict. Create contrast entirely through value differences.

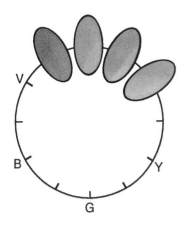

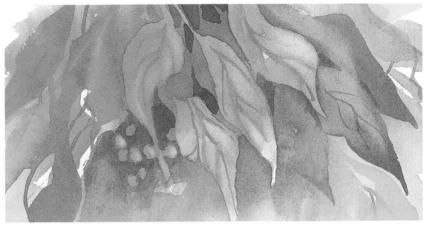

ANALOGOUS

With three or four neighboring colors, you can easily achieve harmony and mood because of the close relationship of the colors. Mixtures invariably result in warm and cool versions of each color. Mixtures are also bright and clean because there is nothing to dull them. Achieve contrast primarily through value differences, not color.

Permanent Rose, Scarlet Lake and Cadmium Orange

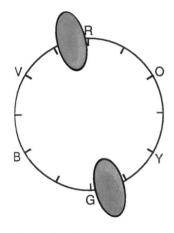

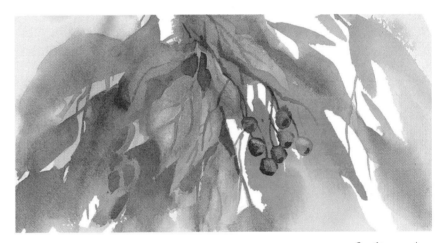

COMPLEMENTARY

Opposite colors enhance each other with the greatest chromatic contrast possible. Dulled colors produced by mixing the two are harmonious because they contain some of each of the pure parent colors. Create additional contrast through value changes.

Sap Green and Permanent Rose

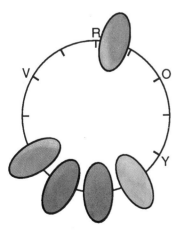

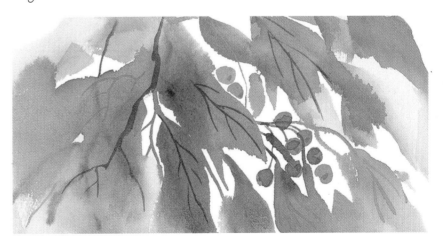

COMPLEMENTARY ANALOGOUS

You can add color and purity contrast to the harmony of the analogous scheme with a complementary color. A wide range of interesting grays can be produced by mixing or mingling the complementary color with the analogous colors.

Cobalt Blue, Phthalo Green and Sap Green vs. Cadmium Red

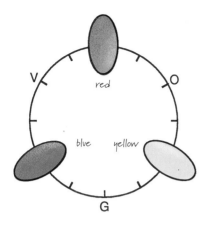

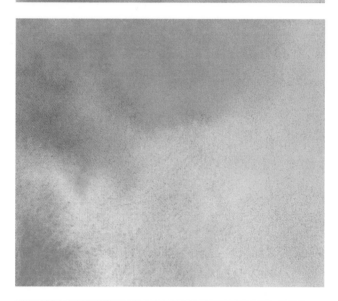

Intense Primary Triad
Phthalo Red, Indian
Yellow, Phthalo Blue

Delicate Primary
Triad
Permanent Rose,
Aureolin Yellow,
Cobalt Blue

TRIADS

A triad is a combination of three hues in a triangular relationship on the wheel. Triads offer the widest range of unique color combinations. They also offer the best chance of producing "mud" when you mix too many colors together at once, or if one of the colors is opaque. You can achieve harmony by allowing one color to dominate and using only the other two colors for mixing with that color. Contrast is by color, value and purity.

PRIMARY TRIADS

These are the most versatile triads because you can (theoretically) mix all other colors from these three: red, yellow and blue. However, choosing primary colors is not just a matter of selecting any red, yellow and blue. In most cases, each of these hues has a bent toward being either warm or cool. The selection you make will determine the type and quality of colors they produce when mixed together.

Many artists like to have warm and cool versions of each of the primary colors on their palettes, so they can mix clean, brilliant colors. They start with the palette on the left and then add a selection of favorite convenient secondary, "unsaturated" and "blackened or whitened" pigments, if they wish.

The following are some primary triads that you may wish to consider.

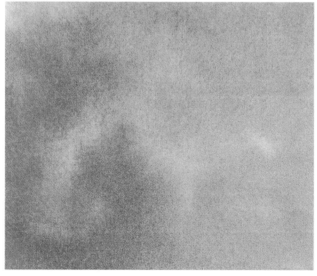

Weathered
(Unsaturated) Triad
English or Venetian
Red, Raw Sienna,
Indigo

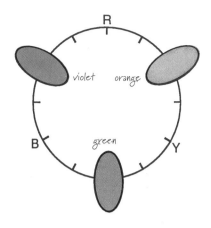

SECONDARY TRIADS

These are unusual triads made up of secondary colors. The results are not what you would think if you are new to mixing. Two primary colors make a secondary color, but two secondary colors do not make a primary. However, they do create a wonderful range of grays.

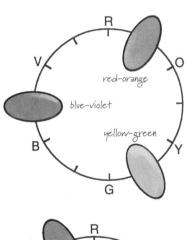

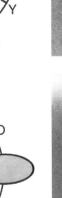

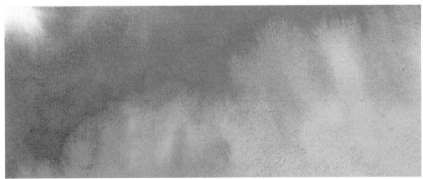

INTERMEDIATE TRIADS

As pure colors, these may be quite startling next to each other, but when mixed they produce extraordinary results. These are a challenge to use, but the expressive results are worth a try.

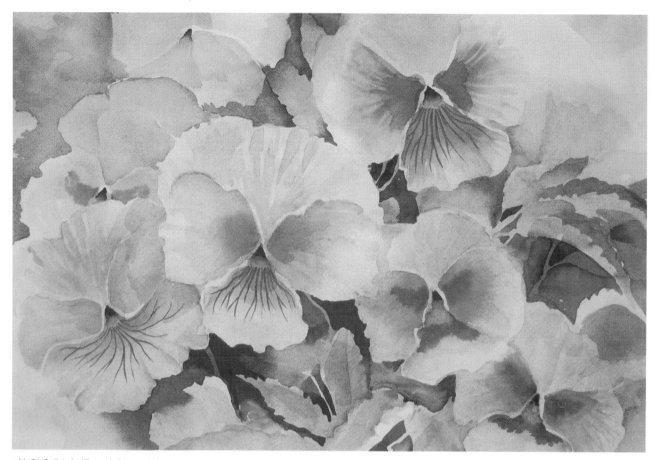

VARIETY AND HARMONY
In Pansies the repeated flowers create a random pattern with variety in the color combinations. I made certain to clearly define the intersections of edges at the center of each flower, as well as the edges of each petal.

Pansies started as a loose wet-in-wet field of intermingling colors from which the flowers developed. The gradation of colors resulting from the blending adds appeal to each flower. Warm and cool colors intermingle throughout the flowers, creating a balanced harmony.

PANSIES
11" x 14" (28cm x 36cm)
Collection of the artist

A SIMPLE PRINCIPLE FOR CLEAN, BRILLIANT RESULTS

It is important to know the relative positions of the colors on the color wheel (see page 95). To mix a secondary or intermediate color that will have maximum brilliance, choose two colors that are as close as possible to the color you want to mix. For example, in Diagram A on page 105, I produced violet by mixing red and blue, but the degree of brilliance you achieve depends on which red and blue you choose. For maximum brilliance you must find a red and blue that both have a hint of each other in themselves. In this case, Ultramarine Blue contains a hint of red that warms it, and Permanent Rose contains a hint of blue that cools it.

Another way to think of it is to look for two colors such that each contains a hint of the end result you are after. The farther away on the color wheel colors are from the color you want to mix, the duller the results will be. This is because as the colors you mix get farther away from the color you want to achieve, they invariably begin to contain hints of the target color's complement. See Diagram B on page 105.

GRADATION

In composition, gradation is a gradual transition from one color or value to another. Our eyes delight in gradations from one color to another.

DIAGRAM A: MIXING BRILLIANT SECONDARY COLORS

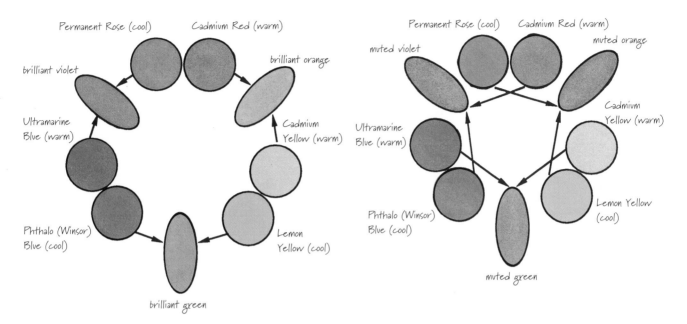

Permanent Rose (cool)

Cadmium Red (warm)

brilliant violet

brilliant orange

Ultramarine Blue (warm)

Cadmium Yellow (warm)

Phthalo (Winsor) Blue (cool)

Lemon Yellow (cool)

brilliant green

DIAGRAM B: MIXING MUTED (GRAYED) SECONDARY COLORS

Permanent Rose (cool)

Cadmium Red (warm)

muted violet

muted orange

Ultramarine Blue (warm)

Cadmium Yellow (warm)

Phthalo (Winsor) Blue (cool)

Lemon Yellow (cool)

muted green

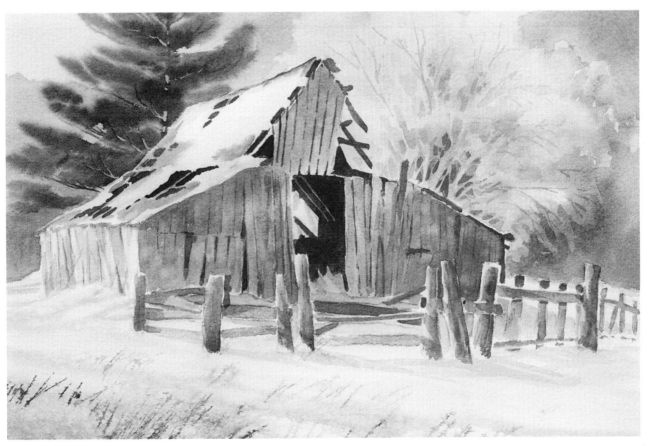

PATTERN AND GRADATION CREATE BALANCE

The barn boards and fence of Southwest Homestead create a pattern that has variety in size, position and spacing. Notice how the broken rafters and intersections in the fence attract your attention. The walls gain interest with a gradation from warm browns to cool gray. The warm wood, grass and tree against the cool snow, evergreen and sky provide a psychological balance.

SOUTHWEST HOMESTEAD
11" x 14" (28cm x 36cm)
Collection of the artist

Ways to Approach Composition

Everyone develops his or her own methods for tackling pictorial composition. On the following pages are three basic approaches that I use.

Approach One: Working From Real to "Abstract"

Most two-dimensional art is an "abstraction" to a certain degree, since it is only the representation of three-dimensional reality. This approach is what I use when I wish to make a picture about an existing subject, be it real (from life) or in a photograph.

Consider the subject or photo in front of you. Think about the elements and principles of composition as you know them, along with your intuitive sense of design, to decide how you will arrange the components into a pleasing composition as you see it.

KEEP OPTIONS OPEN WHEN USING REFERENCES

Though I never use someone else's painting for reference, you can learn from copying photos and others' work. However, when you gain control of the medium and an understanding of composition, wean yourself from this method of picture making. Use photos, magazine pictures, slides, models, etc., only to develop ideas. Use whatever material you wish as a starting point but not for the end product. Develop a composition from several references or views of a subject to get the details you want. Take what you need to create an *interpretation*, but don't restrict yourself to literal translation. Until you make changes to your references, you cannot claim ownership to the picture. That's when the creative process begins and you can call yourself an artist.

Reference material can get in the way of painting. For example, committing to every detail of a photo is a sure way to stifle the nature of this medium. Even if you are working on a commission where a literal translation is necessary, try to leave some areas unplanned so you can innovate during the painting process. For most of my work, I put references aside and refer to them as little as possible once I have a sketch on my paper. This way, the painting surprises me with each stroke by developing on its own.

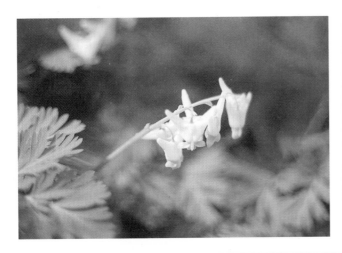

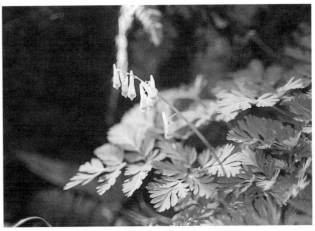

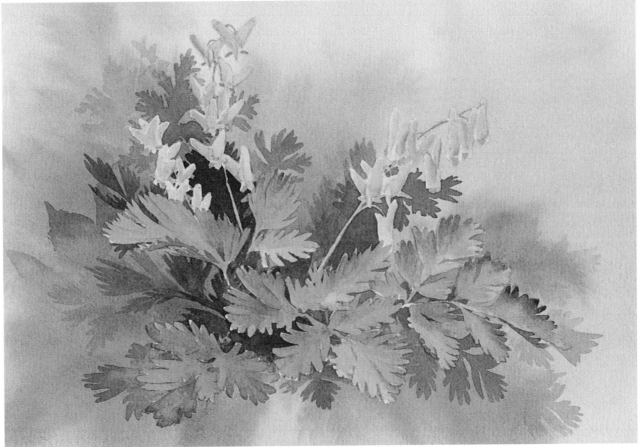

DUTCHMAN'S BREECHES

I often use more than one photograph for reference. In viewing the first one, I became interested in the way this delicate wildflower bore its blossoms, but I needed the second picture to define the laciness of its leaves. The important thing is that photos gave me the detail, but I created my own composition.

DUTCHMAN'S BREECHES
11" x 14" (28cm x 36cm)
Private collection

WHAT GRABS YOUR ATTENTION?

When you scan through photos or references, there are always those that grab your attention. Sometimes only a portion of a photo appeals to you. Something may elicit an emotional response, such as the colors, the lighting, a memory of a pleasant experience or a feeling you want to incorporate into your painting.

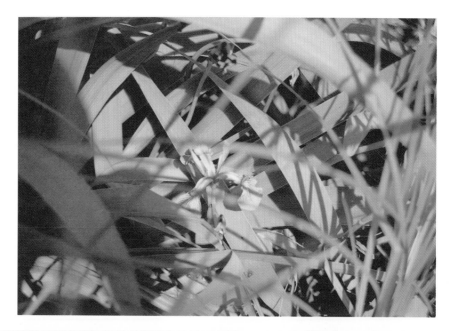

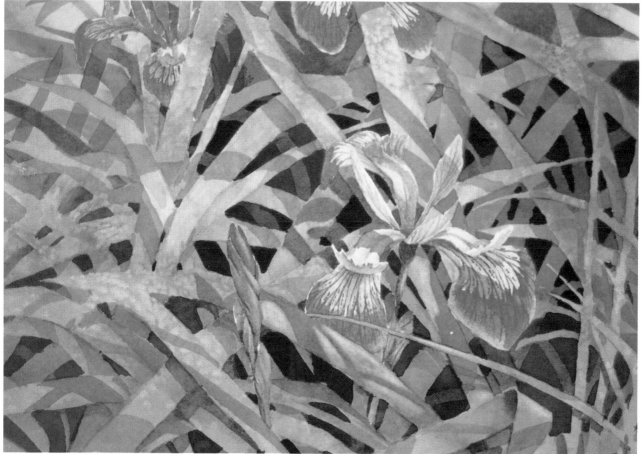

WILD FLAGS
This wild iris grows along the edges of lakes and bogs. In the photo, I became interested in the dense foliage that seems to head in every direction while almost cradling the flower. Using the photo, I created my own flower(s) and foliage arrangement.

WILD FLAGS
11" x 14" (28cm x 36cm)
Private collection

HOW ARE VISUAL ELEMENTS ARRANGED?

Next, determine how the visual elements in your reference—lines, shapes, colors, values, patterns, etc.—cause this emotional effect. What is the mood in the photo? What colors are evident? Where are the shapes? Can you see the value pattern when you squint?

Composition is about relationships, comparisons and contrasts, so look for these things in your photos. You need these answers, because they form the basis of your interpretation of the photos.

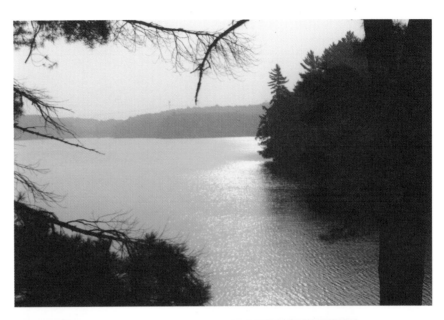

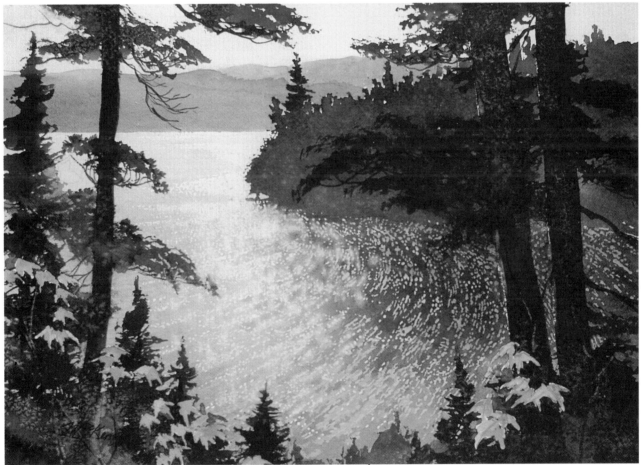

SHIMMERING LIGHT, PLEASANT MEMORY
It was the shimmering light on the water that attracted me here, as well as the pleasant memory of a park in which I had once camped. I added more foreground trees and emphasized the wind direction in the waves. I created the sparkle effect on the water by softening some of the dots of light that I had saved by masking.

POINT AT OSTLER LAKE
11" x 14" (28cm x 36cm)
Private collection

SKETCH VARIOUS IDEAS FOR COMPOSITIONS

Take what you want from your references. Alter and manipulate them to make the strongest statement. Make several thumbnail sketches until you arrive at a composition that best captures the appeal the reference material held for you.

HOLD YOUR HORSES

Only start sketching after you have taken the time to really look at and think about your subject. If possible, walk around and study it from different points of view. Don't rush right up to a subject and record everything that's before you. If you do, you probably will record a lot more than necessary, and you will record everything with equal importance.

Once you have begun to sketch, don't let the desire to get painting override the time you spend exploring compositional ideas and alternatives. Continue to look, sketch and think about your subject. Thumbnail sketches will give you a chance to experiment with the arrangement of shapes, values and lines. Remember, the first sketch you make usually is not the best solution or composition you can come up with, so make several before you decide which to do.

What is the value arrangement? Squinting will allow you to see the big value shapes. Identify the light (including white), middle and dark (including very dark) value areas. Remember that light (white) areas will attract viewers' attention in a composition, particularly when they contrast with the very dark darks. Outline major value shapes in a sketch.

What is the direction of the lighting? Since cast shadows usually are part of a realistic composition, you may want to change the direction of the light to improve the composition (you have artistic license to do this). Adjust values for contrast, for interest and to emphasize your focal point. Add detail. Redraw, if necessary. Transfer to watercolor paper.

VIEWING WITH INTUITION

Let your intuitive inner eye seek out its own sense of what is profound and beautiful. In viewing, you must keep asking yourself, "What in particular, in what I am seeing right now, is causing an emotional attraction for me?" It is those aspects that you will want to include in your work. Keep looking inwardly as you scan outwardly.

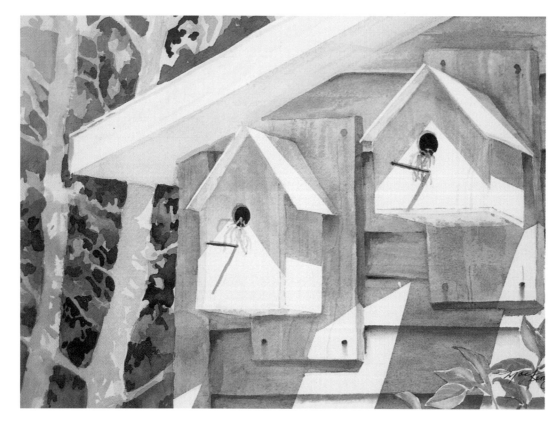

SUMMER
APARTMENTS
11" x 15"
(28cm x 38cm)
Collection of
the artist

COMPOSING WITH A VIEWFINDER

A viewfinder is a piece of cardboard or plastic with a rectangular hole in the middle. Use it to frame a subject, scene or part of a photo to locate a composition. This eliminates peripheral detail so you can focus on the subject. Think about your subject and composition as you look through the viewfinder. Here are some considerations, in addition to others mentioned throughout this chapter, to help dissect your subject and guide you to a stronger composition:

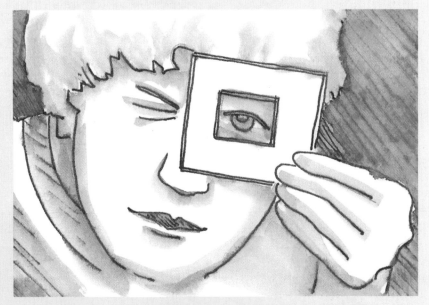

What would make a good focal point? Is there enough contrast around it to emphasize your focal point? Will you need to create more contrast to emphasize your point of interest?

Would it help if you transformed something? For example, could you enlarge, distort or eliminate some aspect of the subject or scene? Is there something new you could introduce?

View the subject from different vantage points. Move up, down and behind the subject, if you can.

What format and proportions best suit the subject? Should it be horizontal or vertical?

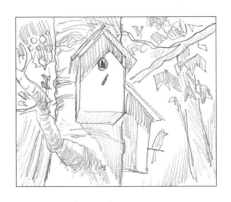 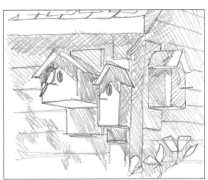 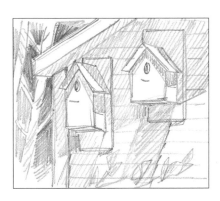

TAKE THE TIME
You will never know if there was a better composition for your idea unless you make the effort to explore variations. I went through several before settling on one for Summer Apartments.

DEMONSTRATION OF APPROACH ONE: WORKING FROM REAL TO "ABSTRACT"

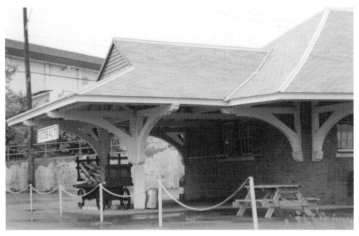

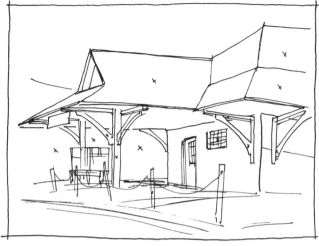

1. SEE THE BIG SHAPES AND VALUES.

The subject for this demonstration is an old railroad station on the Ontario Northland Railway line in Cobalt, Ontario. I see the station as a giant geometric mushroom offering protection beneath its massive top. I find the curving roof braces a wonderful contrast to the straight lines of the roof, while the shadow of the roof provides an opportunity for some great value contrasts. Analyze the station, looking for major lines dividing the subject. These are usually the edges of major value shapes, which you can read more easily if you squint. Think about lights, mediums and darks.

2. OUTLINE BIG VALUE SHAPES IN A SKETCH.

Also notice how smaller shapes relate to larger shapes. Think of changes in the arrangement that will produce a stronger composition. Keep in touch with what you would like as your center of interest—in this case, I chose the baggage wagon—and the values surrounding it that will enhance it. Eliminate what you feel is unnecessary, such as the picnic table. Note the direction of the light and where it falls on your subject. Mark these lights and sunlit areas with an X.

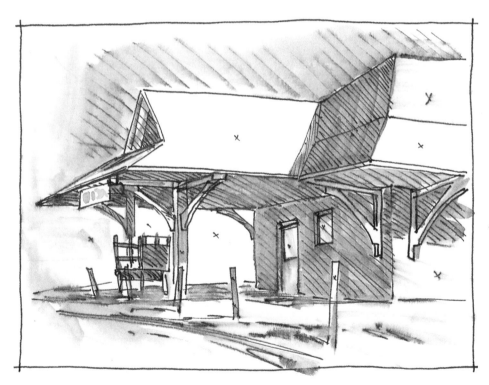

3. ADD VALUES TO YOUR SKETCH.

For my sketches I used a fountain pen with blue-black ink. To represent different values I varied the density of the hatch marks. A wet brush easily dissolved and spread the ink in each area to produce a wash in the value I wanted. I saved the X areas as white paper and made sure that the greatest contrast was still in the focal point area. Squint. Continue to study the smaller value areas of your composition, knowing that each needs to be lighter or darker than what is next to it in order for the viewer to see it. Don't be afraid to change the value of an area if it improves perception and value dominance.

4. ADD OR REARRANGE FOR MORE INTEREST.

I decided to add the lone figure as well as window detail, telephone pole (angled for character) and sundry freight. The figure became the major focal point, and the baggage wagon, secondary. At this stage I also added in the darkest values where needed. As is often the case at this stage, I needed to redo my sketch to clearly show the changes in subject matter, arrangements and values that I now wanted. I reminded myself that I was not working on a final solution but evolving toward one, and redrawing is part of that journey.

Now work up two or three other compositions that explore variations in value, subject arrangement and even style, because invariably it will be number two or three that you will like best of all. Remember, value patterns are the result of light direction. If you change the value pattern you are effectively changing the light source. Make sure that cast shadows are consistent with any new light source.

When you are satisfied with your sketch, transfer it to watercolor paper using as few light pencil lines as possible or very thin nonstaining paint. You can erase pencil lines later with a soft gum or synthetic eraser.

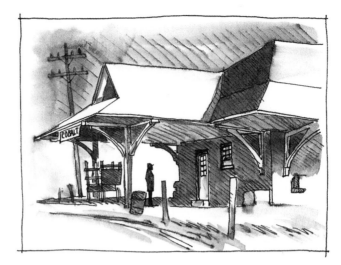

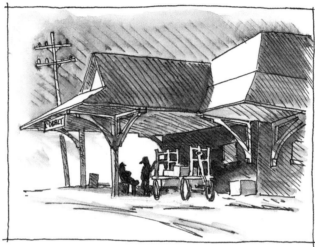

value and subject variation

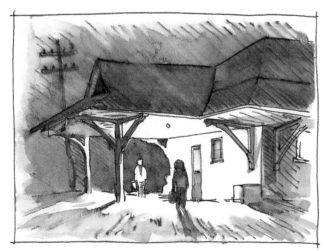

subject and time-of-day variation

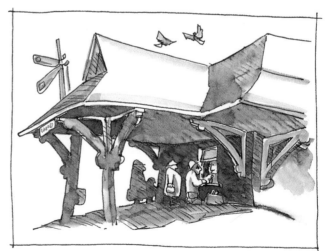

subject and style variation

Approach Two: Working From "Abstract" To Real

With this approach you allow your imagination and intuition, along with your knowledge of composition, to generate ideas. This time you do not start with a subject, view, time or place in mind but instead start with abstract sketches. Using additional free sketching, intuition and imagination you gradually move toward a real idea. The less you block your intuition in this process, the more easily it flows each time you use it. This approach is valuable when you are nowhere near a subject—on flights, in waiting rooms, in coffee shops, etc. All you need is a piece of paper and your imagination.

STEP ONE: DEVELOP ARRANGEMENTS IN THUMBNAIL SKETCHES

The first step in this process is to arrange shapes and lines in small abstract thumbnail sketches. From these come ideas for pictures which is step two. There is no right or wrong way to do this. Listen to your intuition as you decide where marks should go.

I will show you five variations on how to begin and complete this approach. You always start by putting down random marks in some particular way in your thumbnail sketches.

STEP TWO: WHAT COULD IT BE?

Examine your thumbnail sketches one at a time. Turn your imagination loose, and squint at each sketch. Ask yourself, "What could it be?" Turn the sketch and look at it from all angles, increasing the odds of seeing an idea you could develop.

EXPERIMENT WITH REDRAWING YOUR SKETCHES

You may add more lines or shading to your sketch. Let your mind make suggestions. Redraw sketches.

Clarify the images your mind creates. Don't stop at the first one. More ideas will come if you look for them. Experiment with the arrangement of values and shapes.

PUT INTUITION IN CONTROL

Let your imagination and intuitive senses of composition assume control. The hardest part about this is believing in your ability to do it. The second-hardest part is shutting off that little left-brain voice that says, "This is stupid. It won't work." It takes courage to step into the unknown and trust what you find, particularly when the unknown is within you.

WORK SKETCHES INTO REAL SUBJECTS

In the final stage of this process, let your imagination and your mind's abilities make sense out of your random marks. In other words, your imagination will harvest the visual seeds that your intuition has planted. With practice, you will develop your own method of working abstract sketches into real subjects, and in the process you will discover the endless supply of ideas for pictures that resides within you.

RESEARCH FOR DETAIL AND ACCURACY

Let me emphasize that this "abstract to real" approach is to help you develop an idea for a composition. It will not produce the finished, detailed sketch that you will need for a painting. Once you have an idea for a composition, you must do the research necessary for detail and accuracy. For example, my composition may suggest a floral arrangement. I must now decide what kinds of flowers I want and research them so I can draw them with accuracy. My composition may have suggested a building. It is up to me to find an appropriate building that I can use for reference.

COMPOSING WITH INTUITION

This is the phase of picture making where you decide how to portray your vision. It is during this process of organizing and arranging the parts of your picture that you can use intuition in partnership with your experiences and analytical art knowledge to make some of the decisions. This applies to preliminary sketching as well as the painting stage. Here is an example of a picture developed from an intuitive abstract sketch.

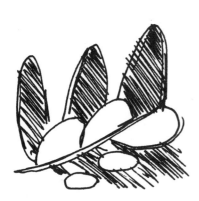

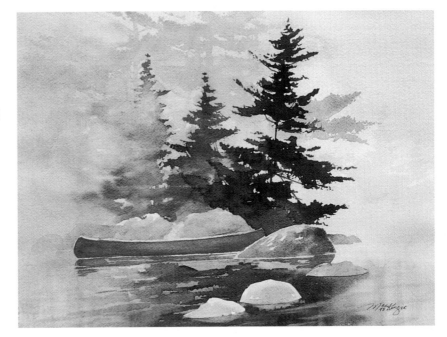

VARIATION A: PUT DOWN SHAPES, LINES AND SHADING

Put down a pattern of overlapping shapes from one side of the frame to the other (Column 1). There is no restriction on the size, number or location of shapes, but they must be similar. Suggest movement by adding lines that flow through the arrangement of shapes and off the paper (Column 2). These can be of any type or direction and may suggest depth or movement. Arbitrarily shade sections (Column 3). Establish greater contrast around one shape. This will become a focal point. Shade values for other parts.

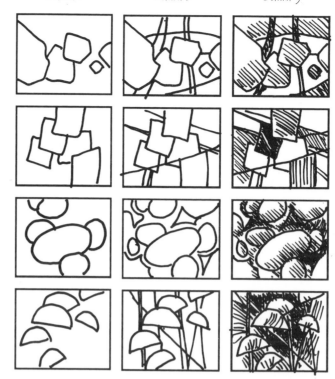

Column 1   Column 2   Column 3

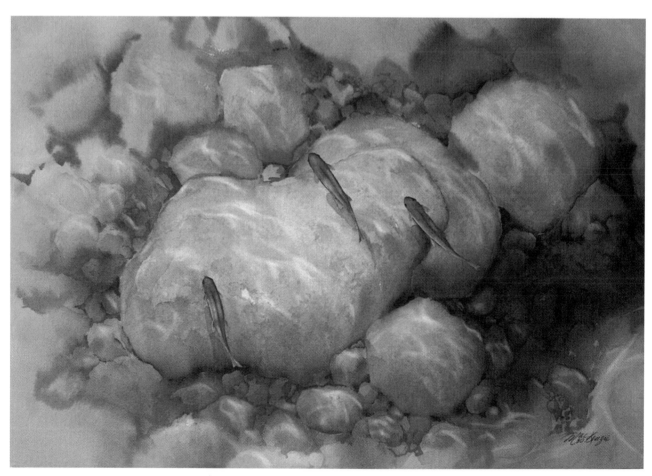

PAINTINGS DEVELOPED FROM VARIATION A

Just to give you an idea of how approach two works, here are two examples of real paintings that eventually developed from the abstract sketching of Variation A.

CURRENT EXPLORERS
15" x 22" (38cm x 56cm)
Private collection

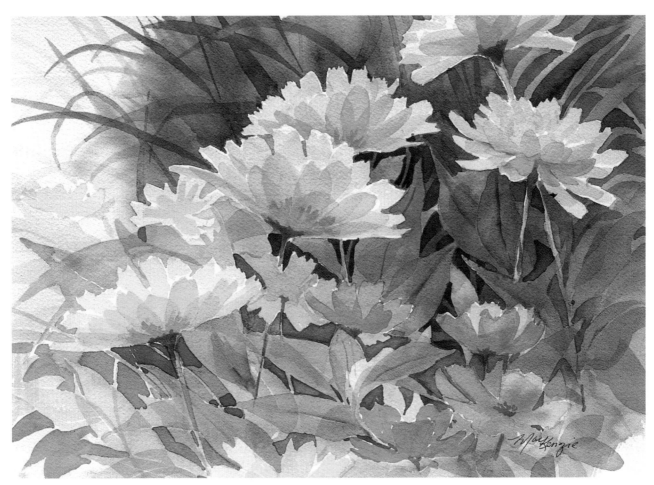

SUMMER DANCERS
11" x 15" (28cm x 38cm)
Private collection

VARIATION B: SHADE AND EMBELLISH SHAPES

Arbitrarily shade two or three dark, irregular shapes, beginning from different sides of your frame and protruding into the picture (top row). Think of this as negative space, and focus on the white area. Using your intuition, add marks and shading to make the white shape more interesting. Do not make something real yet, just embellish the shape (bottom row).

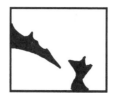

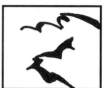

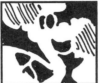
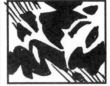
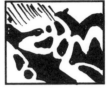
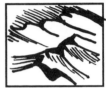

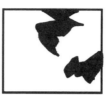

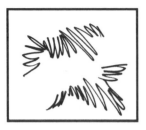
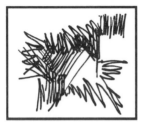
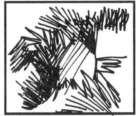

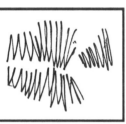
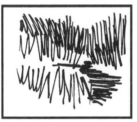
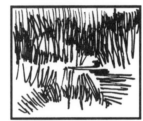

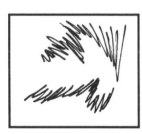
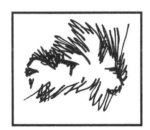
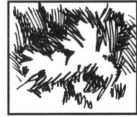

VARIATION C: DEFINE AREAS WITH LINES

This is a very quick process where I make a series of parallel or fanning hatch marks that vary in size, direction and darkness. This is similar to Variation B, but instead of using dark shapes to define a light area I use a series of lines. I start with light marks and gradually get darker and darker by adding more lines. In doing so, I automatically add value to my developing composition.

VARIATION D: START WITH A HOOK SHAPE

Here I started with a hook shape that entered the picture space from one of the sides. As you can see, there are many ways to do this. I then embellished the path of the hook with random shapes and marks that are similar in nature—jagged, circular, swirling, hatch marks, etc. I know that the eye will follow the hook to its tip, making it a perfect place to put a focal point later. There are endless variations on the same hook.

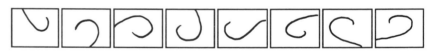

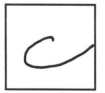
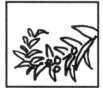
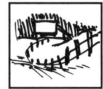
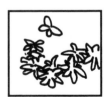

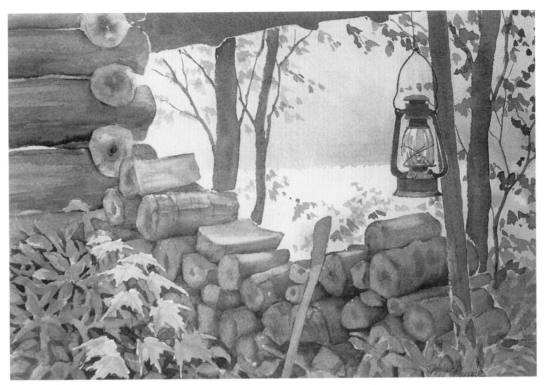

FINAL RESULTS OF TWO VARIATIONS
Here are two final results on the same "hook" composition.

SUMMER LIGHT
11" x 14" (28cm x 36cm)
Private collection

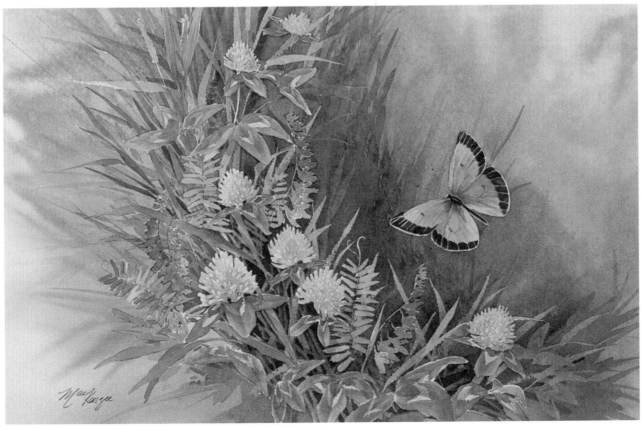

SULFUR
11" x 14" (28cm x 36cm)
Private collection

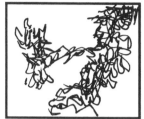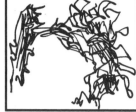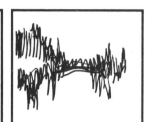

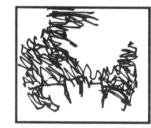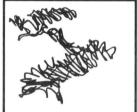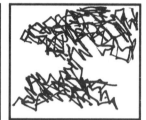

VARIATION E:
CREATE A BRIDGE
Create a "bridge" from one area of the picture to another without lifting your pencil. Bridges can go in many directions. Start from one side. Draw marks with a continuous line that extends toward another location. Let your instincts guide your pencil. Your bridge may have vertical and horizontal protrusions that reach to the margins. Don't make a perfectly symmetrical bridge, but one where one side is larger and more intricate than the other. Do not center it either.

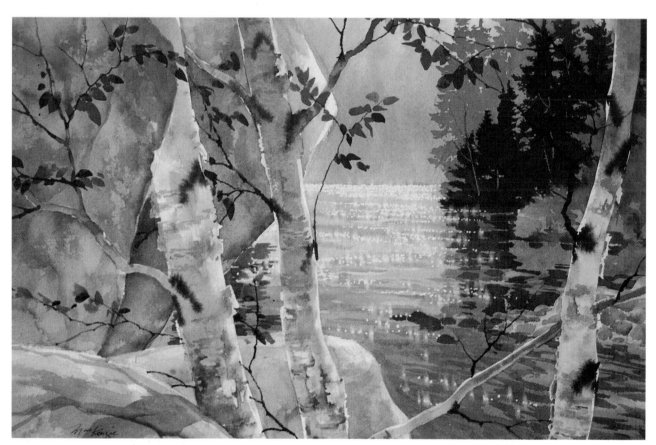

PICTURE DEVELOPED WITH BRIDGE COMPOSITION
Here's an example of a picture that was developed with a bridge composition. Note how the larger mass on one side of the picture connects to a lesser mass on the other.

ROCK'S EDGE
15" x 22" (38cm x 56cm)
Private collection

MANY IDEAS FROM ONE THUMBNAIL
A single thumbnail sketch can generate more than one idea for a picture.

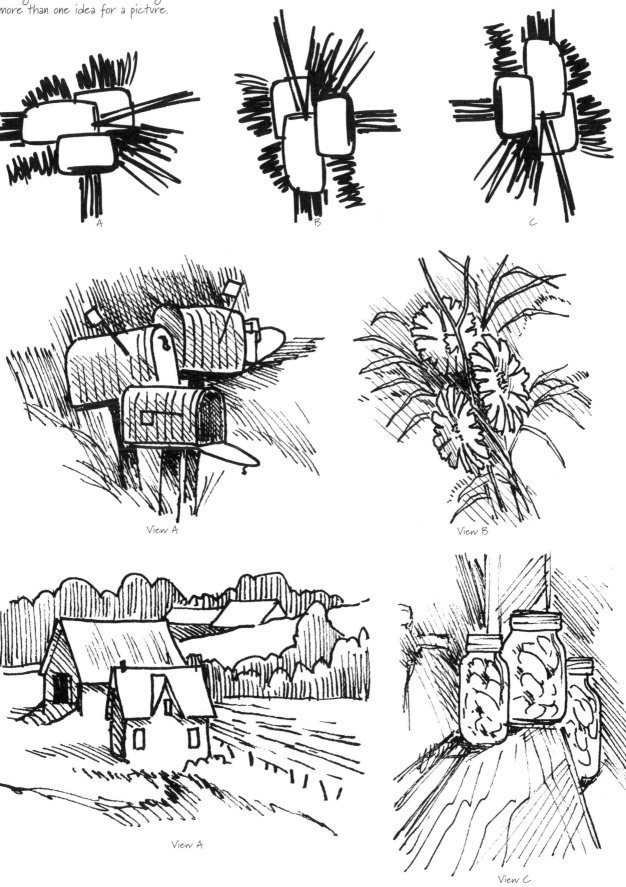

A

B

C

View A

View B

View A

View C

Approach Three: Working From Memory and Imagination

This is a combination of Approaches One and Two. Look inside yourself, to the endless selection of images you have already stored away from a lifetime of experiences.

The picture you produce does not have to be an accurately detailed record of a specific thing or place. Your prime objective is to recapture the essence of an experience as you recall it.

Our memories have emotions attached to them. The stronger the emotions attached to a memory, the more vivid the visual image you have, and vice versa. Therefore, this process will work best with topics or experiences about which you feel very strongly. Familiarity improves your memory. Your images of flowers improve if you take up gardening. You will know more about painting mountains if you see and paint them frequently.

Close your eyes and imagine yourself returning to an enjoyable place. Let the images and impressions of that place flash before you.

Define the underlying emotions that you remember about this situa-tion, then look for the causes of those feelings. Perhaps it was the quality of the colors, the tempera-ture, the time of day, the feel of the wind, the sunlight or some unique atmospheric conditions that impressed you. Use these things to recapture the essence of this place in a picture.

QUICKLY MAKE A THUMBNAIL SKETCH

Choose a specific aspect that appeals to you. Quickly make a thumbnail sketch that captures the basic layout of this image. Begin to enhance the image by defining and arranging shapes and values to approximate your memory or simply to suit your liking. Imagination and artistic license obviously play a major role in this part, as does knowledge of design, but uppermost in your thoughts should always be the recapturing of an emotional experi-ence. In your sketch, incorporate some of those influencing elements you identified earlier in the process. Since you can achieve some of them only with color and painting tech-niques, you might have to wait until the painting starts before you can incorporate those aspects.

IMPROVING THE QUALITY OF MEMORY

An important spin-off of this approach is that in the future you will be more observant when you are in a situation that has potential for a picture. By making a conscious effort to observe detail and relation-ships, you will make later recall easier and richer.

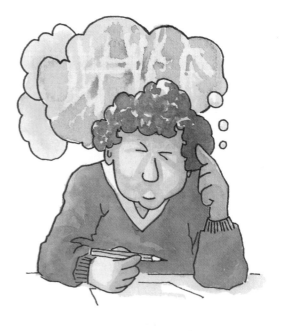

SKETCH COMPOSITIONAL VARIATIONS AND DETAILS

Redraw a "memory" sketch several times in order to explore compositional variations and clarify details. Remember, no matter how good your recall, you still may have to improvise in areas where you cannot remember details. On the other hand, knowing that memory is an impression of an experience colored by feelings, if you work from memory you can work without the distractions of peripheral details. What you do not remember exactly, you render the way you want it to be or the way the picture needs it to be. Your imagination can manipulate and generate an endless stream of images that add to what you remember.

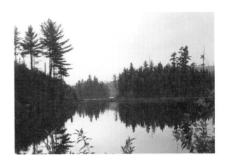

EXAMPLES OF WORKING FROM MEMORY

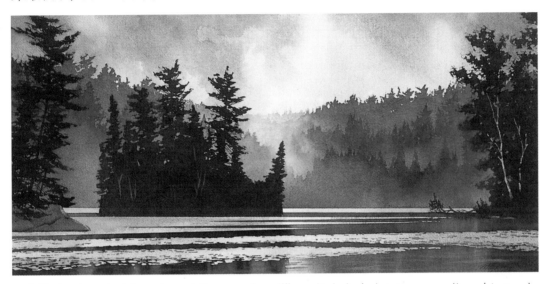

SOLITUDES
11" x 22" (28cm x 56cm)
Collection of the artist
Photographer: Ken Dobie, Kevanna Studios

In Solitudes, I wanted to go beyond the pervasive stillness that dominates so many northern lakes and say something of the spirit that moves across the water and land.

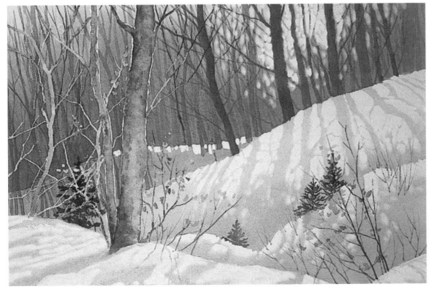

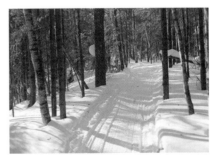

I have spent many hours on the winter trails near my home. Winter Rays is an impression from one such outing. In it my objective was to recapture the moment in which the warmth of the winter sun spread out before me.

WINTER RAYS
11" x 15" (28cm x 38cm)
Private collection

Developing a Series of Paintings

Sometimes a subject or concept is so rich that it warrants more than one attempt to capture it—your group of pictures could become a series. Some features common to most paintings include subject, value and lighting (see pages 110–113), distance from subject, point of view, values, shapes, patterns, lines, colors, techniques, etc. To do a series, keep as many features as you can the same while using one major aspect as a variable. Often there are one or two minor variables, but in the end the pictures should look as if they belong together. The five series that follow explore interesting variables.

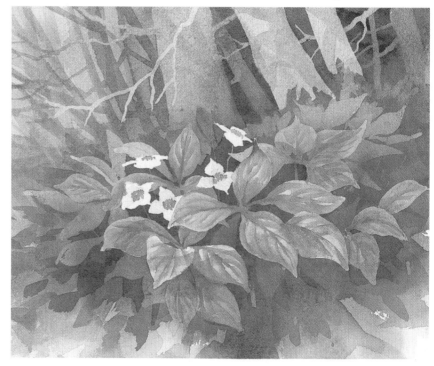

MAJOR VARIABLE: SEASON
The technique (multiple masking—see page 56) and the subject (woods) remain the same.

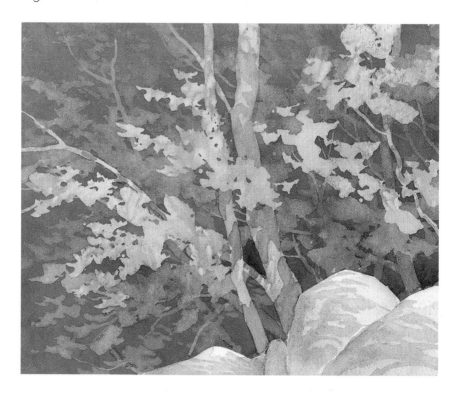

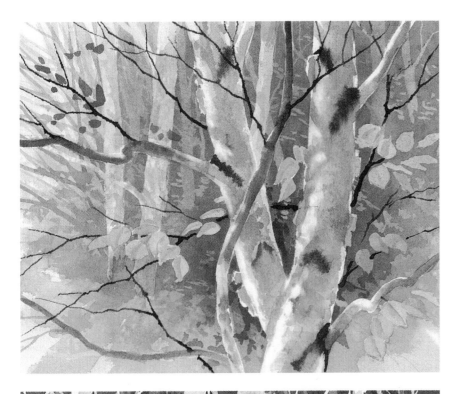

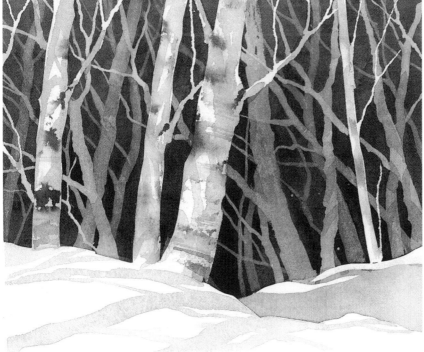

MAJOR VARIABLES: DISTANCE FROM
SUBJECT AND POINT OF VIEW
Minor variable was composition. The rest stayed the same.

MAJOR VARIABLES: FLOWERS AND COLORS
The technique, numbers of blooms, point of view, style, distance from subject and technique are the same.

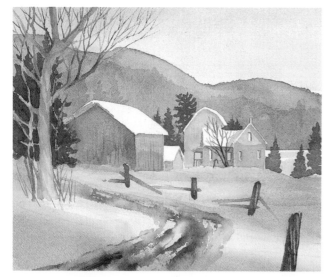

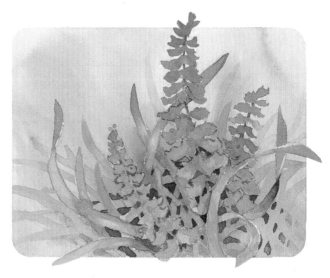

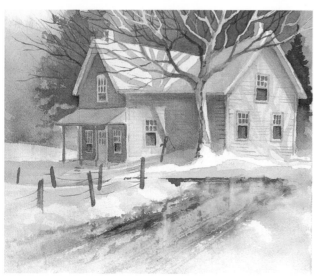

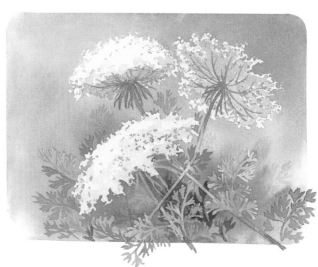

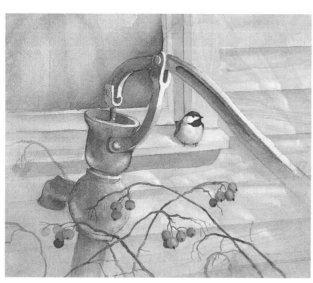

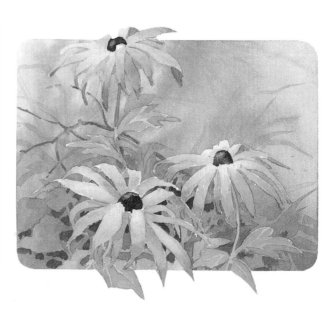

MAJOR VARIABLES: TEXTURES, PATTERNS AND COLORS

In this painting, the general subject (a door and window), the season and technique are the same.

MAJOR VARIABLE: COLOR SCHEME

Composition, style, season, etc., remain the same.

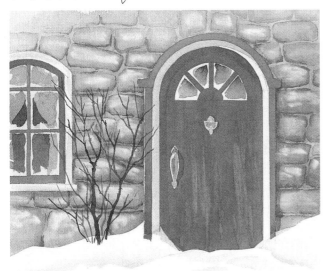

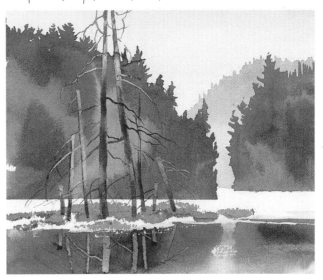

Phthalo Green, Red Rose Deep, Raw Sienna

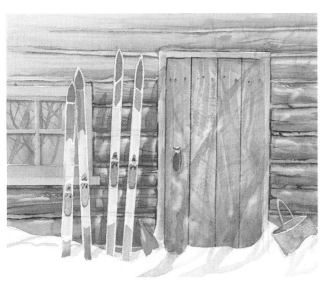

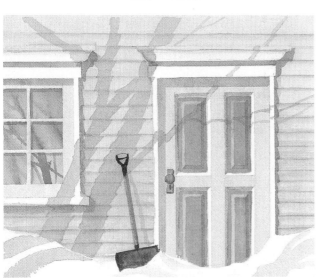

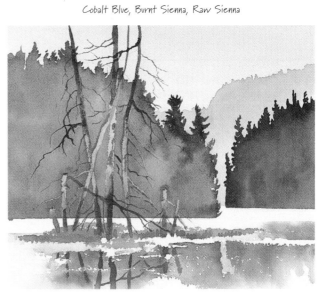

Cobalt Blue, Burnt Sienna, Raw Sienna

Indigo, Indian Yellow, Cadmium Red

PAINTING WITH INTUITION

Every time you decide to do something, you open doors to other possibilities. This does not mean you have to deviate from your plan when painting, but be aware of options and your intuition can help you decide which way to go. When you pick up the brush to add color to a wet area, realize that you could choose a different brush, a sponge or a knife. You could pour on the paint or spatter it with a toothbrush.

Sometimes you set your direction, then close your eyes and mind to other possibilities. You see any variation or happy accident as a mistake that you must correct, instead of an opportunity on which to build. Keep your mind open and your intuition ready to chart a new direction. Remain open to opportunity and options. Let your intuition play a role in the decisions you make.

Intuition vs. Planning

Beginners and experienced painters alike often tighten up when faced with a new challenge. They squirt out a millimeter of paint, hunch over their work with a steel grip on their smallest brushes, and work away, wet on dry, in terror of making a mistake.

Watercolor can be a difficult and sometimes bewildering medium unless you learn to lighten up a bit. The following pages take a close look at things you can do to improve your spontaneity and, in turn, increase your enjoyment of the medium. It even suggests ways to save pictures, just in case your spontaneity runs amuck.

INTUITION

Artists rightfully draw on knowledge gathered from experience to make decisions. Yet there is a deeper level of knowing that resides in your subconscious that you can access as well—it is your intuition. Intuition is not a substitute for experience, however, because the more you understand about perception, composition and techniques, the more informed your intuitive decisions will be. Pay attention to the rules, but do not ignore your intuition. Think of the creative process as a bridge between rules and some insight trying to be born of a greater wisdom that resides within us all.

Unfortunately, you cannot will creativity, insight or intuition. All you can do is will yourself to approach your work with daring and the openness of mind that invites them in.

Listen to your intuitive sense at all stages of the picture-making process. This is a major challenge, because it means trusting and believing in your own good judgment. The more you call upon your intuition

for direction, the faster and clearer it will come.

PURSUING THE VOICE FROM WITHIN

We artists have images of how we would like to paint. No matter what your skill level, the desire to express ideas in a way different from what you are currently doing seems to be common. A preferred style of expression swirls in and out of consciousness as you work. A successful painting is not your final accomplishment, just another level of achievement on the way to your goal, which may seem vague at times. However, the vision, along with the joy of painting, leads you on, to keep you coming back again and again to attempt to achieve it. The diligence with which you pursue your vision determines your artistic growth. This goes beyond mastery of manual skills and techniques.

When my students describe how they would like to paint, the vast majority see images that are freer, looser and livelier than what they are currently producing i.e., more spontaneous. Spontaneity suggests confident, deliberate and intuitive movement or action. Artists who work spontaneously seem to know instinctively what to do. Every move is confident, as if they are directed by a force unseen. They move quickly, seemingly focused on the whole work and unconcerned with little details until the time is right. They know where they are going, and they seem to know how to get there. Working more spontaneously means trusting your intuition.

No one can make you more spontaneous unless you want to be, but having chosen watercolors, you at least have chosen a medium that is highly sympathetic to spontaneity.

PHYSICAL AND MENTAL BLOCKS TO SPONTANEITY

A PALETTE WITH SMALL WELLS

A palette with small wells will not allow you to use those nice new big brushes you have just run out and bought. Sorry about that, but it will definitely slow you down if you can't get at your paint.

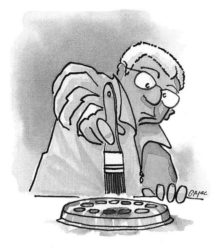

LET YOUR WORK REFLECT YOU

The desire to have your work mirror yourself, and not just the subject, is the essence of the creative process, the essence of being an artist, the essence of finding your inner creative self. It is all about finding and making your "self" visible.

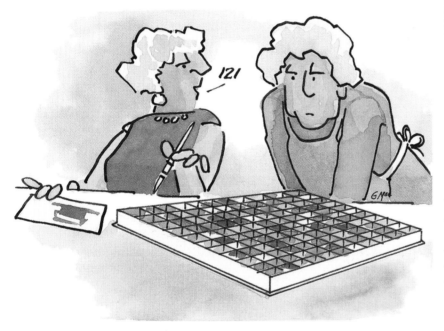

TOO MANY DISORGANIZED COLORS

A palette with too many colors contributes to confusion. A smaller selection of basic colors will reduce hesitation when making color decisions. You can produce mixtures yourself. See Setting Up Your Palette on page 97.

TOO LITTLE PAINT ON THE PALETTE

You will interrupt your painting flow if you have to search for more paint. Watercolors will not go bad if you leave them to dry on the palette. The odd color may crumble in time from repeated re-wetting, but this is a small inconvenience compared to reaching for a color that isn't there while you are painting. The amount of paint you put out is an indicator of how serious you are about succeeding. Examine the palettes of experienced painters. They put out lots of paint because they know they will need it, particularly when they use their large brushes.

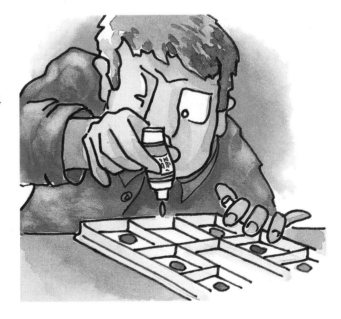

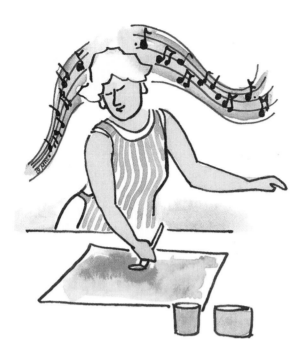

RESTRICTED MOVEMENT FROM SITTING DOWN

Sitting down keeps you from using the full movement of your arms and body. The term spontaneous suggests acting out your impulses. It is hard to do this if you are sitting on it. Also, the larger your piece of paper, the more physically demanding the painting process and the more important that you get full arm movement behind your brushes. Sitting down really does cramp your style and your spontaneity, but when you stand you should raise your table to hip height and stand on a cushioned mat to minimize back and leg stress.

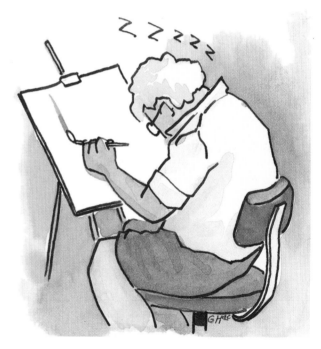

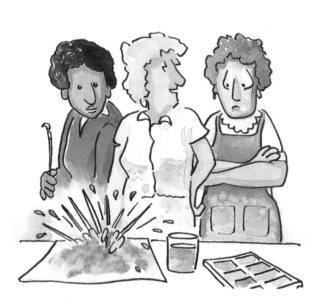

INTERRUPTIONS AND DISTRACTIONS

Constant interruptions will break your flow and concentration. As hard as it may be, you must try to find a time and place where there will be minimal distractions, particularly conversation with others. Have you ever noticed how hard it is to stay focused in a workshop situation where other people want to carry on a conversation? Some may prefer to work in silence, while others find music a powerful tool for remaining centered on this right-brain activity.

FATIGUE

Being tired is a real killer of spontaneity. Painting is a process that demands great mental strength and physical stamina. Working spontaneously is the most demanding because you must be constantly alert and totally involved in the process.

Life often leaves little time and energy for painting. However, artists who paint on a regular basis and for sustained periods of time are likely to be freer in their approach than those who paint only occasionally. When you return to painting after a long break, it takes time to get back in the swing of it. If you feel as if you have almost forgotten how to paint, it is highly unlikely that you will approach it spontaneously.

WORKING ON ONLY ONE PAINTING AT A TIME

It is easy to overwork a picture when it's the only one on which you are working. Have several on the go at any one time. If things are not going well or you are not sure what to do next, put one away and work on another. When you return to the original, your fresh view often will indicate what you need to do. At any time, I have twelve or more paintings at various stages of completion.

Stop work on a painting when you reach a "high" and all is going well. Walk away with your attitude one of "winning," and you will be eager to get back to it. If you have only one painting, you have to quit when things are not going well. Your feeling is of defeat, and it will be hard to get back to painting.

BRUSH SIZE AND WORKING SMALL

Over-reliance on small brushes will also slow down spontaneity and produce an overworked appearance. You will spend more time carrying paint to the paper than you will spreading it around. If you have become comfortable producing small paintings, chances are you are also overusing small brushes. By increasing the size of your pictures, you will be obliged to use larger brushes and bold strokes to cover large areas quickly. This is particularly critical in the beginning stages of a work when you often want to deliver a lot of paint for a background passage. As a rule of thumb, try to paint as long as you can with your biggest brushes (1½" to 2½") and save the small ones for detail at the end.

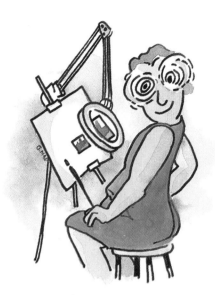

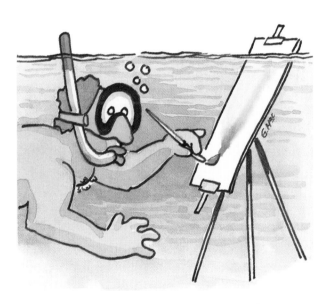

ALWAYS USING THE SAME TECHNIQUE

If you always work wet-on-dry, you are missing out on the medium's most exciting feature. It's the wet-in-wet approach that helps produce much of the free and spontaneous appearance of your work. This is understandable, because it's in this state that the paint takes on a life of its own. The pigments flow and react to water in ways that you cannot always plan. These techniques demand a give-and-take attitude while you remain open and ready to react spontaneously and intuitively to opportunities and possibilities that the medium presents.

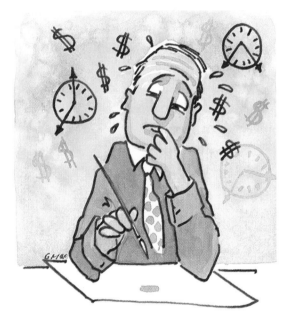

WORRYING ABOUT WASTE

You might waste valuable time and materials if you take chances and ruin your picture. You're right—you just might. You might lose lots of paper and paint and time, but that's the price and the chance you have to take. Painting more freely is about taking chances, and this is just one of them. By "wasting" time and materials, you will open creative doors you never knew existed. You will derive far greater enjoyment from the painting process because you will grow and learn much faster. You will want to paint often, so you will produce far more work that, along with better planning, will quite likely reduce the chance of wasting time and materials in the long run.

THE SMELL OF FEAR

Besides physical blocks to spontaneity, there are some very real and powerful mental blocks, chief among them being fear: fear of making a mistake, embarrassment, ridicule, exposing deep secrets and artistic inadequacy. Take your pick. Any one of these phantoms is enough to scare the living "spontaneity" right out of anyone. We spend a lifetime developing all means of protection for our egos. We will do anything to avoid embarrassment. Why would we ever want to let our guard down and compromise ourselves like this? Because it's the price we all must pay in order to break loose and soar.

To work spontaneously we must screw up our courage and stare down these phantoms. In truth, most of your fellow artists do not spend a lot of time worrying about your inadequacies anyway. They have enough problems dealing with their own. They will, however, envy your strength of conviction and the results you get.

WHERE ARE YOU GOING?

Think of painting as taking a week-long vacation. Most of us would not just walk out of our homes, jump in the car and wander merrily down the road for seven days without knowing where we were going. Many of us paint this way, then wonder why we never seem to get where we want to go.

Working spontaneously does not mean working without a plan. If you want to successfully arrive, you must at least have a general idea of where you want to go—that is, what you want to say or capture and how it will appear. This may mean exploring the subject with thumbnail sketches or value studies first to find or clarify a plan that will best express your vision of the subject.

PLANNING KEEPS YOU IN CONTROL

For that week's trip you would undoubtedly give some thought to a destination. You might consider various routes and stopovers along the way. You would consider the things you need to take and maybe even things to do at various stages on your way. You feel more comfortable if you think about these details. You also know that if your plans are flexible enough to take advantage of some of the unexpected little treasures that might pop up, you will get even more enjoyment from the journey. If you plan ahead, refer to travel brochures and make reservations in advance, it allows you in some small way to feel that you are in control of your destiny. You are more confident that your trip will be a success.

You must also consider beforehand how you are going to get where you want to go and in what sequence. That is, what techniques will you use, and in what order? What colors would best convey the feeling you wish to express? What size and format will the picture be?

Don't forget supplies. Have you put out enough paint on the palette? Have you located the main brushes and other tools you will use in the process so you don't have to interrupt the flow while you hunt for them?

All successful artists develop unique ways of planning their work, not because someone told them to, but because they have found advantages to doing so. Take the time to think out your painting beforehand. You will be able to work with greater confidence while still remaining open to options and opportunities that come your way.

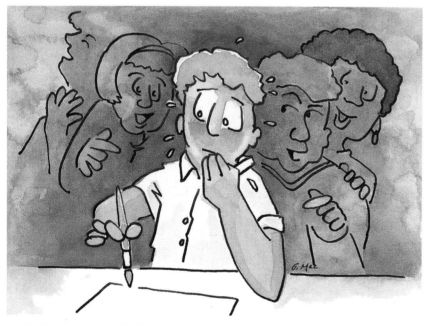

THE PHANTOMS OF FEAR

STAY OPEN TO POSSIBILITIES

When you paint, there is no guarantee that you will arrive at the exact location you had planned. The only guarantee is that if you have not done some planning beforehand, you will not even come close or will quite likely end up in the ditch. Painting is a nebulous process of compromise and surprise. You must accept destinations that are not quite the way the brochure describes them but nevertheless quite acceptable.

REALISM

Not every painting has to be a super-realistic depiction of an actual subject. Paintings can be born of your mind's eye, memory and imagination. They can be a compilation of things and places. You can render them in whatever way you desire. Realism that reflects a slavish adherence to the literal appearance of the subject is not a measure of quality. This is realism for realism's sake and is more a measure of the painter's technical skills than of his or her creative abilities.

You should strive to produce work that reflects the creative decisions you have made, be it in a realistic fashion or any other. Even paintings that contain high realism can have passages that suggest a spontaneous approach. Images that reflect our "self" have an all-important emotional impact not usually found in literal "copies" of a subject.

DEVELOPING A STYLE

The style of your work is a reflection of your personality and physical dexterity. It will develop naturally, over time, as you learn to trust your innate ability to make intuitive artistic decisions regarding subject, composition, color and techniques. Don't be surprised if you develop several styles. After all, you see the world in different ways. Why shouldn't you be able to express yourself likewise? Remember, precious gems have many facets.

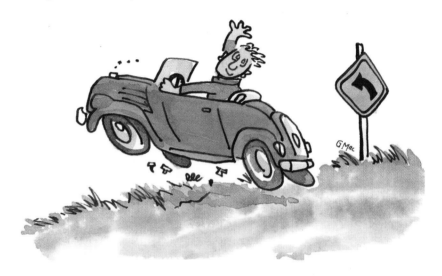

To Save Or Not To Save

Let's face it. No matter how much you want to resurrect a work, the reality is that you cannot save all works, and to waste time trying will only add to your frustration. This section is also about determining which pictures may be worth saving, which ones to forget and the techniques to try.

ANALYZING THE PROBLEM

Squint. This eliminates distracting detail so you can study values, big shapes and major lines.

Mirror. Try looking at your work in a mirror. It provides a fresh view of your work.

Stand back. This also eliminates much detail, allowing you to see problems with value and unity. If things fade out or are unclear at a distance, that may be your problem.

Reducing glass. This is just a concave lens. Hold it up and view your work through it. It allows you to see your work at a distance—but in detail. This may help you spot confusing patterns, edges and values.

Turn down the lights. This is a good way to check values and big shapes. The basic structure and focal point should be discernible even in low light.

The "L" with it. Cut an old mat at opposite corners to make two Ls. Lay these on your work and play with the format. Eliminate or save what you want.

Put it away. Getting a problem picture out of sight for a while often helps. When you come back to it, any problems with the work will stand out immediately, but just for a second or two.

Rose-colored glasses. Viewing your work through a piece of red acetate helps you see the value of your colors and any problems between them.

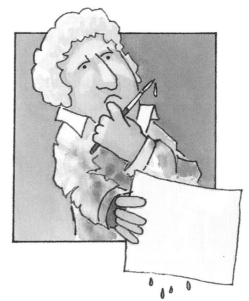

MAKING CHANGES—
FIRST, THE BAD NEWS...

The following problems are nearly impossible to change, even with a great deal of effort. Just turn your paper over and start again.

- mistakes in perspective, structural or perceptual logic
- poor position of major shapes
- the size of objects
- tight brushwork that says "over worked"
- too many colors
- colors that have become muddy
- staining colors where you wanted to lift paint
- paper that has lost its sizing (a substance that limits absorbency of watercolor paper) or developed mold
- scratched and overworked surfaces
- masking that is sloppy or has torn the paper

...NOW THE GOOD NEWS

You can usually correct the following common problems without too much risk. Essentially, any method that maintains the freshness and spontaneity of a work while remaining indiscernible, is acceptable.

Problem:
Run-Backs and Hard Edges

Action
Let the paper dry completely. Wet only the area of concern and gently scrub the edge of the run-back (water spot or blossom) or hard edge with an old, stiff synthetic brush. If you use a new one, you will ruin its tip. When the edge disappears, blot with a tissue. If it was a run-back, you may now replace color to this damp area. A natural elephant's ear sponge or soft toothbrush may also work. Use lots of water, and scrub gently in a circular motion. If the paint was a staining color, you may not be able to remove it without going right to white paper.

Next Time
Keep an eye on damp areas. They are most vulnerable to excess moisture that comes in contact with them. Keep a large, damp brush handy to fade out hard edges before they can dry.

Problem:
Incorrect or Ineffective Values

Action
By squinting, you will see the area or objects that need greater contrast. Darken one or the other with a color already used. You can use an all-over, transparent glaze to join small or fragmented patches of similar values into larger masses.

If you must lighten an area, you can remove paint using water and a soft sponge. Staining colors are the hardest to remove. You may need to redefine the dark edges that border the area you have scrubbed. Do so when everything is dry.

Next Time
Plan your values with a thumbnail sketch beforehand. You need only worry about a few values—lights (including white), mid-values and darks (including black). By limiting your palette, you will have to make more contrasts by value instead of colors alone. Get in the habit of squinting at your work as you paint.

Problem:
No Particular Mood Evident

Action
Dominant temperature, brilliance (purity) and value of colors determine mood. The position and types of shapes and lines (movement) also contribute to a picture's mood. You can usually change colors and values. Try glazing most of the painting with a transparent color in the temperature you wish. Don't overdo it. Save some white, particularly near the focal point and other areas. Soften the edges of the glaze area. The darker the glaze, the lower the total value of the painting becomes.

Next Time
Decide the feeling you want before you start, and select your color scheme accordingly (see page 114). A thumbnail sketch can help you choose the dominant value for the work (see page 122).

Problem:
Focal Point Hard to Find

Action
The eye sees all parts of the picture equally because you have evenly distributed values, details and colors. You can subdue and unify unnecessary detail by scrubbing back or glazing over with a transparent color. Increase the detail and contrast around the center of interest. This can be a problem if you have made it very small. To move the viewer's eye into the focal area, try glazing and darkening the corners and sides of the picture with a cool color.

Next Time
Save your detail and highest contrast for the center of interest. Other areas should help the viewer focus on this spot by being less attention grabbing.

Problem:
Highlight or Dark Detailing Missing

Action
Squinting will point out where you need values. Scrub out highlights with a small hog hair scrubber and water, or carefully scrape with a razor blade. Paint in darks as needed, particularly next to areas you want to highlight.

Next Time
You might consider masking in order to save some of the highlights.

Problem:
Misplaced Looseness

Action
The edges, in particular the corners of major shapes, need care so the viewer can read them easily. A loose edge may read as sloppiness. If you mangle a lot of major edges and corners, it may be easier to start again.

You may be able to clean up sloppy edges by scrubbing with a small hog hair scrubber. When dry, redefine the edge with paint. For a precise edge, use the edge of a piece of clear acetate as a mask and scrub the area with a wet toothbrush. Blot excess water immediately.

Next time
Save loose edges for less-important areas and parts of shapes where you want the eye to keep on going.

Problem:
Paint Splatters

Action
Only worry about the ones that are really distracting, that you cannot work into your composition. Be very careful with the ones sitting on heavy-colored backgrounds. You don't want to replace a dark splatter with a white blotch. Splatters on very light backgrounds are the easiest to remove.

Carefully wet the spot with water and let it stand a moment. Depending on the size of the splatter, gently scrub with an old, stiff synthetic brush, a soft toothbrush or a hog hair scrubber. If the spot is on a heavily colored background, you may need to scrub off a larger area with the soft toothbrush and then repaint it. Make sure the edges of the removed area fade smoothly into the surrounding colored area.

Problem:
Small Paint Dots

Action
Carefully pick off with the tip of a craft knife and then erase.

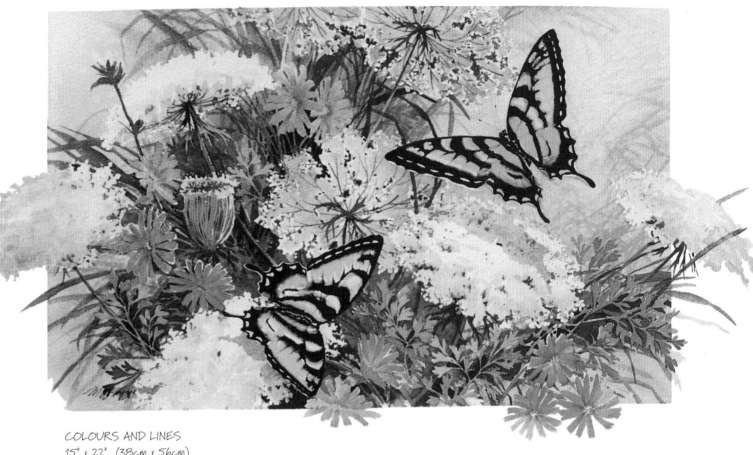

COLOURS AND LINES
15" x 22" (38cm x 56cm)
Private collection

Gallery

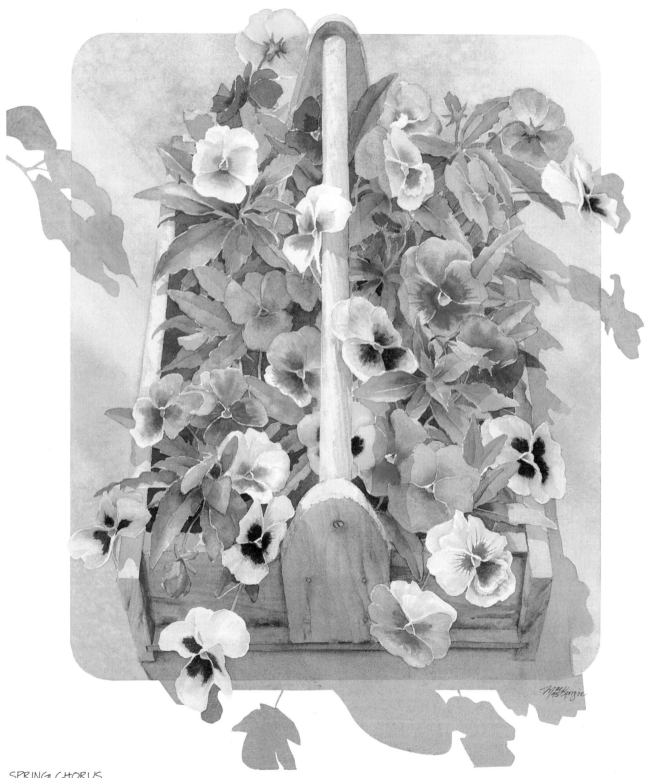

SPRING CHORUS
19" x 22" (48cm x 56cm)
Collection of the artist
Photographer: Kevin Dobie, Kevanna Studios

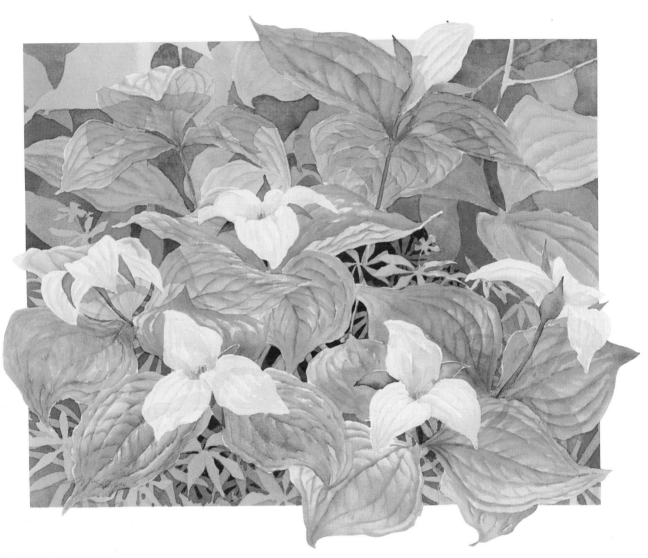

PLAYERS OF SPRING
19" x 22" (48cm x 56cm)
Collection of the artist
Photographer: Kevin Dobie, Kevanna Studios

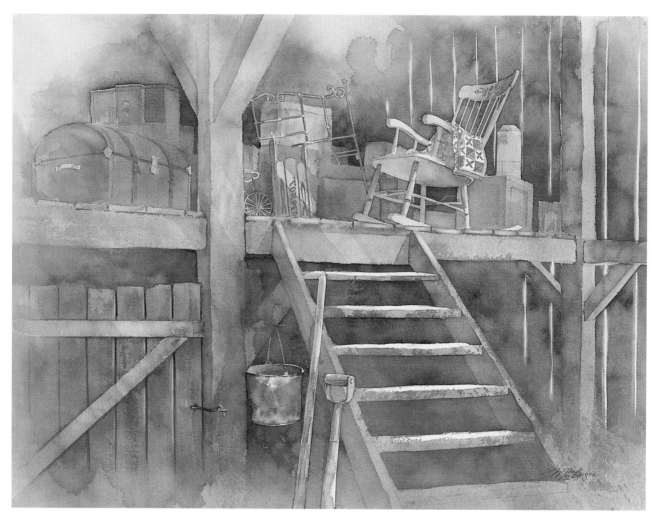

MEMORIES
22" x 30" (56cm x 76cm)
Collection of the artist
Photographer: Kevin Dobie, Kevanna Studios

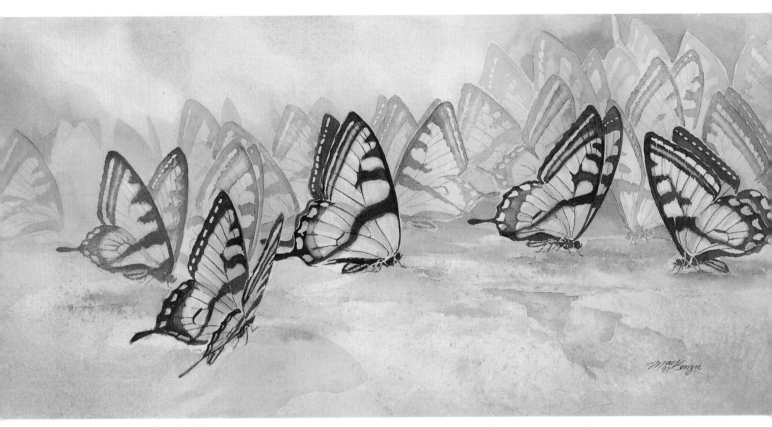

GATHERING OF THE CLAN
11" x 22" (28cm x 56cm)
Collection of the artist
Photographer: Kevin Dobie, Kevanna Studios

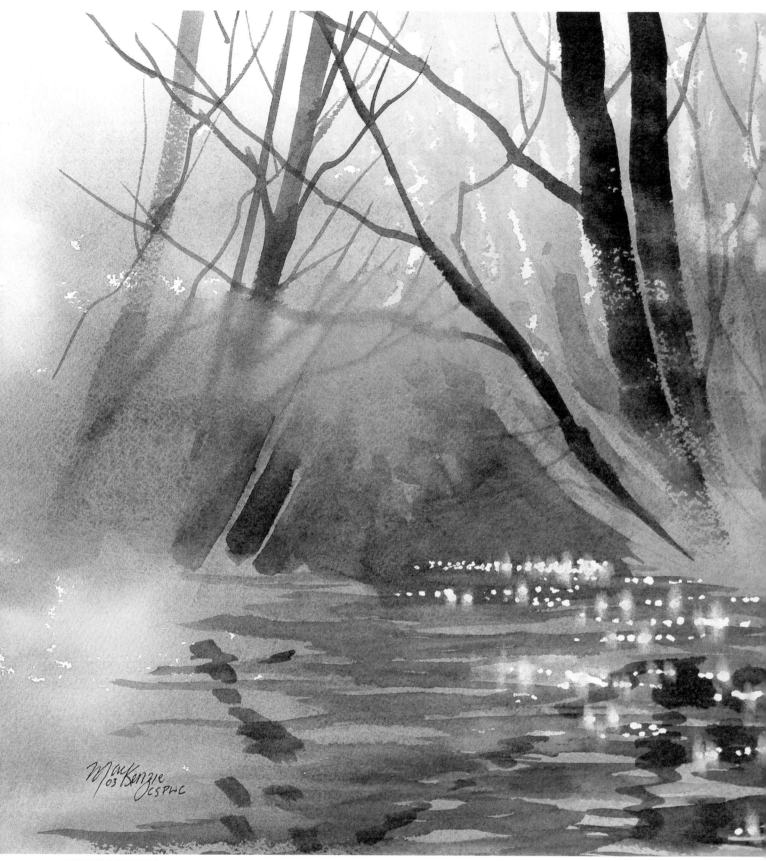

SPRING MEDLEY
11" × 14" (28cm × 36cm)

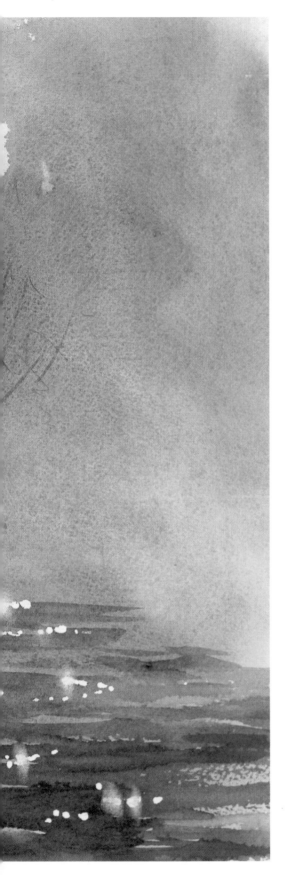

The
Watercolorist's
Essential
Notebook
Landscapes

Gordon MacKenzie

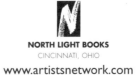

NORTH LIGHT BOOKS
CINCINNATI, OHIO
www.artistsnetwork.com

Acknowledgments

The best way to learn something is to teach it, and the best way to teach is to learn from your students. With this in mind, I acknowledge all that I have learned over the years, both directly and indirectly, from my students. I also wish to recognize the many dear friends and colleagues whose real and spiritual support over the past five years has made this book possible. And a special thanks to Pam Wissman, acquisitions editor, who made the opportunity happen.

Production edited by Stefanie Laufersweiler
Designed by Lisa Holstein
Production art by Lisa Holstein
Production coordinated by Mark Griffin

Metric Conversion Chart

To convert	to	multiply by
Inches	Centimeters	2.54
Centimeters	Inches	0.4
Feet	Centimeters	30.5
Centimeters	Feet	0.03
Yards	Meters	0.9
Meters	Yards	1.1
Sq. Inches	Sq. Centimeters	6.45
Sq. Centimeters	Sq. Inches	0.16
Sq. Feet	Sq. Meters	0.09
Sq. Meters	Sq. Feet	10.8
Sq. Yards	Sq. Meters	0.8
Sq. Meters	Sq. Yards	1.2
Pounds	Kilograms	0.45
Kilograms	Pounds	2.2
Ounces	Grams	28.3
Grams	Ounces	0.035

About the Author

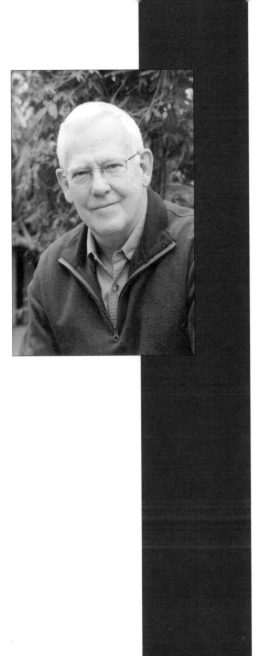

Gordon MacKenzie is a native of New Liskeard in northern Ontario. He now lives in Sault Ste. Marie, Ontario, where he maintains his painting and closeness to the outdoors. Even though it precluded any formal art instruction, the remoteness of northern Ontario became the inspiration behind Gordon's work. His paintings reflect his emotional bond with the natural world.

"An artist's work is a reflection of their personal aesthetics; the ordinary things that have extraordinary and hidden beauty, meaning and significance just for them. These perceptions are set at an early age, and for me it was the spirit of remote Northern lakes and forests speaking in breathtaking images for the eye and timeless silence for the soul."

Gordon received his first formal art training at the Ontario College of Art and Design while certifying as a visual arts specialist in education. Work in a variety of media followed, but none captured the transient and ethereal nature of the land as he saw it until the early 1970s when he switched to watercolors. He has been a devoted watercolorist ever since.

Gordon has now retired after thirty-three years as a teacher and art consultant for the Sault Ste. Marie Board of Education. As a graduate of Laurentian University and a specialist in art education, he has taught ministry of education and university-level art education courses for teachers for many years. With over twenty-five years of teaching private adult watercolor workshops as well, Gordon has earned a reputation as a first-class artist and instructor. Gordon has had twenty-six solo watercolor shows in Canada and the U.S., and his work appears in many private and corporate collections throughout Canada, the U.S., Europe, Africa and the Far East. He has received honors in several American shows, including that of the Detroit Institute of Art and the American Artist annual competition. He is a member of the Canadian Society of Painters in Watercolour and author of the very successful *The Watercolorist's Essential Notebook* (North Light Books, 1999).

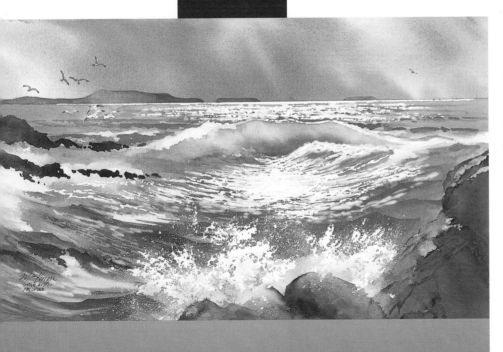

Dedication

For Jane,
who taught us all how to live
this life, and now guides our
hearts from afar.

DEPARTURE
11" × 19" (28cm × 48cm)

Table of Contents

Introduction.................................149

1 The Medium, Tools and Techniques...151

Before We Start.................................152
Pigment Characteristics.................................153
Paint Quality Chart.................................155
Brush Types.................................156
Brush Techniques.................................158
Water.................................160
Fading Out.................................162
Graded Washes.................................164
Palette and Paper.................................165
Negative Painting.................................166
Masking.................................168
Combining Masking Materials.................................169
Painting With Palette Knives.................................170
Painting With a Sponge.................................171
A Treasury of Techniques.................................172

2 Composing a Landscape Painting ...175

How Do I Go From Painter to Artist?.................................176
Color Characteristics.................................180
Color Wheel.................................181
Color Schemes.................................182
The Quality of Sunlight.................................183
Light Effects.................................184
Creating Atmosphere/Mood.................................185
Perspective.................................186
Surface Patterns That Lead the Eye.................................188
Using a Model for Perspective.................................190
Dynamics: Are There Any Signs of Life?.................................191

Contrast.................................193
Priming the Imagination.................................195

3 Landscape Elements ...199

Painting Water.................................200
    Making Waves
    Wave Direction and Surface Patterns
    Interrupted Flow
    Sparkling Waters
    Masking Ripple Marks
    The Laws of Reflection
    Calm Reflections
    Techniques for Dynamic Water
    Sea Spray
    Rapids

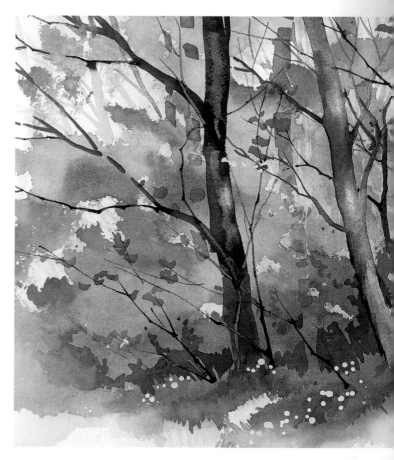

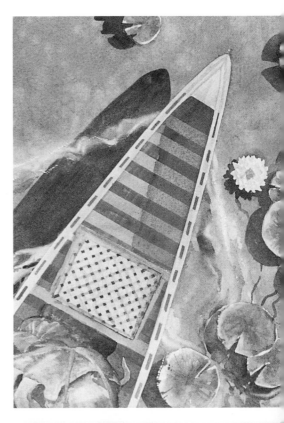

Big Water

Patterns in the Foam

Whitecaps

Capping and Breaking Waves

Seeing Into Water

Painting Underwater

Painting Skies 230

Wet-in-Wet Skies

Making Cloud Bottoms by Fading Out

Making Billowy Clouds

Graded Washes

Lifting Paint

Lifting Color for Northern Lights

Spraying and Tilting

Dropping Water or Paint

Painting the Land 244

Rocks

Reflected Light on Rocks

Trees

Deciduous Trees

Painting Deciduous Foliage

Branching Options

Coniferous Trees

Painting Coniferous Foliage

Palm Trees

Combining Techniques for a Meadow

Ferns

Tree Trunks

Tree Lines and Seasonal Forest Scenes

Lighting in the Forest

Backlit Forest Meadow

Edge of the Forest

Country Roads

Snowstorm in the Forest

From Dusk to Dawn

Under the Stars

Winter Hills

Autumn Glow

Mist in the Hills

Arid Hills

Snowy Mountains

Index 282

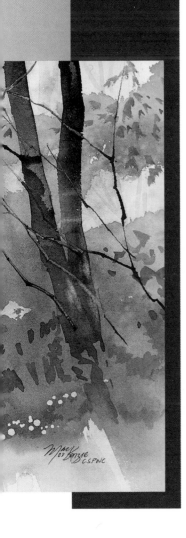

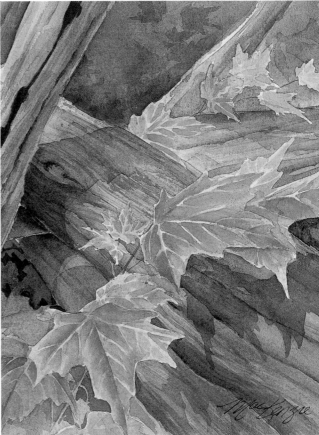

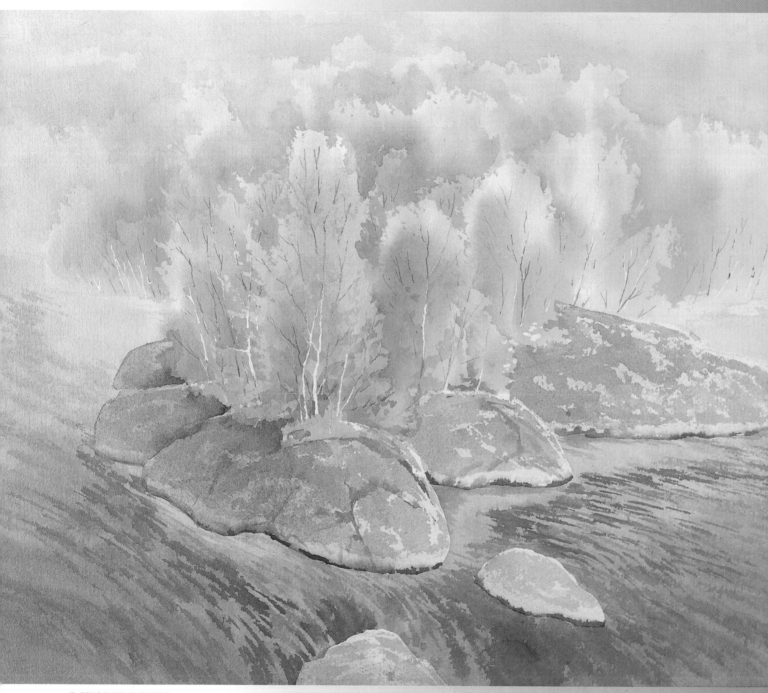

OCTOBER POINT
15" × 22" (38cm × 56cm)

Landscape painting is our interpretation of how the land has energized us. Deep within our being it touches chords, which are then played out as images on our paper.

—Gordon MacKenzie—

Introduction

I am sorry if you bought this book thinking that you would become a full-blown artistic wonder overnight just by reading it. The arts are about doing, making and creating something, and that takes time. It also takes practice—lots of it. To assume that every piece of paper you use should end as a masterpiece is like assuming that every time a violinist picks up the instrument he or she must perform a flawless concerto.

They say that you will learn something from every painting regardless of how it turns out. Believe me, there have been many, many times when I have learned a lot more than I really wanted to from a painting.

And the lessons are often on just one small aspect of the total picture. This book tries to address this way of learning. It reflects what I have noticed about students' needs in workshops. They want to see the finished picture but they also want specifically to learn about painting such things as rocks or reflections or storm clouds. They ask about color qualities and compositional processes. They want to know about techniques that will help them make better pictures, and they want to know what is going on in my head when I create. (That one is a bit of a mystery in itself.)

All these things help them focus on their particular needs, but what I also want them to do in workshops and with this book is stand back and see the whole picture-making process for what it is. For in the end, it is not about how well you can paint but how much you have grown. In the final measure, it is not the number of accolades you gain but how well you share and celebrate the gift of the creative spirit.

There are three sections in this book. Chapter one deals with the essential techniques and information that you need to work with watercolors. Chapter two is about taking control of your composition. Chapter three comprises the biggest part of this book and covers the specifics of painting water, sky and land. Each is dealt with separately so that you can focus and experience numerous ways of portraying just that element. As often as possible, I have tried to show more than one way of doing something. That will leave you with a lot of partial pictures, but these can be added to and completed later if you wish.

Please remember that what value you get from this book does not depend on which exercises you do today but the variations of your own that you paint tomorrow. In that sense, this book is only a stepping stone, a doorway, a reference point. It is up to you to move forward.

And so, I wish you good luck and good fortune on your creative journey. May the path lead you to places of profound joy and personal fulfillment.

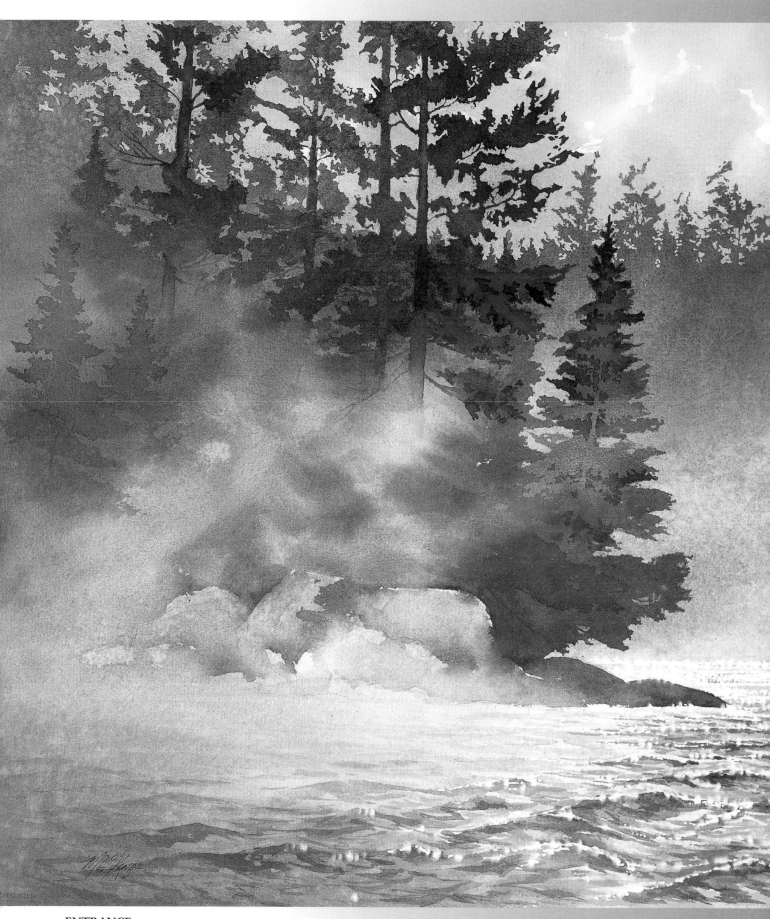

ENTRANCE
22" × 30" (56cm × 76cm)

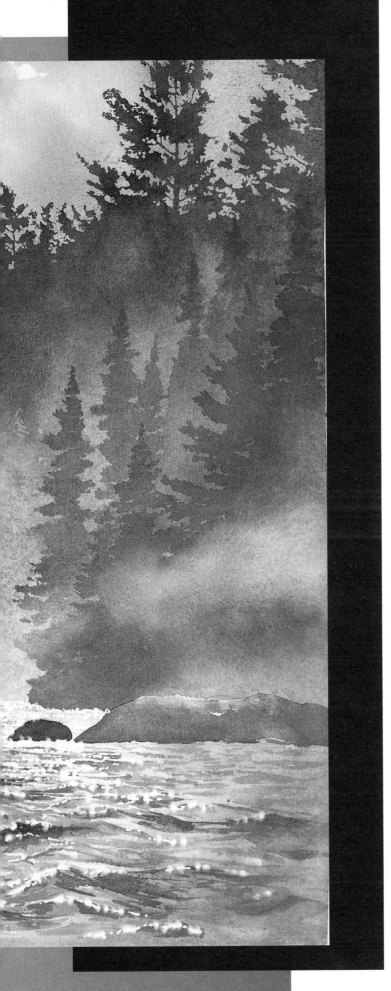

The Medium, Tools and Techniques

1

Watercolor: a process of applying colored water to a piece of paper so that you can watch, spellbound, while it evaporates; a quest to experience all the subtleties and nuances of diluting paint.

Right.

You're probably thinking that you should have taken up something a little more dynamic, like knitting, but please read on. For all the simplicity at its core, watercolor is still a most powerful medium that is more than capable of capturing every mood and vision you can imagine.

This chapter is a summary of the medium, tools and essential techniques and procedures that you will need for painting in watercolors in general and for working through the specific exercises and demos found later on.

Before We Start

THE MEDIUM

On countless occasions I've had non-watercolorists make the comment, "I understand that watercolors are the hardest medium to work with," to which I reply in all seriousness, "Why of course, by all means, they are indeed extremely difficult to handle. It takes an extraordinary amount of talent, unbelievable patience and a really winning personality to handle this medium." If they don't catch the tongue-in-cheek of my reply, then I let them live on with their delusions. Ironically, the most important part of my reply is the part about personality, because so much of what is personality is attitude, and in watercolors, attitude is everything.

Even the medium has an attitude. Try to beat it up, push it around, force it to perform to your will, and it will turn on you. It will take the joy right out of your days and rob the hours of your nights. Only when you assume the role of student to the medium and partner in the creative process will you set the stage for endless growth and discovery in watercolor.

THE TOOLS

Just about anything that will apply, move or lift paint has been tried in watercolor. Traditionally, brushes of all shapes and sizes have been the tool of choice for watercolorists, but if one is not too mired mentally in tradition, there are other ways of delivering and manipulating paint and water—such as palette knives, toothbrushes, sponges, cloth, found objects, syringes, even sticks. In fact, after hands and fingers, sticks were the tool of choice for many years until some distant ancestor decided to add hair to theirs. Can you imagine the uproar of traditionalists vowing never to try those newfangled gimmicks called 'brushes'? Things haven't change much, but in watercolor you are free to push the boundaries on those days when you feel a brush is just not enough. By the way, buy the best sticks you can.

THE TECHNIQUES

"Techniques" or "procedures" simply means the alternative ways of applying, manipulating and removing paint. You might see some referred to as "tricks" from time to time, as if they were the unpredictable results of happenstance, sort of secret shortcuts for lazy painters in a hurry. Understand that they are anything *but* this. They are indeed the result of very creative and very knowledgeable minds determined to let the characteristics of the medium work their magic. These artists are determined to let the paint share in the creation of the work. They know that the techniques are there only to support the visual statement, but they also know that the proper technique, just as the proper brush, can free them from needless brushwork so that they can focus on their creative flight.

Ms. Swampgas decides to modify her paint stick.

Pigment Characteristics

Knowing a paint's characteristics puts you at a distinct advantage. For example, transparent colors maintain their luminosity because they allow light to pass through and reflect back from the paper. On the other hand, opaque colors block the light. The more opaque a color, the more it blocks light, especially if it is built up in layers.

If you want to glaze one color on top of another so that you can see the colors mixing, use transparent colors of any strength or thinned opaques. If you want to produce a really dark color that has depth, use full-strength transparent colors. To capitalize on the beauty of opaque colors, avoid multiple layers if applied full strength; otherwise, thin them out (e.g., work on wet or damp paper) to reveal their hidden beauty.

Adding an opaque color to a mixture will invariably turn it to mud.

If you plan to lift paint back to white paper as part of your technique, avoid the staining colors. If you wish to lift one color of a mixture to reveal a second color below it (by scraping with a knife, blotting, etc.), then use a stainer and non-stainer mixture. If you wish to lift color and leave an after-image of the same color, use all stainers.

PIGMENT NUMBERS

The pigments used throughout the world for all sorts of color work are given letter/number codes. The letters indicate the pigment's hue. For example, PB means "pigment blue." The numbers are those assigned internationally for that pigment material. The codes are the easy way to remember complex pigment names.

The quality of pigments varies considerably, and although not all pigments need to be permanent (for example, when printing colored flyers for the newspaper), we do want the best durability possible for our paintings. An unreliable color will usually fade with time or moisture, but some darken or shift color. An unreliable color is unreliable no matter what extenders, binders or other pigments it is mixed with.

Interestingly enough, paints made with quality pigments cost no more than those without. As more artist have become aware of pigment reliability, the quality of paints on the market have improved.

Transparent Staining		Transparent Low- or No-Staining		Semi-Transparent Low-Staining		Semi-Opaque to Opaque Low-Staining	
Phthalo Green	PG7	Viridian	PG18	Lemon Yellow	PY3	Permanent Red	PR101, PR102*
Phthalo Blue	PB15	Cobalt Blue	PB28	Quinacridone Gold	PO48, PO49		
Prussian Blue	PB27	Ultramarine Blue	PB29			Cadmium Red Light	
Thioindigo Violet	PR88 MRS	Quinacridone Red Quinacridone Violet (Rose and Ruby paints)	PR209	Gamboge (original, new or hue)	*	Cadmium Red Medium	PR108
Indian Yellow	*		PR192			Cadmium Red Deep	
Aureolin	PY40		PV19	Raw Sienna	PBr7	Cadmium Scarlet	*
			PR206	Burnt Sienna	PBr7	Cadmium Orange	PO20
			PR207	Raw Umber	PBr7	Cadmium Yellow Light	
				Sap Green	*	Cadmium Yellow Medium	PY35, PY37
				Hooker's Green	*	Cadmium Yellow Deep	
				Ultramarine Violet	PV15 (better to mix PB29 + PV19)	Yellow Ochre	PY42, PY43
						Venetian Red English Red Indian Red	PR101
						Burnt Umber	PBr7
						Phthalo Yellow Green	*
						Permanent Yellow Green	*
						Cerulean Blue	PB35 or PB36
						Indigo	*
						Payne's Gray	*
						Chrome Oxide Green	*
						Sepia	PG17
						Naples Yellow	*

* These colors are mixtures and vary with the manufacturer.

PIGMENT CHARACTERISTICS CHART
The reliable colors in this chart are grouped according to their staining abilities and opacity. Pigment numbers are shown to the right of each color for your reference.

Once you start looking at pigment numbers on your paint tubes, you will realize that there is a lot of duplication out there.

WHAT'S IN A NAME?

Over the past several years numerous paint manufacturers have reintroduced colors that were once very popular but had fallen into disrepute because of the unreliable pigments they contained. They knew the marketing value of an established and popular name and so reformulated their colors to keep those names while satisfying an increasingly more informed market. However, there are still many of tubes of unreliable paint being put out there under the same popular names, so we really must read those labels. The "Common Culprits" chart shows some of these reintroduced names. Double-check to make sure they contain none of the pigments I recommend you avoid.

A-SHOPPING WE WILL GO

You really don't need the numbers of the reliable pigments when you go shopping. All you need are the ones to avoid. Unfortunately they don't often list pigment numbers in catalogs or on websites, so it becomes hard to know what you are buying from these sources. If that's the case, check out the chart on the next page. It lists the more reliable colors from many of the major suppliers. By the way, the pigments below represent only about 25 percent of the pigments available for paintmaking, which means that there are a lot of good ones out there.

Carefully Check These Common Culprits

	Yellow	Indian Yellow, Gamboge (new, original or hue)
	Red	Crimson Lake, Scarlet, Vermillion, Permanent Red
	Violet	Mauve, Violet
	Green	Phthalo Yellow Green, Permanent Yellow Green, Hooker's Green, Sap Green

Pigments to Avoid

	Yellow	PY1, PY1:1, PY12, PY13, PY17, PY20, PY24, PY34, NY24, PY55, PY100
	Orange	PO1, PO13, PO34, PO65
	Red	Every red pigment number below 100 except PR88MRS. Plus: NR4, NR9, PR104, PR105, PR106, PR112, PR122, PR146, PR173, PR210
	Violet	PV1, PV2, PV3, PV4, PV5AL, PV23, PV23BS, PV23RS, PV37, PV39
	Blue	PB1, PB4, PB66
	Green	PG1, PG2, PG8, PG12
	Brown	NBr8, PBr8, PBr24

Pigments By Any Other Name...

If you have any of these colors, you won't need to buy Phthalo Blue (PB15):	
Talens	Rembrandt Blue
Lukas	Helio Blue
LeFranc Bourgeois	Hoggar Blue and Hortensia Blue
Maimeri	Berlin Blue
Pebeo	Cyanin Blue
Holbein	Antique Bronze Blue
Daler-Rowney	Monestial Blue
Winsor & Newton	Winsor Blue and Intense Blue
Schminke	Brilliant Blue
American Journey	Joe's Blue

If you have one of these colors, you also have a tube of Quinacridone Violet/Red (PV19):	
Schminke	Permanent Carmine, Rose Madder, Ruby Red
Da Vinci	Permanent Rose, Carmine, Alizarin Crimson, Red Rose Deep
Grumbacher	Carmine Hue, Thalo Red, Thalo Crimson
LeFranc Bourgeois	Crimson Lake, Ruby Red, Carmine Permanent
Lukas	Primary Red
Winsor & Newton	Permanent Rose
American Journey	Alizarin Crimson

Paint Quality Chart

This chart summarizes paint quality according to ASTM (American Society for Testing and Materials) standards for a wide range of commonly used colors from various manufacturers.

Legend:
- excellent
- very good
- good
- questionable
- not recommended
- not available

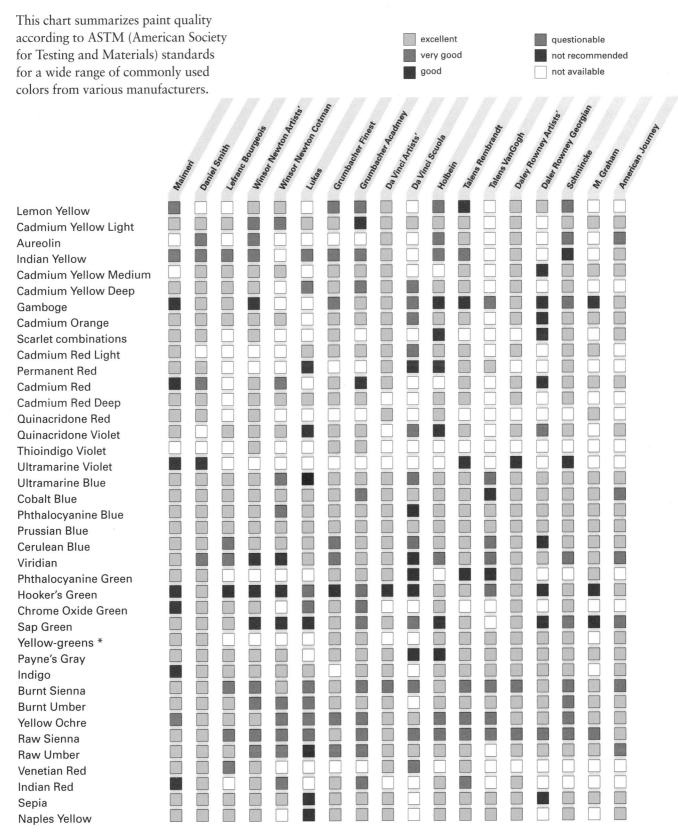

*Phthalo Green, Permanent Green, Leaf Green, Spring Green, May Green, Cinnabar, Green Gold

Brush Types

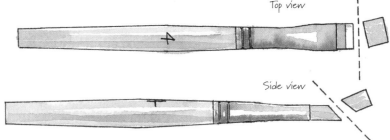

Top view

Side view

Your brush is your connection between you and your painting. I strongly recommend that you buy some basic, good-quality brushes and keep them just for watercolors.

BRUSH FIBERS

Brushes are constructed with natural or synthetic fibers or a blend of these two types.

Natural fibers cover quite a range, from the kolinsky red sable, the best performing and most expensive watercolor brush of all, to the inexpensive, coarse hog-hair bristle at the other end of the spectrum. Natural fibers vary greatly in their flexibility, but all are excellent at holding moisture and releasing it slowly. Because natural fibers can lose their rigidity when wet, some can be awkward to work with.

Synthetic fibers that make an excellent, inexpensive brush have more spring or "snap" to them but hold less moisture and release it more quickly than natural fibers. For the best of both worlds, try those made with a blend of natural and synthetic fibers.

BRUSH SIZES

Misconception: A big brush is just for making big marks. Wrong. A big brush can produce some surprisingly tiny marks if you use just the corner or tip. The real difference between sizes is that the big one holds more paint. Therefore, when choosing brushes, buy a couple of big ones right from the start. The majority of experienced artists paint mostly with their biggest brushes—in order to quickly lay down juicy pools of paint without constantly reloading—and save their small brushes for detail at the end.

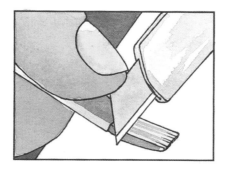

HOG-HAIR BRISTLE BRUSHES

A hog-hair bristle brush allows you to make marks that have natural looking edges. This is important when depicting natural things that have irregular edges, such as rocks, clouds, foam, foliage, fields, etc.

If you plan to try the demos in this book, you may as well go out right now and buy yourself a couple of hog-hair brushes. You will find them in art stores, catalogs and websites in the gesso/oil paint/acrylic/mural/brush sections. You will not find them in the watercolor section because they are not considered a watercolor brush. They are also known as "China" bristle. They range in size from a tiny no. 2 flat acrylic brush to a 3-inch (75mm) flat wash brush. You can sometimes find them in hardware stores masquerading as housepainting brushes. They are generally inexpensive.

THE SCRUB BRUSH YOU MAKE

This type of brush is one of the most valuable for cleaning up edges and adding highlights to your painting. You will need a sharp razor knife and a no. 2 or no. 4 flat hog-hair bristle brush. Let it soak in water for about five minutes to soften the bristles. Hold the brush on the edge of a table. Place the blade straight across the bristles but tilted back. Cut the bristles off by pushing the blade forward hard with the thumb of the hand that is holding the brush. The chisel edge is so that you can scrub off a fine line with the leading edge, or turn it over and scrub out a much larger area. Always scrub with lots of water.

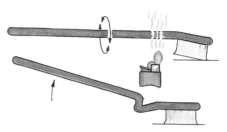

OLD TOOTHBRUSH

These are great for gently lifting paint in an open area or through a stencil. It also comes in handy for spattering paint. You can make it more functional if you bend the handle upward. Gently heat the handle and bend to the desired angle. Cool under running water.

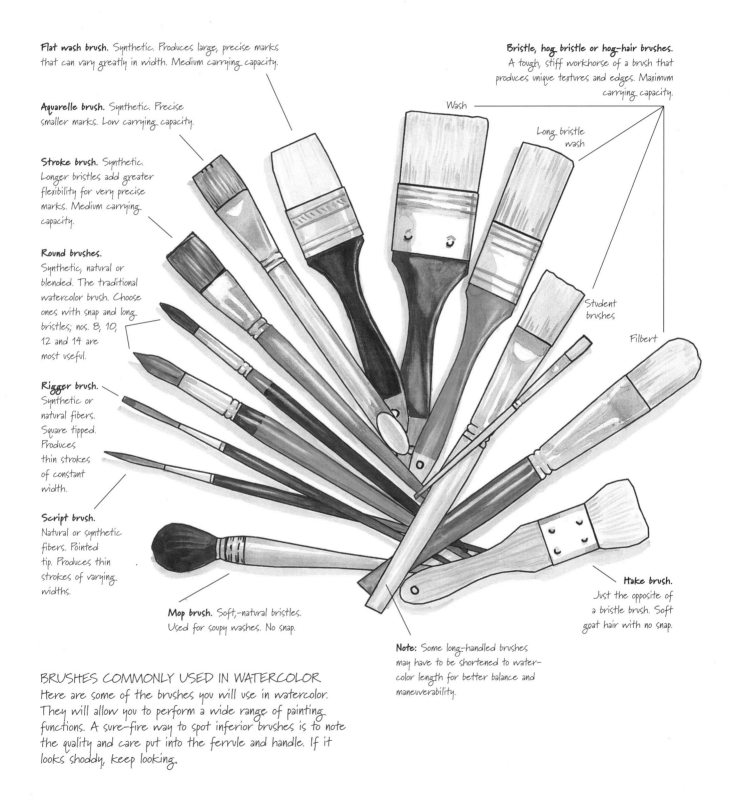

Flat wash brush. Synthetic. Produces large, precise marks that can vary greatly in width. Medium carrying capacity.

Aquarelle brush. Synthetic. Precise smaller marks. Low carrying capacity.

Stroke brush. Synthetic. Longer bristles add greater flexibility for very precise marks. Medium carrying capacity.

Round brushes. Synthetic, natural or blended. The traditional watercolor brush. Choose ones with snap and long bristles; nos. 8, 10, 12 and 14 are most useful.

Rigger brush. Synthetic or natural fibers. Square tipped. Produces thin strokes of constant width.

Script brush. Natural or synthetic fibers. Pointed tip. Produces thin strokes of varying widths.

Mop brush. Soft,-natural bristles. Used for soupy washes. No snap.

Bristle, hog bristle or hog-hair brushes. A tough, stiff workhorse of a brush that produces unique textures and edges. Maximum carrying capacity.

Wash

Long bristle wash

Student brushes

Filbert

Hake brush. Just the opposite of a bristle brush. Soft goat hair with no snap.

Note: Some long-handled brushes may have to be shortened to water-color length for better balance and maneuverability.

BRUSHES COMMONLY USED IN WATERCOLOR

Here are some of the brushes you will use in watercolor. They will allow you to perform a wide range of painting functions. A sure-fire way to spot inferior brushes is to note the quality and care put into the ferrule and handle. If it looks shoddy, keep looking.

Brush Techniques

Learning to use brushes to their fullest extent is one of the best ways to unlock the potential of this medium. It's amazing how people will pay good money for a new type of brush and then use it like all their other brushes—like a windshield wiper.

GETTING A GRIP
The worst habit that painters can get into is holding their brushes in only one way, such as like a pencil. They are missing out on what the brushes can really do, sort of like owning a sports car and only using it in the driveway. It takes a conscious effort to change your angle of attack (or grip) to vertical or underhand, but the payoff is being able to paint more freely and make marks that are more "painterly."

WORKING VERTICALLY
By holding a brush vertically, you can easily make marks that vary in width and direction. These marks constitute "real" painting, where as little as a single stroke can create a leaf, flower petal or tree trunk. This is just the opposite of the cautious coloring-book approach, where a shape is first outlined and then filled with color—usually with an under-sized brush. Break yourself of that habit as soon as you can by mastering strokes made in the vertical.

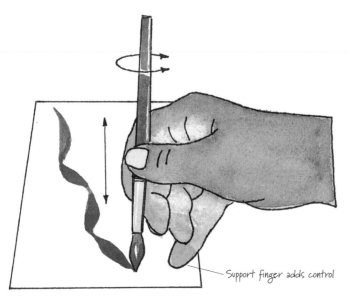

Support finger adds control

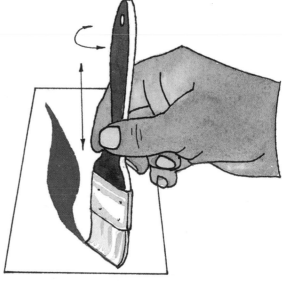

VERTICAL ROUND BRUSH
Holding your brush vertically allows you to take full advantage of the tip of a round brush. By dropping a finger you can control the pressure on the tip, and therefore the width of the line it produces. By twisting the brush through the stroke, the mark will end with a very sharp point.

Don't lift your brush until you have finished the stroke. Many of us have the bad habit of lifting our brush as we approach the end of a stroke, which produces a very weak, ragged finish. Practice making long strokes that vary in width and direction, such as blades of grass.

VERTICAL FLAT BRUSH
By holding a flat brush vertically and twisting ninety degrees through the stroke, you are able to make marks that vary greatly in width. If you also increase the pressure as you make the stroke, the width will be even greater. This technique is extremely useful for painting leaves, waves and flower petals.

WORKING UNDERHAND

Many artists find it far easier to create shapes when holding the brush underhand, particularly if they are standing up. Experiment with different angles and pressure applied. *Caution:* Avoid pushing your brush. The texture of the paper can grab and snap the fine tips off your synthetic brushes.

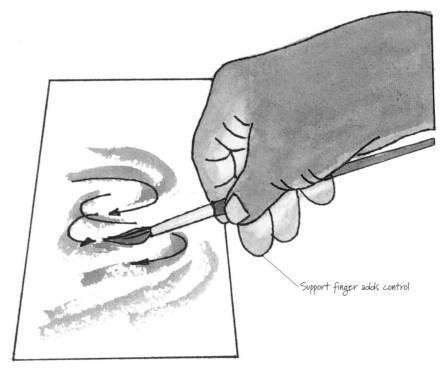

Support finger adds control

UNDERHAND ROUND BRUSH
Holding a round brush underhand allows you to make irregular drybrush-type marks with the side of the bristles. This technique can be used to texture rocks, bark, foam, clouds, etc. If the brush is dragged sideways in a line, it produces an irregular-edged shape that serves well for a rough-barked tree trunk.

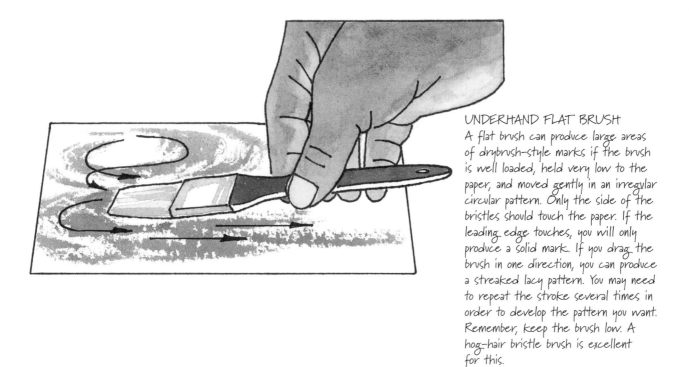

UNDERHAND FLAT BRUSH
A flat brush can produce large areas of drybrush-style marks if the brush is well loaded, held very low to the paper, and moved gently in an irregular circular pattern. Only the side of the bristles should touch the paper. If the leading edge touches, you will only produce a solid mark. If you drag the brush in one direction, you can produce a streaked lacy pattern. You may need to repeat the stroke several times in order to develop the pattern you want. Remember, keep the brush low. A hog-hair bristle brush is excellent for this.

Water

SO, WHEN DO I WET MY PAPER?

If you want your colors to blend together or your strokes to have soft edges, then wet the surface before you add paint. This is called *wet-in-wet* or *wet-on-damp* painting.

When you want controlled, clearly defined brushstrokes, then paint on a dry surface (*wet-on-dry*). Of course, as soon as you put down paint you are creating a wet area into which you can now paint wet-in-wet.

The danger with painting large, complicated areas wet-on-dry is that some parts of your paint may dry to the damp stage or more before you have completely finished them. This can cause all sorts of problems, from backruns or "blossoms" to hard edges when you do add more paint. If you cannot work a bead of paint from one area to the next to avoid this, then it might be wise to pre-wet the areas to be painted. It is not necessary to wet all the way to the edges of the shape. When you add paint, you can go beyond the wet area to create the precise edge needed.

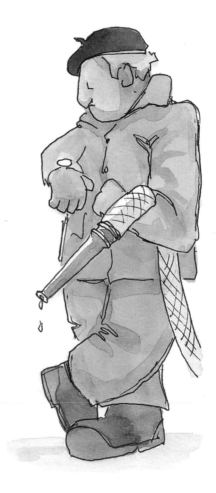

Always have water at the ready.

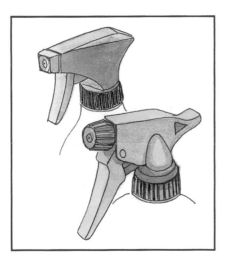

CHOOSING THE RIGHT SPRAY BOTTLE

This may seem trivial, but it's the difference between a technique requiring water spray working or not working. In most cases you'll want a sprayer that lays down a coarse pattern of drops so that when the paint meets the water, it will follow irregular lacy paths. If you use a small atomizer-type sprayer, all you are putting on the paper is a fine mist that is not wet enough to move paint. If you move in closer to apply more, all you get is a small, solid wet spot.

The two types of sprayers pictured here are found in most drug or variety stores and are quite effective because of their versatility. If you squeeze the trigger slowly on these, you get a coarse spray. If you squeeze it hard, you produce a large, fine spray that will wash paint right off the paper. Experiment with the distance from the nozzle to the paper when spraying.

WETNESS TERMINOLOGY

ON YOUR PAPER

- **Flooded:** a sheet of water that even obscures the texture of the paper.
- **Wet:** paper is shiny with water, but texture of paper evident.
- **Damp:** a dulled shine, perfect for many techniques.
- **Moist:** shine is gone, but paper still has moisture; a dangerous time to work.

ON YOUR BRUSH

- **Sopping:** brush goes directly from water to paper; OK if you are pre-wetting your paper.
- **Wet:** brush is wiped once or twice on the edge of the water container.
- **Damp:** after wiping the brush on the edge of the water container, excess moisture is squeezed or pulled out. Brush can still moisten the paper.
- **Moist:** only enough moisture remains to hold the brush in shape. Great for lifting color.

HYDRODYNAMICS: THE LAW BEHIND IT ALL

One of the most important things for new painters to learn is that there are different degrees of wetness, and that these differences determine the effect we get when they meet. This is the basis for most of the techniques we use. Whether the technique works or not depends on your awareness and ability to control the amount of wetness involved.

There is only one law of physics to remember: *When two unequal bodies of moisture meet, the greater wetness will always flow into the lesser.*

It doesn't matter where or what they are. For example, paint or water will flow off a brush onto a surface if the brush is wetter than the surface. Paint or water will flow from the surface onto the brush if the brush is drier than the surface.

You will not get much flow if the two areas are of similar wetness. Only when there is one that is much wetter than the other will there be flow.

Often the flow is from a large wetness on the paper into a less wet area beside it, put down with another brush. We call this "fading out," or "softening an edge."

Below are examples of textural and blending effects created by just one aspect of hydrodynamics: adding water or paint to a damp/painted surface. There are many more for you to discover, as you will see later in the book.

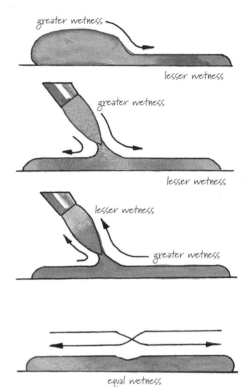

HYDRODYNAMICS

Hydrodynamics: the direction of flow is always from the greater wetness to the lesser wetness.

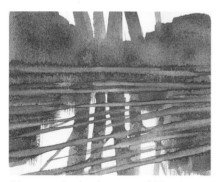

Strokes of pale blue were laid onto damp reflections using the edge of a flat synthetic brush.

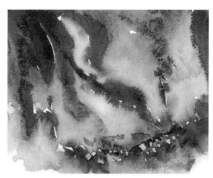

Background color was quickly painted beside and between the wet color of the flames and allowed to mingle.

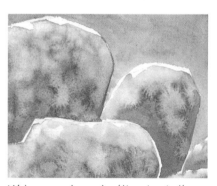

Water was dropped with a brush tip onto the damp blue-brown paint on the rocks.

Fading Out

There are many occasions in watercolor when you want to fade out or soften the edge of a colored area. For example, you may want more eye movement throughout your picture. You can do that by softening a few of the hard edges on shapes as it's being painted. Fading out is like added a passageway or invitation for the eye to move on. Clouds are a perfect example of shapes that have some hard and some soft edges.

We can also use this technique to make the viewers see only what we want them to see.

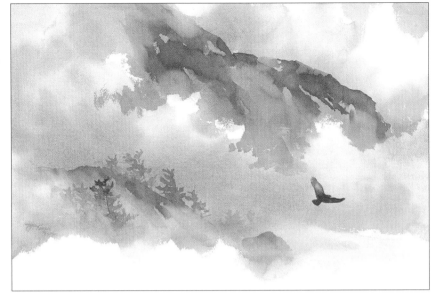

FADING OUT FOR EASE OF TRAVEL
Fading out an edge is like opening a visual gateway on a shape. Your eye sees the hard edges but still moves freely about the picture.

FREEDOM
15" × 22" (38cm × 56cm)

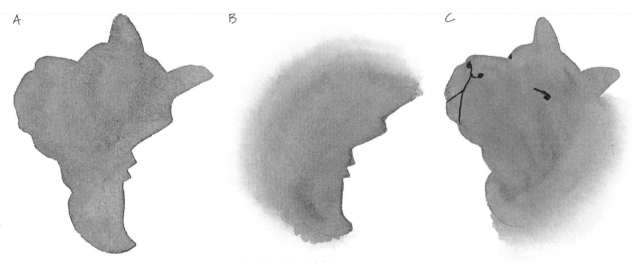

A B C

FADING OUT TO CONTROL WHAT THE VIEWER SEES
Fading out edges can direct the viewer's eye to see what you want it to. The eye focuses on hard edges; therefore, if I don't want the viewer to notice an edge, I will fade it out. For example, if I paint an irregular shape on the paper (figure A) you may not know what it is until I fade out one side or the other (figures B and C).

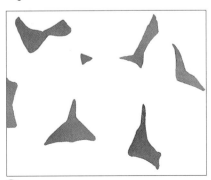

D

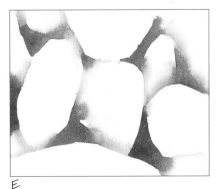

E

THE TRICK OF PERCEPTION
This trick of perception is used continually in watercolors. In figure D are some random marks. In figure E you can see what they mean once I soften some of the edges, or, in other words, tell you where not to look. Fading out is also the method to use to model a shape with shadows.

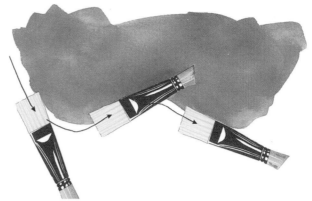

GETTING IT RIGHT

If two bodies of unequal moisture meet, the wetter area will overflow into the drier area in order to balance out the system. So, if you want an area to fade out, you must use a brush that is less wet than the painted area.

There are a few other things you must also get right. One is the direction in which you move the damp brush. Follow the shape or contour of the painted area. Don't reach into the paint and drag out color.

Also, be careful how close you get to the wet paint with the damp brush. All you are trying to do is lay down a damp strip that will attract the wetter paint, so just tickle the edge of the paint. It may take several passes with the damp brush in order to moisten the paper enough. Once the paint begins to move, make your strokes farther and farther out.

It's best if you have your damp brush ready to go as you're laying in the area you want to fade out. If your damp brush is working as soon as the paint is down, you're more likely to succeed. Remember that the drier the paint gets, the less willing it is to flow and the harder it is to get a less wet brush to move it. Therefore, get to fading out quickly and, by all means, do some practicing.

DOS AND DON'TS OF FADING OUT
Remember that your brush must be less wet than the painted area you're trying to fade out. Follow the contour of the wet paint, just tickling the edge of the painted area.

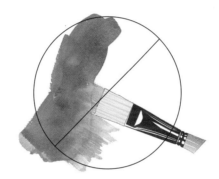

Don't reach into the paint to pull it out.

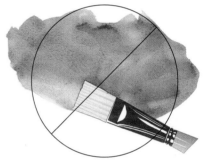

If you go too far into the paint, your damp brush will just soak it up.

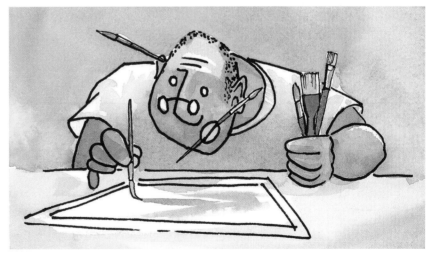

READY TO FADE OUT
Have a damp brush ready before you even put the paint down.

Graded Washes

A *wash* is a solid sheet of color. A wash over a previously painted surface is called a *glaze*. A *graded wash* is a wash that changes in hue, value, temperature or intensity from one section to another. A graded wash does not have to be developed along a horizontal line as shown on this page. It is possible to have one that is curved or circular. You will use all of these techniques in this book.

THE 15-PERCENT SOLUTION

This is a method that I use because it works so quickly on a graded value wash. If you want to smooth the gradation even more, tilt your board slightly as you work. Use a large 1½-inch to 3-inch (38mm to 75mm) flat wash brush and any color.

GRADATING ONE COLOR INTO ANOTHER

You can also gradate one color into another by playing both ends against the middle.

1. Make a Few Strokes

Load your brush with color and paint a couple of strokes across one edge of your dry paper.

2. Reduce the Pigment by 15 Percent

Quickly dip the brush in your water container and wipe it on the container's edge twice. This will reduce the concentration of pigment on the brush by about 15 percent. Now make a few more broad strokes across the paper starting on top of the last one put down.

3. Finish Laying the Graded Wash

Work your way down the paper, repeating the dip-and-wipe process. To fade the color faster, make fewer strokes between dips. To fade more gradually, wipe the brush against the edge of the water container only once.

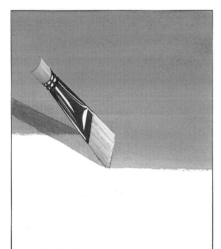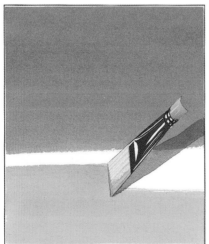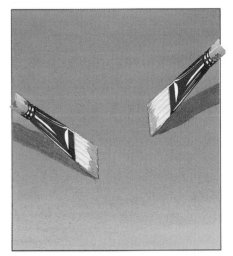

1. Lay Down the First Color

Paint the first color on the top two-thirds of the paper using long, horizontal strokes.

2. Lay Down the Second Color

With a fresh brush, paint the second color on the bottom of the paper and work your way from the bottom up toward the first color.

3. Blend the Colors

Continue painting the second color right over the first one until you're about one-third of the way into it. Keeping your brush on the paper, reverse direction. Move back and forth until the colors blend.

Palette and Paper

YOUR PALETTE

A palette is more than a place to park your paints. The physical design greatly affects the way you paint.

THE ANATOMY OF A GREAT PALETTE— WHAT TO LOOK FOR

1. **Big wells that will let you access your paint with large brushes.** If you wish to work more freely and spontaneously, you will want to use large brushes. Your palette should have large wells to accommodate them.
2. **Flat wells.** Sloped or basin-type wells allow dirty pigments to accumulate around your clean paint. Flat wells allow dirty pigments to run off your paint.
3. **A large mixing area.** You need plenty of room to mix all the color you need.

PAPER

There is not room in this book to delve into every type of watercolor paper on the market. All I can give you are some basic guidelines for finding the paper that best suits the way you want to work. It will involve some experimentation on your part.

First, let me point out that eight out of ten times it's the *paper* that determines the success of your painting. High-quality paints and brushes, fancy brushwork and a smashing color scheme won't do a bit of good without a suitable surface. What you are working can make the difference between success or failure.

That means that you need to pay attention to your paper. It means that you shouldn't scrimp when buying it. The most common mistake that new beginners (and eternal beginners) make is using cheap paper. They figure that if they are just beginning, they can make do with the cheap stuff. Wrong. When you are beginning, you need all the help you can get. It's like the fella who takes up skydiving and figures that since he's just beginning, he can make do with the cheapest parachute he can find. Give yourself a break. Buy quality paper.

HOW DO I RECOGNIZE QUALITY PAPER?

Good-quality paper should be 100-percent acid-free (pH neutral) rag (cotton), mould-made or handmade. The acid-free quality will help it endure the test of time.

There are many brands on the market that meet this criteria. Less expensive papers are invariably made on machines using wood fibers (cellulose) which are put down in layers to build up the thickness. Not only do these cellulose fibers not hold moisture for very long (a critical aspect of many techniques), they will also separate if scrubbed, taped or masked. As would be expected, some mould-made papers now contain treated wood fibers (cellulose), or synthetic (polyester) fibers. You be the judge.

You will need a paper that holds moisture long enough for you to perform whatever techniques you wish. Cotton fibers have the greatest water retention. The thicker (heavier) papers will allow you to work at a technique longer because they hold more water and dry more slowly and consistently, with less warping in the process. The thickness of the paper may affect surface quality in some brands. While most 300-lb. (640gsm) papers tend to be impervious to any technique, the same cannot be said of lesser weights for all brands. That means that you must experiment with several brands in this lighter weight range to find the one that best suits your way of working.

You will find many types in the 140-lb. (300gsm) range that are quite suitable, especially for half-sheet paintings or smaller. Test a single sheet, though, before you buy a truckload.

Watercolor paper comes in three common surfaces:
• Hot-press (smooth)
• Cold-press (medium textured)
• Rough (heavily textured)

Texture affects the appearance of brushwork and detail, so experiment here, too. I typically stick with the middle-of-the-road option: cold-press.

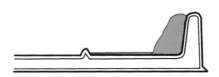

PLACING PIGMENT
Squirt your paint out along the back wall of the well so that it stays well above the dirty pigments below.

Negative Painting

Whenever you save a light shape by painting around it with a darker color, you are negative painting.

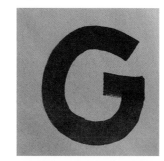

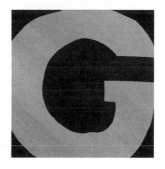

UNDERSTANDING THE PROCESS

I have a small piece of paper and a felt marker with which to make the letter "G."

One way to do this is to print "G" on the paper (top right). Another way is to black out everything that isn't "G" so that what is left makes the letter (bottom right).

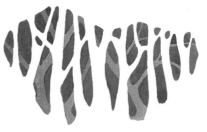

A LITTLE PRACTICE

Try writing your own name using a ballpoint pen and scrap paper. You don't have to work large to see the effect. What you are doing is creating words without actually writing them. If you can do that, then you can paint in the negative, because negative painting is the same thing, only with objects. You are making the shape of an object without actually putting paint on it. After mastering words, try simple objects like a house, ladder, bird, flower, and so on. All you need is a ballpoint pen.

WHAT ISN'T THE LETTER

If I wanted to do my whole name, I would first divide a long rectangle by the number of letters in my name and then black out what isn't each of the letters. The black represents the negative shape or space.

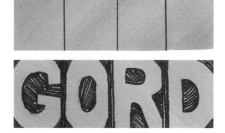

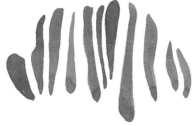

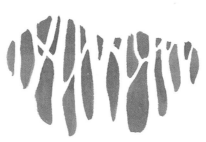

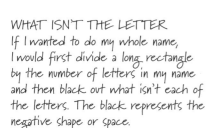

CREATE BRANCHLESS TREE TRUNKS

Using any dark-colored paint and a no. 8 or no. 10 round brush, make vertical strokes that represent the negative spaces between light-colored tree trunks. Try to vary the sizes and shapes of the dark lines and light spaces left between, kind of like a freeform bar code.

CREATE TREE TRUNKS WITH BRANCHES

Try again, only this time imagine that some of the light spaces branch into sloppy "Y" shapes. Make a row of these where again the sizes, angles, shapes and spacing are varied.

FILL OUT YOUR FOREST

Now, working within only the dark negative shapes, add a second set of even darker marks to define the space between more tree trunks deeper in the forest. It might help to lightly sketch these first.

IMPROVE YOUR CHANCES OF SUCCESS WHEN NEGATIVE PAINTING

1. In the beginning, allow lots of space and room to grow. In the exercise on page 166, you may have noticed how crowded things became when trying to indicate the negative shapes for trees farther back. Conclusion: when you are going to have several layers of negative painting, always start with large spaces around a few close shapes. If you try to save (go around) too many small shapes at the beginning, it becomes difficult to paint meaningful shapes at deeper layers.

2. To increase the illusion of depth and add interest to your composition, make the transition into the background a gentle one. You do that by slowly darkening your layers of color. If you go dark too quickly, it becomes difficult to go darker with subsequent layers. In reality, there is no need to mix darker and darker colors for each layer. Since these are transparent paints, two layers are twice as dark as one. Therefore, using approximately the same value for each layer will cause a natural darkening as layers build up.

3. Be careful with your color choices. If you layer one complementary color on top of another, you will dull that layer and all subsequent layers. When negative painting, you are always safe layering colors that are close to each other (analogous) or that aren't direct complements.

4. Remember that it is permissible to sketch your objects before painting the spaces around them. With experience, the amount of sketching will decrease as you let each mark tell you were to put the next.

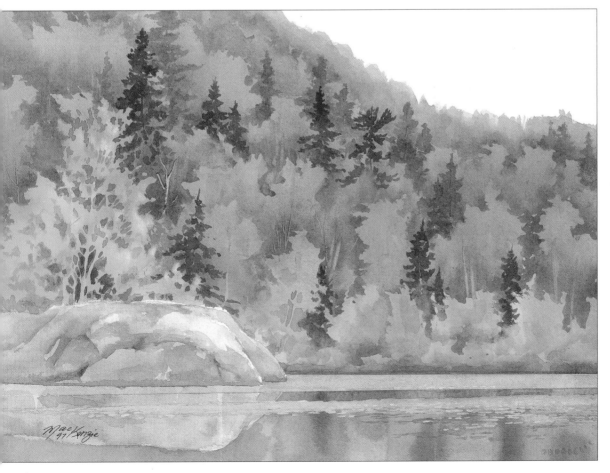

OVERLAPPING LAYERS IN NEGATIVE PAINTING
Whenever shapes are overlapped, part of each shape is positive and part is negative. In this hillside scene, the lighter positive treetops and branches are defined by the darker negative parts of the trees behind. This dark green was sponged around what I wanted to leave for trees, then faded upward.

Masking

Masking may not have the same appearance as negative painting, but it has the same goal—preserving a lighter shape by painting around it. The two types of masking material that I use most are brown plastic packing tape and masking fluid.

I use the tape for large shapes or ones with precise edges. I use masking fluid whenever I have some small, irregular, intricate shapes or ones with less precise edges to save.

Sometimes when I have a large area to protect that has irregular edges, I will use tape for the central core and masking fluid around the edges.

USING MASKING FLUID

Masking fluid is liquid latex that can be applied over a shape to preserve it. Once dry, paint will not penetrate it. After the paint is dry, the dried fluid can be removed by rubbing with your fingers, an eraser or rubber cement pickup.

That's the theory, anyway. In reality, masking fluid *can* let paint through if it has been applied too thinly or had air bubbles in it during application because you shook it before you applied it. (The bubbles later break to let paint through.)

Use tinted masking fluid (such as the blue-gray types) so that it can easily be seen on the paper. Masking fluid can be applied with sharpened sticks, a sponge, a palette knife, a paintbrush or a brush handle. If you use a brush, make sure to protect the bristles by soaping them first and then washing well with soap as soon as you are finished.

USING PACKING TAPE

This technique does not work on machine-made papers or some of the more expensive softer types. Test

CUTTING THE TAPE

In order for packing tape to work for masking, you must be able to cut it and remove it easily. A very sharp knife is a must. I recommend small razor knives with the snap-off blades. Use the slot in the handle cap to snap off a section of the blade. The blade must be able to cut the tape with the least amount of pressure. If you have to push hard, you will go through the tape and right into the paper.

To remove tape from the paper, carefully lift a corner with your knife and then, pinching it against the blade with your other forefinger, lift upward. Sometimes warming it with a hair dryer eases the lift.

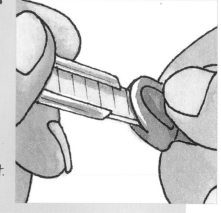

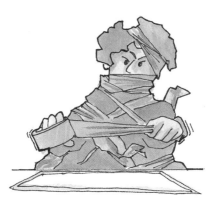

Packing tape: You know the stuff.

your paper first to see if the tape lifts paper when removed. I've found that Arches paper works best with this material, but you can experiment with various brands. I recommend using the brownish tape which is translucent instead of the transparent type which is hard to see on the paper. I also recommend buying the cheapest (thinnest) brand, which will follow the texture of the paper better than heavy-duty tape.

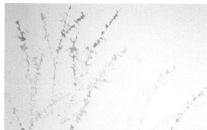

SPRAY AND APPLY
Here, masking fluid was applied to a water-sprayed surface with the edge of a palette knife. The fluid spread rapidly every time it hit a water drop.

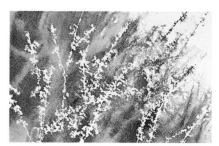

PAINT AND LIFT
When the masking was dry, darker colors were painted over it. When they were dry, the masking was removed.

Combining Masking Materials

This demonstration outlines the procedure for applying packing tape and masking fluid. I suggest that you practice with each before diving into a complex landscape. Please note how the razor knife should be held when cutting the tape.

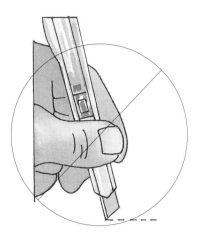

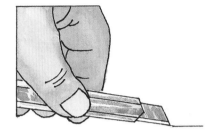

HOLDING THE KNIFE PROPERLY
To make this work, you must hold the razor knife like a butter knife so that as much of the blade as possible is cutting the tape. If you hold it upright like a pencil, all you'll do is tear the tape. It's like trying to cut with a pin.

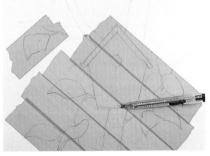

1. Apply Tape

Cover your sketch in rows of overlapping tape. To cut the tape, simply poke it with your knife and it will break off easily. Only push the tape down lightly at this point.

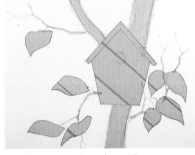

2. Remove Surplus Tape

Remove surplus tape by lifting the edge with your knife and peeling it up. Firmly press down the remaining tape. Apply masking fluid for intricate or irregular shapes like twigs.

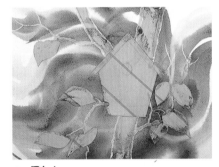

3. Paint

After the masking fluid is dry, paint the background.

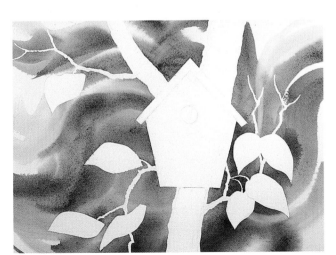

4. Remove Masking Materials

When everything's dry, remove the tape and masking fluid. You can now paint the saved areas.

Painting With Palette Knives

It is important that the knives you use for painting have good stiffness, offset handles and a variety of tips. A wimpy blade won't push paint. An offset handle allows you to access and mix your paint more easily and to use your knife on its side. Having knives with tips of different roundness will allow you to make lines of various widths.

If you are going to paint with your knife, it must be cleaned of all old paint, oxidation and body oils. To do this, scrub the bottom of the blade with a wet piece of 250- to 400-grit waterproof sandpaper. Use lots of water. New blades have coats of varnish that require extra scrubbing to clean. Once a blade has been thoroughly cleaned, it only takes a quick touch-up to remove oxidation or body oils before each use.

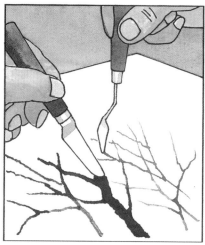

APPLYING PAINT
To apply paint, first load your knife with paint by placing it face-down in a puddle of concentrated color on your palette. (The color should have an ink-like consistency.) If color does not stick to the entire bottom side, the knife is not clean enough. Once loaded, hold the knife almost vertically and drag it across your paper. The roundness of the knife tip determines the line width.

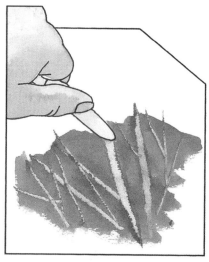

SCRAPING PAINT
To scrape or push paint back, you need as stiff a blade as possible, which means that you may have to support the blade with your thumb. This works best when the paint is just beginning to lose its shine.

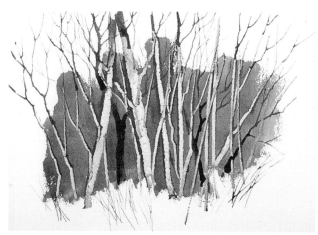

TREE TRUNKS AND LIMBS
I started with a small patch of concentrated color on my watercolor paper. While the paint was damp, I started at the bottom and scraped upward to make tree trunks. I varied the size, position and shape of the lines.

The knife carried some paint (trunks) above the patch. Again using my palette knife, I applied some concentrated color to create more tree trunks and smaller branches beyond the original patch.

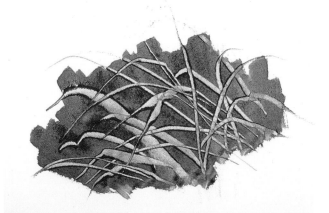

EXPERIMENT WITH STAINING COLORS
Scraping paint can teach you quite a lot about staining and nonstaining colors. Here I laid down a patch of Phthalo Green and Phthalo Blue and immediately painted over it (and mixed into it) with Burnt Sienna, a nonstainer. Once the area had dried to damp, I scraped back the color. The green and blue stained the paper, giving the blades of grass some subtle color.

Painting With a Sponge

Painting with a sponge can create unique, useful textures, but it's also a great way to lay down color fast. A sponge can carry a lot of moisture and pigment. Once the paint is applied, it will also stay wet for a longer period, so you can practice other techniques like scraping, spraying with water, adding salt, etc.

The best type of sponge to use is cellulose (plant fiber) because it holds more paint and releases it more consistently than a plastic sponge. The holes are also more varied in size.

Because they stiffen as they dry, cellulose sponges are usually packaged in a plastic bag with a moisturizer. Cellulose sponges come in blocks and can be found in the housecleaning or automotive section of your grocery store.

When you're ready to use your sponge, dip it in water and then mix paint on your palette. Unless you fancy colored fingers, I recommend wearing a latex glove; this process does bring you in direct contact with the paint.

It's very important that the sponge is well loaded with moisture (the amount of pigment you need will vary, of course). To make marks on your paper, touch the sponge to the surface lightly. Too much pressure obliterates detail. You can touch with the full face, the tip or an edge of the sponge. Each position produces a different mark. Create shapes by building up your marks.

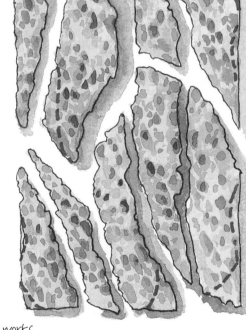

SLICE
Slice off a ¾-inch (19mm) thick slab with a utility knife. Try to cut so the end grain is in the face of the sponge; the sponge will be easier to tear this way.

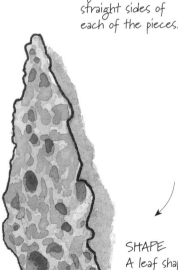

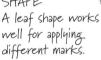

TEAR
Tear the sponge slice into smaller pieces. Pick off the square corners and straight sides of each of the pieces.

SHAPE
A leaf shape works well for applying different marks.

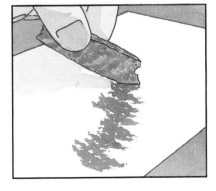

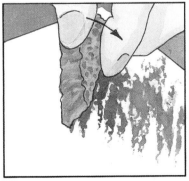

APPLY
You can apply paint using the side or the tip of the sponge.

171

A Treasury of Techniques

The following are but a handful of textural and blending effects that you can get with watercolors once you learn to control the processes and tools discussed in this chapter.

Take time to try these and, by all means, experiment on your own. You will see many of these again in chapter three.

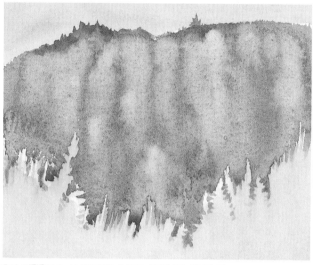

DROPPING WATER INTO DAMP PAINT
Water was dropped from a brush along the top edge of the hill while the paint there was still damp. Tilting the board allowed the water to leave light streaks.

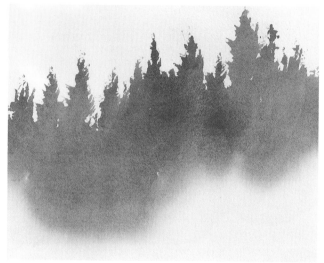

FADING OUT WITH A SPONGE
An area that has been sponged, such as this tree line, can easily be faded out for effects such as fog because the paint goes on quickly and stays wet longer.

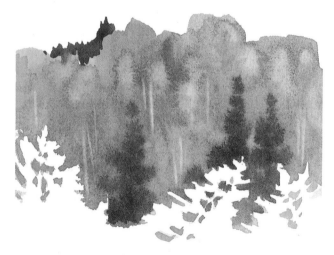

DROPPING WET COLOR INTO WET COLOR
Lighter color was dropped into damp forest color. The dark evergreens were added while the surface was still damp. The foreground was created using negative painting.

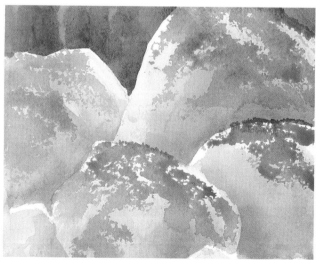

SPONGING ON TEXTURE
A sponge can add texture to objects, like the moss on these rocks.

SPATTERING ON PAINT

I sprayed the surface with water first, then spattered paint with a toothbrush. Packing tape applied beforehand protected the surrounding areas. Try this technique for rocks.

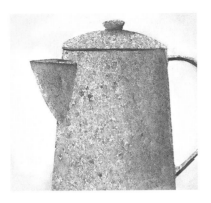

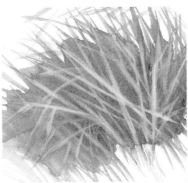

MOVING AND REMOVING COLOR

Using the edge of a damp, flat synthetic brush, I moved and lifted out paint from the dark patch of grass.

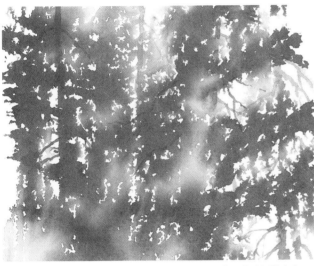

APPLYING PAINT ON A PARTIALLY WET SURFACE

Lacy vertical marks were made with the side of a wet hog-hair brush (see page 74), then a dark green was applied with a loaded sponge. This color spread rapidly into the wet areas. A few trunks and branches were added to suggest a backlit forest.

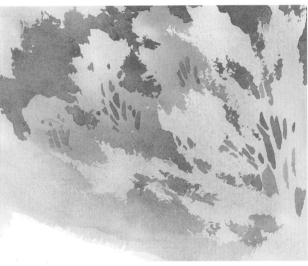

NEGATIVE PAINTING

After laying down the background in light colors, I added trees by painting the negative space using a sponge and a small brush with darker color.

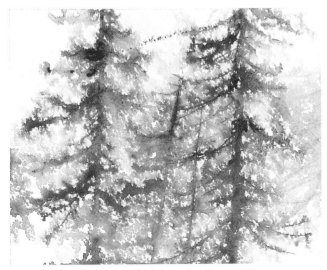

APPLYING PAINT WITH A PALETTE KNIFE

After spraying the paper with water, I applied paint with the edge of a palette knife.

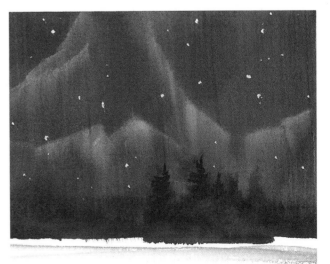

LIFTING PAINT WITH A DAMP BRUSH

While the color was still wet, I lifted it with the edge of a damp, flat synthetic brush. With this technique, be careful to keep the brush clean and not wetter than the surface.

173

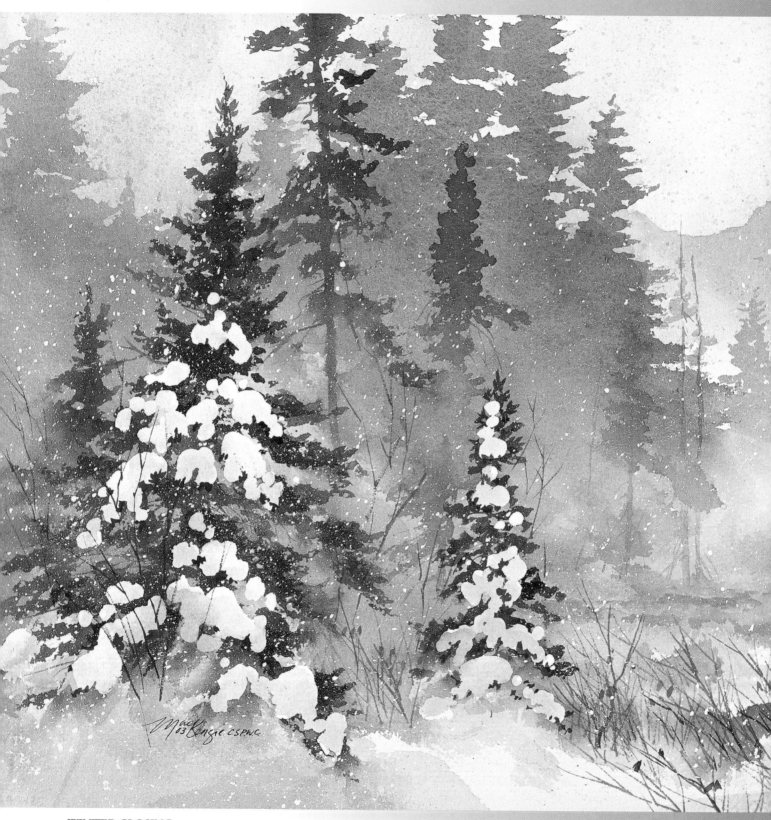

WINTER CLOSING
15" × 22" (38cm × 56cm)

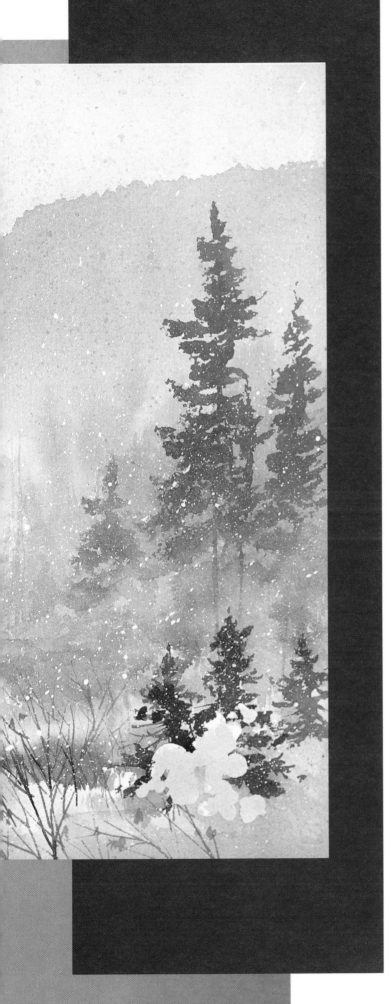

Composing a Landscape Painting 2

Gaining control of your composition is the essence of becoming an artist. Taking responsibility for how all the parts and pieces of your picture are arranged and depicted is what sets you free.

Let's get it straight: There is no shortcut or sure-fire formula for putting together pictures.

We can study the Masters and schools of art and apply what knowledge we can from them, but in the end we will realize that they were simply a reflection of their times. Composition has always been a measure of artistic freedom or lack thereof, and as such, is an evolving process. It reveals the knowledge, abilities, likes and dislikes of the individual artist at the time. In the end, what you will learn from art history and hands-on experience is that the indomitable creative spirit is universal, timeless and unique to each of us. The tremendous diversity of visual expression that we are heir to is proof that there is more than one way of doing things.

It may seem as if I am trying to avoid revealing all the secrets of composition, but I'm not. In fact, shortly I will share many of them. I know that some of you want and need some rules and guidelines to follow at this point and that is fine, so long as you realize that they are only crutches, and borrowed ones at that. Sooner or later you'll need to—no, want to—give them up. In time and with practice, you will reach the point where you won't want to follow somebody else's way of doing things.

The process of composing is an exercise in self-discovery. The more you learn to rely on yourself and your own intuitive preferences, the faster you'll gain artistic independence and freedom.

How Do I Go From Painter to Artist?

Composition is the process of arranging shapes, lines and colors "in order to convey your visions or ideas. But it goes beyond that. There are things, almost magical, that can happen with the arrangement of these elements. But this kind of knowledge takes time and experience to acquire. That's what this journey is about.

I have a friend who referred to the process of composing a picture as "plotting" her picture. She might be closer to the truth than she knows. There might be something slightly sinister in the mind games, optical illusions and visual trickery you play on the viewer, as if "plotting" the great crime of the century. (So, what do we do with the evidence? We hang it.)

The journey you are on is about learning to rely more and more on

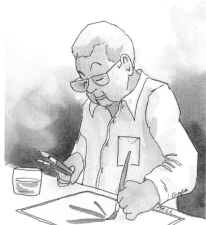

The primary source of quasitonic vericulum is only comparative to the equilibrium of narrative and humanological conquests into supraspastic revelations of inter-garafraxic normalcy. Are you getting all this?

No, but I **am** getting a shovel.

our own intuition and knowledge base and less and less on others.' It's about recognizing that your limitless creative and imaginative powers make you far more than a biological camera. But being creative and imaginative can be hard to do because it means acknowledging

IT'S LESS COMPLEX THAN YOU THINK... REALLY
Composition may seem like a mysterious bunch of contradictory and confusing picture-making rules concocted by a bunch of obscure dead artists or obtuse live ones... but it doesn't have to be.

your own independence and self-worth. For many of us, that's a big hurdle. For some of us, it is a dangerous one as well.

"But I might make a mistake."

So what? You are probably the only one who knows or even cares. Do you really think that others are concerned with what you do on your pieces of paper? They've got their own pieces of paper to worry about. As for the critics who don't even try—learning to ignore them is the kindest thing you can do for them.

Meanwhile, try to remember this:

You have always known how to compose pictures.

You did it as a child and you never forgot.

What you have lost is the memory and nerve to follow your instincts when making a picture.

What you have temporarily forgotten is how to play.

What you grew instead was an ego that demanded protection from embarrassment at all costs.

But it is time to take back command, responsibility and freedom for your compositions

—because no one else will.

ART IS "ME" MADE VISIBLE
Growing from painter to artist is about honoring the child of the universe within you who just wants to play.

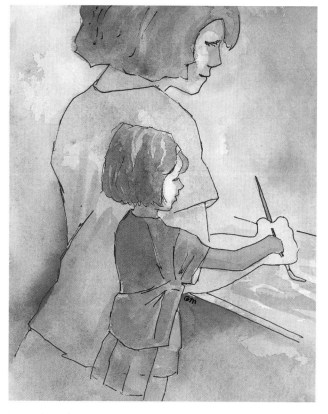

STARTING DOWN THE ROAD

The evolution from painter to artist occurs on many fronts simultaneously.

It's important to recognize that a primary method of learning is imitation. Many of the techniques we're capable of today are a direct result of copying someone else in varying degrees. It's a way for beginners to gain confidence; it allows them the experience of painting without having to worry about technicalities.

However, art is ultimately about *self-*expression. Somewhere between relying on others and artistic freedom is a path that we all walk.

As convenient as it is to rely on others, it is imperative that over time you break away from using other people's things—their paintings, their photos, their reference material—to using your own. This can be a long process, so the sooner you make the decision to pursue self-expression, integrity and uniqueness, the sooner you'll be able to call yourself an artist.

WEANING YOURSELF

To wean yourself of other people's materials, ask yourself, "What is it that I like about the painting? What is it in the way the artist handled the subject that appeals to me?" This is probably the aspect you want to imitate. Anything else can be altered and adapted.

Start building your own database. Start collecting pictures that can be used for reference. Start taking your own photos. By all means start sketching, because there is no better way to improve your ability to see than to draw.

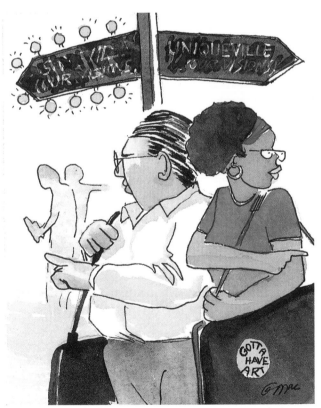

OK, we have to decide—are we going to be painters in Copyville or artists in Uniqueville?

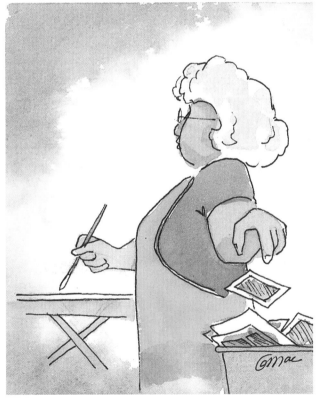

Letting go means taking command.

USING YOUR OWN REFERENCE MATERIAL

As you gradually build and use your own photo/sketch reference base, remember you can always:

- **Eliminate** stuff. Sometimes less is more.
- **Simplify** stuff. Would fading out or obscuring certain parts produce a stronger composition? Would a few details be more appealing than having everything in detail?
- **Combine** bits of material from several photos or sketches into one picture.
- **Rearrange** objects or group isolated objects for stronger compositional units.
- **Adjust** the colors to suit your own tastes or the mood you want to create.
- **Change** the atmosphere, season, time of day or direction and quality of the light source.
- **Add** movement to your work by positioning shapes and lines at an angle to the picture frame. Set up paths for the eyes to follow.
- **Zoom in** on a single item or area of interest, or expand different aspects of an idea.
- **Multiply** a single object into a full composition, such as creating variations of a single flower to form a bouquet.

Throughout this stage, you will undoubtedly become more and more familiar with the language of art (the elements and principles of design) and use it to strengthen your composition. However, you will use intuition more and more to confirm various aspects of your composition. That is, "Does it feel right?"

SELF-CRITIQUING

As your experience, self-confidence and art knowledge grows, so does your desire and ability to self-critique. You will automatically ask yourself questions such as:

- Will the viewer be able to see clearly what I want them to see? (i.e., Am I close enough to the subject, Are the colors, sizes, contrasts and movements effective?)

- Have I put visual energy and excitement into my picture to hold the viewer's interest?
- Have I left areas of mystery in my work to stimulate the viewer's imagination?
- Have I created an effective mood or atmosphere in my work that enhances the subject?
- Have I chosen an interesting point of view?

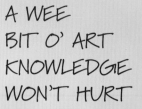

A WEE BIT O' ART KNOWLEDGE WON'T HURT

When planning a composition, an artist has only so many tools to work with. We call these tools the "elements" of design. They are color, line, value, shape and form.

With these tools, an artist is able to create certain effects within a painting. These effects are referred to as "principles" of design. The principles are mood, perspective, balance, variety, unity, contrast or emphasis, rhythm and movement. For example, you may decide to use colors to create mood, or aerial perspective, or variety. In a similar way, lines could create linear perspective, movement or rhythm.

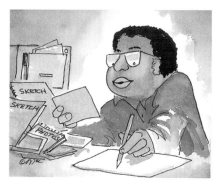

Start using your own reference base and you'll grow as an artist.

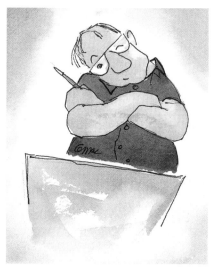

Trust your ability to self-critique.

COMPOSING LANDSCAPES FROM WITHIN

This means looking within yourself for ideas of what to paint. It means using your imagination, memory and experiences along with art knowledge to develop a painting. Art knowledge is applied in a subconscious, intuitive way as you give priority completely to what "feels right." Even if you are working from a real scene, your picture will be a reflection of how that scene stimulated you. You are now in full control of your composition.

Reference material is now there to support an idea that has come from your imagination, your experiences, your memory. Theories of composition are there to confirm your intuition. The landscapes composed *from* within have become the landscapes that *are* within. This way of creating will come with time and experience.

FINALLY, THE SECRET

The speed with which you proceed from painter to artist depends on three things: your painting frequency, your painting frequency and your painting frequency. The more you paint, the faster you grow. It's that simple.

WHAT IS INTUITIVE PAINTING?

You cannot will creativity, or insight, or intuition. All you can do is approach your work with a daring and open mind that will invite them in.

When a viewer looks at a painting, they don't realize that they are really looking at the result of numerous intuitive decisions made by the artist throughout its entire creation. Decisions, such as how the subject should be portrayed or transformed to suit their vision; drawing upon their subconscious inclinations to design their layout; listening to their inner voice when they choose their colors and make technical choices; are all intuitive acts that are well hidden in the final work. Viewers are not aware of the communion that took place between the medium and the artist's intellectual, physical and spiritual capacities.

I do not believe, therefore, that "intuitive" painting is a unique style, appearance or procedure, but instead simply describes the frame of mind the artist was in during the picture's creation. I don't think that select schools of painting were given sole ownership of intuition. I believe that it is there for us all to use, regardless of how we choose to express ourselves.

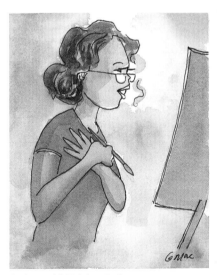

DISCOVERING THE LANDSCAPES WITHIN
You did not come into this life as a team. You came as an individual—to explore, experience and grow your way through all it has to offer. Making pictures is simply a way for you to express the perceptions, feelings and values of that individual point of view.

In your own Bosom you bear your Heaven and Earth and all you behold; tho' it appears Without, it is Within, in your Imagination...

—William Blake

Color Characteristics

When painting, the least useful information about a color is its trade name. What is more useful is knowing that color's characteristics. There are four characteristics of color you should be familiar with: hue, value, intensity and temperature. When the paint starts flying, you'll find yourself asking, "Does my picture need a dark or light color there? Should it be warm or cool? Should it be pure (intense) or dulled? What hue will I use?"

Paint characteristics—the effect of a pigment rather than its color—are also important.

HUE
Hue is the name of the color in its purest and simplest form—red, blue, green, blue-green, yellow, etc. It's what best describes its location on the color wheel (see the next page).

VALUE
Value is the lightness or darkness of a color. In watercolor, you lighten a color (or create a tint) by adding water. To darken a color, mix it with another dark color. You can also darken with black or blackened colors (such as Indigo or Sepia), but it's easy to kill a color that way.

INTENSITY
Intensity is the brilliance or saturation of a color. A color can be dulled—never undulled—by adding its complementary color (the color opposite of it on the color wheel). Mixing complementary colors in the right degree produces different grays.

TEMPERATURE
Temperature is the warmth or coolness of a color. About half the colors on the color wheel can be grouped into a warm family (reds, oranges and yellows) and half into a cool family (violets, blues and greens). Red-violet and yellow-green can be either warm or cool depending on the neighboring color.

Just to confuse things, each hue has a warm or cool bent depending on whether they slide slightly around the color wheel towards the red-orange (hottest) or blue-green (coolest) colors. So, it is possible to have a cool red or a warm blue by adding a touch of blue to the red or a touch of red to the blue.

Color Wheel

This wheel indicates the relative placement and temperature of the paints I regularly use.

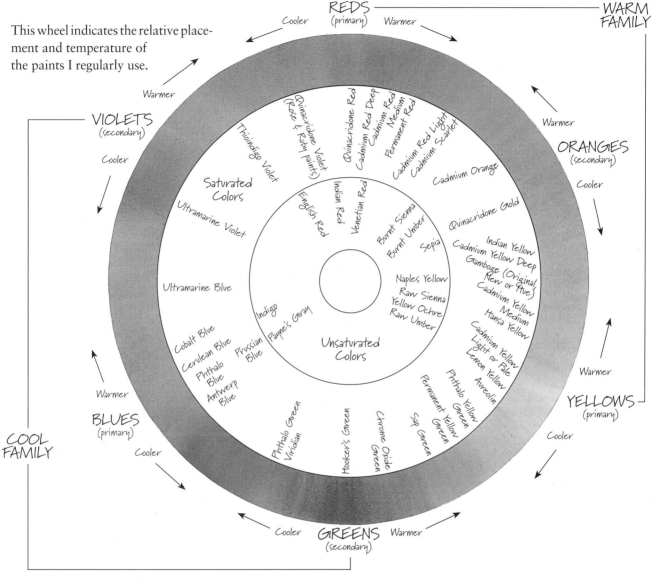

REDS (primary)

Cooler ← → Warmer

WARM FAMILY

VIOLETS (secondary)

Cooler

Warmer

ORANGES (secondary)

Cooler

Saturated Colors

Quinacridone Violet (Rose & Ruby paints)
Thioindigo Violet
Ultramarine Violet
Ultramarine Blue
Cobalt Blue
Cerulean Blue
Phthalo Blue
Antwerp Blue
Prussian Blue
Indigo
Payne's Gray
English Red
Indian Red
Venetian Red
Burnt Sienna
Burnt Umber
Sepia

Quinacridone Red
Cadmium Red Deep
Cadmium Red Medium
Permanent Red
Cadmium Red Light
Cadmium Scarlet
Cadmium Orange
Quinacridone Gold
Indian Yellow
Cadmium Yellow Deep
Gamboge (Original, New or Hue)
Cadmium Yellow Medium
Hansa Yellow
Cadmium Yellow Light or Pale
Lemon Yellow
Aureolin
Phthalo Yellow Green
Permanent Green
Sap Green

Naples Yellow
Raw Sienna
Yellow Ochre
Raw Umber

Unsaturated Colors

Phthalo Green
Viridian
Hooker's Green
Chrome Oxide Green

BLUES (primary)

Warmer

Cooler

COOL FAMILY

Cooler ← **GREENS** (secondary) → Warmer

Warmer

Cooler

YELLOWS (primary)

A BASIC PALETTE LAYOUT

Included on this palette are warm and cool versions of the primary hues—red, yellow and blue. By having both temperatures, you're better able to mix a wider range of colors, and it provides you with more options when choosing color schemes.

To mix a brilliant color, use two other colors that are as close to it as possible on the color wheel. For example, to mix a pure green, use a cool blue (Phthalo Blue) and a cool yellow (Lemon Yellow). To mix a dull green, use a blue and yellow that are farther away on the wheel (Ultramarine Blue and Cadmium Yellow Medium, for example).

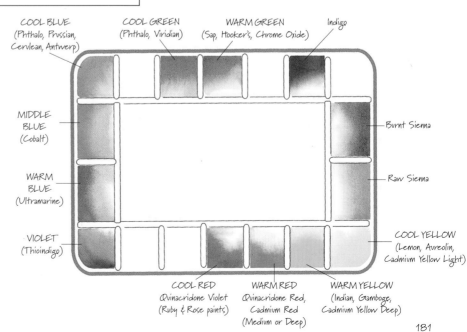

COOL BLUE (Phthalo, Prussian, Cerulean, Antwerp)

COOL GREEN (Phthalo, Viridian)

WARM GREEN (Sap, Hooker's, Chrome Oxide)

Indigo

MIDDLE BLUE (Cobalt)

Burnt Sienna

WARM BLUE (Ultramarine)

Raw Sienna

VIOLET (Thioindigo)

COOL YELLOW (Lemon, Aureolin, Cadmium Yellow Light)

COOL RED Quinacridone Violet (Ruby & Rose paints)

WARM RED Quinacridone Red, Cadmium Red (Medium or Deep)

WARM YELLOW (Indian, Gamboge, Cadmium Yellow Deep)

Color Schemes

This is something that you really don't need to know until you have had a few years of painting experience. However, once you want to use colors more effectively, then it is worth browsing through this information.

This is not to say that you have to use one of these traditional color schemes every time you paint a picture. What I am saying is that with the use of a color scheme, your picture will exude a greater sense of harmony and unity, provided you stick to the plan you have chosen.

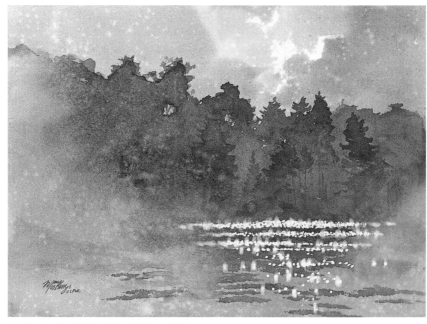

COLOR SCHEME IN PRACTICE
This painting was done with a triad of Permanent Rose, Cobalt Blue and Raw Sienna.

DAVE'S POND
11" × 14" (28cm × 36cm)

TIP

Avoid opaque colors in triads and complementary-analogous schemes. They lead to muddy colors when mixed with more than one other color.

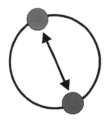

MONOCHROMATIC
This scheme uses value differences of one color to create contrast within a picture. For maximum range, start with a dark color.

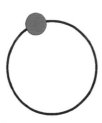

COMPLEMENTARY
Opposite or complementary colors provide maximum chromatic contrast next to each other. When mixed, they produce a range of dulled versions of each other. A balanced mix produces a gray.

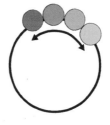

ANALOGOUS
There is bound to be harmony when all of the colors are related to each other. This is a good scheme for emphasizing a particular temperature.

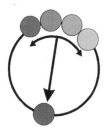

COMPLEMENTARY-ANALOGOUS
You get harmony from the analogous side and balance or accent with the complementary side. Intermixing produces a wider range of dulled colors and grays.

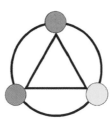

TRIAD
Any three colors in a triangular arrangement produces the widest range of mixed colors and unique grays.

The Quality of Sunlight

It's possible to control different
types of sunlight in your picture
by controlling shadows, detail and
color purity.

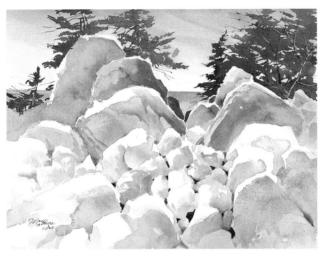

FULL-STRENGTH LIGHT
Under clear, bright conditions, the sky is blue, colors are
pure, and edges and some details are sharp. In the brightest sunlit areas, detail is obliterated. Values are extreme
throughout. Most color play is found in the shadowed areas.

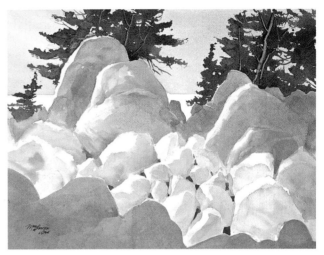

ACCENT LIGHT
This is when small areas are momentarily accented as the
sun breaks through the cloud cover. At sunset, when the sun
breaks through heavy clouds, we have the same accent light
illuminating the trees, hilltops and clouds in the east. This
light adds a real drama to your paintings. Varying values and
pure colors adds strong contrast. Evening light can bathe
the accented areas in a harmonizing, soft pink-orange glow.

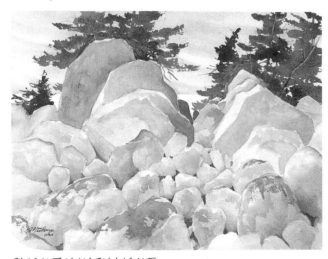

SLIGHTLY HAZY LIGHT
With this type of light, the level of detail and sharp
contrast begin to decrease in the distance. The darkest
values tend to be in the middle ground and foreground.
With decreased light comes a slight decrease in the
purity of colors. Now I can show detail, like the moss on
top of the rocks.

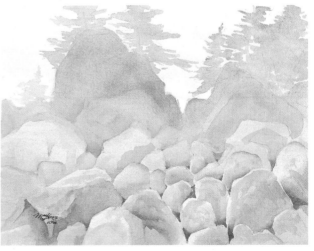

DIFFUSED LIGHT
With the increased humidity of foggy/blizzard conditions
comes a decrease in detail, sharpness and value contrast
throughout. Shadows are warmer, softer and lighter. The
darkest values are in the foreground. Colors are duller and
more subtle.

Light Effects

As artists, we know that we're really only painting what light reveals to us. But it is not sunlight that gives Earth its unique appearance—it's skylight. On the moon, where there is no atmosphere, the light effects are very harsh. It's very bright where the sun shines and very dark where it doesn't, except for a touch of reflected light. On Earth, the atmosphere diffuses some of the incoming sunlight, which in turn lights the whole daytime earth softly and indirectly. We call this skylight, and its condition greatly affects what we see, feel and paint.

LIGHT DIRECTIONS

The pictures below illustrate the characteristics of a sidelit, frontlit and backlit subject. Here the subject, a post and rock, have no cracks, texture or local color to interfere with the light effects.

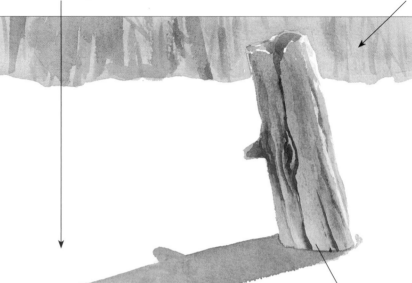

Direction of skylight   Direction of sunlight

reflected light

WHAT DOES SKYLIGHT LOOK LIKE?

Imagine a fence post in the middle of a field of snow on a clear sunny day. The shadow on the back of the post and the one cast on the snow represent the only areas the sun can't reach directly. The source of light here is skylight, and its color is a reflection of the sky color. In this case, it's a cool blue-gray.

As sky conditions (atmosphere) change, so too does the effect of sunlight and skylight.

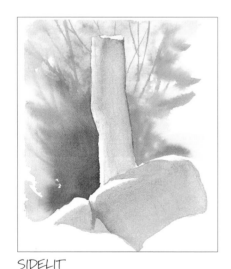

SIDELIT

One side of the post and rock are left white for sunlight. Shadows on the back side are cool near the top and warmer and lighter near the bottom to suggest reflected light. Cast shadows blend into local shadows. The background is darkest next to the highlights.

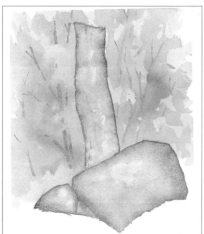

FRONTLIT

Here, the sunlight coming from behind the viewer creates shadows around the edges of the rocks and post.

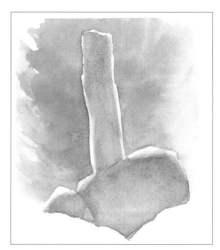

BACKLIT

Light from behind the subject can silhouette or give it light edges. Shadows are cool near the top and show warm reflected light near the bottom.

Creating Atmosphere/Mood

By altering colors and clarity in your painting, you can create distinct types of mood, also referred to as atmosphere. The amount of humidity, snow, rain or smog in the air determines the quality of light that gets through it and in turn the types of colors and details we see. Establishing a distinct mood will bring character to your paintings.

To intentionally create a desired mood, first decide on the dominant *temperature* you want for your picture, then the dominant *value*, then the *clarity* (level of detail). The value (lightness or darkness) and clarity will dictate the light, which will dictate the intensity of the colors in turn.

For example, if I want a warm picture that is primarily light and choose a clarity that is sharp, then I will use colors that are mostly pure. I would also do a lot of wet-on-dry painting for sharpness, show distant detail, and model shapes with shadows and highlights. Sharp clarity implies that the scene is well-lit.

On the other hand, if I choose a clarity that is hazy, then most of my colors will be dulled because of subdued lighting. I'll use lots of wet-on-damp techniques that produce soft edges, and my background shapes will become flattened like silhouettes.

TIP

A center of interest will stand out if some of its characteristics are opposite to the atmosphere.

1 Temperature	2 Value	3 Clarity	4 Intensity	5 Lighting
WARM cheerful vibrant vigorous exciting friendly earthy	**LIGHT (high key)** ethereal spacious optimistic delicate yang	**SHARP** (wet-on-dry painting predominates in all grounds) low humidity distant detail shapes modeled with shadows and highlights crispness	**PURE (vivid)** powerful loud lively clean youthful	Full Strength
—BALANCED MIX—	—BALANCED MIX—	—BALANCED MIX—	—BALANCED MIX—	Accent or Flood
COOL clean refreshing calming distant restful	**DARK (low key)** mysterious foreboding weight strength closeness dignity power yin	**OBSCURED** (wet-in-wet or wet-on-damp painting predominates in background and middle ground) high humidity limited vision mystery closeness quietness shapes flattened like silhouettes	**DULL (grayed)** subdued conservative mature quality dreaminess subtleness	Diffused

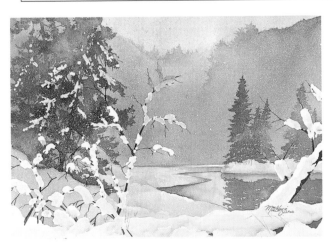

DECISIONS, DECISIONS
These steps will help you understand and develop atmosphere in your pictures. The characteristics of each variable are also indicated.

THE ATMOSPHERE OF THE PAINTING
Despite the snow, this painting evokes closeness, a warmth or coziness, and serene solitude. This is because of the diffused lighting, subdued clarity and warm, dull, midvalue colors.

SUN FLURRIES
14" x 22" (36cm x 56cm)

Perspective

Let me point out first that perspective or perception of distance is only an illusion and not a prerequisite to picture-making. However, that illusion adds dynamics to your work by moving the viewer's eye within and in and out of the picture.

Since most landscape painters want some form of this visual deception in their work, I will review a few of the basics that don't require a ruler.

ELEVATION

Whenever we make a picture or scene, we do so from a particular point of view. The elevation of that view determines what we are able to see. Some things in the view can be seen from above, others from below. To indicate where we want the eye level to be in our compositions, we use an imaginary horizontal line called the "Eye Level Line" (E.L.L.). It is the level of the artist's and viewer's eyes in relationship to the scene.

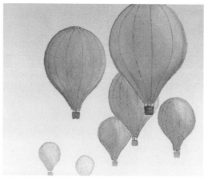

DISTANCE CHANGES OBJECTS
As things move into the distance, they appear smaller, lose detail and sharpness, and become lighter, cooler and grayer in color.

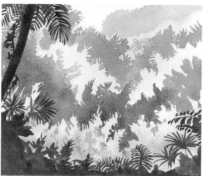

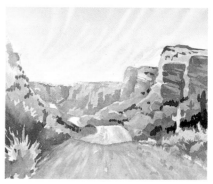

LINES CREATE DISTANCE
Linear shapes and edges on the surface of the land (such as roads, rivers, canyons, furrows, ridges and waves) will lead you merrily off into the distance.

OVERLAPPING SHAPES
A series of overlapping shapes or grounds will create a sense of distance. Darkening the foreground or showing only part of an object in the foreground will give the viewer the feeling of peering deep into a private world.

 E.L.L.

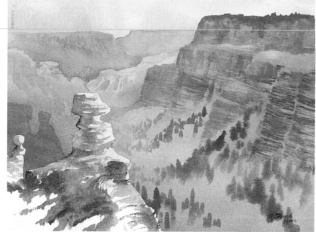

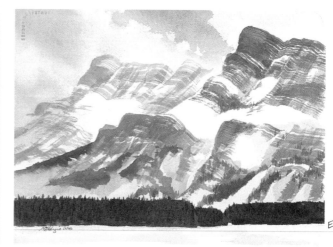

E.L.L.

WHAT'S BELOW
A high eye-level line emphasizes what's below. In this case, the emphasis is on the quiet depths of the canyon.

CANYON GLOW
11" × 14" (28cm × 36cm)

WHAT'S ABOVE
A low eye-level line emphasizes what's above it. This can be useful for spectacular skyscapes. This painting's E.L.L. reinforces the majesty of the towering mountains.

ALBERTA APRIL
11" × 14" (28cm × 36cm)

EYE LEVEL LINE (E.L.L.)

Unless you are a cubist, there is only one E.L.L. for each picture. Do not confuse the E.L.L. with the horizon, which is where the sky meets the earth. Only if you are looking out over a large body of water or a plain will the horizon be the same as the E.L.L.

Here's an example. Also watch what happens to our sense of elevation as we raise the E.L.L. by adding more distant shorelines to the composition below.

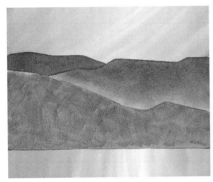

LOW EYE LEVEL
The top edge of a large plain or body of water is usually the E.L.L. The horizon is where sky meets the land.

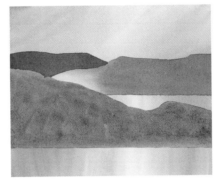

RAISED EYE LEVEL
Now the E.L.L. is the distant shoreline, and you see more water surface.

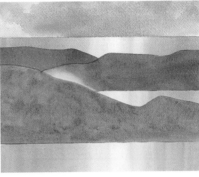

HIGH EYE LEVEL
We can see even more of the water's surface as the E.L.L. and the horizon become one.

OBJECTS IN OR ON WATER

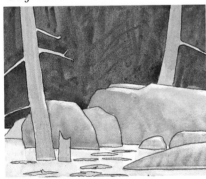

LOW EYE LEVEL
If your eye level is low, the objects that are sitting on or protruding from the water's surface—including land masses—will appear stacked up and have fairly straight bottoms.

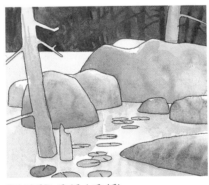

RAISED EYE LEVEL
As the E.L.L. rises, you'll see greater spacing between the objects. Most importantly, the closer they are to you, the more angle and curvature you will see in their baselines.

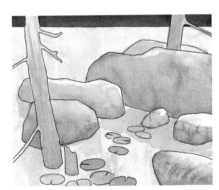

HIGH EYE LEVEL
An even higher E.L.L. allows you to arrange the objects into a pleasing layout, like furniture.

Surface Patterns That Lead the Eye

There are often parallel lines (e.g. waves, furrows) or rows of shapes (e.g. clouds, plants) in our environment that we can use to create the illusion of distance if we put them in perspective. We know that if we look down parallel lines, they appear to converge toward some point in the distance. The point at which they appear to meet is called a vanishing point, and that vanishing point is on the eye level line.

THE FAN PATTERN

If you wish to dramatically increase energy, movement and distance, try laying out parallel lines or rows in your picture in a "fan" pattern.

To do this, secure your paper to a flat surface and lightly draw a desired eye level line that extends well beyond the picture plane. Pick a vanishing point on that line, and then, using a large ruler, draw light lines across your paper while rotating it on the vanishing point. It is important that the lines that are nearly horizontal are drawn close together. As the pattern fans out, the lines become further and further apart. Please realize that these lines are only guidelines for positioning your waves, furrows or clouds so they'll create the illusion of distance without looking bent out of shape.

With practice, you won't need a ruler. You'll be able to sketch light guidelines freehand with the full sweep of your arm.

TIP

The best way to see the pattern in waves or furrows is to look at them through a viewfinder. Note the angle of the waves or furrows compared to the rectangular opening.

THE FAN PATTERN AND GRADATION
Gradation also leads the eye. When combined with the energy and movement of a fan pattern, it becomes even more effective. The types of gradations are endless. Most often a gradation involves color, but you also see gradations in size, shape, pattern and detail.

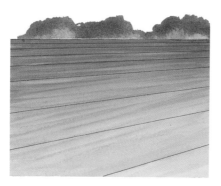

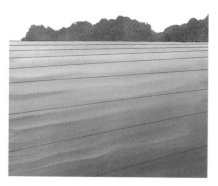

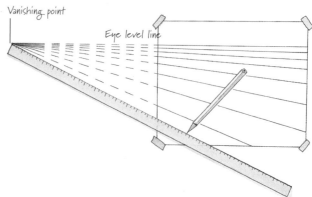

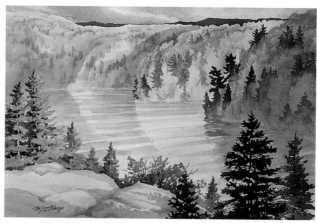

SURFACE PATTERNS AT WORK
Here is an example of how a fanned surface pattern can lead you into a picture.

VANTAGE POINT
11" × 14" (28cm × 36cm)

THE OLD ZIGZAG GAME

One of the most effective ways to lead the viewer through the picture is with a zigzag pattern. It can have as many turns as you want, but even a couple will do.

Think of back roads, meandering streams and canyons as big, wide zigzags. Make them extra wide in the foreground so that the illusion of distance can be more effective. Using a viewfinder will show you that these things are a lot wider in the picture space than you think they are.

Zigzag patterns are not always sharply defined streams and roads. Sometimes, they occur like stepping stones, in the form of lily pads, clouds, waves or puddles.

OVER THE HILL AND THROUGH THE WOODS

You can give the impression of an undulating and twisting road by not showing all of it, as demonstrated in the exercise below.

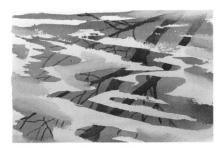

ZIGZAGGING A PATH
The zigzagging puddles lead us right across the picture. The reflections unify the puddles.

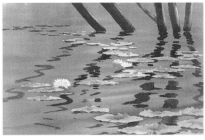

TWO ZIGZAGS
There are two zigzags leading the eye through the painting: the line of the water lilies and the broken reflections of the trees.

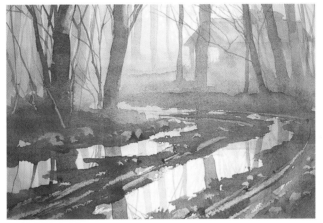

MOVEMENT AND DISTANCE
It's a zigzag route to this shack. The murkier distance and zigzag path creates a sense of distance. Zigzags provide a sense of movement in the otherwise still, chilled scene.

SUGAR SHACK MORNING
11" × 14" (28cm × 36cm)

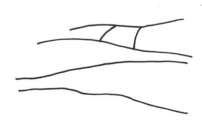

FIRST SECTION
First, draw a few ridge lines. These represent the top of rises in the roadway. Starting from the top one (which will be the ridge farthest away), draw the portion of road that leads up to it from the ridge below. Make sure that you taper the section.

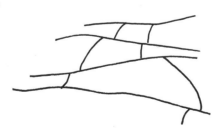

SECOND SECTION
Continue to add road sections as you work toward the front. Make sure that each section starts wider than the section above it. Don't worry if your road turns out wider in the foreground than your paper. This adds to the illusion of depth.

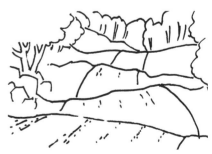

LAST SECTION
The more you offset the road sections, the more twisted the road becomes. The greater the differences in size between each section, the deeper the valley between them. Adjust the ends of the ridge lines to suit the landscape desired.

Using a Model for Perspective

This method of drawing objects in perspective is so simple that some people will consider it illegal. What you are going to do is make a simple model of your subject and hold it above your paper with one hand while tracing around it with the other. I will use a butterfly as an example because I've used those many times.

First, let me point out that I began this method not because I couldn't draw butterflies, but because I wanted to be able to freely play with the arrangement and position of them in my composition. By taping model butterflies to sticks,

I could manipulate the arrangement until I found one I really liked. This method saved a lot of sketching and erasing time, but I still had a problem: How do I get my arrangement onto the paper?

The answer was simple: While holding the butterfly above the paper, I closed one eye and lightly traced around it as though it were on my paper. It wasn't perfectly drawn, but the butterfly's perspective would be accurate and in the position I wanted. I could refine the details later.

The hardest part of this process is keeping your head and hand steady. The solution I found for this was to

rest my hand on a stack of books and then make a conscious effort to move my eyes rather than my head while drawing.

I also found that if I had already sketched parts of my composition before doing this, the benefit was even greater because I could see the model in relationship to its setting.

Normally, I would frown upon the process of tracing because it implies the copying of someone else's work, but in this case, you're only tracing your own arrangement of a piece of work.

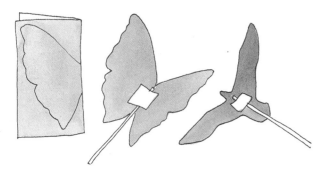

GIVE IT A TRY
Use heavy paper or cardstock to make your model. Butterflies or birds are easy because they're symmetrical and can be cut from folded paper.

Start by folding your paper in half and drawing half a butterfly or bird along the folded edge. Cut it out and add a small stick along the fold so you can manipulate it without getting your hands in the way. Curve the bird's wings to make them more realistic.

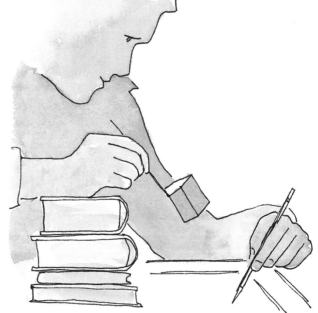

HOLDING STEADY
The trick is keeping a steady hand and head, and closing one eye. Here, the paper model of a building is being sketched.

Dynamics: Are There Any Signs of Life?

In most cases, it is not *what* you paint that creates energy; it's *where* and *how* you paint it. The best way to get and hold the viewer's attention is to make your picture exciting to look at. We call the energy that a picture exudes *dynamics*, much like a person exudes personality. Pictorial dynamics are not an arbitrary set of rules, but a reflection of how the human eye perceives the world. Using the principles of perception, experienced artists add energy and character to their work. You can, too.

A dynamic picture results from using a definite atmosphere, movement and strong contrasts. For now, let's focus on movement.

MOVEMENT

The human eye is attracted to movement. Including some type of movement—even if it's just implied movement—will add excitement.

We perceive vertical elements—particularly lines and edges—to be stable or balanced. We perceive horizontal lines and edges as quiet and inactive. The edges of your paper or "frame" will be perceived as stable and calm. Anything in your picture placed at an angle to the frame will be perceived as unstable or in the process of moving. This adds energy to your composition.

But don't get carried away—character could also mean lively, gently flowing, dancing, ascending, swirling, floating, and so on. Movement can and should be portrayed according to what suits the statement you're trying to make about your subject.

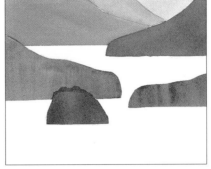 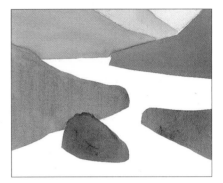

HORIZONTAL VERSUS DIAGONAL
The horizontal shorelines of the land masses on the left have a powerful calming effect. By angling the masses, you not only add implied energy but physical movement as well, by causing the viewer's eyes to follow a zigzag into the distance.

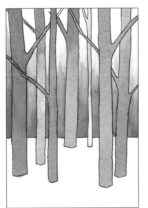 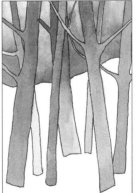 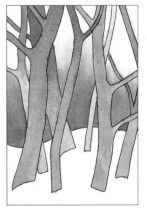

VERTICAL, LIGHTLY ANGLED, HEAVILY ANGLED
The same trees can have different character depending on how they are shaped and positioned. Note how the type and position of the horizon also affects the feel of the picture.

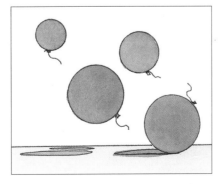

SUSPENSION THEORY
Objects that are in suspension will suggest motion in progress. This is an old cartoonist's trick, but it will work for you, too. Spray from waves, birds in flight and swirling leaves all add a fantastic sense of motion to a picture. Adding a shadow helps with the illusion.

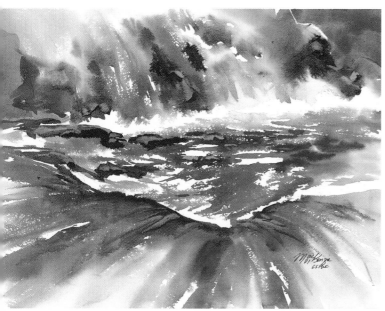

POWERFUL ENERGY
There are not many horizontal or vertical lines in this stream study, but the angles and diagonals give the impression of the water's rushing power.

STREAM STUDY
14" × 22" (36cm × 56cm)

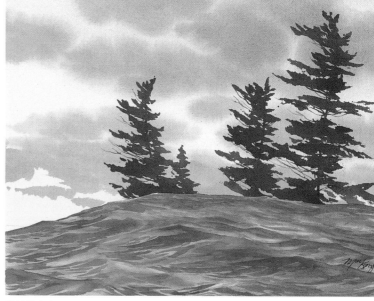

SWELLS
The gentle curves in the waves, the top edge of the swell and the tree trunks produce a flowing sensation in this picture. By overlapping the trees with the wave, I am implying that the wave swell is rising in front of you. The drop in the top edge suggests that it is moving to the left.

SUNSET SWELLS, LAKE OF THE WOODS
11" × 14" (28cm × 36cm)

ANGLES AND LEAVES
Here the angled rails, combined with the bird and leaves in suspension, imply explosive action.

RAILS END SURPRISE
19" × 22"
(48cm × 56cm)

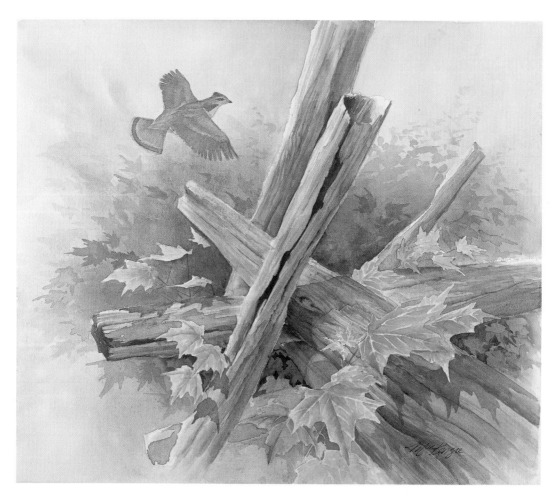

Contrast

Contrast is the primary way in which the brain distinguishes things. The stronger the contrast, the more it attracts attention—and vice versa, which is why low-contrast camouflage works.

Contrast in value is the most common form of contrast used by artists. In fact, the compositional and painting process is one of constantly arranging and modifying the values of various parts of the picture so that an adequate degree of contrast exists among them.

Sometimes values must be modified from how they appear in reality to what is needed in the picture to make a stronger composition. Just squint at your work; if certain areas blend into each other, you may need more contrast. If you make the shadows darker than they are in actuality and lose a little more detail in the bright highlights, you're simply

making the scene more dynamic.

Placing colors of opposite temperatures next to each other is another form of visual contrast. The contrast becomes even more effective (and subtle) if the colors are mingled together by dropping or stroking one into the other.

In the visual world, contrasts are endless. For every condition there is an opposite—look for it and use it to establish contrast. The stronger the contrast(s), the more dynamics you add to your picture.

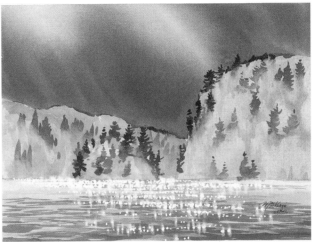

LAKE COUNTRY AUTUMN
11" × 14" (28cm × 36cm)

CONTRASTING TEMPERATURE, VALUE AND PURITY
To lighten and brighten a color to make it stand out, add some dark, dull color to the background. This dark, dull, cool sky makes the autumn hills flame.

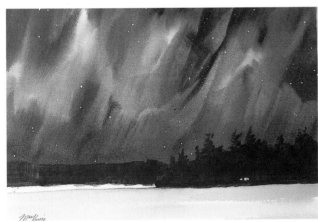

CONTRASTING VALUE AND ENERGY
The lake is a calm horizontal stretch of white. In contrast, the sky is mostly dark with light-valued diagonals for the northern lights and white pinpricks for stars.

SOLAR SYMPHONY
11" × 14" (28cm × 36cm)

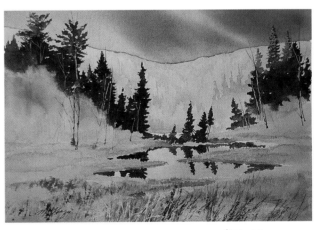

CONTRASTING TEMPERATURE AND VALUE
Here, the warm and cool colors contrast and mingle to produce a subtle glow. The dark pines stand out starkly against the light middle ground and foreground and lead the viewer's eye through the painting.

SNOW BEFORE ITS TIME
11" × 14" (28cm × 36cm)

THE MAGIC OF PROXIMITY

When colors are in close proximity, they tend to exaggerate each other's difference. For example, I can make one color appear much lighter by making its neighbor darker. I can make one appear more pure by dulling the mate, or cool one by warming the other. For whatever reason, the brain wants to create maximum contrast between everything it sees.

This can work to great effect in your painting. To lighten a sky, darken the trees, clouds, hills or whatever is in front of it. The bottom line is this: You can often achieve the changes needed in a color by doing just the opposite to its background.

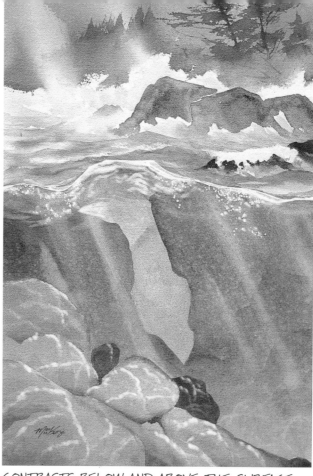

THE CALM BELOW
14" × 11"
(36cm × 28cm)

CONTRASTS BELOW AND ABOVE THE SURFACE
The contrast here is very intense. Where all the colors below the waves harmonize, the colors above contrast. More importantly, above the waves, there are varied details and sharper edges, as well as the violently crashing waves. Below, all is calm. The edges are rounder, the detail more vague and the movement seems limited to the spliced light dancing on the rocks in the foreground.

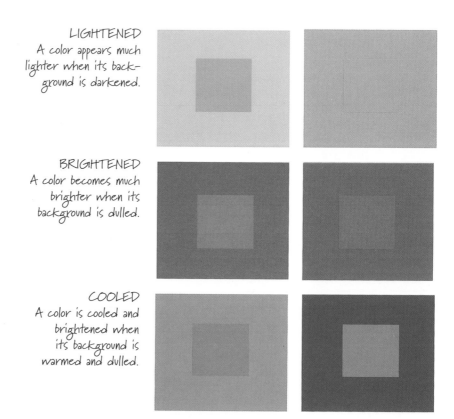

LIGHTENED
A color appears much lighter when its background is darkened.

BRIGHTENED
A color becomes much brighter when its background is dulled.

COOLED
A color is cooled and brightened when its background is warmed and dulled.

Priming the Imagination

If you have children you know that growth does not occur in a smooth, continual flow but in spurts, usually triggered by the purchase of new clothes. The creative process is no different.

Each time I reach a new level, there is great excitement and lots of things to try and places to explore. After awhile, things slow down and I start to lose interest in the way I am presenting my subjects. The creative drive is still there, but it's hard to find a worthy focus.

I am not always sure of how to get to the next level—or even what that level may be—so I explore variations on this one that will challenge me and keep me painting. I know for sure that I will not make the next leap unless I do this.

These are some of the approaches I have used to prime my imagination and get me moving again. Hopefully they will work for you, too. It's the way the game is played by beginner and professional.

Maybe if I bought some new clothes…

CHALLENGE YOURSELF

I like to set up a challenge for myself with each painting I do. In fact, I have always felt that my best pictures are the ones in which I have had to solve a problem. It doesn't always have to be nuclear physics—just something to challenge my inventiveness or imagination for that particular picture. Sometimes the problem arises from the subject I'm working on, and sometimes the challenge precedes the subject. Either way, I'm driven to better myself.

LISTEN TO MUSIC

Music speaks directly to the soul. Close your eyes and focus on the feelings and fleeting images generated by your music. Try to connect those feelings to any setting or scenario that your imagination might be generating as you travel. Have a sketch pad handy and, without breaking the mood, gently record the movements and rhythms of the music and any bits of images you are able to capture.

You may not get an idea for a picture with each piece of music, but you will at least experience the combined power of music and your imagination.

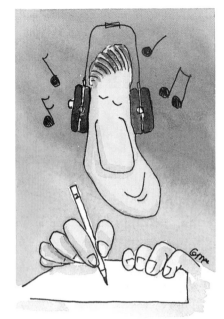

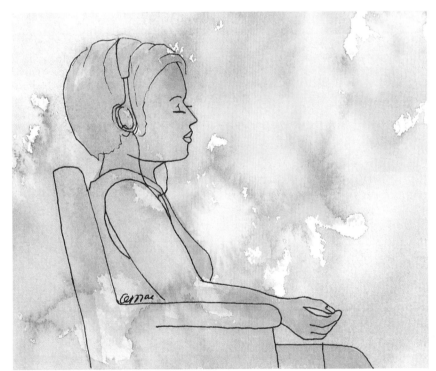

PRACTICE MEDITATION

Meditation is a natural extension of using music to stimulate the imagination. It just might turn out to be the most valuable addition to your painting process that you can make. This exercise does more than clear the mind. It can also be a time to receive intuitive information, a time for our inner self to speak when we have quieted our loud, conscious mind. But be ready: Your inner self speaks quickly and gently. It's easy to miss or dismiss it.

Don't expect meditation to work immediately. It takes practice, but the payoff is big. There are many meditation tapes and CDs out there that combine music and natural sounds that will teach you how to relax, visualize and "walk through" your inner landscapes. As French postimpressionist Paul Gauguin said, "I shut my eyes in order to see."

EXPERIMENT FROM PAPER TO IMAGE

Other than the printed page, printed information can take many unique forms such as maps, building plans, theater tickets, travel brochures, menus, invitations, sheet music—the list goes on and on. For each of these pieces of paper, there are endless image possibilities. Create a picture where you combine the piece of paper and the image that it brings to mind for you into one picture. You may have to do some research for the piece of paper and image(s) you use—and do lots of pre-sketching and planning to find a suitable composition—but then again, the challenge to create a unique image is what it's all about.

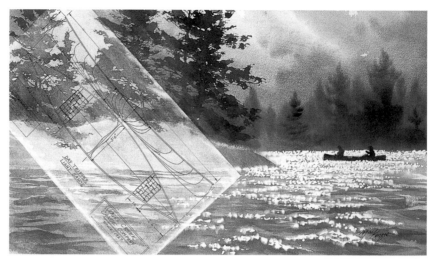

COMBINE PLAN AND PAINTING
Here are the plans for a canoe combined with the end result. The plans were drawn out on the paper first with a waterproof/lightproof pen. When dry, the picture was painted. When the picture was dry, I outlined the plans with packing tape and then removed color by gently scrubbing with a wet sponge and blotting with a paper towel. Using staining colors in the picture left the best after-image.

ROUNDING THE POINT
14" × 16" (36cm × 41cm)

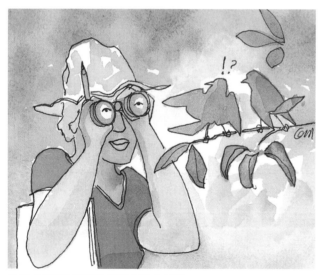

COMPOSE WITH BINOCULARS
Using binoculars or field glasses to find a subject for painting is not much different from using the zoom feature of a good camera, except the enlargement is easier to see because you are using both eyes. Besides having the effect of eliminating peripheral detail like a simple viewfinder, binoculars can also blur unimportant details in the background and foreground. They also flatten a three-dimensional subject into two dimensions. This effect makes the subject look like overlapping paper cutouts, which can help you define layers or grounds in your composition.

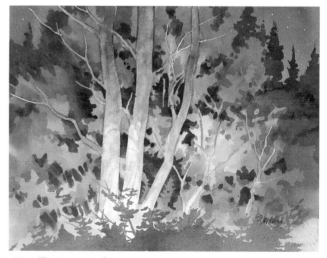

TRY PAINTING FROM DUSK TO DAWN
This special time of day—after the sun has set, through the darkened night and to the break of dawn—holds promise for some truly powerful visual effects in your paintings. Without the usual overhead light of the daytime sun, you must illuminate your picture with such light sources as street lights, campfires, house lights, moonlight and candles.

FOREST LIGHT
11" × 14" (28cm × 36cm)

TRY SOMETHING DIFFERENT

I believe that we paint the best pictures when we paint about what we have experienced and know best. Within that framework we should continually challenge ourselves to explore beyond the norm for different, fresh ways of presenting our subjects. You have a license to do anything you want. Use it. For example, when was the last time you tried…

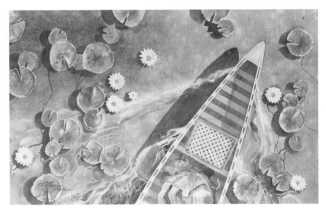

INTO THE SHALLOWS
22" × 24" (56cm × 61cm)

…an unusual viewpoint of your favorite subjects? From above, below, inside out, in silhouette, cross section, multiplied, close up, in fog, at night, etc.?

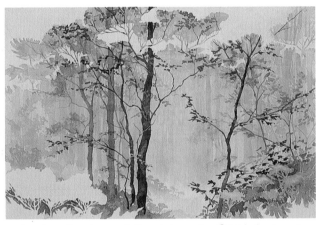

…changing the shape of the picture plane? This is done by masking border areas with packing tape or masking fluid so that the remaining picture space is not the usual rectangle.

FLOWERS OF THE FOREST
14" × 22" (36cm × 56cm)

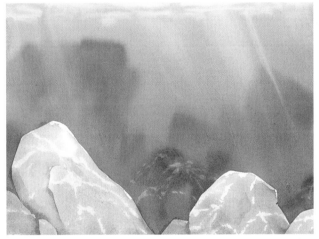

…looking below the surface? Landscapes do not have to be on dry land. Anyone who has snorkeled or done scuba diving will attest to the beauty under the sea just waiting to be painted, especially with watercolors.

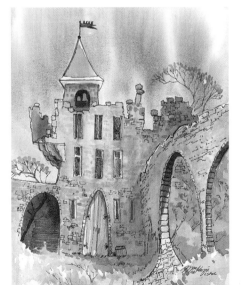

…distorting or exaggerating a subject—sometimes referred to as caricature? This invariably adds a lighthearted note to your work. They also offer you a chance to work like an illustrator with pen or brush and ink plus your watercolors.

In fact, when was the last time you mixed watercolors with another medium? Consider colored pencils, water-soluble crayons, wax crayons, waterproof markers, chalk or oil pastels, torn paper, fluid acrylics or gouache, all of which are compatible with traditional watercolors.

ST. POLYCARP, FRANCE
14" × 11" (36cm × 28cm)

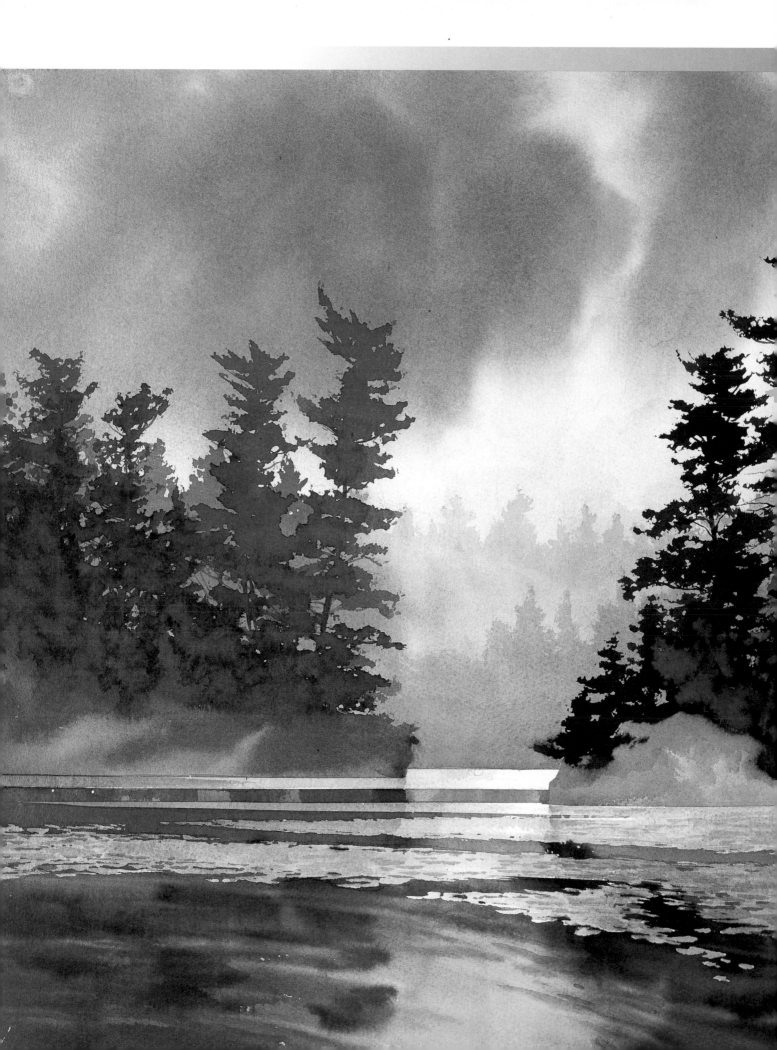

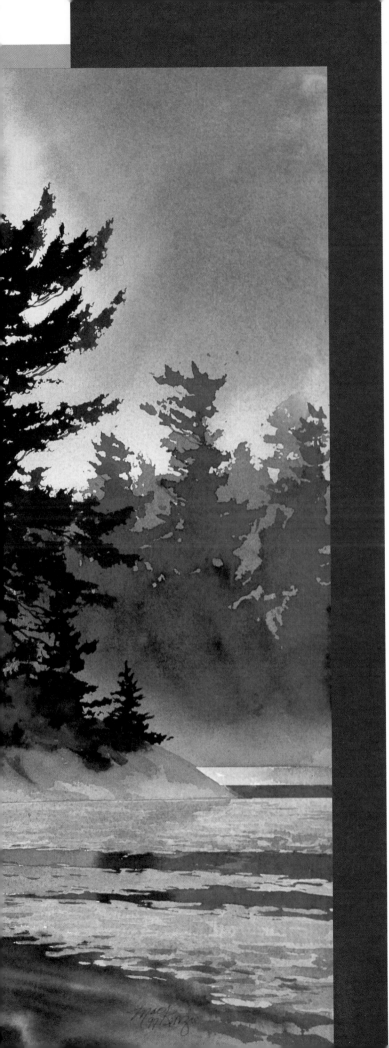

Landscape Elements 3
Water, Sky and Land

This chapter examines, one at a time, the choices or variations you can use within the three major aspects of a landscape painting—water, sky and land. The numerous exercises and examples will better enable you to handle any of these elements when it becomes a dominant player in your picture.

SENTRIES OF THE HEART
19" × 22" (48cm × 56cm)

Painting Water

Water, next to air, is the most vital element for our survival. It is the earth ingredient that has most shaped the development and movement of civilization. It is fitting, therefore, that we somehow honor the magic, majesty and enduring energy of this element in our paintings.

Water can be one of the most complex characters you can add to a picture. It can also be the star that steals the show. Because it can play so many roles, from tranquil pond to pounding river, there are a wide variety of techniques involved that are specific to water. But beyond the techniques, there is other knowledge you must grasp. Recognizing and using the patterns that water follows or creates is one example. Perspective of a flat surface is another.

Exploring the exercises and demos that follow will have you awash with confidence to use water as a major element in your paintings.

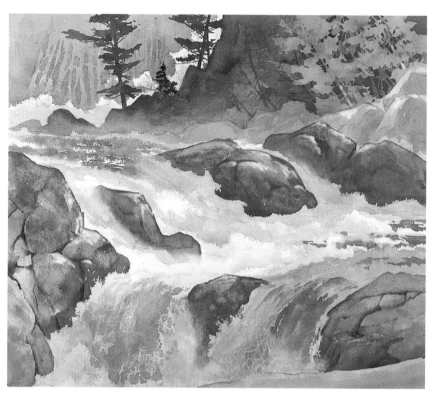

CYCLE OF LIFE
19" × 22" (28cm × 36cm)

MATERIALS USED FOR WATER EXERCISES

Surface
- 140-lb. (300gsm) cold-press paper, mostly 11" × 14" (28cm × 36cm)
- Rigid board for mounting paper

Paints
- Burnt Sienna
- Cobalt Blue
- Indian Yellow
- Permanent Rose
- Phthalo Blue
- Phthalo Green
- Raw Sienna
- Sap Green

Brushes
- ¾-inch (19mm) or 1-inch (25mm) synthetic flat
- 1½-inch (38mm) to 2-inch (51mm) synthetic flat
- ¾-inch (19mm) hog-hair bristle
- 1-inch (25mm) hog-hair bristle
- 1½-inch (38mm) to 2-inch (51cm) hog-hair bristle
- Assorted rounds (synthetic or synthetic/natural mix), nos. 8 to 14
- Small scrub brush (To make one, see page 16.)
- Flat synthetic stroke brush

Miscellaneous
- pencil
- eraser
- masking fluid
- rubber cement pickup
- water-filled spray bottle
- paper towels
- packing tape
- popsicle sticks or tongue depressors
- razor knife
- hair dryer
- piece of cellulose sponge
- stiff palette knife
- small piece of coarse sandpaper
- toothbrush
- thin sheet of acetate

Making Waves

Before you get swept away by the water exercises, practice making some basic wave marks that can be used on everything from calm waters to surging tides.

SHOWING PERSPECTIVE

For the sake of perspective, graduate your marks and the spaces in between from very large at the bottom of your paper to tiny near the top. There should be more undulation in the foreground and very little in the distance. Also, the color should lighten as you move into the distance. This aspect is very easy to do if you simply let your brush run out of paint as you work up the paper. Or, begin light in the distance and darken the mixture as you move forward. Unfortunately, one brushful of color won't paint your whole picture. You'll have to work from bottom to top along several paths.

TIP

This is a great time to let the rhythm of dance music get you in the flow. It's best to stand up so that you have the full movement of your arm. Besides, it's hard to dance sitting down.

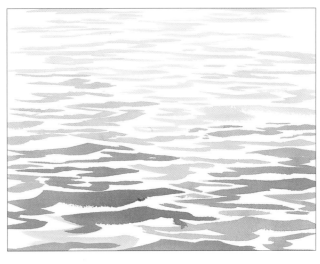

REAL WAVES
Vary the size, spacing and darkness of your marks, and try to avoid overlapping them. As the surface fills up, place the marks so that they interlock.

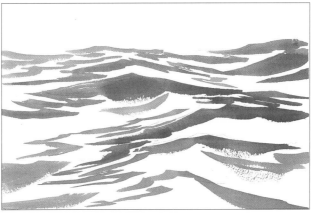

VARIATION
These marks can be used on larger swells as well as calm water. Notice the variety in the length and spacing of the waves.

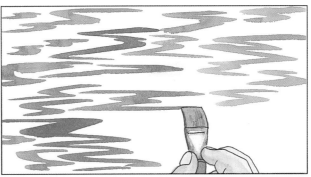

THE BASIC MOVE
Holding your flat brush as shown, move it from side to side, making a loose, broken zigzag pattern. Work your way up or down the page. Concentrate on varying the length of the individual strokes as well as the length of any continuous strokes.

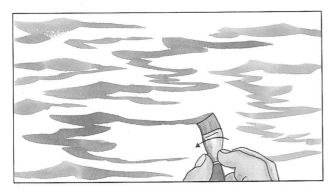

ADDING A TWIST
To make your marks look more like waves, add a small twist to your strokes. Do this by turning the brush ever so slightly upward at the rise of each wave, whenever you change direction, or at the end of each stroke. This will vary the width of each mark and create a more undulating appearance.

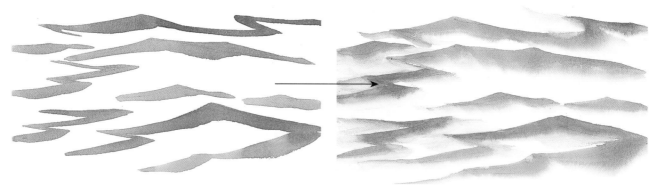

MODELING WAVE MARKS

To make the foreground waves look more three-dimensional, soften the bottom edges and ends of the closer major waves with a damp brush. In order for this to work you will have to fade out the marks while the paint is still wet. Therefore, paint only a couple of waves at a time before fading them out.

CALM WATERS TO LIGHT CHOP

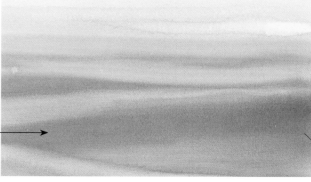

BEGIN WITH A BACKGROUND

With any color you want for the water, paint a smooth graded wash from dark in the foreground to light at the horizon. Make two of these. Let one dry and use the other while it is still wet for the wet-in-wet process shown at right.

CREATE SWELLS

To indicate gentle, rolling swells add some darker horizontal streaks to the damp graded wash. You could also lift off light streaks with a damp brush. Let dry.

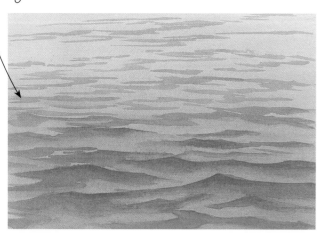

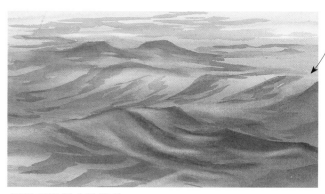

ADD WAVE MARKS

When the paper is dry you can start laying in wave marks in a loose zigzag pattern using a 3/4-inch (19mm) or 1-inch (25mm) flat synthetic brush loaded with a more concentrated charge of the color. Start with the larger waves in the foreground and work upward to fewer, flatter, smaller waves in the distance (left). For the wave swells, paint the wave marks to suit the direction of the swells (above).

Wave Direction and Surface Patterns

The secret to painting realistic water is to have the waves and ripples appear to be following a consistent pattern. This pattern, which invariably involves perspective, is used as a rough guide for the placement of waves, ripples, sparkles and reflections. It is not the intent that you follow these lines exactly when putting in your waves. They need only follow the general direction and spacing.

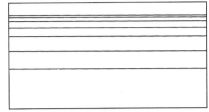

SPACE BETWEEN LINES CREATES DISTANCE
This simplistic pattern illustrates how to create the illusion of distance by decreasing the distance between the rows of waves.

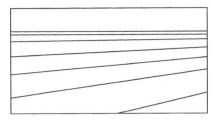

DIAGONAL LINES CREATE MOVEMENT
A pattern that runs at a diagonal to the frame adds energy to your work, but note that these lines are not parallel. They run to a common point outside the picture plane, the vanishing point.

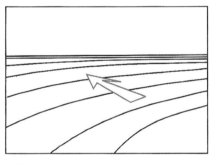

Offshore

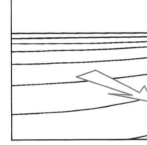

Onshore

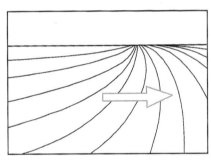

Passing in front

BENDING THE LINE EMPHASIZES WIND DIRECTION
Once you can draw wave guidelines diagonally, it's not much of a leap to draw the lines slightly curved because our arm naturally wants to move like a windshield wiper anyway. Turn your paper to take advantage of this wiper-like movement. This produces wave patterns evident when the wind blows diagonally away from you (offshore), toward you (onshore) or sometimes across in front of you.

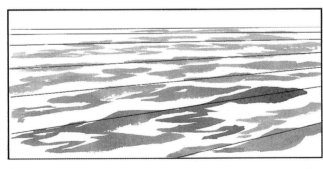

A

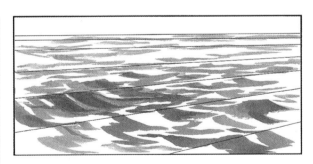

B

TWO WAYS TO PLACE THE WAVES
There are two ways of positioning your wave marks. One is to follow the angle of the guidelines (figure A). The other is to keep your marks more or less horizontal and follow the converging path of the lines (figure B). It's your choice. The wave marks are the zigzags you practiced earlier.

Interrupted Flow

Often the wave flow is interrupted by islands, rocks, points of land and such. The next time you're near a large body of water, pay attention to wave direction. You will be amazed at how much you will see when you are looking for something specific. A viewfinder will be of great value by giving you a firm horizontal/vertical reference base. It is always surprising to see what unexpected angles the lines for moving water can have.

TIP

Look at your sketch in a mirror. If it looks alright there, then chances are it is.

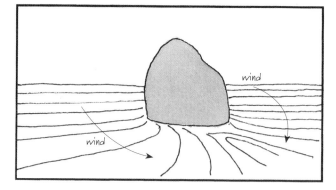

CALM WATERS
Wave patterns change when the water encounters land forms.

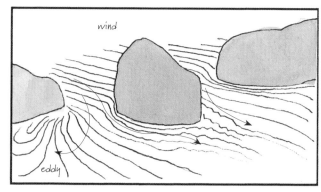

TURBULENT WATERS
By comparison, choppy water flowing around obstacles makes a slightly different pattern.

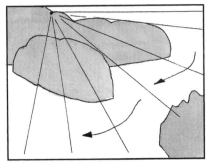

PRE-PAINTING SKETCH
Here, I set the horizon or eye-level line near the top of the picture plane for a high vantage point. The wave pattern lines rotate around a vanishing point located on this imaginary line. Following these rough guides, I sketched slightly curving lines to indicate wind direction and to suit the contour of the land. I used these lines a reference when applying masking fluid for the sparkles. (See the next page for more on that procedure.)

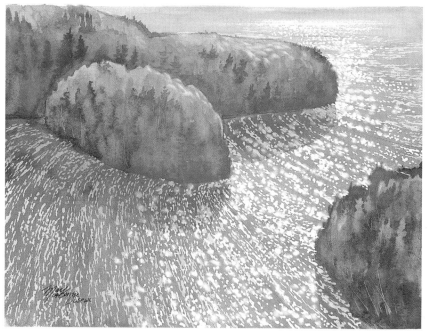

SPARKLES FOLLOW THE FLOW
Here the waves indicated by the sparkles curve around the point and into the bay.

DIAMOND DANCE
11" × 14" (28cm × 36cm)

Sparkling Waters

The best way to see sparkles dancing on water is to squint as you look. Note the pattern they make because you are going to use masking fluid to re-create that pattern.

COLOR NOTE

When mixing together the three colors of a triad, you will get various dulled colors. What kind depends on which color is most dominant in the mix. If it is blue, then the result will be a dulled blue. If it were red, then a dulled red. If red and blue are equally dominant, then you will get a dulled mauve.

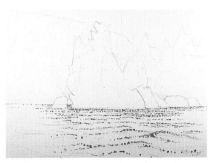

1. Sketch and Apply Masking

Sketch your plan and indicate the crests of a few major foreground/middle-ground waves. Apply dots of masking fluid for the sparkles using the butt end of a small paint brush. Cluster your dots in varying sizes along the crests of the waves, with a few scattered in between. As you work into the distance, make your dots smaller and your rows closer together. You may wish to leave gaps for calm areas among the sparkles.

This can be a mind-numbing process, but stick with it and try not to be stingy with your dots. Every one represents a sparkle. Without them, the water won't shine.

2. Choose Colors

The palette used here is the triad Cobalt Blue, Raw Sienna and Permanent Rose because I wanted fairly transparent, non-staining colors. More important than a preconceived color for water is the use of correct value, intensity and temperature to suit the atmosphere you want. For a sunny day, use mostly pure forms of your triad colors or mixtures of only two colors at a time. For a warm, hazy atmosphere—which is the case here—mix all three colors to produce a dulled dark and warm color (here, dulled mauve).

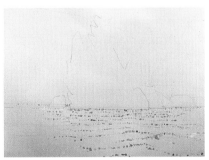

3. Paint the Water and Sky

With your dulled mauve, paint a graded wash from dark in the foreground to light in the distance. Paint past where the far shore would be. Paint a sky that would suggest a soft, warm light by adding more yellow and water to your mix. Let dry.

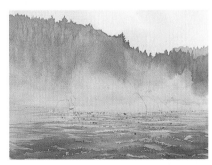

4. Add Land and Detail the Waves

Paint the top of the distant land with a darker mixture of your triad colors. While still wet, fade it out downward into the mist. Model the backsides of the larger waves with a more concentrated color.

205

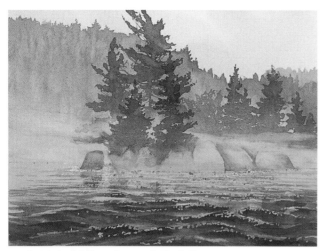

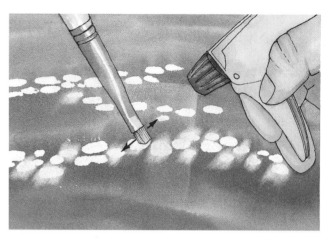

5. Add Middle-Ground Detail

Continue with the same dulled triad mixture. To continue the illusion of a hazy atmosphere, paint the hills and middle-ground trees as single masses. For depth, use darker and darker colors as you come forward. Keep the rocks light for contrast.

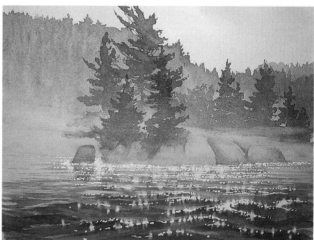

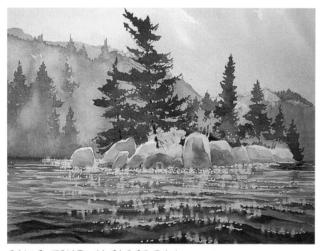

SAME TRIAD, CLEARER DAY
This painting was done with the same triad but here the more pure colors were used or only mixed two at a time. There is more value contrast and detail shown because it's a clearer day.

MORNING DANCE TWO
11" × 14" (28cm × 36cm)

6. Create Sparkle

When the paint is dry, remove the masking fluid from the dots with an eraser or rubber cement pickup.

To achieve the illusion of light on the water's surface, spray the whole area with lots of water—literally a small lake—and then soften *some* of the dots by scrubbing with a small hog-hair scrub brush. Be consistent in the direction of your scrubbing. Unless you have painted with a lot of heavy opaque colors, nothing will move under this extreme wetting unless you touch it with your scrub brush.

When you have finished scrubbing as many dots as you want, pour off the water and blot—don't rub!—the surface with a paper towel.

MORNING DANCE ONE
11" × 14" (28cm × 36cm)

Masking Ripple Marks

Ripples are the marks made by light breezes on a calm surface. You could save the entire ripple area with masking fluid, but I have found that if I use packing tape for the core of these areas and masking fluid along the edges, I can save a lot of time and masking fluid. Besides, the tape produces far more precise lines and edges that are needed on distant ripple areas.

Warning: Test your paper first. Packing tape will not work on some papers. Arches is one of the brands recommended for this process.

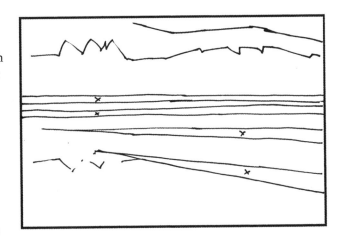

1. "X" Marks the Spot

Sketch the areas or shapes that you want to save as ripple areas. Use a ruler to get the distant areas straight. For this exercise we'll keep it simple.

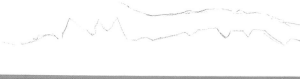

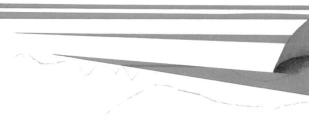

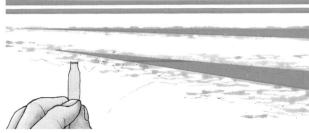

2. Apply Packing Tape

Apply overlapping pieces of packing tape over the designated area. At this point, press down lightly. Don't worry about a few wrinkles. Carefully cut the packing tape with a razor knife according to your guidelines and remove the unwanted pieces. Now, firmly press the taped areas. You should be able to see the texture of the paper in the tape.

3. Apply Masking Fluid

Apply masking fluid along the edges of the taped areas in the foreground and some in the middle ground. It's easy to apply with a popsicle stick or tongue depressor that has been carved with a chisel edge. You are trying to create a gentle gradation between the ripple area and the calm area. Make sure that the hard edge of the tape in the foreground is completely obscured with masking fluid. Let dry.

TIP

If you have not worked with packing tape before, you can save a lot of headache by reading pages 168–169.

3. Paint the Sky, Hills and Reflections

Paint the sky and its reflection a pale Raw Sienna. Let dry.

Paint the land and hills simultaneously. Wet these areas and apply patches of Raw Sienna, Burnt Sienna and Indian Yellow to represent distant autumn trees. Paint the reflected patches with the same colors. While still wet, paint a blue-gray (Cobalt Blue + Burnt Sienna) around the warm patches.

On the land, define the hilltop. In the water use vertical strokes to suggest reflection. While the painting is still damp, add darker evergreens using Cobalt Blue and Sap Green.

4. Complete the Painting

Remove the packing tape first. Lift the corner with a knife blade. Warming it with a hair dryer will ease its release. Remaining masking fluid can then be removed with a rubber cement pickup.

Paint the ripples a pale Cobalt Blue because they indicate the sky above you, not the sky at the horizon. In the foreground, darken the ripple marks in the lighter ripple area and reflected sky area. This eases the transition between ripples and calm water.

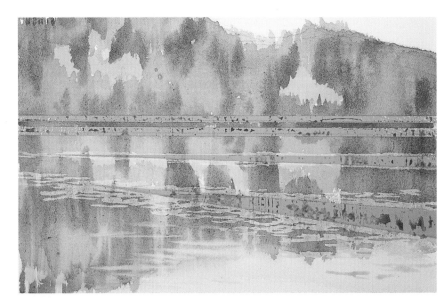
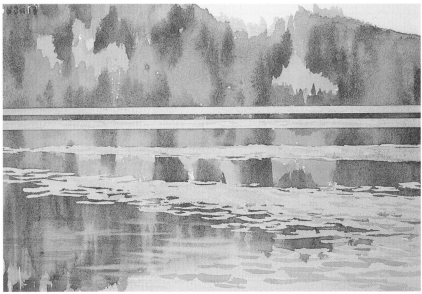

RIPPLE STUDY
11" × 19" (28cm × 48cm)

The Laws of Reflection

When you are working with water, there are four hard and fast characteristics of reflections that you must use in order for the water to look authentic.

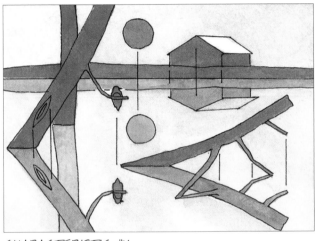

CHARACTERISTIC #1
On a body of water, a reflection is always directly below the thing being reflected.

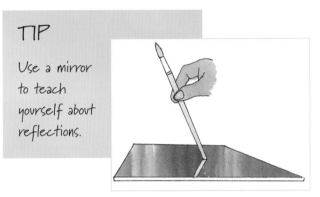

TIP

Use a mirror to teach yourself about reflections.

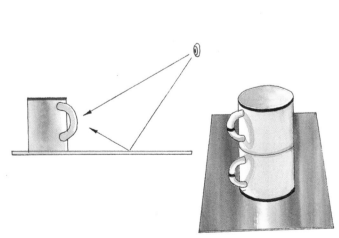

CHARACTERISTIC #2
The reflection is rarely the exact same as the object being reflected. The reason is that the reflection is a different view of the object—actually, a view from below. This is something to keep in mind particularly for foreground and middle-ground reflections.

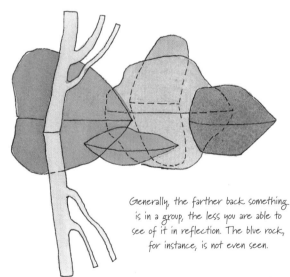

Generally, the farther back something is in a group, the less you are able to see of it in reflection. The blue rock, for instance, is not even seen.

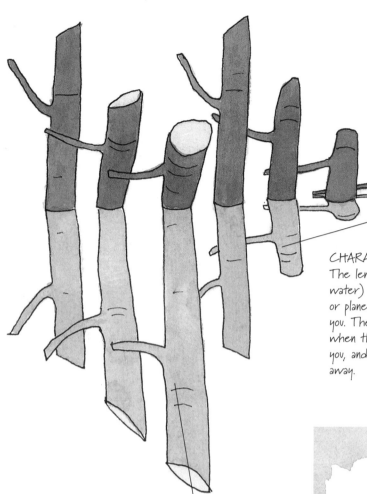

Note how the reflection is actually behind the tree when it has fallen away from us.

Reflections become shorter when the object tilts away from us.

CHARACTERISTIC #3
The length of a reflection (in calm water) depends on whether the object or plane is tilted toward you or away from you. The reflection gets longer and wider when the object or plane is tilted toward you, and shorter and narrower when tilted away.

Reflections become longer when the object tilts toward us.

CHARACTERISTIC #4
Reflections become elongated when the surface of the water develops ripples. Each wave acts like a tiny moving mirror that is able to reflect objects over a greater area of the water. The result is a reflection that is much longer than the object.

To create light distant reflections, wait until the painting is dry, then lift off horizontal marks by rubbing with a damp sponge. Use pieces of paper as stencils to preserve straight edges. When dry, you may need to touch up some of the ripple marks.

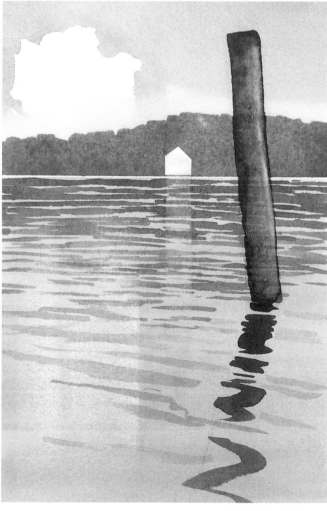

Calm Reflections

There are many degrees of "sharpness" in calm reflections. In this back-lit subject, the reflections are somewhat less than mirror-perfect.

1. Prepare the Background

Mask out the canoe with packing tape or masking fluid. For the forest background, paint a graded wash that transitions from warm green (Sap Green + Indian Yellow) to cool green (Sap Green + Phthalo Green). Let dry.

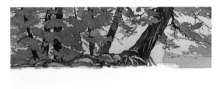

2. Add Trees

Sponge or brush on dark foliage with greens ranging from Sap Green near the light to Phthalo Green at the edges. Leave some white areas for the shoreline rocks. When dry, paint the rocks, dark trunks and limbs between the clumps of foliage with a dark blue-gray (Cobalt Blue + Burnt Sienna). Use a palette knife to add texture to the trunk and to define the tops of the rocks.

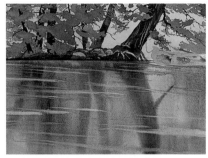

3. Paint the Reflections

This is one long, continuous step, so prepare pools of paint before you start.

Gradate a wash of Cobalt Blue from dark in the foreground to light in the background. While wet, brush on bold vertical strokes of greens, starting with yellow-green and then using dark warm and cool greens. Leave some areas of blue (reflected sky) showing.

While still wet, paint the trunks with a dark gray-brown (Cobalt + Burnt Sienna). When this dries to the damp stage, lift off a few light ripple lines with the edge of a damp flat synthetic brush. Follow with a few strokes of blue with the same brush. Let dry.

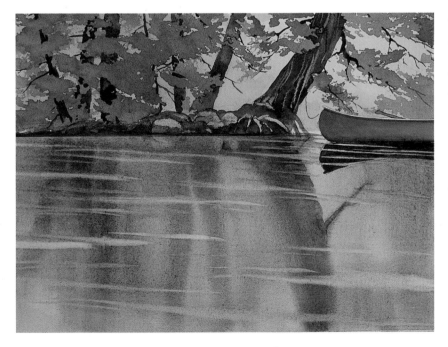

4. Finally, the Canoe

Remove the masking and paint the canoe in a red that is darkened with a drop of green. Paint its reflection with the same color, leaving gaps for ripples. Sharpen the edge of the tree reflection near its base.

Techniques for Dynamic Water

There are many ways to paint moving water, from wave swells to crashing rapids. The next few pages show the main techniques.

WET-IN-WET

The two examples below use wet-in-wet methods of depicting moving water.

TIP

A zigzag on the water can act as a guide for placing wave marks. Major wave stokes flow away from this mark, leaving a light ridge for the eye to follow.

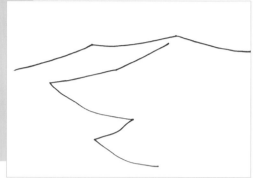

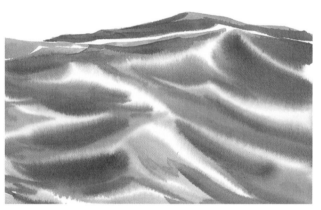

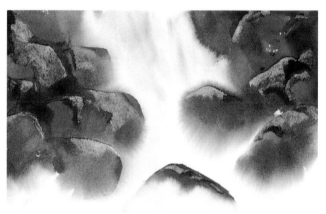

WAVE SWELLS

For this wave exercise, wet the paper only as far as the top of the sea, which you will notice is not perfectly horizontal. When you start painting the wave, first define the hard top edge of the water by painting just beyond this wetted area. This will give it a hard edge against the sky.

For the wave marks, use a 2-inch (51mm) synthetic brush well-loaded with concentrated color (e.g. Phthalo Blue). It is important that you paint the marks quickly with bold strokes, leaving space between them. Each mark will diffuse but not quite meet its neighbor. The result is a light pattern of lines that defines the movement and undulations of the water. Strokes can be varied by holding your brush vertically and turning it while increasing the pressure up and down as you make the stroke. While the blue waves are still wet, add a few smaller strokes of darker green on top for emphasis.

WATERFALLS AND RAPIDS

Completely wet the paper and define the water flow with a few pale blue strokes. When this dries to damp, paint the rocks with any dark, concentrated brown-blue mixture (e.g. Cobalt Blue + Burnt Sienna) using a 2-inch (51mm) flat synthetic brush. Leave a path for the water. When that dries to damp, model some rocks by scraping back with a palette knife. After it has dried completely, go back and clearly define the top edges of rocks in the stream with more dark color. Fade out into the rocks. Then paint the top of the foreground rock, soften along its bottom edge and scrape the top.

DRYBRUSHING

The only difference between dry-brushing and traditional wet-on-dry painting is the angle at which you hold your brush. Both brushes are well-loaded with paint, but with wet-on-dry you hold the brush upright and use the tip to apply paint in a solid stroke. For drybrushing, you apply paint in a broken pattern with the side of the brush. For this technique, it helps if you use a brush with long, coarse bristles, such as a hog-hair or badger.

The trick (There is always a trick.): Stand up and move your entire arm and body. This ensures that the brush will remain at the necessary low angle throughout the stroke.

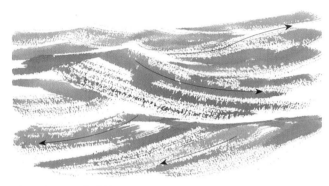

FLOWING WAVES
For drybrushed waves, use long, sweeping strokes. Notice how the change of direction in the strokes adds variety to the movement of the waves.

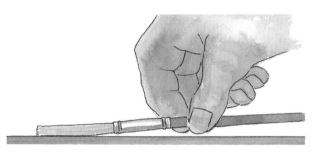

A LOW-ANGLED BRUSH
To paint with the side of your brush, you must hold it low to the paper. A 2-inch (51cm) hog-hair brush with long bristles is excellent for this process. Ironically, this method of drybrushing is not done with a dry brush. It is done with a well-loaded brush that drops a lot of paint from its side.

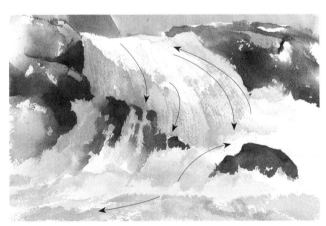

RAPIDS
Drybrushing adds texture and movement to a stream. While the first marks are still damp, apply a second different-colored layer on top for variety. You may find it more effective to pull some of your strokes upstream. Add the rocks after the water dries.

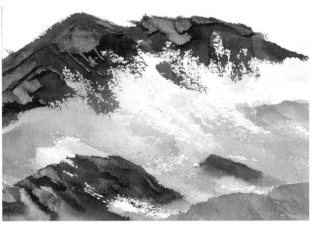

CRASHING WAVES
First, paint the wave area a pale blue and let dry. Using a midvalue blue, drybrush pattern and movement on the waves. When this is dry, drybrush a dark brown-gray (Cobalt Blue + Burnt Sienna) for the rocks. Paint your first strokes downward to make a lacy spray, and then carry the paint upward to build the rock shape. When this dries to damp (starts to lose its shine), scrape some lighter rock faces with a palette knife.

PARTIAL WASHES

Yes, Virginia, there is such a thing as a partial wash. It's basically dry-brushing with clean water, except you add color after you make the stroke. Partial washes are fantastic for creating foam, sparkle, water movement and ice.

One of the beautiful features of a hog-hair (bristle) brush is the loose pattern of water that it lays down when dragged on its side. This pattern, or partial wash, can then be used to carry paint that is dropped into it into a loose broken pattern that can be used in many places in your landscape. Because the brush is dragged, it makes a linear pattern that defines movement in the water as well.

The longer the bristles on your hog-hair brush, the better this process works. The colors dropped in can vary, but all should be concentrated for maximum contrast and prepared *before* you put down your partial wash.

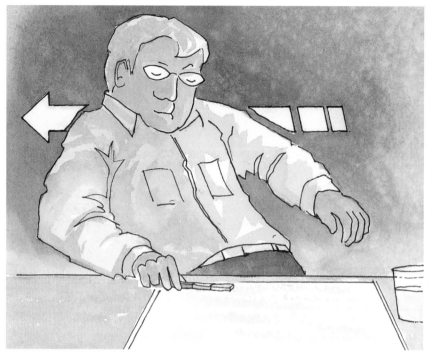

LAYING DOWN THE WATER

To apply a partial wash, drag your brush—well-loaded with water—across your paper. Try not to lift your brush as you go, otherwise water will come off the leading edge and give you a solid wet mark. Repeat the stroke until you are satisfied with the coverage in the desired area. Standing up makes it a lot easier to make a consistent mark across the paper.

Getting this water pattern down is the most important part of this process. If you get too much water on the paper, you won't have any sparkles when you add the paint. On the other hand, if you don't put down enough lacy pattern, you won't get the colors to flow. Practice makes perfect. Use the backs of old paintings if they are not too buckled.

ADDING COLOR

Let the water do the painting. Your job is to deliver lots of paint to the partial wash as soon as it's down, and let the water do the rest. Use a large, well-loaded flat synthetic brush. Hold it vertically and just touch it to the paper lightly. As soon as it finds water, the pigment will burst out of the brush to create wonderful patterns. Hold the brush in the direction of the wash. Keep reloading color and dropping it as long as you want.

Finally, if necessary, soften the edges of the wash with a damp hog-hair brush so that it blends into its surroundings.

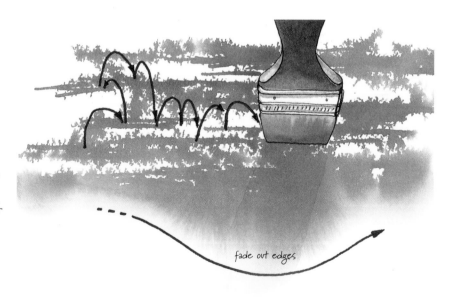

fade out edges

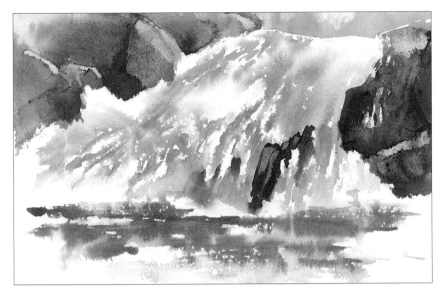

WATERFALLS

In this example the partial wash defined the direction of flow for the water-falls and the pool at the bottom. Once color was added to the partial wash, the edges were softened with a damp hog-hair brush. The rocks were painted when the washes were dry.

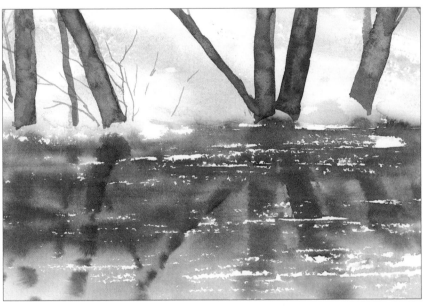

CALM REFLECTIONS

This horizontal example started with a fairly wet partial wash resulting in only a few small dry areas. Notice how you can use more than one color for your water if you have them mixed before you start the partial wash. The edges of the wash area were softened with a damp hog-hair brush. This produced the soft edge of the snow bank at the top. The tree reflections were painted last while the surface was still damp. Care was taken not to paint over dry spots.

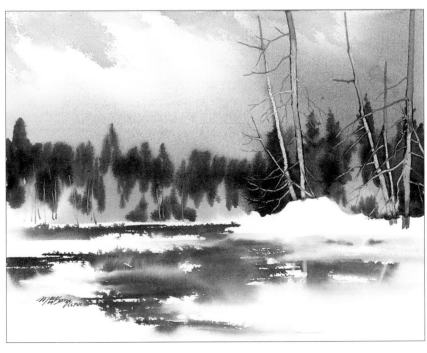

DEPICTING ICE

Here the partial wash captures the transition between ice and open water.

Sea Spray

Active water crashing into land often produces spray. This evidence of energy in nature can add a note of excitement and energy to your pictures.

Here are two ways to create that dramatic effect: one with rough sandpaper and one with masking fluid.

SANDING FOR FINE SPRAY
For this technique you need a dark background against which to contrast the spray. In this case, we will use the sky and dark rocks.

1. Paint the First Wash and Lift the Spray Area

Pant a midvalue-blue wash over your entire paper. While this is still wet, use a damp brush to lift an irregular white area where you want the main body of spray to be. Let dry.

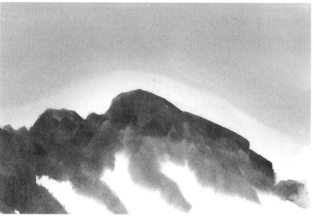

2. Develop the Rocks Around the Spray

Wet only the bottom part of the spray area. When this dries to damp, paint the rocks so that their tops are hard-edged on the dry paper and their bottoms are blurry in the damp area. Use a dark color (Cobalt Blue + Burnt Sienna) to define light fingers of spray in front of the rocks. While the rocks are still damp, scrape with a palette knife for highlights and texture. Let dry.

3. Sand Out the Foam

Use a small piece of coarse sandpaper, a little nerve and a lot of pressure with your thumb to sand from the white foam area out into the darker background.

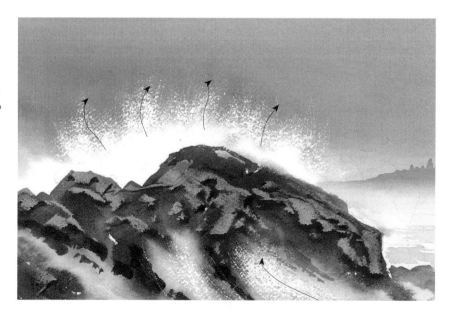

MASKING FOR SPRAY

You can create a fairly intricate scene with crashing water by masking the foaming water part with a sponge and spattering masking fluid with a toothbrush for the finer spray.

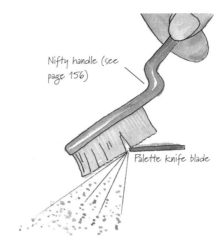

Nifty handle (see page 156)

Palette knife blade

THE KEY TO SPATTERING SUCCESS

The trick to spattering paint or masking fluid with a toothbrush is to push the bristles across the blade of a palette knife that is held horizontally. This prevents big drops from falling off the back of the blade.

1. Sponge On the Heavy Spray

To produce the irregular lacy mark for foaming water and heavy spray, use a torn piece of cellulose sponge to apply the masking fluid. Pour the masking fluid onto a plastic lid to make it easier to get at with your sponge. Moisten your sponge and touch just the face of it to the masking fluid. Gently "print" a lacy pattern on the paper for the spray. This is the end of the road for the sponge, so work quickly to build your pattern of spray.

2. Spatter On the Fine Spray

Touch just the ends of the bristles of your toothbrush into the masking fluid in your lid. Use your thumb or palette knife to spatter masking fluid around the edges of your sponged area. Wash your toothbrush immediately so the masking fluid doesn't dry in the bristles.

3. Add the Water and Background

Paint the water and rocks whatever colors you wish, but try to establish a dark contrast for the spray. Let dry.

4. Remove Masking and Finish

Remove the masking fluid with a rubber cement pickup. Use a small scrub brush and water to soften the bottom edges of the masked areas so they blend into the rest of the water. Apply a few shadows to the foam with pale blue.

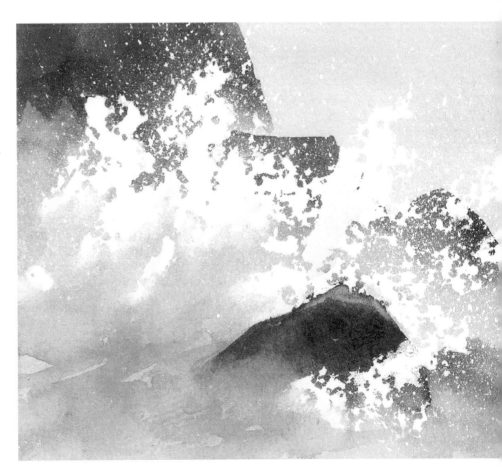

Rapids

Painting rapids or falls is a good example of how we often get better results by painting what the picture *needs* instead of what we actually *see*. Most rapids and waterfalls have a lot of midvalue- and dark-colored water. Add to this the darkness of rocks, sand or silt that it passes through, and you may find your pristine water looking more like a sewage outflow.

To combat this, I use a lot more white and light colors in the water and a wider range of values and temperatures in the environment. We all know that the rougher the water, the foamier it is, so by painting water that is lighter than normal, you'll also be adding some rip-snorting action to your picture.

COLOR NOTE

In this exercise, I used Cobalt Blue for blue, Sap Green for green, Permanent Rose for red, Burnt Sienna for brown, and Raw Sienna for yellow because all of these are nonstaining and fairly transparent.

1. Plan the Flow

Make a thumbnail sketch that indicates an interesting flow through the picture space.

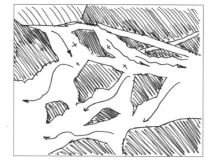

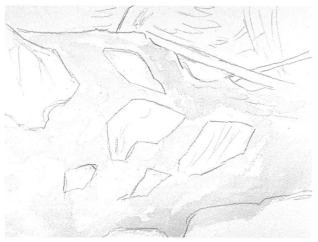

2. First the Water

After lightly sketching your plan onto your paper, you are ready to paint the flow in your stream. Use the side of a 2-inch (51mm) flat hog-hair brush loaded with a pale blue-green-brown mixture. Starting at the top of the rapids, quickly drag the brush (drybrushing) downstream, following the undulations of the flow. Save lots of white paper. This does not take long and immediately sets up the dynamics for your picture. Fade out some of the edges of these lacy marks with a damp brush. Let dry.

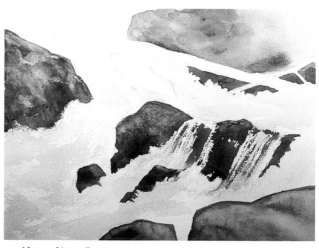

3. Now the Rocks

Paint the surrounding land and rocks to define the water's edge and movement. Start with the area behind the logs with colors that will allow for negative painting of trees and rocks later. Next, paint the rocks with a mixture of brown, red and blue. Paint one rock at a time so that you can focus on how it meets the water and its textures. (Create texture by dropping water into the damp paint.)

Keep the tops of the rocks hard-edged. At the water's edge, they can either be softened with a damp brush or given an irregular hard edge with the side of a bristle brush. Load your bristle brush with rock color and drybrush the water flowing over the central rock. Soften the marks with a few strokes of a damp brush.

4. Background and Turbulence

Negative paint to suggest trees and foliage in the background. Draw tree trunks and branches with a pencil first if you wish.

Define turbulence in the waves and foam with the side of a small hog-hair brush loaded with pale blue-green gray (blue with a touch of brown and green). Fade the top of each mark upward with a damp brush. In the foreground turbulence, add a few holes in the froth.

Paint what can be seen of the distant foliage and sky. Paint the logs a pale blue-yellow mix. Darken under the logs and where they are wet.

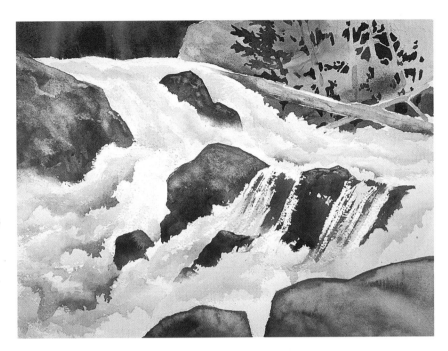

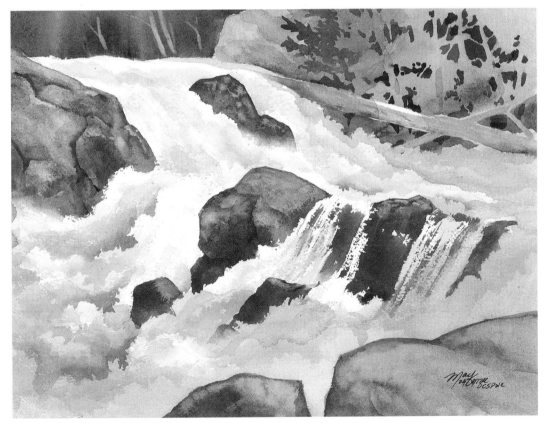

5. Details and Shadows

When completely dry, add detail (cracks, indentations, etc.) to the rocks. The final touch when it is completely dry is to add shadow. Mix a thin blue-gray and quickly glaze it across the lower part of the rapids using your 2-inch (51mm) hog-hair brush. This gives the impression of unseen hills or trees that intimately surround the scene. It also forces the eye to focus on whichever part of the rapids you want the viewer to see, which in this demo happens to be the upper part.

Big Water

If you haven't already done so, I strongly recommend that you practice making wet-in-wet waves with your 2-inch (51mm) flat synthetic brush before starting this painting.

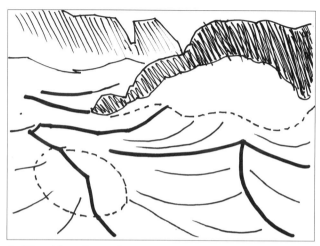

1. Plan Your Layout

Draw lines where you want the tops of the major swells. These lines will serve as a starting point for the direction of minor ridges and valleys. You might also want to indicate where you want to preserve white areas for foam and spray.

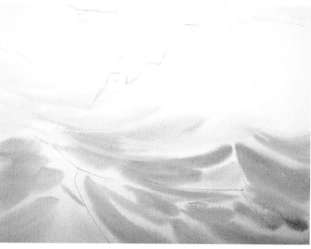

2. Lay In Wet-in-Wet Wave Marks

Wet the entire paper. When it dries to damp, load a large flat synthetic brush with a midvalue blue-green (Phthalo Blue with a touch of Sap Green). Boldly lay in the dominant strokes that flow away from or between your major ridges. Focus on varying the length of the strokes and leaving space between each. Reload your brush and continue with smaller, lighter strokes right into the background. The spaces left between strokes and along the tops of ridges provide soft white lines that define the movement of the waves. Make sure to leave white for areas of crashing waves. Let dry.

3. Paint Where the Land Meets the Water

Across the front of the rocks you will combine flowing colors and drybrushing. Wet the left half of the spray area, being careful not to go beyond the rock shape at the top and left end (refer to outline). Load a flat bristle brush with a dark blue-brown mixture. When the wet area dries to damp, paint the top of the rocks just outside the wet area on the left side. Bleed this color down into the wet area, giving the impression of soft spray. Start at the left, and continue along the rock face until you reach the dry area.

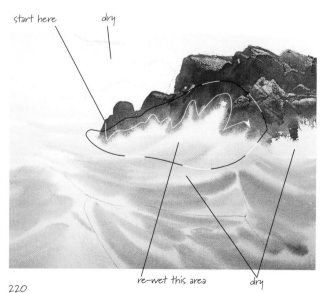

start here   dry

re-wet this area   dry

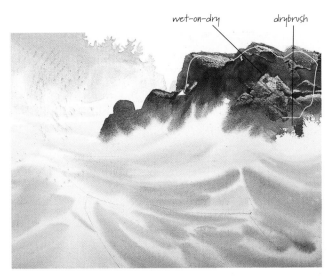

wet-on-dry   drybrush

4. Develop the Rocks and Background

When you reach the dry area on the right, lower your brush and paint an irregular lacy edge with the side of the bristles (drybrushing). Reload if necessary. Return your brush to a vertical position and continue to carry this dark color upward and then back toward the left. Create a hard edge for the top of the rocks. While this is still damp, scrape back some rock faces with your palette knife.

Paint the background land a paler blue-gray (blue plus brown). Make the bottom of this mark irregular. As soon as it is painted, use a damp brush to fade out the bottom edge into the waves or fog.

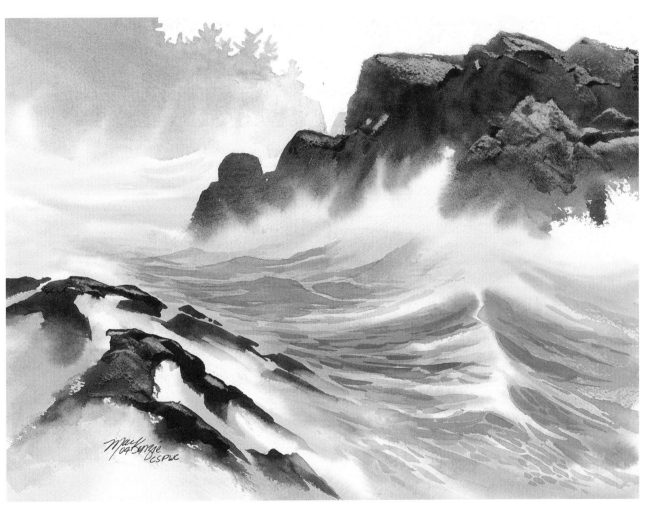

5. Finish With Foreground Detail

Paint the protruding foreground rock wet-on-dry, as if it were fragmented. While it is wet, soften the bottom edges of the fragments with a damp brush. When this dries to damp, scrape out some rock highlights with a palette knife.

To finish, add some darker wet-on-dry wave marks and holes in the froth that follow the swells.

Patterns in the Foam

Active water often produces foam and bubbles that create interesting patterns of movement on its surface. These can be painted one bubble hole at a time; however, the objective here is not to create holes in the ocean but the illusion of lacy ribbons of foam on top.

Practice on sketch paper or the back of an old painting. Use a no. 10 or larger round synthetic brush and a pool of any dark color you want.

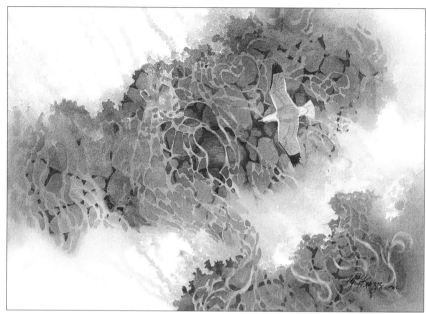

ROCKY BOTTOM
The illusion of floating foam is enhanced when some of the rocks on the bottom are painted in the holes of the foam. Paint some large holes in your foam so that you can do this sort of thing.

SURF RIDER
11" × 14" (28cm × 36cm)

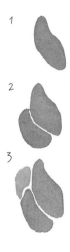
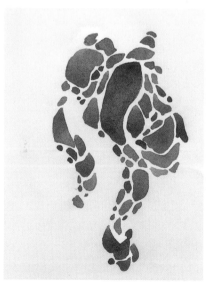
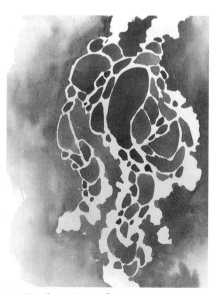

1. Start the Shapes

Paint one large, smooth, irregular shape. Paint a second that fits perfectly against it without touching it. Paint a third of a different size that fits into the first two.

2. Continue Adding Shapes

Add shapes, consciously making them different in size and position and an irregular distance apart until you have created a large cluster of bubble holes. Try to keep the value of the holes about the same.

3. Define the Foam

Make the white lines stand out by painting around the cluster and fading out into the background.

In a finished painting, the background would probably have some color already.

Whitecaps

In this exercise you will use a paper towel rope to lift off color in the shape of whitecaps by pressing it firmly onto the painted surface with both thumbs.

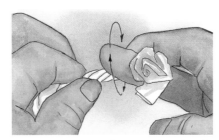

Grab the corner of a paper towel and twist it into a tight rope.

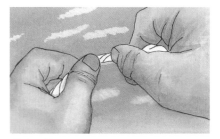

Blot with your paper rope.

1. Paint Background Wash and Blot Whitecaps

Paint a wash that gradates from blue in the distance to blue-green up close. Use nonstaining colors, such as Cobalt Blue or Ultramarine Blue and Sap Green or Raw Sienna. Leave some of the foreground white if you wish to have foam around rocks on the beach.

Quickly twist a paper towel into a tight rope (see diagrams). While the paint is still damp, blot white-caps with the rope, starting in the foreground and working toward the distance. Make your marks larger (by loosening the rope) and farther apart up close, and smaller and closer together in the distance.

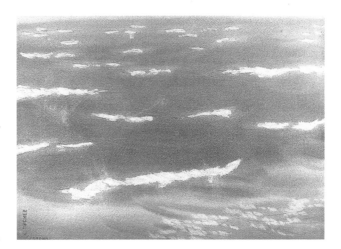

2. Develop With Darks and Shadows

When the painting has dried, lay in darks along the tops of the major waves and under the white-caps. Notice that since a wave usually drops in height as the whitecap forms, it makes sense to paint the part that isn't breaking higher. Fade this dark color down the wave and into the valleys.

Lay in some shadow on the whitecaps as well. To indicate movement between the waves, use drybrushing or a flat synthetic stroke brush loaded with a darker color to make smaller wave patterns. Add water texture (dry-brushing) around the beach area and paint any rocks desired.

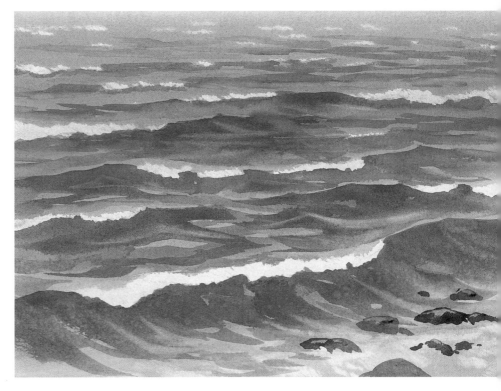

Capping and Breaking Waves

WHITECAPS

Rows of whitecaps can be masked out using a sponge and masking fluid (next page), but in these exercises you will paint around them using a hog-hair brush. Cobalt Blue and Sap Green were used because of their nonstaining transparency.

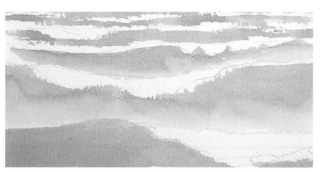

1. Save the White Caps

Start by painting around the bottom of a foreground white cap using a well-loaded hog-hair brush. Carry this color to the left and right to finish the top edge of the wave. Since waves decrease in height when they break, make the rest of the wave slightly higher. Carry color downward until you get to the foam of spent waves in front. Define the waves farther and farther back by repeating this process but stopping at the top of the wave in front. Don't forget to decrease the size and spacing of distant waves.

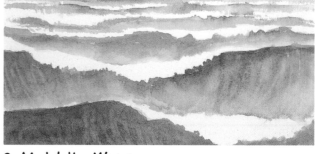

2. Model the Waves

Darken underneath the whitecap with more concentrated wave color. Fade downward into the trough. While this is damp, water can be painted on the foreground wave slopes in lines to help suggest the contour of the wave and valleys. After all is dry, add shadow to the foam.

BREAKING WAVES

Big waves often roll or break after they have capped.

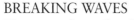

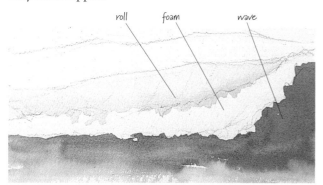

1. Save Room for the Roll

Make a sketch showing room above the foam for a roll in the wave. Paint the wave a darker blue-green at the top and underneath the foam, fading downward into the trough. Paint the roll area pale blue.

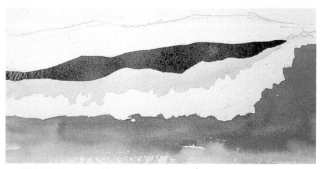

2. Paint the Roll

Paint the top area of the roll a solid dark blue-gray. Go immediately to step 3 on the following page.

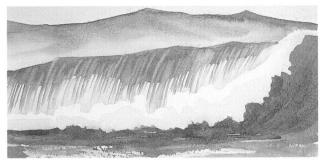

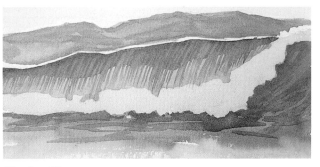

3. Paint the Lines on the Roll

Make curved lines with a small, damp, flat synthetic brush. Start the stroke in the dark area and draw it down into the light part. Stop the line where you want the top of the foam to start. Clean your brush as needed. Repeat this over and over along the length of the roll.

Drybrush a pale blue-gray texture onto the foam area. Darken it around the bottom edges.

Option One

If you want your waves to have front or overhead lighting, then continue by putting in background waves that are dark near the top and fade into the valley so that it contrasts the breaking wave.

Option Two

It is not unusual when the sun is low in the sky to see light coming through tall waves. I call this split-second treat the "jewel" of the wave. If you wish to include this illusion of transparency, you must do three things:

1. Paint the wave in the background dark but leave a small space between it and the top of the roll. This will look like sun bouncing off the edge.
2. Paint a pale green over the roll area. Darken this toward the ends.
3. Add more blue shadow to the foam section since it will be out of the sun.

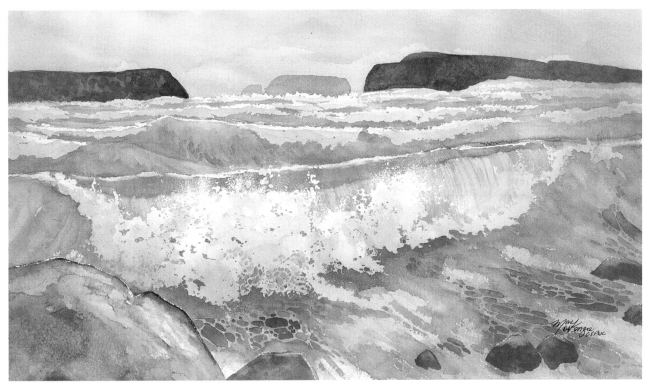

MASKING FLUID TECHNIQUE
Here is an example of waves capping and breaking where the foam was saved with masking fluid that was applied with a sponge.

SUPERIOR, NORTH SHORE
11" x 19" (28cm x 48cm)

Seeing Into Water

Painting the illusion that you are seeing into water is a lot like looking through a Venetian blind. Imagine that the surface of the water is just such a blind—painted blue to reflect the sky. When ripples form on the water, it's like opening the blind. Suddenly, you can see the blind as well as the world beyond through the slits.

This is a wonderful example of the principle of closure, where the viewer perceives whole objects though only a part is shown. Good fun!

COLOR NOTE

In this exercise, I used Cobalt Blue for blue, Sap Green for green, Permanent Rose for red, Burnt Sienna for brown and Raw Sienna for yellow. These are all nonstaining and fairly transparent.

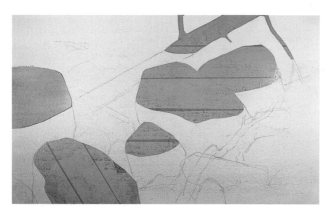

1. Mask the Rocks and Paint the Reflected Sky

Use packing tape to preserve objects so you can paint the water freely. Notice that because we are looking down on the objects, you can see the front curves of the rocks as they enter the water.

After the tape that masks the shapes has been pressed down firmly, paint a graded wash from dark blue in the foreground to light blue in the background. This represents a reflection of the sky. Worry about other reflections on the water's surface later. Let dry.

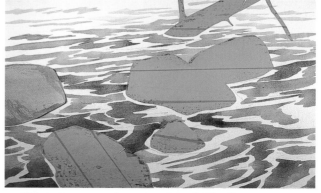

2. Paint the Openings in Your "Blind"

Mix a midvalue, warm greenish brown to represent the color of the water and the bottom that you are able to see through the water. Use a 1-inch (25mm) to 2-inch (51mm) synthetic flat to paint freeflowing and broken zigzags. Try to make them follow the edges of the protruding objects and key into each other. Make more big dark shapes in the foreground and gradually make them smaller and fewer as you work up the paper. For realism, soften the edges of some of these dark marks as you go with a damp brush. Let dry.

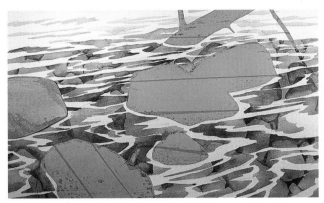

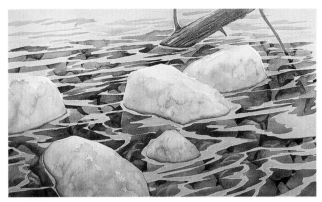

3. Paint the World Below

Now create the scene beyond the blind. Draw in natural extensions of the protruding objects, but only in the green areas. Take advantage of the dark marks to show the edges and junctures of more rocks and sunken treasures.

Working only in the green areas, define the visible edges of underwater rocks by painting an even darker greenish brown mixture around them. Intersections of edges and corners are important. Fade out the marks to make some edges stand out. Work slowly. Keep in mind that, due to lighting, a rock is sometimes painted darker than its background.

4. Add Finishing Touches

Remove the tape from the rocks and log. To paint the rocks, first wet them and then drop in pale yellow, brown, red and blue. Let these colors intermingle. When they get to the damp stage, add drops of water for texture. When this dries, paint a dark line with the same colors along the rocks' (and tree's) juncture with the water. Fade this upward.

To make the blue marks more interesting, paint slightly darker blue marks inside them. With a small scrub brush, lift some highlights from the tops of the underwater rocks.

WET-INTO-WET OPTION
This is an example of what you get if you paint the dark greenish brown marks on the blue reflected-sky background while it's still wet. Everything else is done the same way.

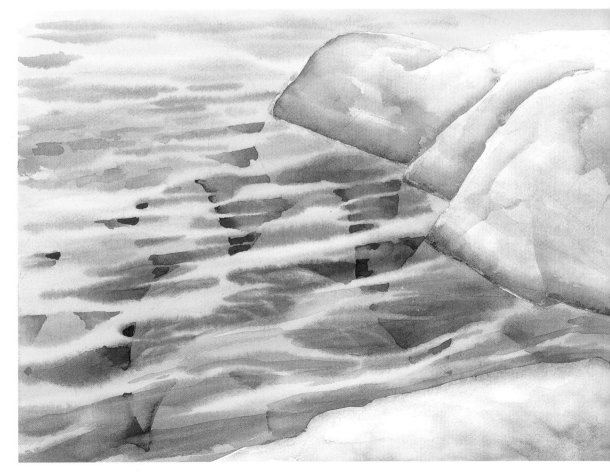

Painting Underwater

No, you don't have to hold your breath for this one, but the results can be breathtaking.

The underwater world is one of phenomenal beauty and one often ignored by painters. There is intrigue, mystery, even fear of what lies beyond our limited vision in this watery world. In fact, it is that unique shallow depth-of-field that characterizes the illusion of being underwater. Only things in the foreground are in sharp focus. The rest are silhouetted and blurry. For painters, that means lots of wet-in-wet painting.

In this world it is common to see shafts of light passing through and striking the upper surfaces of things below. Sometimes underwater structures are darker than their background, sometimes lighter. Regardless, the difference in value between them becomes less and less the further away the structures are.

Color variety is not a big thing underwater. Brightly colored objects are limited to the immediate foreground. Most of your picture will be painted in monochromatic color or analogous mixtures of blues, greens and browns. What is more important than color variety is color value and temperature. Generally objects will be warm and light up close, and cool off and darken in the distance. Water will be lighter near the surface than in the depths.

There is no such thing as one way to paint underwater any more than there is one way to paint above it. This exercise is a generalization of techniques that will help you jump in.

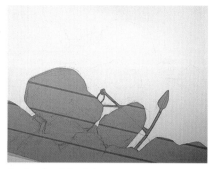

1. Apply Masking

Use packing tape or masking fluid to save foreground shapes that you want to have hard-edged or lighter.

COLOR NOTE

All colors used are transparent. Sap Green, Raw Sienna and Burnt Sienna are non-staining (therefore lift easily), while Phthalo Blue leaves an pale blue after-image because it stains.

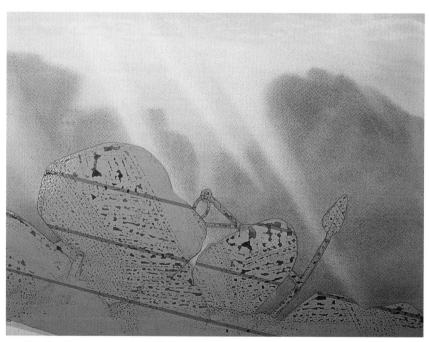

2. Begin Background Colors and Shapes

Wet the entire paper. Paint a graded blue wash from dark along the bottom to pale along the top. Immediately use a twisted paper towel to lift off a few light wave lines from the underneath side of the surface above.

While still wet, use a large, flat hog-hair brush loaded with a darker version of the background color to add a few background shapes. Start at the top of the shape and work the color downward until it blends with the background color.

While the paint is still wet, use a large, damp hog-hair brush to lift off the suggestion of a few parallel shafts of sunlight. Start at the top and pull downward. Clean your brush for each stroke and make sure that it is just damp. Don't get carried away. Let dry.

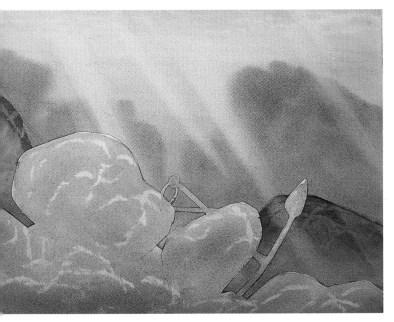

3. Paint Middle-Ground and Foreground Rocks

Paint some middle-ground rocks using a bluish green (Phthalo Blue + Sap Green). Start painting at the top of the rock and then fade downward. Lift off some curved ripple lines with a twisted paper towel. Remove any shafts of light that you want to pass in front of this rock. Let dry.

Remove the masking material, then carefully wet the entire masked area. This will prevent hard edges from forming when you apply a pale brownish green (Burnt Sienna + Raw Sienna + Sap Green) to the entire rock and anchor area.

While still wet, remove light curved and criss-crossing ripple lines from the tops of the rocks with a twisted paper towel. Let dry.

4. Model the Rocks and Add Details

Model the rocks by using a darker version of the three colors used to paint them. Start by darkening the cracks and holes between them and then fading this color upward onto the rocks. Try to avoid covering your ripple lines. When this dries, add Phthalo Blue to the mix and use this to define the darkest shapes and holes between the rocks and the anchor.

Optional Fish
Cut several tiny willow-leaf-shaped holes in a piece of thin acetate. Using your scrub brush and water, lift some of these shapes at random spacing so that they create a flowing pattern. When dry, add a few darker shapes amongst them for fish in the shadows.

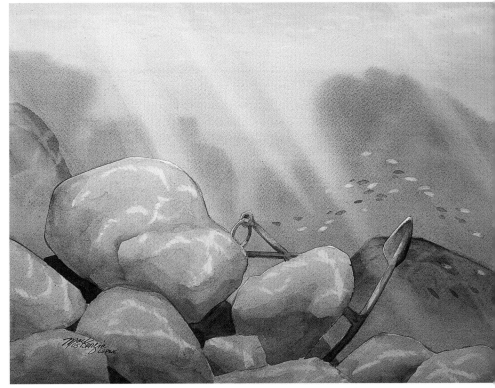

HOOKED IN THE PAST
11" × 14" (28cm × 36cm)

229

Painting Skies

Look up. There are grand atmospherics being staged overhead. The sky is the environmental background for your picture, and as such does much to create the desired mood and drama in your work. Be aware of the unlimited range of choices you have when you make the sky a major player in your picture.

Skies do not normally take a long time to paint. Don't feel guilty and think you have to hang around poking at it for a while. Generally, skies are no place to dilly-dally. Get in, get the paint down and get out. If you want to add more paint, wait for it to dry.

It's important that you use large brushes that can deliver a lot of paint in a hurry with the fewest brushstrokes. It's also useful to have your colors already mixed on the palette so that you don't have to hunt for them during the painting process.

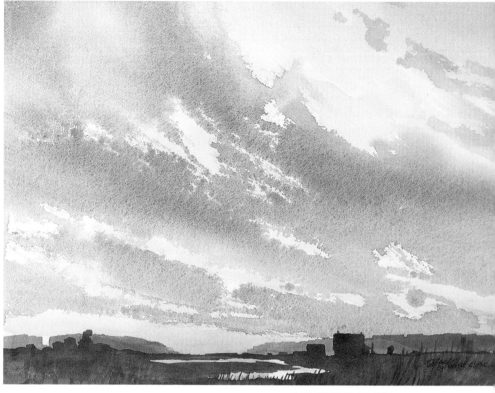

BAR RIVER FLATS
11" × 14" (28cm × 36cm)

MATERIALS USED FOR SKY EXERCISES

Surface
- 140-lb. (300gsm) cold-press paper, mostly 11" × 14" (28cm × 36cm)
- Rigid board for mounting paper

Paints
- Burnt Sienna
- Cobalt Blue
- Indian Yellow
- Indigo
- Lemon Yellow
- Permanent Rose
- Phthalo Blue
- Phthalo Green
- Raw Sienna
- Sap Green
- Sepia
- Ultramarine Blue

Brushes
- ¾-inch (19mm) or 1-inch (25mm) synthetic flat
- 1½-inch (38mm) to 2-inch (51mm) synthetic flat
- ¾-inch (19mm) or 1-inch (25mm) hog-hair bristle
- 1½-inch (38mm) to 2-inch (51mm) hog-hair bristle
- Assorted rounds (synthetic or synthetic/natural mix), nos. 8 to 14

Miscellaneous
- block sponge
- packing tape
- razor knife
- paper towels
- water-filled spray bottle
- small piece of coarse sandpaper

Wet-in-Wet Skies

To make these skies, let paint flow and mingle freely on the wet surface. This works best if you have your colors mixed in pools before you wet the paper. Tilting the surface also gets things moving, but tilting in too many directions will blend everything together and lead to muddy results. *Note:* If you wish to have water or land in your scene, save the hard edge with tape.

TIP

To wet your paper quickly and evenly, use a very wet block sponge. The next best option is a large natural-fiber brush such as hog, badger or goat. Avoid using a synthetic brush because it doesn't carry as much and tends to drop it all in one place.

MOTTLED WET-IN-WET
For the shadows of clouds, paint a mixture of Cobalt Blue + Burnt Sienna onto a wet background. Lay in the color in blotches using a well-loaded, large hog-hair brush. Leave white spaces between your blotches. Notice that a suggested diagonal movement made with brush marks and tilting adds energy to the sky at no extra cost. This process does not take long.

WET-ON-DAMP SKY HOLES
Start as you did for a mottled wet-in-wet sky, but when it gets to the damp stage, quickly paint a few blue sky holes in the white areas. Notice that they are larger near the top of the paper and diminish in size and darkness near the horizon.

WET-ON-DRY SKY HOLES
Start as mottled wet-in-wet, but let it dry before painting the sky holes in the white areas. Create irregular shapes by using the side of a large hog-hair brush well-loaded with blue paint. Soften a few edges as you go with another damp hog-hair brush. Lighten the blue near the horizon.

WET-IN-WET DRAMA

To achieve dramatic contrast, keep the clouds dark along a light horizon. Wet the sky area and brush on juicy, pure strokes of Cobalt Blue, Permanent Rose and Raw Sienna. Let these colors mix on the paper to produce grays in some areas. Use a large brush so that you can move quickly with bold strokes that suggest upward movement in the clouds. While this is still very wet, tilt your board and, using a small brush, carry the sky color down to create the treetops of the distant shore by painting the spaces between them. Blot with a rolled paper towel to create rays of sunlight in the sky. Sponge on the dark foreground trees after the sky is dry.

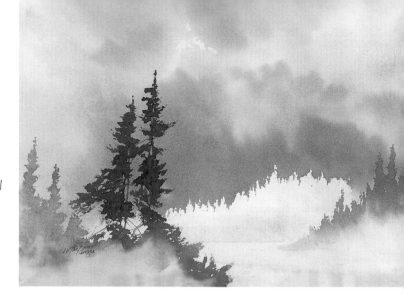

WET-IN-DAMP MOONLIT NIGHT

This uses the same wet-on-damp technique from the previous page except that the colors are darker and a moon is added.

Save the moon first (see diagram). Wet the paper and brush on patches of dark gray for the cloud shadows. While this is still wet, paint the dark sky color (Indigo + Cobalt Blue or Ultramarine Blue) using a well-loaded hog-hair brush. Place this dark color in the white areas between the cloud shadows, particularly around the moon. This color will flow toward the gray but leave a halo of white around the clouds. When the sky is dry, glaze a wash of blue-gray over the entire clouds that are farthest from the moon. Fade out the glazing as you approach the moon. This leaves the greatest contrast around the moon.

In this example, the sky color is also used for the water. Sparkles were made by sanding the water when it was completely dry (see diagram). The darker land is a mixture of Indigo and Sepia. Remove the masking from the moon and, if you wish, pick out a few stars with the tip of a razor knife.

SANDING FOR WATER SPARKLES

This isn't a sky technique, but you may wonder how the water sparkles were created in the painting above. Using a ruler as a horizontal guide, press down hard on a small piece of coarse, folded sandpaper positioned against the ruler. Drag it quickly along the ruler to create your sparkles. It may take several swipes to remove enough paper. Work your way down the paper. Use a soft eraser to clean the area.

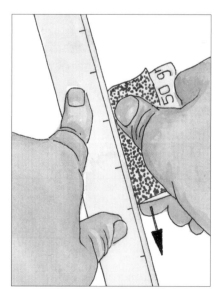

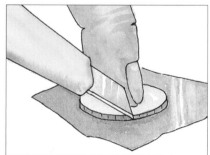

SAVING THE MOON

Place a coin over a small piece of packing tape where you want your moon to be. Gently cut around the coin with a razor knife. Remove the coin and excess tape, and press the moon shape firmly.

Making Cloud Bottoms by Fading Out

When heavy clouds roll in, they're often so thick that all you see are their bottom sides.

1. Paint the Cloud Bottoms

Mix a gray from Cobalt Blue + Raw Sienna. This gray can be cooled with more blue or warmed with more brown. Make an irregular mark across your paper to represent the bottom of a distant cloud. Fade this upward with another damp brush. Let dry.

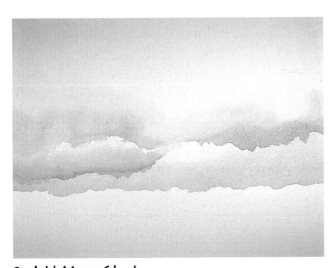

2. Add More Clouds

Repeat the process in step 1 with more clouds, letting them dry between applications. Vary the width and length of each cloud mark.

3. And a Few More

As you work your way up the sky, the clouds should normally become larger, warmer and darker. Their edges also become more irregular. Let dry.

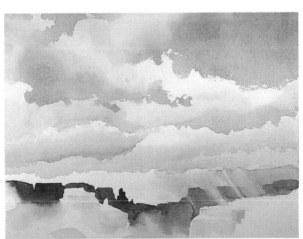

4. Add Sky Holes

Some pure blue sky will make a good contrast against all the grays. Try some if you'd like. The sky under the clouds will probably be a warm white (pale Raw Sienna).

Rain

If you want distant rain falling, paint some of the sky underneath the clouds a dark, cool gray. Fade this out along the horizon and, while wet, lift out some streaks with a damp brush. When this dries, paint the land so that it fades out into the rain cloud.

233

Making Billowy Clouds

Here are two techniques for painting billowy clouds. If you look at the clouds in the photo, you will notice that in some places the billows are light against a darker background and, in others, dark against a lighter background. Each is painted in its own way.

LIGHT BILLOWS AGAINST A DARKER BACKGROUND

These types of clouds will give you plenty of practice fading out color. It's also the rare occasion when you will be doing a lot of brushwork in the sky. The challenge is to make it look as if you hadn't.

Sooner or later you are going to realize that you are doing the same thing over and over again. This is the same process used to paint the bottoms of clouds on the previous page. The only difference is how you look at it. Now, the bottom edge of the dark mark defines the top of a light billowy cloud below it.

The gray used for the cloud shadows is a very pale mixture of Cobalt Blue + Burnt Sienna or Raw Sienna.

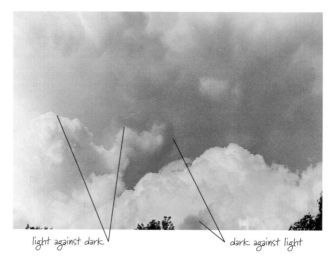

CLOUDS LIGHT AND DARK
Sometimes clouds are light against a dark background, and sometimes vice versa.

light against dark   dark against light

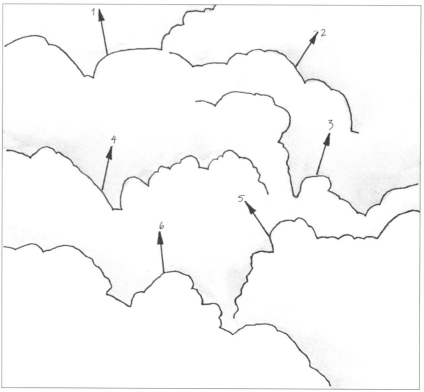

THINKING THROUGH THE PROCESS
Start with the billows at the top of the cloud mass and work your way down. Don't try to plan where each billow will go; place them where they feel right. Focus on making the bottom edge of your mark as irregular and interesting as possible because it will become the top of another cloud. Try to make a conscious effort to vary the length, width and position of the marks and the distance between them. If your sky looks like a squadron of flying snakes, you don't have enough variety and you are not likely fading out each mark appropriately.

You will notice as you work your way down the paper that one mark will often fade upward and partially obscure the mark above. That's okay; it adds to the realism and variety. Give the impression that your clouds continue right off the paper instead of trying to neatly contain them within the picture plane.

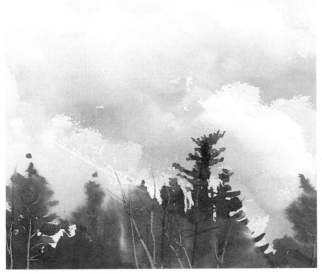

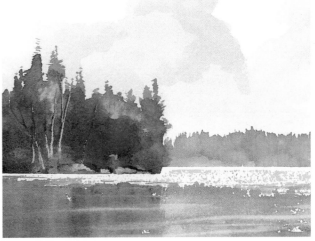

HEIGHTEN THE DRAMA
Extra drama and contrast can be created by using darker gray on some of the bottom clouds. A touch of blue sky defines the top of the cloud mass, while dark trees put everything in perspective.

ADDING SHADOWED CLOUDS ON THE HORIZON
Paint light, billowy clouds as before, but leave a light area near the bottom of the sky. When this is dry, paint the silhouette of shadowed clouds on the horizon with the same blue-gray used for the first part. When this dries, add billows to these clouds with more blue-gray.

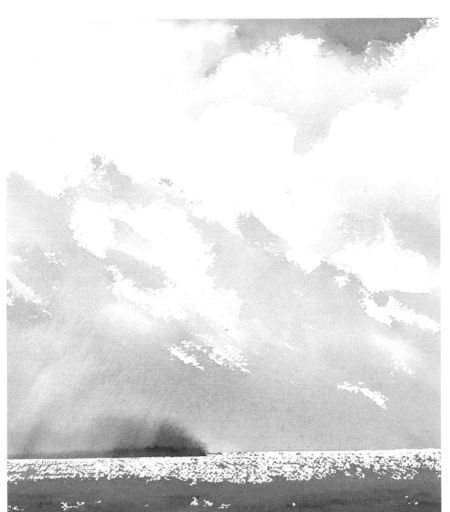

A STORM-FRONT VARIATION
Instead of adding more billowy clouds along the horizon, you could add a storm front. To do this, sweep in a dark layer of blue-gray clouds from the horizon up. Use the side of a large, well-loaded hog-hair brush.

To add to the illusion of an approaching rainstorm, paint some dark land or hills while the darker gray clouds are damp. Immediately use a damp hog-hair brush to lift falling rain marks from the clouds and land by stroking from the horizon up.

DARK BILLOWS AGAINST A LIGHTER BACKGROUND

Unlike the toplit clouds where entire billows are created one at a time, the billows on these front-lit clouds are painted one *cloud* at a time. Your picture will likely have more than one cloud, and each is treated separately.

Again, the grays used for the cloud shadows are made with a very pale mixture of Cobalt Blue + Burnt Sienna or Raw Sienna. The process seems to work best with a synthetic round brush no. 12 or larger.

1. Prepare the Cloud

Thoroughly wet the shape of a single cloud. Drop paint along the outer edges of the wet area using a no. 12 synthetic round loaded with a concentrated blue-gray. The color will diffuse into the wet area, leaving a dark, hard edge to the cloud. Vary the width of this shadow area by dropping more paint in some areas than in others.

2. Leapfrogging Magic

Continue painting with the same brush without reloading it. Start picking up paint from the dark edges and carry it in toward the white, wet center of the cloud using continuous leapfrog-type strokes. These marks that mimic the edges of cloud billows produce tiny, soft, subtle billows on the face of your cloud. The front-lit illusion is strengthened when your paint gets lighter and lighter as your brush runs out of pigment toward the center of the cloud.

As an option, try placing a drop of clean water in the light billow centers when the paint dries to the damp stage. This can create some interesting backruns and feathered edges in your clouds. Don't worry about the bottom of the cloud at this point.

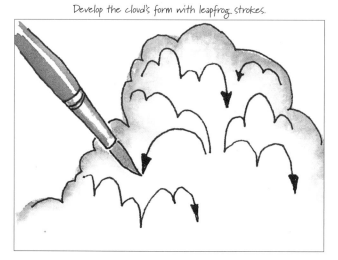

Develop the cloud's form with leapfrog strokes.

What the result looks like

3. Add More Clouds, Background Sky and Cloud Bottoms

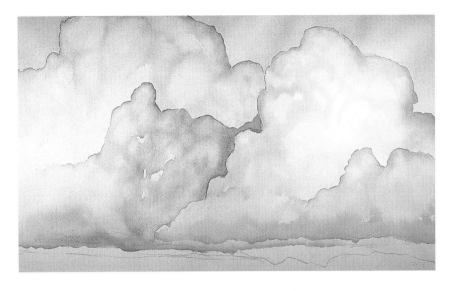

Add More Clouds

Paint more clouds using the procedure from steps 1 and 2. You will find it easier to work from foreground clouds to background clouds. I intentionally warmed up the background clouds just to show you that the temperature of these clouds can vary. This is particularly true of the clouds are bathed in the warm accent light of evening or morning.

Add Background Sky

If you wish to have an even color for the sky, first wet the entire sky area and then add concentrated color with a 2-inch (51mm) flat synthetic or hog-hair brush. Carefully paint to the edge of the clouds. Tilting helps distribute color evenly.

If you wish to have cirrus clouds high in the background, paint the sky as if it were solid blue and then invert, tilt and spray it with water in a couple of areas near the top of the clouds. The paint will flow off the paper, leaving the light streaks of cirrus clouds in the background.

Add Cloud Bottoms If Desired

It is not always necessary to show the bottoms of the clouds. For example, if you want a dramatic storm on the horizon, paint your hills and trees where the bottoms would be.

If you do want bottoms on your clouds, paint them the same as the tops by first wetting the area, dropping paint along the edge and working it upward. The only difference is that the bottoms are flatter. Clouds in the background will have bottoms that are lower in the sky than the foreground clouds.

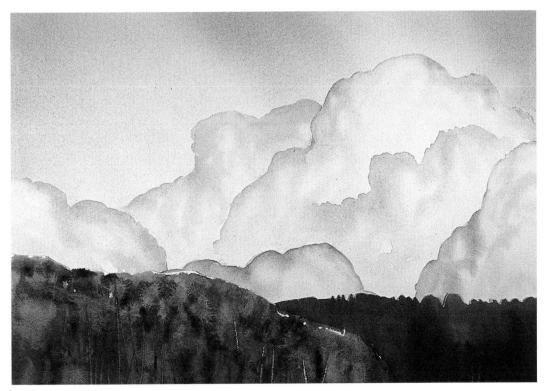

A DISAPPEARING ACT
Land can obscure the bottoms of clouds.

Graded Washes

A graded wash makes a great sky on its own or is the start for many others. The trick to smooth color gradation, if that's what you want, is to tilt your board so that gravity and the water can do the work. As usual, work quickly with a large brush, and make strokes that go right off the paper.

1. Start With a Graded Sky

Every sunrise or sunset is different. About the only consistent feature is the gradation from cool color to warm as you approach the sun. In this exercise, gradate the pale background wash from Cobalt Blue at the top to Permanent Rose, then to Indian Yellow.

2. Add Graded Clouds

Gradate the clouds cool to warm, but make them duller and darker than the sky. Mix all three sky colors to make a mauve-like gray. Use this for the top clouds. Gradually work your way down, adding more clouds. As you go, first pull more red into the gray mixture, then more yellow. For a smoother gradation, don't clean your brush each time you add a color. For more realism (thanks to the pollution level), darken the horizon area with more dulled mauve.

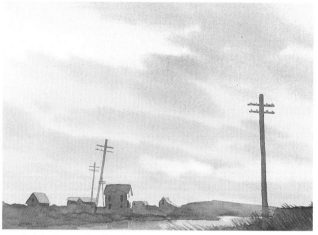

3. Add the Final Touches

While still damp, paint a few strokes of pale Lemon Yellow in the sun area and for highlights under the clouds. The contrast of adding dark land will make the sky seem brighter.

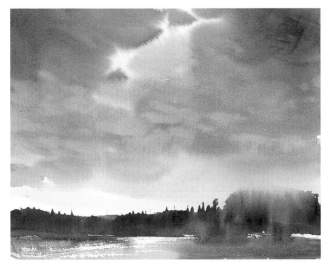

GRADED CLOUDS ON A TONED BACKGROUND

Wet the sky area. Add Raw Sienna near the horizon and fade this out upward to just clean water at the top. While this is still wet, use a large, flat hog-hair brush loaded with concentrated, dark blue-gray (Cobalt Blue + Burnt Sienna) to brush on the clouds. Gradate from large, dark strokes at the top to smaller, paler strokes near the bottom. (This happens naturally as you run out of paint.) Leave some of the pale yellow sky showing.

When this dries to damp, highlight the open sky and undersides of the clouds by touching them with the corner of a hog-hair brush loaded with pale yellow-orange (Indian Yellow + Permanent Rose). Land can be added now or later for contrast by using dark, concentrated sky colors.

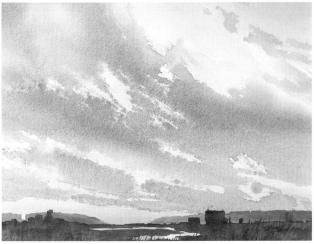

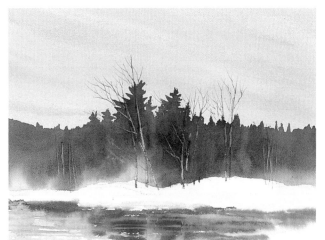

DRYBRUSHING OVER A WASH

Paint a pale graded wash from Raw Sienna at the horizon to Cobalt Blue at the top. Add a hint of mauve (Permanent Rose + Cobalt Blue) near the horizon. Let dry.

Mix two puddles of gray using Cobalt Blue + Raw Sienna: one a bluish (cool) gray, the other a brownish (warm) gray. Load a large hog-hair brush with either one and repeatedly drag it on its side across the sky to create a bold, lacy pattern. Following a sweeping diagonal will add dynamics to your picture.

Immediately pick up some of the other gray and repeat so that the grays blend here and there. Softening edges with another damp brush will add realism. Painting distant hills a blue or mauve before doing the foreground will add depth to your scene.

HOT-IN-COLD WASH

Instead of doing a progression of colors for a background wash, start by giving your sky a consistent wash of midvalue Cobalt Blue. Immediately reload your brush with any yellows, pinks and oranges and stroke this across the blue. It will push the blue aside and take on a wonderful glow.

For the sake of harmony, use dark, concentrated sky colors for the land and reflections.

Lifting Paint

Sometimes removing paint from a
picture is the best way to achieve
results. In both examples below, a
rolled paper towel was used.

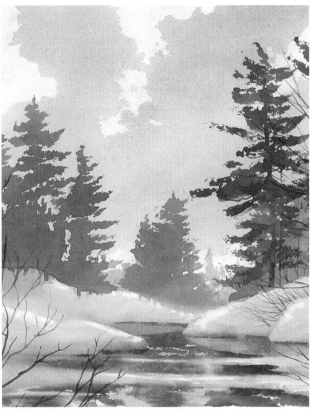

LIFTING COLOR FROM A GRADED WASH

These are the clouds caught in the glow of early evening
or morning before the sun is in the sky. Use nonstaining
colors (Cobalt Blue, Raw Sienna, Permanent Rose) to paint
a graded wash from cool blue above to warm hues near the
horizon. Immediately create holes between clouds by blotting
with a rolled paper towel. To take off big areas, roll the
towel across the surface. Work quickly and reposition your
towel continually so that a clean portion is always being used.
The light holes should have a slight blue cast.

In case you didn't realize, this is negative painting, except
you are removing paint instead of adding it.

Trees were painted with Phthalo Green and Burnt
Sienna using a torn piece of cellulose sponge.

LIFTING SILVER LININGS

Start with a loose, mottled wet-in-wet background using
Cobalt Blue with a hint of Raw Sienna. (Any nonstaining colors will work.) While this is still wet, remove paint in
an irregular line by blotting with a twisted paper towel.
The light shape represents the light breaking through the
clouds, or the clouds' "silver linings." To improve the illusion,
darken the clouds that are silhouetting some of the edges
of this light patch. The darker you make these edges, the
brighter the light patch will appear. In other areas of the
blotted shapes, blend the edges into the surrounding clouds.

Lifting Color for Northern Lights

It is possible to capture the gossamer nature of northern or southern lights by lifting paint with a flat synthetic brush.

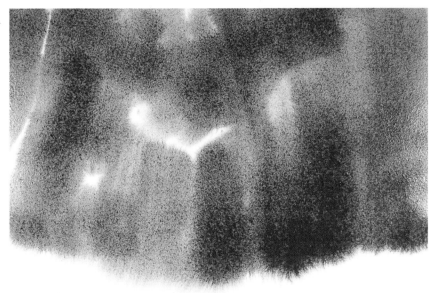

1. Prepare the Background

Start by mixing a large batch of very dark color (e.g., Indigo + any blue or Permanent Rose + Phthalo Blue and Sap Green).

Since you may need extra time to work on this exercise, I suggest working on a waterproof surface and wetting both sides of your paper. Don't bother taping it down since the water will make it adhere it to the surface.

Apply your color liberally to your paper using a large hog-hair brush. Leave narrow, curved light areas between strokes.

2. Lift for the Lights

While still moist, use a large, damp synthetic brush to extend the light areas upward. The trick is to hold your brush on the light band for a couple of seconds before dragging it up ward. This allows the brush to pick up more color at the start which produces a light bottom on the band. Repeat this process of lifting color with vertical strokes as you work along the light band. Keep your brush clean and damp. While the sky dries, pick out some stars with the tip of a razor knife. Paint the tops of the hills and trees and fade these downward into the night.

Variation: Try this on a piece of paper that has been toned pale yellow-green and let dry.

241

Spraying and Tilting

Here's a quick, fun way to create a dynamic background for a sky. This process does not take long; you must move quickly and avoid overworking. The key to success is how you spray and the type of spray bottle you use.

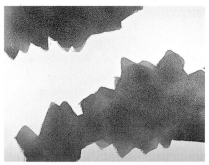

SETTING THE STAGE
With a big, well-loaded brush, put down a heavy mass of dark paint along the top or bottom or across the middle of the sky. Leave at least 50 percent white.

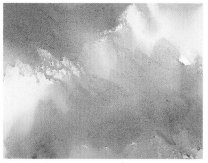

SPRAYING AND TILTING
Apply a coarse spray of water along the edges of the dark areas. Tilt the paper to direct the flow back and forth. Try to maintain the same direction of flow. Spray more as necessary to keep things moving. Stop while you still have lacy patterns trailing across white paper. Lay it flat to dry.

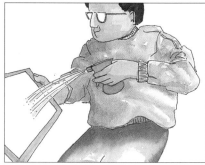

SPRAYING NOTE
To get a coarse spray, go lightly on the trigger and keep your distance. Pretend that you are making it rain on the paper. Do not use a small atomizer for this job.

DROP IN A "LAND-SHAPE"
This is a great example of how almost anything will do for a sky. Here I dropped a lake scene "land-shape" in front of it. A land-shape is the land portion cut from an old picture. In sky workshops I keep a few on hand so that students can instantly see how great their skies really are once they are shown as the atmospheric backdrop they are intended to be. Make some of your own.

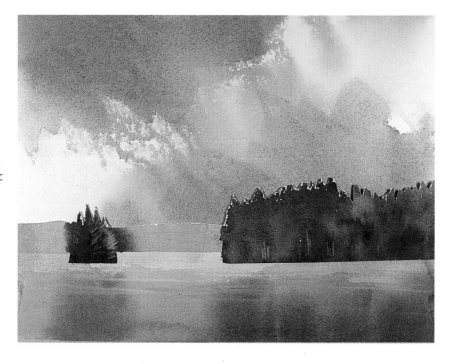

Dropping Water or Paint

These are some of the simplest skies to paint. Start by wetting the sky area and laying in a graded wash with a nonstaining color.

When the surface starts to lose its shine, load a large brush with water or paint and let it drip off the brush onto the paper. The water will expand on the wet surface to resemble closely packed clouds, producing a wonderful mottled sky.

For the sake of perspective, try to make the drops at the top of the sky big and the ones near the bottom small.

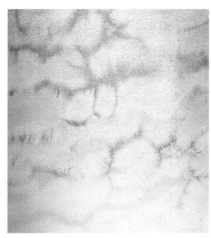

DROPPING WATER ON COLOR
The background for this sky was a graded wash of Cobalt Blue to Raw Sienna. While the wash was still damp, I dropped in water to create the cloud effect.

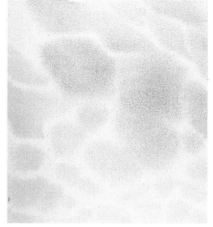

DROPPING COLOR ON WATER
When the clouds are in front of the sun, they appear darker than the sky. I wet the entire surface, then loaded a large brush with a pale gray and dropped in color by just touching the brush to the wet surface. The drops of color expand but leave a light line between each one.

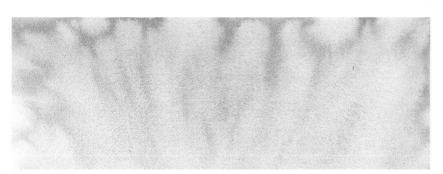

DROPPING AND TILTING
Here, I laid the drops of water in vertical rows. Tilting the paper flowed them together in streaks

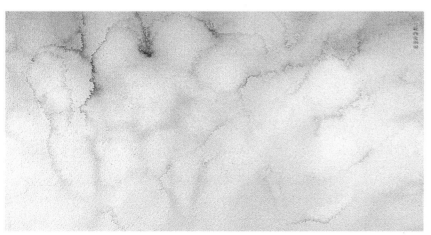

REPEATEDLY DROPPING WATER
Here, I repeated the process of dropping water into the paint several times. Each time I waited until the paint dried to the damp stage before adding more drops of water.

Painting the Land

The land is the host and humans merely guests.

—Chinese proverb

This part of the chapter examines various aspects involved in painting the land. It is your job to take the examples used here and, if necessary, modify them to suit your corner of the world. After all, you are the best authority. But first look here for the underlying lessons in procedure or technique that may help you see and capture your own unique view of our natural host.

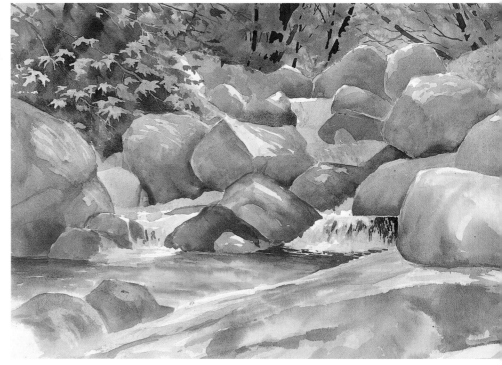

WATER MUSIC
15" × 22" (38cm × 56cm)

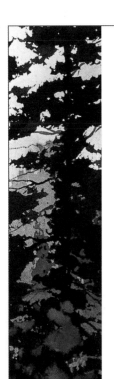

MATERIALS USED FOR LAND EXERCISES

Surface
- 140-lb. (300gsm) cold-press paper, mostly 11" × 14" (28cm × 36cm)
- Rigid board for mounting paper

Paints
- Burnt Sienna
- Cadmium Orange
- Cadmium Red Light
- Cerulean Blue
- Cobalt Blue
- Indian Yellow
- Indigo
- Lemon Yellow
- Permanent Rose
- Phthalo Blue
- Phthalo Green
- Raw Sienna
- Sap Green
- Sepia

Brushes
- ¾-inch (19mm) or 1-inch (25mm) synthetic flat
- 1½-inch (38mm) to 2-inch (51mm) synthetic flat
- ¾-inch (19mm) or 1-inch (25mm) hog-hair bristle
- 1½-inch (38mm) or 2-inch (51mm) hog-hair bristle
- Assorted rounds (synthetic or synthetic/natural mix), nos. 8 to 14
- Any size rigger or script liner
- Small scrub brush (To make one, see page 156.)

Miscellaneous
- vinyl glove
- razor blade
- stiff palette knife
- razor knife
- cellulose sponge
- water-filled spray bottle
- thin sheet of acetate
- pencil
- eraser
- masking fluid
- rubber cement pickup
- toothbrush
- packing tape
- paper towels
- scrap paper

Rocks

There are a few ways to handle this common landscape feature. In most examples, the rock area is textured or patterned in some way and then cracks and modeling are applied.

FIST AND SCRAPE
This technique that works for tree trunks works even better on rocks.

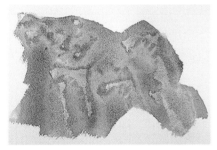

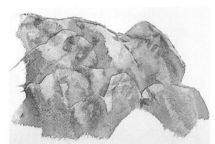

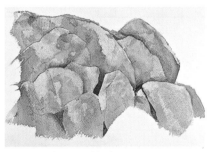

1. Get Right Into the Paint

Paint the rock mass a medium-to-dark gray. Immediately push the edge of your fist or knuckles into the paint. I recommend wearing a vinyl glove for this.

2. Start Scraping

While this is still damp, use a razor blade or palette knife to scrape back the top surface of rocks. Make sure they coincide with the outside contour of the rock mass.

3. Brush Details

After you have washed your hands (if you didn't wear a glove), use a darker form of the gray and a fine brush to paint the deep cracks and to emphasize light edges.

SPATTERING FOR BEDROCK

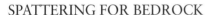

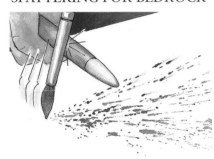

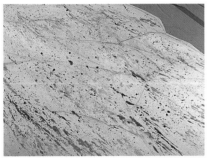

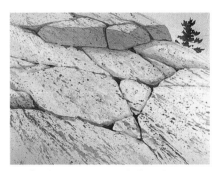

SPATTER TECHNIQUE
Load a large brush with color and gently tap it on another brush handle. Do it at a low angle so that the spatter fans out across the paper, giving direction to the texture.

Be warned: This can get really messy because of the kickback spray that goes all over your paper. Protect nonrock areas with paper or tape.

1. Spatter the Background Colors

Sketch your rocks and then paint over with a pale, mottled Cerulean Blue/Burnt Sienna wash. Let dry. Spatter with pale and concentrated forms of the same two colors.

2. Add Cracks and Shadows

Paint the shadows and cracks for the rock with the same two colors mixed. Paint irregular lines and fade each upward from the crack. Repeat with darker concentrated color to deepen the crevices.

BEACH STONES

Here's an approach that was also used for clouds.

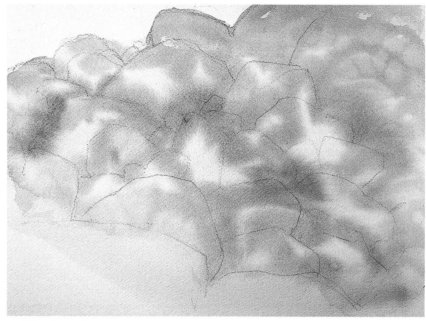

1. Play Leapfrog

For this mottled background, mix any concentrated gray from a triad and apply it with a round brush in random "leapfrog" fashion all over a damp rock area. Don't try to follow the rock shapes. Stop while there are still light areas left in the pattern.

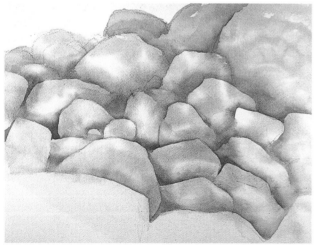

2. Define Rocks

Define one rock from another by outlining them with a more concentrated gray and fading out into the rocks behind. Work from the bottom up.

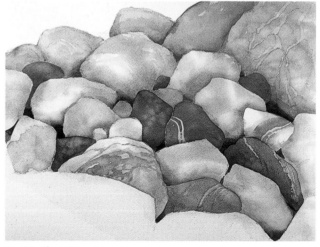

3. Refine Rocks

Darken some of the rocks. Glaze a hint of different color on others. Create veins by direct positive and negative painting as well as painting and scraping with a palette knife. Try water spots, too. Redarken the deepest crevices.

Reflected Light on Rocks

This is one of the most dramatic effects to use with rocks. You will capitalize on how warm reflected light can illuminate areas that are in shadow and give the impression that the objects themselves are giving off light.

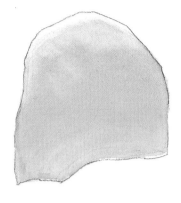

PAINTING THE COLOR OF REFLECTED LIGHT

To create the effect of rocks that are bathed in reflected light, you must blend cool and warm colors on the shadow side of the rock. A band of pale, cool color (blue) is painted near the top of the rock and a pale, warm band (orange) is painted along the bottom. In the middle, where the two meet, blend them together to produce a gray. Fade out the top edge of the blue band.

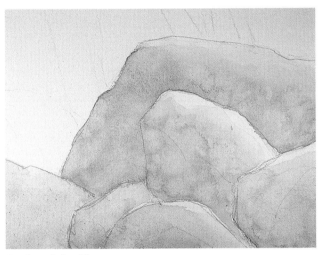

1. Gradate It

Work one rock at a time until all have a gradation from cool near the top to warm at the bottom. Let dry.

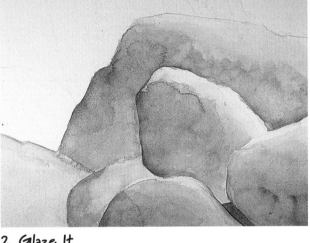

2. Glaze It

Darken the edges and the shadow side of each rock by glazing with a warm gray. Texture with water drops while this layer is still damp.

3. Shadow It

Add cast shadows using a flat synthetic brush and a dark, cool gray. Notice how the cast shadows of the trees out of view blend into the rocks' shadows on the shadowed side.

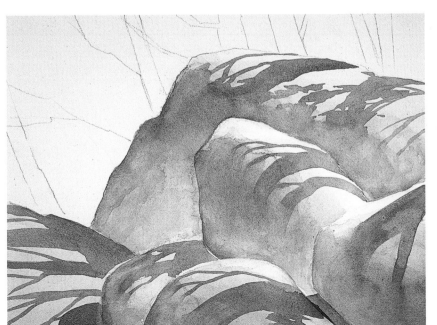

Trees

Trees are like actors in the cast of a play who bring energy and reality to the performance. They will perform for you in your paintings as well if you take the time to make them look believable and position them so that they can best play the role intended for them.

Making trees look believable has a lot to do with understanding that the primary function of the trunks and limbs is to reach up and out far enough to hold their leaves in the sunlight. All species do this in their own way, but it wouldn't happen if the trunk, branches and twigs didn't graduate in size as they got farther away from the base. Your tree won't look very real either if the branches don't quite connect or are overlapped at a joint.

GROWTH PATTERNS

The problem that most people have with making trees is that they are still influenced by the icons for "tree" that they developed as a child. It is time to look at trees with a more critical artist's eye. What you will find are a couple of common, simple growth patterns. By seeing and following these patterns, you can improve the character and believability of the players on your stage.

Deciduous and coniferous trees have their own patterns, each affected by age and environment. With age, trees exaggerate their growth as if celebrating their survival. Bases broaden and limbs thicken, twist and distort as they extend their reach. If growing by themselves,

they will reach a fullness of shape. But in the close company of other trees, they will shift their energy to the upper limbs and take whatever shape is necessary to perform their primary function. And, of course, in the face of strong prevailing winds, there is also distortion that mimes the wind itself.

In time, you will discover how each species is a variation on the patterns to follow. Many species fit into the same growth pattern, and the same species can fit into more than one pattern. For example, a maple may have a single central trunk when young but evolve with multiple trunks as it ages, or grow to have everything at the top if it's in a dense forest.

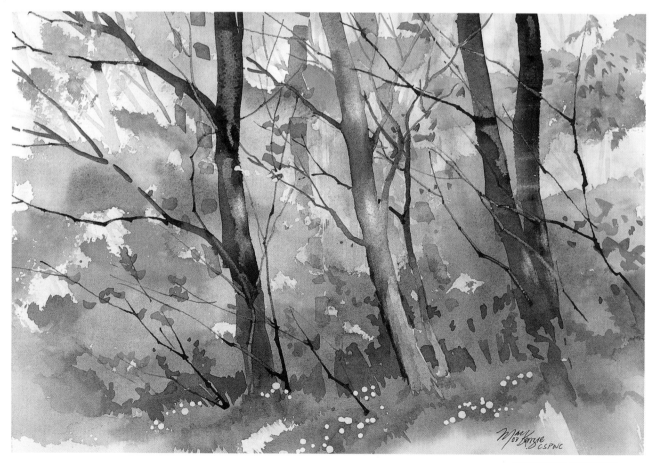

SUMMER RESPITE
11" × 14" (28cm × 36cm)

Deciduous Trees

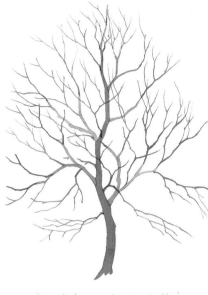

SINGLE VERTICAL TRUNK

Here a central trunk supports branches that tend to head outward before turning upward. The lower branches turn down.

Start by painting a single tapered line from the ground up (red). If this main trunk isn't perfectly straight, it will have more character. Make changes in direction, abrupt or smooth. Use a round or flat synthetic brush or a broad-tipped palette knife.

To this trunk, add a few tapered branches (blue) that grow upward and outward in the same style as the trunk. The width and height of the tree is up to you. Use a broad rigger, fine-tipped round brush or broad-tipped palette knife.

To your branches, add smaller branching limbs (green) to fill out your tree into whatever shape you want. Be consistent with the style of your branches. Use a rigger, a fine round synthetic brush, a sharpened stick or a fine-tipped palette knife.

TIPS

1. Regardless of species, branches are a lot longer than you think they are. Let them run off the paper, and don't forget the ones that grow downward.
2. Pay attention to the angles at which main trunks and branches meet each other as well as their general placement (i.e., opposite or random). There is a consistency in each tree.
3. The shape your tree takes is up to you, but very few are perfectly symmetrical.

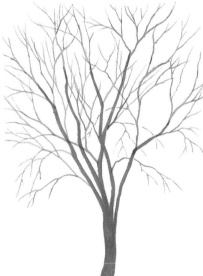

MULTIPLE TRUNKS

In this pattern, more than one vertical trunk either grows from a single base trunk or leaves the ground as a clump. Start with the main trunks (red), which tend to branch upward (blue) before adding smaller limbs (green) that reach outward and down.

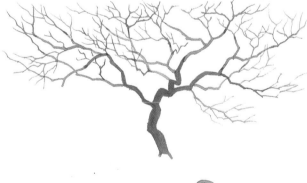

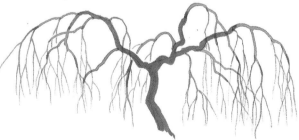

DECIDUOUS TREE VARIATIONS

Sometimes the main trunk is contorted because of the species, its age or weather conditions. As before, start with the main trunk (red) and then add branches (blue, green) that suit the character of the trunk. Sometimes branches head down, as in "weeping" types of trees.

Painting Deciduous Foliage

You will paint better deciduous trees when you understand the structure within them. In most cases, it's best to paint the foliage of a deciduous tree before the trunk and branches, but that shouldn't prevent you from lightly sketching in their locations as a guide for the foliage if it's important for the composition.

Below are just a few ways to add foliage. Try to paint not individual leaves but clumps, and don't forget to leave spaces between the clumps for birds to get through. Generally speaking, the top of the tree is lighter and warmer than the underside. Add details, branches and the trunk after the paint is dry.

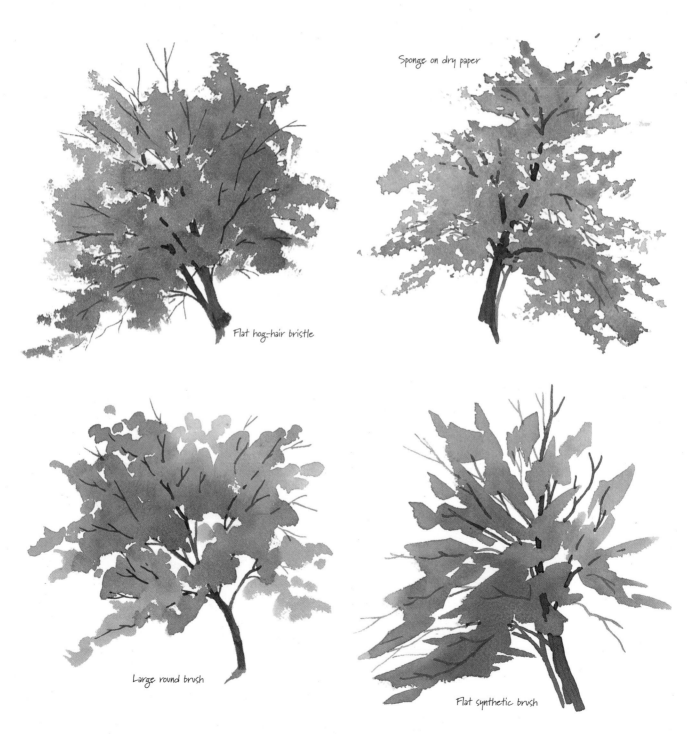

Sponge on dry paper

Flat hog-hair bristle

Large round brush

Flat synthetic brush

Branching Options

The style of branches in your picture conveys a subtle message to the viewer. Are your limbs from haunted forests or a tranquil garden? Are they carrying life or remnants of a former day?

ANGULAR

If you wish to have twisted or sharp angular branching on your tree, try using a rigger or a palette knife. Make the main branch with numerous stops. At each stop, change direction. From each subsequent bend, start another angular branch, and from those angles extend more bent twigs. This type of branching is most common on deciduous trees.

SMOOTH FLOWING

If you want less agitation in your branches, soften the bends. Smooth branches with low-angled joints to give a different feel to your work, regardless of species. These can be made with a round brush, rigger, script liner or palette knife.

SHARP, ANGULAR BRANCHES

SMOOTH, FLOWING BRANCHES

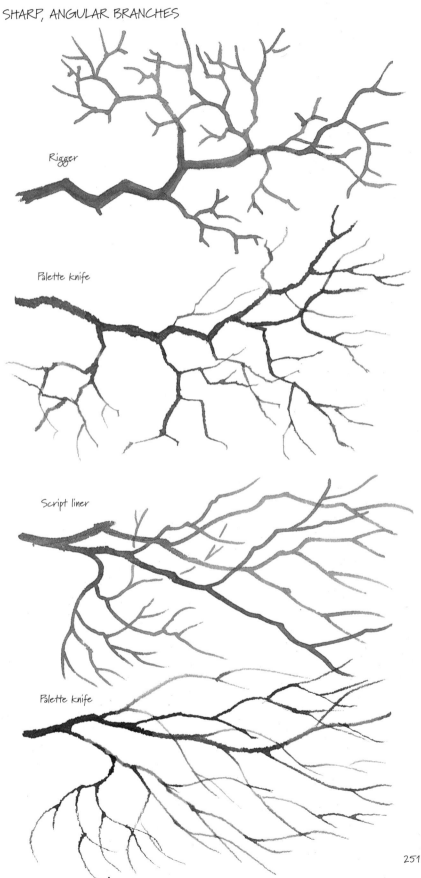

Rigger

Palette knife

Script liner

Palette knife

Coniferous Trees

Although we rarely paint a coniferous tree without its needles, it is nonetheless important to understand its underlying structure. These trees develop around a single central trunk that is usually straighter than deciduous types. It's also important to get the angle of coniferous branches correct. Branches at the top head upward, those in the midsection head outward and then upward, and those near the bottom head downward and then upward. Coniferous branches tend to be shorter, and most branch out flatter than deciduous ones (which allows for space between the branches). Branches on some trees grow out of the trunk nearly opposite each other.

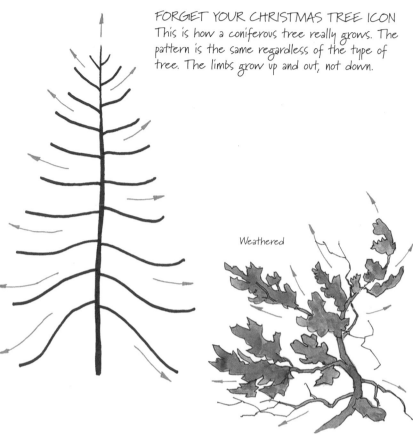

FORGET YOUR CHRISTMAS TREE ICON
This is how a coniferous tree really grows. The pattern is the same regardless of the type of tree. The limbs grow up and out, not down.

Weathered

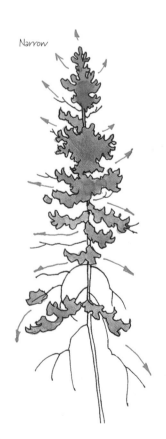

Narrow

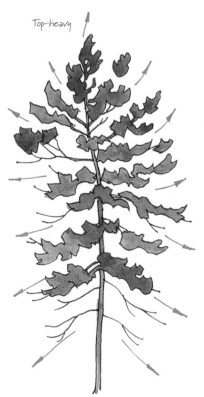

Top-heavy

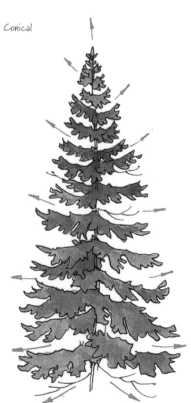

Conical

Painting Coniferous Foliage

Coniferous trees can be painted with a variety of tools and techniques.

SPONGES

One good technique for creating coniferous trees is to paint them with the edge and tip of a piece torn from a synthetic sponge. Start from the top and work down. Occasionally flick the sponge upward to create the effect of nee-dles. Add the trunks after the foliage is painted.

BRUSHES

Each type of brush you have will create a unique tree. Again, start from the top and work down. Add the trunks after the foliage is paint-ed. Flicking a bristle brush upward will suggest clumps of needles.

PALETTE KNIFE

You can also drag the edge of a pal-ette knife that has been loaded with concentrated color across a page sprayed with water. Start by making the trunks and then drawing (well, dragging) one branch at a time. Keep reloading your knife with dark color because the sprayed water will dilute it.

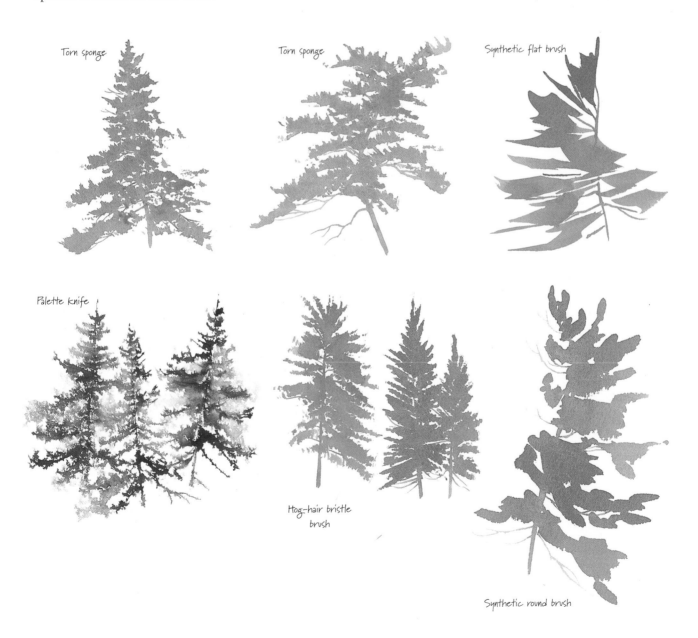

Torn sponge

Torn sponge

Synthetic flat brush

Palette knife

Hog-hair bristle brush

Synthetic round brush

Palm Trees

Sometimes because of age, crowding or species, the leaves or fronds of a tree grow only at the top end of a single trunk. This is the case with most palm trees. For example, the fronds of the coconut tree arch in a radiating pattern, like exploding fireworks.

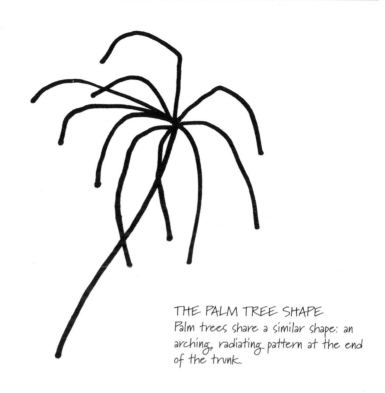

THE PALM TREE SHAPE
Palm trees share a similar shape: an arching, radiating pattern at the end of the trunk.

A TROPICAL
PLANT SAMPLER
Notice how many branches or fronds radiate from a line and/or a center. This is a common tropical growth pattern.

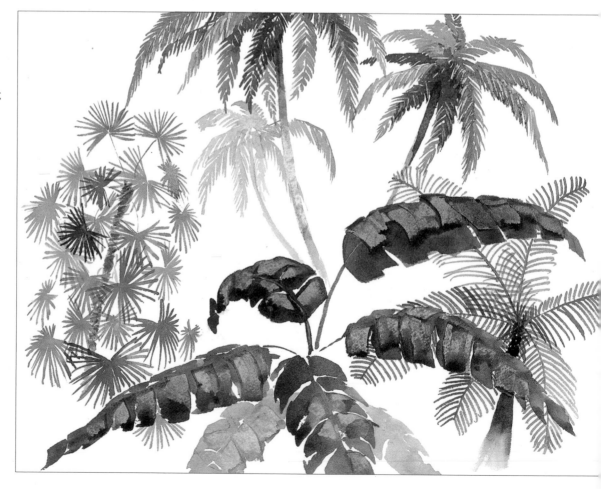

PAINTING PALM FRONDS

Paint your palm trees one frond at a time, using a script liner or round brush and a range of warm and cool greens. Start by painting a fine center line for the frond and then painting the blades with repeated strokes from that center line outward. Keep the general direction of the blades angled toward the front of the frond. The leaves of the banana plant are painted with a small, flat synthetic brush with spaces left between some of the strokes. The palmetto palm has blades that radiate from the tips of the stems.

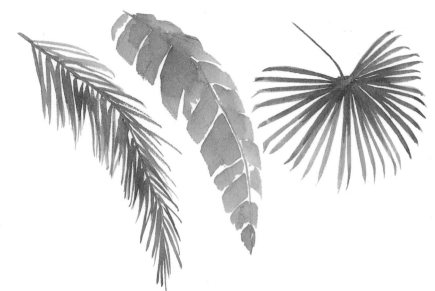

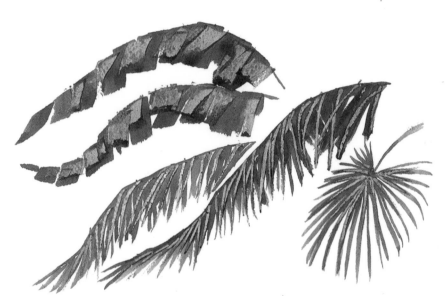

PAINTING THE SIDE VIEW

Sometimes, only one side of the frond is visible. In this case, paint the fronds dark and then scrape back a few light ones with a palette knife or a narrow slice of a defunct credit card when damp. After most of the fronds are painted, add a few darker ones in the underneath shaded part of the tree.

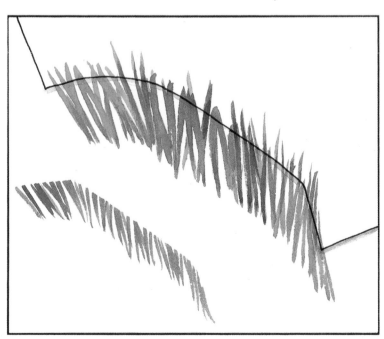

A STENCIL FOR PALM FRONDS

Cut a paper stencil that follows the center line of your palm frond. By painting off this stencil, you create blades that start along a very precise line. Do the opposite side of the frond with the other piece of the stencil. The problem with this method is that you'll be cutting a lot of stencils and waiting until each side dries before doing the next. This gives you precision at the price of spontaneity.

Combining Techniques for a Meadow

One simple technique with a hog-hair bristle brush allows you to make grassy fields with ease, while another technique with a flat synthetic brush creates individual blades of grass.

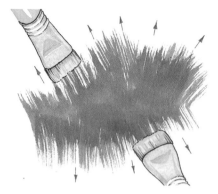

HOG-HAIR BRISTLE TECHNIQUE FOR GRASS CLUMPS
Hold your loaded brush vertically. Make sweeping strokes upward to represent dark positive blades of grass and downward to create light negative blades.

1. Begin in the Distance

Paint a graded wash from pale Cobalt Blue in the distance to yellowish green in the foreground. Let dry.

In the distance, make short strokes up and down with a pale, cool, dull green (Phthalo Green + Cobalt Blue). Leave spaces between clumps of grass as you follow the terrain. Darken some areas, fade out others.

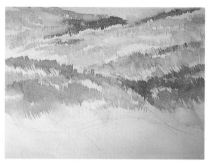

2. Move Forward

As you get closer, add more Sap Green and Burnt Sienna to the mixture and make your strokes longer and varied. Continue to make some patches lighter and others darker, and don't forget to fade out occasionally.

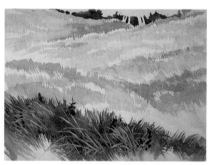

3. Add Foreground Blades

Use a green mix (Phthalo Green + Indian Yellow + Burnt Sienna) to paint an irregular dark patch of grass in the foreground. When this dries to damp, lift some light blades with a damp, 1-inch (25mm) synthetic flat. Work quickly and keep cleaning your brush. Add darker blades of grass and weeds. Try a bit of negative painting for variety and contrast. Add a background forest.

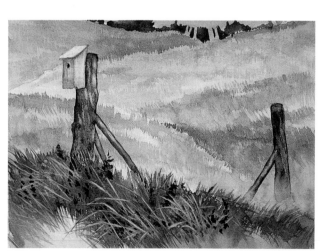

4. Finish the Details

Help model the field and add to the range of greens by glazing pale blues for valleys and yellows for highlights over the meadow. Reinforce perspective by adding something in the foreground, such as fence posts.

VACANCY
11" × 14" (28cm × 36cm)

Ferns

This simple process can be repeated over and over to create a field of ferns. In fact, it can be used to paint fields of any objects that are stacked up against each other. What is important is that you work through the steps quickly. Developing shapes this way is a perfect example of how an object can be both positive and negative. You will see a similarity between this and the previous meadow exercise.

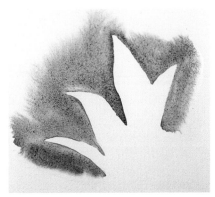

1. Define the Shape

Paint around the basic shape of a clump of ferns with a good load of paint.

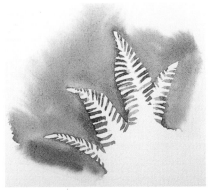

2. Refine the Shape

Immediately draw some of the wet paint toward the center line of the fern using a fine-tipped brush. You are painting these ferns in the negative.

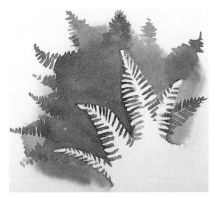

3. Define the Background

While still wet, load your fine-tipped brush with more color and extend the background paint into the positive ferns.

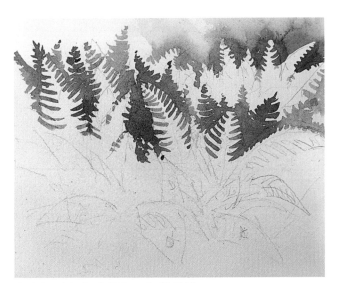

STARTING A FIELD OF FERNS
In a real picture you may wish to sketch the rough location of ferns before painting a light wash of greens over the background. After that dries, you would then paint the light ferns in the middle ground with a row of cool, dark-green ferns behind them, varying the angles of the fronds. Next, you would paint the row of background ferns. These are only painted in the negative, with the background color faded out. A cooler (Phthalo) green was used here.

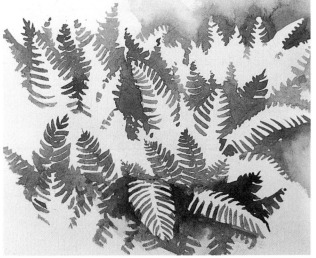

FINISHING THE FERNS
You would reverse the process in the foreground, starting with the dark positive fronds at the back of the clump and working the color down and around light fronds in the foreground using a warmer (Sap) green.

Tree Trunks

Sooner or later, you're going to have to get close to a tree. Here are four ways to handle their surfaces, but there are lots more ways for you to invent.

TRUNK VARIATION #1
First paint the trunk with dark, nonstaining color. When this dries to the damp stage, add large drops of water up the center of the trunk. When this dries to damp again, blot the entire tree. The trunk will be dark around the edges. Add line detail when everything is dry.

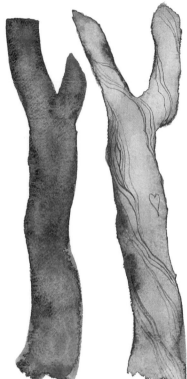

TRUNK VARIATION #2
First, paint the trunk with a dark color. When this reaches the damp stage, scrape with a palette knife. Add pale blue shadows when it dries.

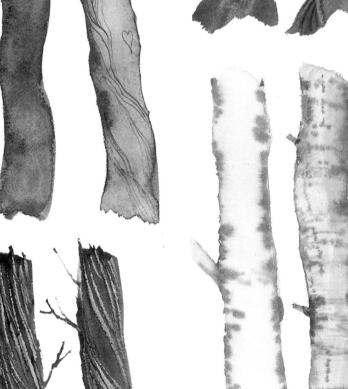

TRUNK VARIATION #3
Paint the trunk in dark colors. As the shine leaves the paper, press the edges of your fist and knuckles into the paint (you can wear vinyl gloves if you like). When this dries, add darker details.

TRUNK VARIATION #4
First, paint the trunk a pale warm color. When it dries to damp, run a fine-tipped round brush loaded with dark color along the edges. Carry the color as dots and lines across the trunk. Add shadows when dry.

Tree Lines and Seasonal Forest Scenes

When you look at a forest, you only see the hint of individual trees. Our objective in these exercises is to create the illusion of a forest without a whole lot of work. You will have an opportunity to use a variety of techniques for trunks and foliage.

For these simple scenes, you'll paint a swath of colors in the rough shape of a forest's edge across the middle of a dry piece of paper. Use large brushes to put down light colors first. While these are still wet, you'll add darker colors for contrast and to define the skyline. When this has all dried to the damp stage, you have the option of manipulating and adding to the colors in many ways (scraping, dropping color or water, blotting, adding salt, etc.). Don't get carried away; using a few techniques is usually better than using every trick in your bag.

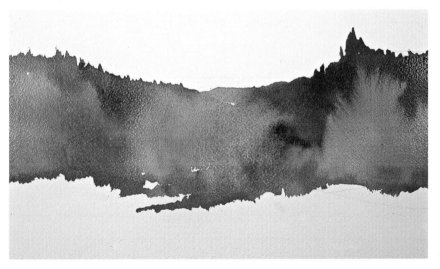

1. Lay Down Autumn Colors

Use vertical strokes to lay down an irregular swath of autumn colors (oranges, pinks, greens, yellows, etc.). Let one color flow into the next.

While still wet, add dark evergreens to establish the top edges of your forest and to create internal contrast.

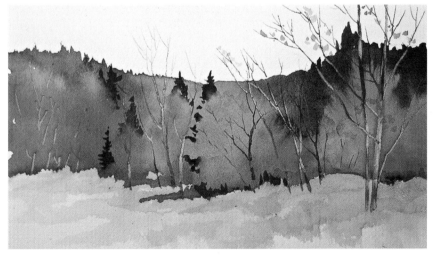

2. Add Detail

To add additional evergreens just paint a portion of their tops and then fade this downward into the forest. Add dark trunks and limbs with a palette knife or brush to complete your trees. Finish the foreground as you wish.

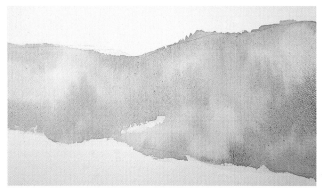

1. Paint the Shades of Winter

Use pale, cool grays to define your forest shape. While this is wet, stroke in a few hints of warm color (siennas, ochres, pinks). Darken the skyline with evergreen treetops and the ground line with darker gray.

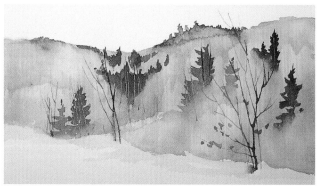

2. Suggest Without Overstating

Suggest some of the subtle edges of the tree clumps and ridges with a medium gray, then fade this out and upward into the background. Let dry.

To simulate bare tree trunks, drybrush vertical lines over your forest with a hog-hair bristle brush loaded with pale gray. Let dry.

Add dark evergreens by painting a portion of their tops and fading them downward into the forest. Extend a few dark tree trunks and limbs above and below the forest shape. Drybrush a few twigs using a pale, warm gray.

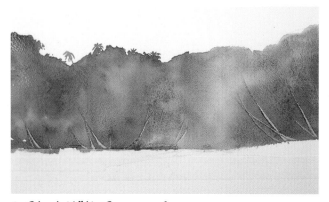

1. Start With Summer Greens

The challenge here is to create a variety of greens. First, put down patches of light warm and cool greens. While wet, dab in dark greens for contrast and also to define the skyline and ground line. Leave a light area so you can paint darker trees in front later. (I used masking tape to save a beach line.) When damp, scrape in a few tree trunks.

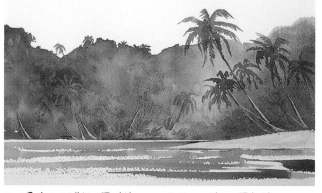

2. Finish With Positive and Negative Painting

Paint the dark positive trees in front of the light area. Negative paint the suggestion of treetops in the background. Add the beach, water and shadows. Mauve is good for balancing all those greens.

Lighting in the Forest

Where you put branches and trunks has a profound effect on the illusion of light direction. This exercise will help you understand the effect. More examples of it are in the tree demos to follow.

1. Prepare the Backgrounds

Pre-paint two backgrounds. To make your backgrounds, first paint a roughly circular gradation of greens that covers your entire paper. Start with light warm greens (Sap Green + yellow) in the center and work to light cool greens (Sap Green + blue) around the outside. Let dry. (You could wet the paper first, but it is unnecessary if you use large brushes and work quickly.)

2. Add the Leaves

When this is dry, sponge on irregular clumps of leaves in dark-to-medium greens. Even though you want about 50-percent coverage of the background, try to make the sizes of the clumps and spaces vary. Let dry.

3. Add Trunks and Branches

Use a no. 8 to no. 12 round and a dark blue-brown mixture. On one background, paint the trunks and branches only in the dark areas. Now your trees are front-lit. To complete the illusion, scrub off a few sun spots on the trunks when they are dry.

On the other background, paint trunks and branches only in the light areas. Suddenly your trees are backlit.

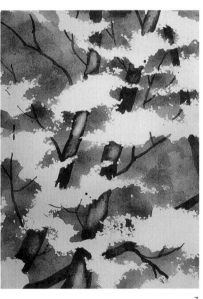

1

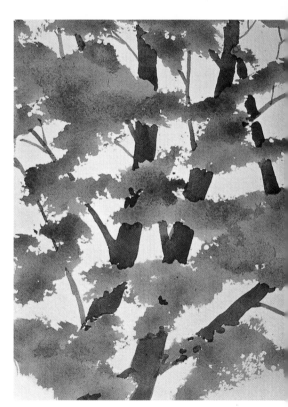

3

Backlit Forest Meadow

The backlit effect, which you just saw in the last exercise, is achieved when dark trunks and limbs are visible in the light patches of your background. We will be doing the same thing here except we will be changing the value and temperature of the dark leaves and trying a different way of painting a meadow.

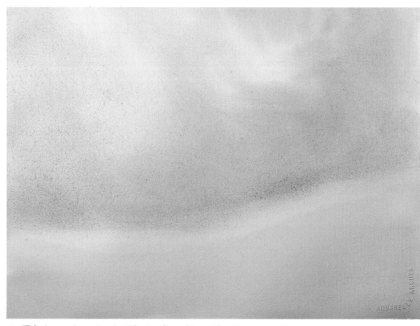

1. Paint a Graded Wash for the Background

Roughly define with pencil where the forest ends and the meadow starts. Wet your paper. Paint a circular graded wash that starts with a pale pink at the light source and gradates to a cool blue-green around the edges. Use Raw Sienna and Permanent Rose at the center, and gradate through yellow-green to Sap Green, Phthalo Green, then Cobalt Blue at the edges. Fade your colors into the meadow area. Let dry.

2. Sponge on the Leaves

Sponge on irregular clumps of leaves that gradate from very dark and warm over the light source, to medium value and cool around the outside. Vary the size and distribution of these clumps. Let this dry, but don't wash your sponge.

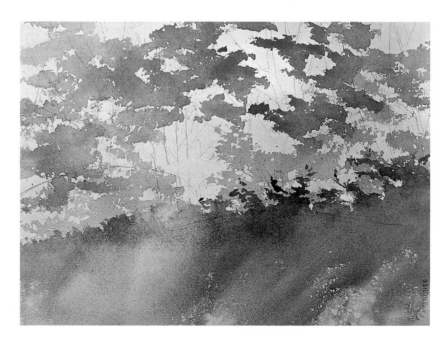

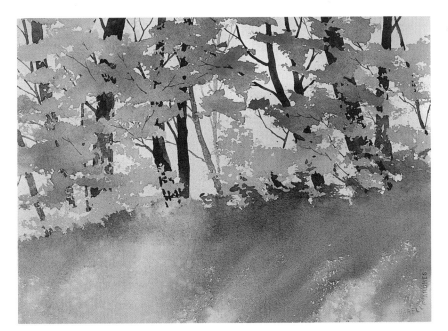

3. Build Foliage and Try a New Meadow Treatment

Sponge more of the dark foliage colors along the top edge of the meadow, covering some of the previously painted foliage. Immediately tilt your paper and spray water loosely along the top of the meadow. Keep spraying until the paint runs down in a lacy pattern over your foreground. Lay your painting flat to dry.

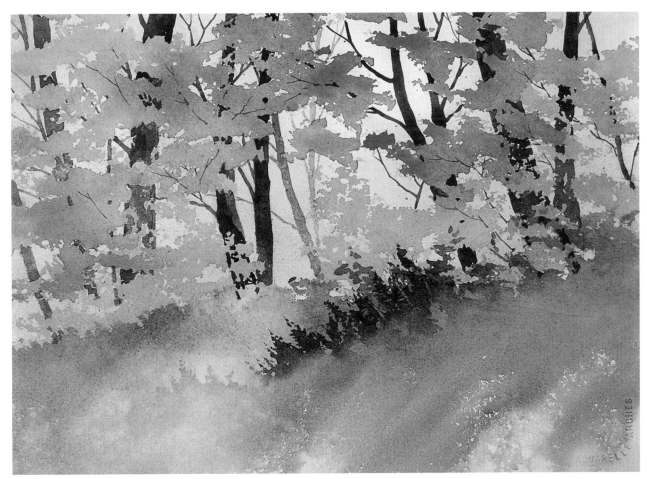

4. Add Final Details

Paint tree trunks and branches in the light areas. Use something, such as a fence, to define the edge of the meadow. Notice that, like the tree trunks, it is not completely visible.

SUMMER LIGHT
11" × 14" (28cm × 36cm)

Edge of the Forest

We could now do a frontlit exercise where all the tree trunks are light against a dark background, but instead we will do one that mixes things up a bit: the base of the tree will be light against dark, but dark against light farther up. You'll see why later.

1. Paint the Tree Area

Paint the tree area in the light mottled colors of the spring season. I chose Raw Sienna, Sap Green and Phthalo Green. The foreground meadow is painted lighter than the forest. Let dry.

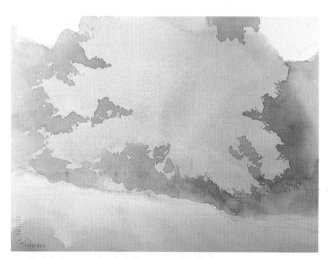

2. Add Irregular Edges and Texture

Use a sponge and/or a large brush and a darker, cooler version of the background colors to define some of the irregular edges of the major trees. Vary the width of your marks and fade them out into the background colors.

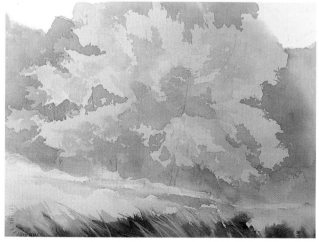

3. Darken the Grasses and Foliage

Use the same process with the same colors to define some even darker spaces in the foliage. Use a brush to carefully paint around the base of major tree trunks. Darken the meadow grass in the foreground with some Sap Green and Burnt Sienna to suggest that the viewer is in the shade. Remove a few light blades of grass with a damp brush. Let dry.

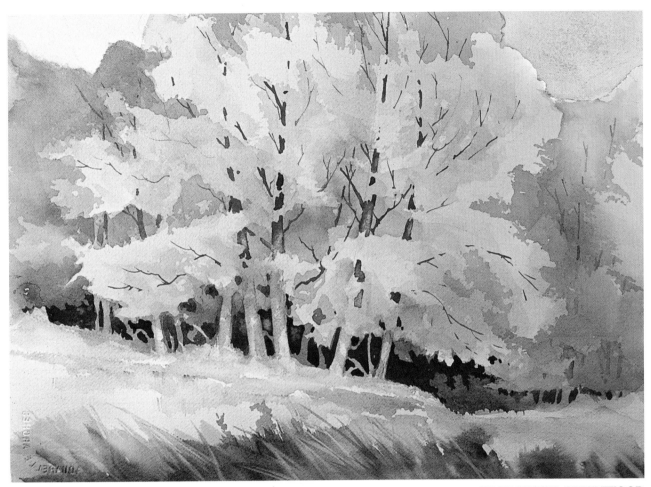

4. Add Final Details

Sponge midvalue marks onto the face of the tree. Fade out some of the edges of these marks. Use very dark color to redefine the bottom of the tree trunks while saving a couple of midvalue trunks inside the forest.

To achieve the front-lit effect, extend the tree trunks and branches into the trees by painting them dark in the lighter valued spaces. When dry, add cast shadows on the lower tree trunks and wipe back a few sunspots on the dark portions. Add sky above the trees and detail to the foreground grasses.

EDGE OF THE GREENWOOD
11" × 14" (28cm × 36cm)

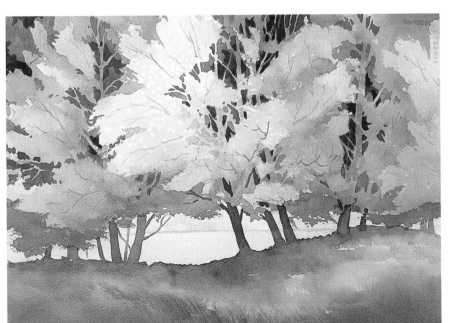

VARIABLE CONTRASTS
This picture is also frontlit, but in reverse of the above painting. Here, the dark trunks and meadow are silhouetted against a light background while light limbs above are set against darkness. Each picture projects its own feeling because of different contrasts.

AUTUMN ENTRANCE
11" × 14" (28cm × 36cm)

Country Roads

The objective here is to capture the feel of a sun-dappled country road.

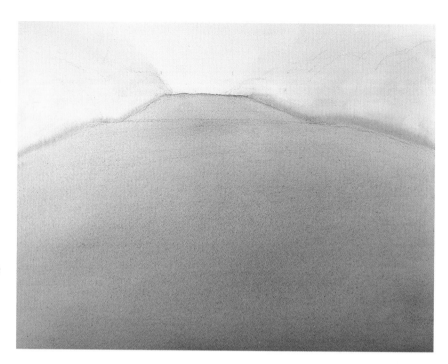

1. Set the Stage

Start by painting the road surface a medium-to-dark warm gray made from nonstaining colors—Cobalt Blue + Burnt Sienna or Cerulean Blue + Cadmium Orange. The darker you make the road, the brighter the sunspots will be. Add a pale yellow-green for the roadsides and sky.

2. Create the Dappled Sunspots

Create sunspots by using a spray bottle to flood the area, then lifting paint with a small scrub brush. These spots are really ovals of varying sizes and brightness. They should fan out in a pattern that adds a sense of perspective to your road.

When this dries, add more color and texture to the foliage on the sides of the road.

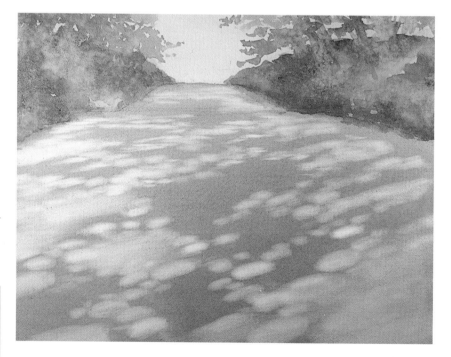

COLOR NOTE

To get the desired colors, make sure you're using a real Cerulean Blue (PB35 or PB36), not a mix of Phthalo Blue (PB15) and white. Read the label.

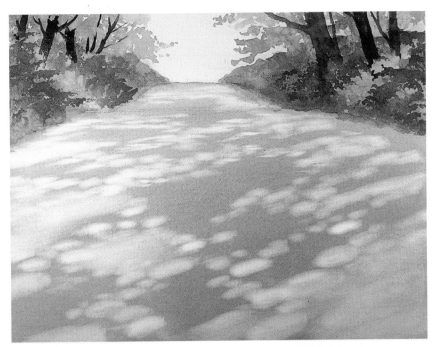

3. Complete Roadside Detail

Create more foliage detail with negative and positive painting. Use a pale blue-green for the distant trees to add a sense of depth. Add dark tree trunks and branches.

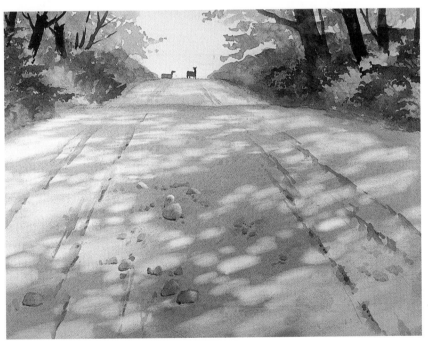

SIGHTINGS
11" × 15" (28cm × 38cm)

4. Paint Rocks and Ruts

Create ruts by painting broken lines with the original road color. Fade these out at random. Darken the rise in the road so that it is different from the road beyond.

Create some stones by painting them darker than the ground, especially on their shadow side. Create others using an acetate stencil and a scrub brush. Start by cutting small curved bits from the edge of a piece of acetate. Use your scrub brush and water and one of the notches in the acetate to remove only a small amount of paint for the sunlit side of the rock. When this dries, paint the remainder of the rock dark.

I've added the deer as a center of interest.

Snowstorm in the Forest

This is very much like painting fog. The many faces of winter offer grand opportunities to play with color temperature and purity. The snow is a mirror for the subtle atmospheres that surround it, from the pure warm and cool colors of a bright sunny day to the dulled subtlety of a snowstorm.

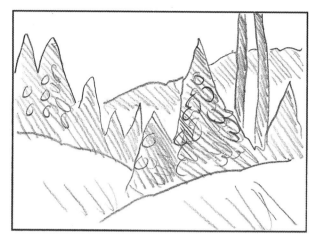

THE PLAN
This is a rough layout for the picture. It helps determine the areas to protect with masking fluid.

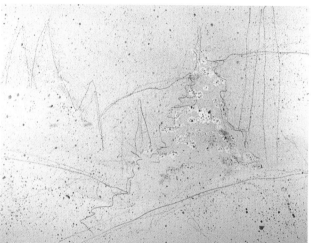

1. Apply Masking

Use masking fluid and a brush to save some snow on the limbs of the nearest trees. For the falling snow, spatter masking fluid over the entire surface with a toothbrush. To avoid accidental drips, try to spatter the fluid onto the paper from outside the picture area. Don't be stingy with your snowflakes. When dry, paint a thin gray (Cobalt Blue + Burnt Sienna) wash over the entire paper.

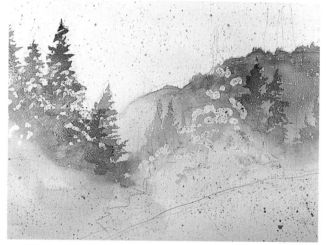

2. Paint Background Hills and Trees

Paint the tops of distant hills in a light, cool, mottled gray (Cobalt Blue + Burnt Sienna). Fade this downward and let dry. Use a brush—or better still, a sponge—to paint the middle-ground trees with a midvalue gray. Treat these as a silhouette and fade them downward.

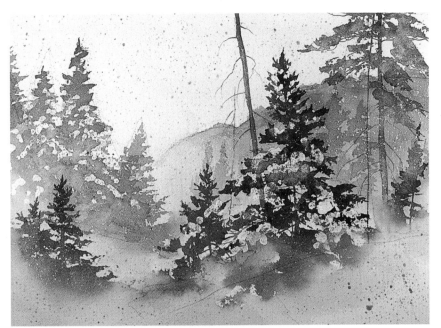

3. Paint the Foreground Trees

Using a sponge or brush, paint the foreground trees with a dark, warm gray that has just a hint of green in it. Try to make the branches match the clumps of snow that you masked out. Fade the bottom of these trees to suggest snowdrifts. Let dry.

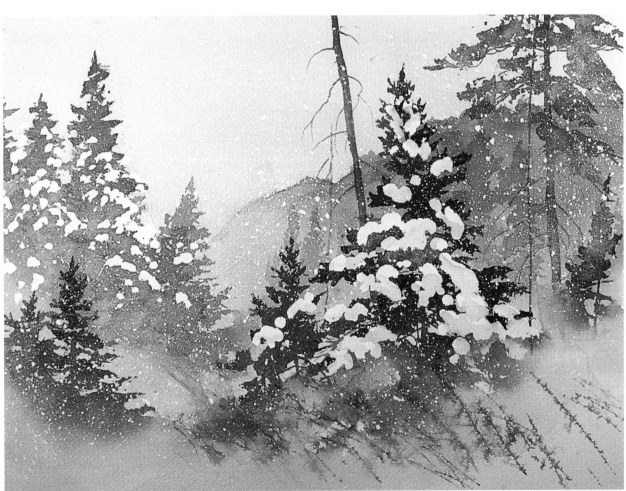

4. Remove the Masking and Add Shading

Spray the foreground with water and paint warm weeds and shrubs with the edge of a palette knife loaded with reddish brown. When everything is dry, remove all masking fluid and shade the undersides of the snow mounds with a pale, cool gray.

ON SILENT WINGS
11" × 15" (28cm × 38cm)

From Dusk to Dawn

It is said that we are children of the light and as such are attracted to it in real life and in visual presentations. But deep within us is also a personal response to the world of darkness. It is that buried sense of what night means to us, with all its assorted mysteries and intrigue, that we are after here.

Paintings set at this time of day have a quality that appeals to an entirely different and deeper level of knowing within the viewer as well. For many, night is not a time of gloom and dread but a time of excitement, fascination and even comfort. It has the ability to stir things in the twilight of our memories that somehow connects us to the distant and long ago.

There are some special factors to consider when depicting this time of day. You must decide on the light sources in your picture; their strength and direction and what they illuminate. You also have to decide how much illumination is necessary to reveal the subject, or how much of the subject can be obscured by darkness and still convey what it is. Detail is not a factor at night. Creating illusion by suggestion is everything.

Some light sources need to be saved by masking while others can be created during the painting process or by scrubbing out later. Glazing can also be used at the end to subdue certain areas while causing the eye to see others.

The following two exercises are an introduction to some of the techniques used in night painting.

COLOR NOTE

Use a triad of Indigo, Permanent Rose and Raw Sienna or Burnt Sienna. When mixed together, these colors produce others that are subdued.

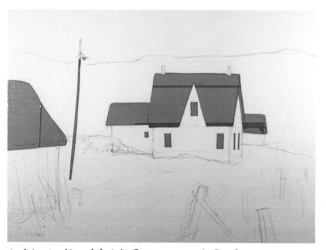

1. Mask the Light Sources and Surfaces

In this exercise, the homestead windows, yard light and the sky are the sources of illumination. Mask these as well as the roofs with masking fluid or packing tape.

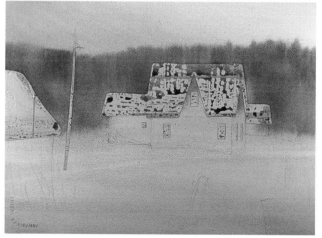

2. Lay In the First Washes

Mix a large puddle of warm gray using your triad colors. ("Warm" meaning the Permanent Rose or Raw Sienna will dominate.) Wet your entire paper and apply the gray over the surface. Use more color to darken the right side of the horizon. Lighten the left side by lifting pigment with a damp brush. Immediately mix a more concentrated form of the gray and paint the background trees. Blend this forward into the fields. Let dry.

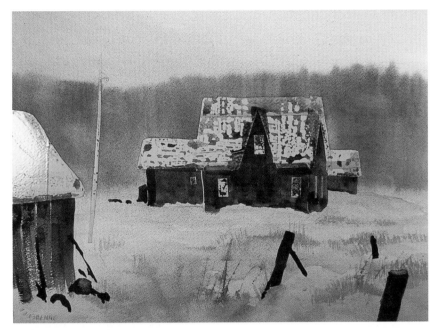

3. Add Grass and the Darkest Values

Use drybrushing with more of the original light-wash color for random clumps of dead grass. Fade out as necessary. Let dry.

Paint the sides of the buildings and yard objects using a dark mix of the original triad colors. Let dry.

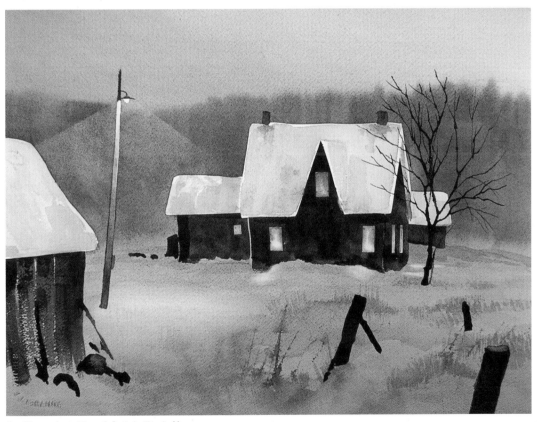

SUPPER'S READY
11" × 15"
(28cm × 38cm)

4. Develop the Light Details

Remove the masking. Gradate the window openings from Burnt Sienna to Raw Sienna in the center. Gradate the lamp pole from dark at the base to light at the top. Paint it dark above the light. Cut a wide "V" out of a piece of paper or acetate. Invert this and lay it over the paper. Use a damp sponge to lift pigment to suggest an area of light rays from the yard lamp. With a small scrub brush, lighten the center of some of the windows and the illuminated areas of snow. Paint the roofs a cooler light gray and then model the ground a bit with the same gray. When everything is dry, paint the tree with a palette knife.

Under the Stars

This night exercise involves masking with masking fluid and painting the transition of colors from dark and cool to light and warm. The light source is a campfire that is unseen but emitting smoke and light that reflects off the tree trunks and leaves.

1. Mask Light Areas and Lay In Initial Colors

Use masking fluid to save the limbs and trunks of the major trees, background rocks and the two figures and tent to the left. When the masking fluid is dry, paint a concentric graded wash that ranges from pale Raw Sienna at the campfire to Sap Green then Phthalo Green at the top of the tree line. Paint over the foreground rock as well. When this has dried, paint the sky a dark blue-gray (Indigo + Phthalo Blue) down to the tree line. Let dry.

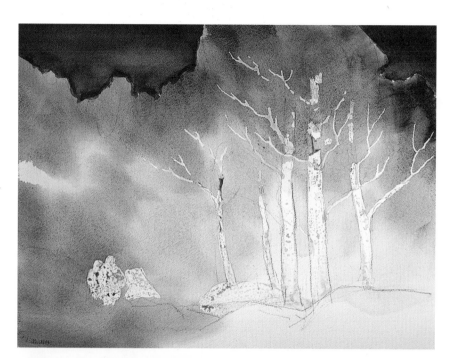

2. Paint the Foliage

Use a sponge loaded with a extra-dark blue-gray (Indigo + Sepia) to define the tops of the distant trees against the sky. Use the bottom of these marks to indicate the lighter tops of closer trees. Soften the back edges of your marks. As you move closer to the light source, add Phthalo Green, then Sap Green, then Raw Sienna and water to your mix so your colors get warmer and lighter as you go. Paint the area around the figures dark. Paint the large foreground rock a warm gray (Cobalt Blue + Burnt Sienna).

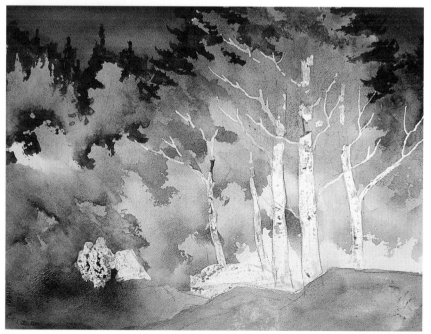

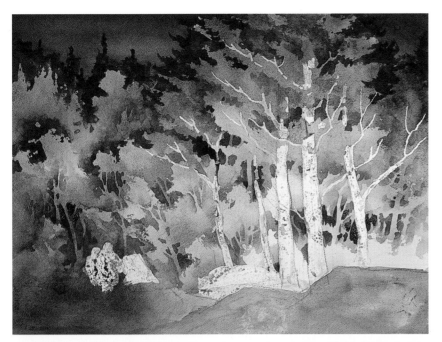

3. Create the Trees with Negative Painting

Take your time to create background trunks, limbs and holes in the foliage using negative painting with your sponge and small brushes. Fade out your dark marks so the lighter edges and limbs will stand out.

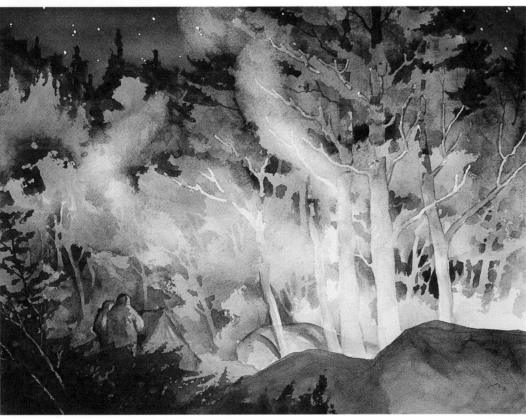

UNDER THE STARS
11" × 14"
(28cm × 36cm)

4. Add Final Details

When dry, remove all masking. Gradate the tree trunks and branches from dark brown at the top to Burnt Sienna, Raw Sienna and then white at the bottom. Paint the figures and tent Burnt Sienna. Let dry.

Cast shadows on the flat middle-ground rocks. Add dark shadows to the figures, tent and foreground rock until they almost blend into the darkness. Let dry.

With a damp sponge or toothbrush, gently remove some wafts of smoke, starting in the campfire area. Sponge on a dark blue-gray (Indigo + Phthalo Blue) for the foreground foliage on the left. Add stars by picking the paper with a razor knife.

Winter Hills

The plan is to have the warm, late-afternoon sun highlighting the hilltops in this winter scene. This is another opportunity to play warm colors against cool.

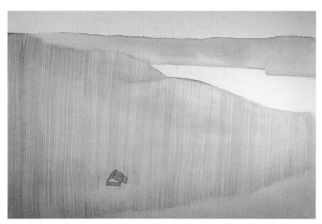

1. Prepare the Background

If you want a cabin in your work, mask its roof with packing tape. Paint the entire land area (not the lake) a pale, dull Cobalt Blue. While this is still wet, add pale reddish brown (Burnt Sienna + Permanent Rose) along the hilltops. Work this in with your brush to push the blue aside. Lift paint to make it lighter. Let dry.

Now comes the part that takes nerve. To capture the illusion of bare trees on the hills, mix a pale, warm gray (Burnt Sienna + Cobalt Blue). Drybrush it from the top of the hill to the bottom using long vertical strokes. A large bristle brush with fanned-out bristles works well for this. Don't paint the foreground ridge. Let dry.

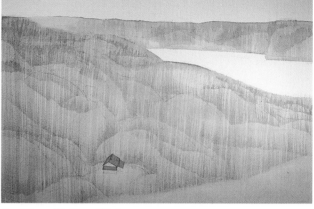

2. Stencil the Ridges

Now for the fun part. To create the illusion of ridges on the hill, use the same brush loaded with warm gray and a few pieces of torn paper as stencils. Place a piece of torn paper on the painting, then, starting on the stencil, drag your brush upward for a short distance. To change the bend of a ridge, simply shift the stencil, but make sure your strokes remain vertical. For the top edge of your hill, make strokes downward. Try to create a natural flow in the location, direction and spacing of your ridges. They will get closer together as you work over the top of a hill or into the distance.

COLOR NOTE

The major colors here are Burnt Sienna and Cobalt Blue. The minor colors are Permanent Rose and Sap Green. These represent two complementary pairs.

EVERGREEN TECHNIQUE USED IN STEP 3
Load your brush and hold it low and flat to the paper. Lower your brush and just touch the paper with one corner of the bristles. Press down lightly and lift off.

The triangular mark that you have stamped on the paper with your brush creates the impression of a distant evergreen. Vary the size and width by changing pressure and angle. By stamping repeatedly, you can create a clump or row of trees.

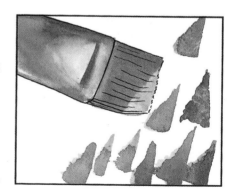

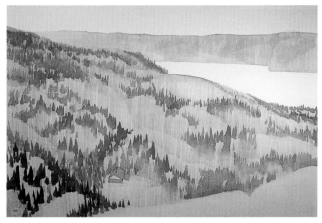

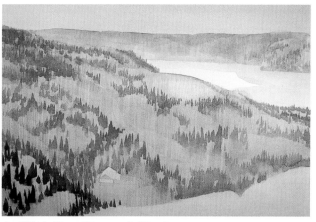

3. Add Evergreens

These evergreens are not actually green. They are a range of warm-to-cool dark grays made by mixing Cobalt Blue + Burnt Sienna. (You could also mix Sap Green + Permanent Rose to get a dark, dull green). Following the brush technique on the previous page, make your trees one at a time or in clusters using a 1-inch (25mm) flat hog-bristle brush. Practice this on a piece of scrap paper first.

4. Paint the Sky and Shadows

Add a few pale evergreens to the far shore. Paint the sky with a pale Burnt Sienna + Permanent Rose.

Remove the masking from the cabin roofs. With a large flat brush, quickly glaze Cobalt Blue over the shadow area in the valley. Use the same color for cast shadows on the lake. Let dry.

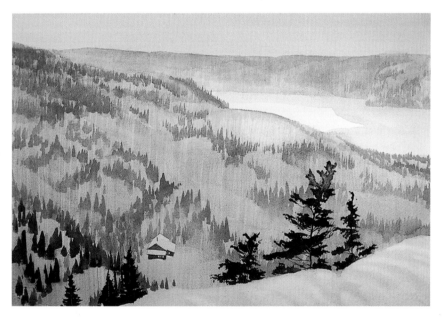

5. Add Finishing Touches

Use your scrub brush and lots of water to scrub back the sun on the foreground ridge. When this is dry, paint the sides of the cabins and a few nearby dark pines (Cobalt Blue + Burnt Sienna + Sap Green). The tops can be lightened by scrubbing the middle of the tree tip, blotting and then adding pale Sap Green.

SOLITUDE
15" × 22" (38cm × 56cm)

Autumn Glow

Do you remember the last time you came home from a drive in the autumn countryside? It was probably not the trees and hills in particular that you remember, but the emotional impact of their colors. Those who have learned to see with their heart know that it is not just single colors but combinations, profound and subtle, that touch chords deep within your being. It is that visually exciting interplay of hues that we are after here. In this exercise, the medium does the mixing in ways we never could.

COLOR NOTE

Prepare pools of the colors before you start. I would suggest pale mauve and yellow-green mixtures, as well as Cobalt Blue, Indian Yellow, Lemon Yellow and Permanent Rose.

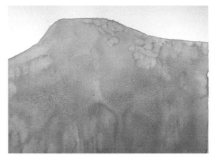

1. Let the Medium Do the Work

Wet the entire hill and paint a mingled wash of pale blues and mauves over the whole area. *Immediately* start dabbing your warm colors into this cool wash using a large round brush, starting with yellows and oranges in the distance. Leave space between your marks so that some blue/mauve can show through. Create "blossoms" in the damp paint with drops of water. You should be getting some wonderful play of warm and cool colors and subtle grays emerging. Stop while it is still fresh. Let dry.

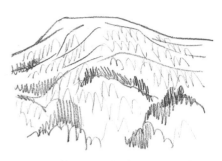

A thumbnail sketch indicates the flow of ridges on the side of the hill.

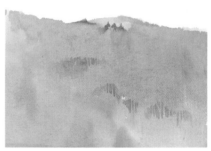

SOMETIMES LESS IS MORE
This is a field sketch I did after I had done two detailed sketches of the same subject. I like this one best of all because it is able to speak freely and differently every time I look at it. It can do this because I have not tried to confine it to one possibility of what it could be.

2. Add Just Enough Detail

How much detail you add to your impression of hills is up to you. You could define the tops of trees or distant ridges by painting dark behind them with a brush or sponge and fading upward. The "dark" could be any mixture of the colors used so far. Those same colors, when concentrated, can produce a dark, dull green that could be used for evergreens. Evergreens are good for contrast as well as leading the eye along ridges.

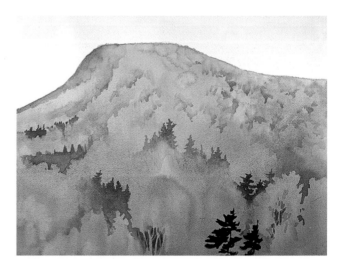

Mist in the Hills

These hills are created by painting their tops dark and fading downward. This will create the illusion of humidity hanging in the valleys. You will be starting with the farthest hills and working forward.

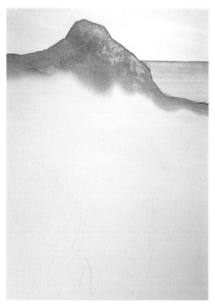

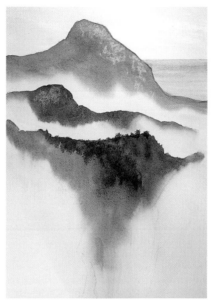

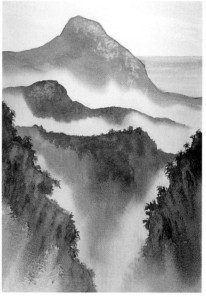

1. Paint the Farthest Hill

If you wish, paint the sky and water now. Since the land dominates, keep them simple. Let dry.

Paint the top of the background hills a dark blue-green (Cobalt Blue + a touch of Sap Green). Make the bottom edge irregular. Immediately wet the area below it with a damp bristle brush to fade out the color. Tilting your paper will help. Add more color along the top if needed.

For texture, try rolling a crumpled paper towel across the mountain while it is still damp. Let dry.

2. Change Color on the Next Ridges

Repeat the same process with the next couple of ridges, letting the paint dry between each. Use a bluish green (Cobalt Blue + Sap Green) for the first one and a greenish blue (Sap Green + Cobalt Blue) for the next. Start indicating vegetation by painting irregular edges on your ridges. Carry this down and fade out in the valley. Go back and add ridge detail now. Let dry.

COLOR NOTE

Except for some yellow-green in the foreground hills, all the land is painted with varying mixtures of Cobalt Blue and Sap Green.

3. Add the Foreground Ridges

Paint the right side of the split ridge first. This time, fade out by spraying. Place a good puddle of concentrated dark green (Sap Green + a touch of Cobalt Blue) along the edge of the ridge. Quickly tilt your paper and spray the edge of the paint. Direct the runoff away from the gorge. Add drops of yellow-green along the top and let these run down. Use a small brush to capture detail along the edge before it dries. When dry, repeat the process of painting and spraying on the left side of the gorge.

When the painting is thoroughly dry (overnight), glaze some of the mist with a pale Cobalt Blue using a large brush and very few strokes.

OUT OF THE MISTS
14" × 11" (36cm × 28cm)

Arid Hills

These hills provide a temperature and humidity contrast with the previous hills. To capture the warm, arid atmosphere, I warmed up my palette with Raw Sienna, Burnt Sienna, Permanent Rose and Cadmium Red Light, and I added Cerulean Blue (which is a dulled blue). I also used a little Phthalo Blue.

COLOR NOTE

To get the desired colors, make sure you're using a real Cerulean Blue (PB35 or PB36), not a mix of Phthalo Blue (PB15) and white. Read the label.

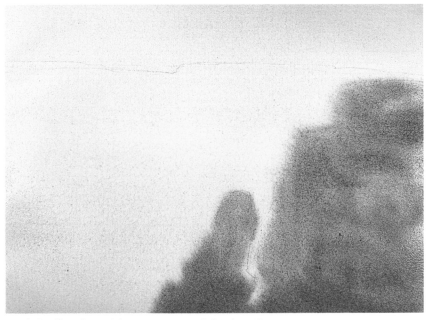

1. Establish the Atmosphere and Major Rocks

Paint a wash over the entire paper, starting with Raw Sienna and Burnt Sienna at the bottom and grading to pale Cerulean Blue at the top. While this is still wet to damp, paint the foreground rocks with concentrated Raw Sienna and Burnt Sienna with a small amount of Cadmium Red Light.

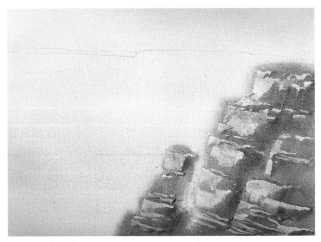

2. Model the Rocks by Scraping

When the foreground rocks dry to the damp stage, scrape back the light layers in the rock faces with a stiff palette knife.

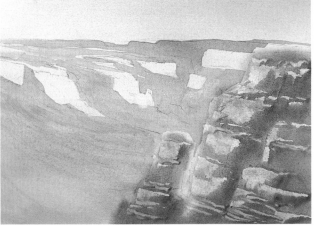

3. Add the Distant Hills

Lightly sketch the distant hills, taking note of the areas you want to stay sunlit. Paint the shadow area as a continuous shape using a pale mix of Cerulean Blue + Cadmium Red Light. Fade out this color as you come forward. Let dry.

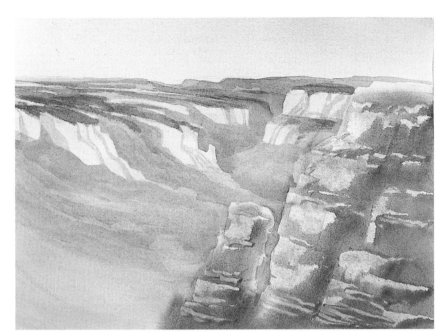

4. Define the Cliffs, Canyons and Ridges

Use a slightly darker version of the Cerulean Blue and Cadmium Red Light mixture to further define the cliffs, canyons and ridges in the distant shadow area. Keep the detail minimal in the sunlit areas. Paint the tops of the mesa and the vegetation on the slopes a pale, cool, dull green (Phthalo Blue + Burnt Sienna) in the distance.

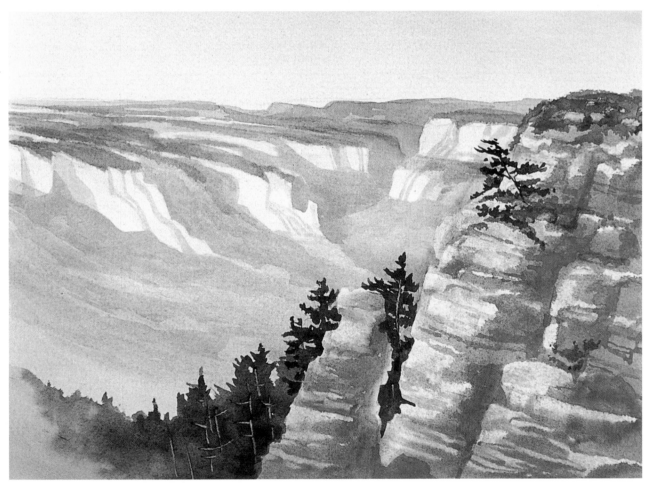

5. Add Foreground Contrasts

Using a darker mix of Phthalo Blue + Burnt Sienna, paint an ascending ridge of trees to contrast with the rock faces. Paint the cracks and crevices in the rock faces using a concentrated warm gray (Cadmium Red Light + Cerulean Blue). Have a damp brush ready to fade out the edges. Drybrush the vegetation using a small hog-hair bristle brush. Glaze major shadow areas with pale Cerulean Blue.

ARID HILLS
11" × 14" (28cm × 36cm)

Snowy Mountains

If you plan to paint mountains beyond this exercise, I strongly suggest that you study the structure of the mountains of your choice. Try to understand what you are looking at. A mountain is more than a two-dimensional chunk of the earth; it's a three-dimensional sculpture in progress. Try to reconstruct how the "artists" of nature—avalanches, glaciers, wind and rain—have wrought a piece of the earth to awe-inspiring beauty.

Reconstruct how gravity has torn away rock and debris from the top of a range and deposited it on the slopes around its base. Look for the strata or layers that are exposed and the pitch at which they are set. These lines define the face of the mountain while indicating places where snow can't cling or vegetation can. Find the major ridges that have resisted the elements. They are the backbone of the work.

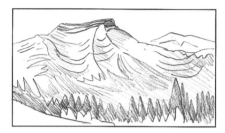

Record major ridges and valleys and strata in your thumbnail sketch.

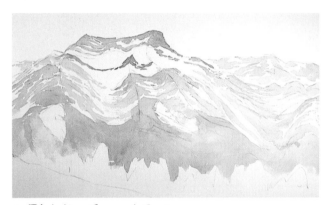

1. Paint the Exposed Rock

Use a large round or 1-inch (25mm) hog-hair bristle brush to paint the exposed rock on your mountains using a cool gray. Here I used Cerulean Blue + Indigo, lightening the value to indicate distant peaks. Carefully work your way across and down the mountains, taking time to capture the essence of the lines and patterns found there. Paint far down the mountainside. Let dry.

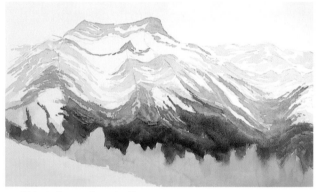

2. Paint the Vegetation

Back up your mountainside and start indicating vegetation with a 1-inch (25mm) bristle brush. Follow the ridges and valleys using a mix that starts as mainly Cerulean Blue with a touch of Indigo and gradates to mainly Sap Green with Indigo near the base. For contrast, leave an area for light trees in the foreground. Paint these yellowish green (Sap Green + Raw Sienna) when the background is dry. Also leave an area for foreground land.

COLOR NOTE

The major colors here are Cerulean Blue, Indigo and Sap Green. The minor colors are Burnt Sienna, Raw Sienna and Phthalo Blue.

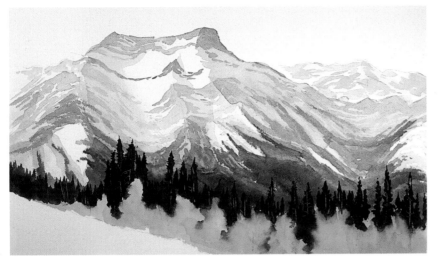

3. Add Mountain Shadows and the Forest

Use a large, synthetic flat brush to add shadows to your mountain with a pale blue-gray (Cerulean Blue + Indigo). Paint the dark evergreens with a concentrated Phthalo Blue + Burnt Sienna mixture. Soften the edges into the foreground bushes and scrape on light trunks with the tip of a palette knife.

TIP

Experiment with brush techniques (how you hold your brush and apply the stroke) on scrap paper before you start. You just might find a better way to make marks.

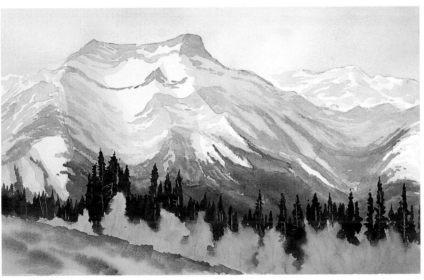

4. Paint the Sky and Final Details

Paint the sky by wetting it all over and then dropping Cerulean Blue at spots along the horizon. Tilt the painting upward so the blue runs off and white areas are left for the clouds.

Paint the foreground land a pale Raw Sienna. While this is damp, touch the area with a brush loaded with a darker green-brown texture and contrast with the light trees.

NEARING BANFF
11" × 14" (28cm × 36cm)

Index

Afternoon Birches, 31
Alberta April, 186
Analogous colors, 101, 167
Arid Hills, 279
Atmosphere, creating, 42, 185
    arid, 278–279
    cool, 52
    See also Mood
Autumn, 276
Autumn Birch, 55
Autumn Entrance, 265
Autumn Walk, 52

Background, 93
Backlighting, 88, 93, 173, 184, 261–263
Backrun. *See* Water blossom
Bar River Flats, 230
Bridge, compositional, 120
Brushes, 18–20, 156–157
    aquarelle, 157
    bristle, 18
    for fading out, 46
    filbert, 157
    flat, 18, 36–37, 49, 89, 156–159
    goat hair, 20
    hake, 20, 157
    hog hair, 18–20, 36–37, 48, 157
    hog hair, using, 156, 159, 173,
        213–215
    holding, 158–159
    masking, 54
    mop, 157
    ox hair, 19–20
    rigger, 18, 35, 157
    round, 19, 34
    sable, red, 19
    sabeline, 20
    script, 18, 35, 157
    scrubber, 42, 45, 156
    sizes of, 18–20, 131, 156
    snap of, 19
    stroke, 157
    student, 157
    synthetic, 18–20, 49, 54
    tooth-, 54, 135, 156
    using, 158–159, 163
    wash, 19–20, 157
    See also Techniques, brush
Brushstrokes
    natural versus synthetic bristles, 46
    practicing, 33
    See also Techniques, brush

Buried Treasure, 77
Butterflies, 55, 83, 100, 137, 141

Calm Below, The, 194
Camouflage, 84
Campfire, 85, 272–273
Canyon Glow, 186
Cast shadows, 76, 86–88, 110
Centers of interest, 65, 85, 185
    multiple, 66
    See also Focal point
Closure, using, 70–71, 73, 77, 226
Clouds, 156, 159, 232–240
    billowy, 234–237
    edges of, 162
    heavy, 233
    light effects on, 240
    negative painting, 73
    storm, 235
Color, 94–105, 178, 180–182
    analogous, 101, 167
    blending, 164
    choosing, 12, 167
    complementary, 101, 167
    emphasis, 95
    fugitive, 12
    gradation, 104–105, 164
    intensity, 94, 180, 185
    juxtaposition, 193–194
    layering, 153
    lifting, 42, 223
    mixing, 62–63, 180–182
    mixing, dark, 153, 262
    muddy, avoiding, 182
    muted, 84
    opaque, 12
    palette, 96–97 (*see also* Palette, color)
    permanent, 12
    primary, 97
    pulling, 46
    purity, 94
    saturation, 12–13, 180
    secondary, 103, 105
    in a series, 126–127
    transparent, 12–13, 73
    as a visual element, 94–105, 109,
        178, 180–182
    See also Watercolor
Color contrast, 98, 193–194
Color harmony, 98–99, 182
Color schemes, 100–103, 180, 182
    in a series, 127

    triad, 102–103, 182, 205
Color temperature, 52, 94–95, 97, 135,
    180–181
    and mood, 185
    in winter, 268–269
Color wheel, 94–95, 181
Colours and Lines, 137
Composition, 175–197
    angles in, 191–192
    binocular, 196
    bridge, 120
    changing, 79
    closure in, 70–71, 73, 77, 226
    considerations, 65–105
    and creativity, 79, 175–179 (*see also*
        Creativity)
    direction in, 80, 88, 203
    dynamics, 191
    hook-shaped, 118–119
    horizon placement in, 191
    intuitive, 115, 179
    leading the eye, 45, 65–68, 82–83,
        162, 193, 219
    light in, 86–87, 92–93, 183–184
    planning, 128–133, 178
    putting together a, 64
    references, visual, 106–109,
        112–113, 177–178
    self-critiquing, 178
    shadows, 88–89, 92–93
    sketching, 110, 276 (*see also*
        Sketching)
    space, dividing the, 66–67
    subject matter, 65–69, 196–197
    and the suspension theory, 191–192
    viewfinder, 111, 204
    See also Experimentation;
        Negative painting
Composition, approaches to, 106–123
    abstract to real, 114–121
    imagination, 122–123, 195
    memory, 122–123
    real to abstract, 106–113
Composition, elements and principles
    of, 178
    arranging, 109
    color, 94–105, 109, 178, 180–182
    color harmony, 98–99, 182
    contrast, 84–85, 98, 109, 178,
        193–194
    focal point, 65–66, 84–85, 136
        (*see also* Centers of interest)

format, 68–69, 197
gradation, 104–105
line, 109, 178, 191–192
mood, 85, 109, 178, 185 (*see also* Mood)
movement, 68, 80, 83, 178, 189, 191, 203
pattern, 81, 109, 188–189
perspective, 178, 186–190
repetition, 81
rhythm, 81
shape, 72–83, 109, 178
value, 84–85, 90–91, 109, 178
See also under specific element or principle
Contrast, 84–85, 178, 193–194
and center of interest, 85
color, 98
value, 84, 90, 182
Creativity, 64–65, 79
obstacles to, 128–133
See also Experimentation; Inspiration; Intuition
Current Explorers, 116
Cycles of Life, 200

Darks, 84, 90–91
fixing, 136
mixing, 153, 262
Dave's Pond, 182
Depth, creating, 42, 167
Detailing, fixing, 136
Diamond Dance, 204
Direction
cast shadow, 88
of shapes, 80
of waves, 203
Distance, depicting, 186–189, 203
line, 186
pattern, fan, 188, 266
pattern, zigzag, 189, 201–203
shapes, 186
See also Depth, creating
Dots, paint, fixing, 136
Drama, adding, 183, 232, 235
Dream Lights, 63
Drybrush. *See* Techniques, drybrush
Dutchman's Breeches, 107

Edge of the Greenwood, 265
Edges, 191
fixing, 135–136

hard, 46, 82, 135
leading the eye with, 82
shape, 78
soft, 46, 82, 161–162
Entrance, 150
Evergreens, 252–253, 259–260, 274–276
Experimentation, 170, 196–197
brush, 281
color, 170
Eye, leading the, 45, 65–68, 82–83, 162, 193, 219

Ferns, 72, 257
Fields, 156
Figure. *See* Subject matter
Fish, 229
Fishing gear, 66
Flight, 83
Flowers, 35, 65, 107–108, 137–139, 158
apple blossom, 86
color, varying, 127
masking, 55
negative painting, 53, 74–75
pansy, 104
repeated, 104
in a series, 126
and shapes, 78
Flowers of the Forest, 197
Focal point, 65–66
fixing a, 136
See also Centers of interest
Foliage, 156, 250, 253
light and shadow, 92–93
masking, multiple, 124
Forest, 259–265, 268–269
See also Trees
Forest Light, 196
Formats, 68–69, 197

Gathering of the Clan, 141
Glazes, 44–45, 164
Gradation, 188
color, 104–105, 164
wash, 44, 164, 238–240
Grass, 158, 256, 264–265
brushstroke, 34
palette knife, 170, 173
Grays, mixing, 180, 182
Greens, mixing, 181, 276
Ground, 72

Hard edges, 46, 82
fixing, 135
Harold's Bench, 79
Headwaters, 42
Highlights, fixing, 136
Hills, 77, 274–279
arid, 278–279
misty, 277
negative painting, 77
winter, 274–275
Homesteads, 105, 126, 270–271
Hooked in the Past, 229
Hue, 94, 180
Human figures, and direction, 80

Ice, 215
Imagination, 122–123, 195
Inspiration, 195
See also Creativity
Into the Shallows, 197
Intuition
composing with, 115, 179
controlling, 114
defined, 128
painting with, 128
seeing with, 110
Intuition, versus planning, 128–133
blocks to spontaneity, 129–131
openness to possibilities, 133
realism, 133
smell of fear, 132
style development, 133

Knife, palette, 28, 49, 54
techniques, 38–39, 170, 173, 253

Lake Country Autumn, 193
Lake Spirit, 52
Leaves, 35–36, 158, 192, 262
edge quality of, 82
Light, 183–184
back-, 88, 93, 173, 184, 261–263
campfire, 85, 272–273
evening, 183, 232
on foliage, 92–93
front-, 184, 264–265
moon-, 232
reflected, 86, 247
shimmering, 109
side-, 184
sky-, 86–87, 184
sponged, 42

subdued, 84
sun-, 86–87, 93, 183
sun-, late afternoon, 274–275
translucent, 86–87
types of, 183, 185
See also Northern lights
Light in the Forest, 30
Lines, 78, 109, 178, 186
   angled versus straight, 78
   brushstroke, 34
   close, 35
   converging, 88
   defining areas with, 118
   flowing through shapes, 116
   and movement, 83, 203
   palette knife, 38
   width of, controlling, 34–37
Liquid Diamonds, 67
Liquid latex. *See* Masking fluid
Local shadows, 86–87

Masking, 30–31, 54–61, 168–169, 217
   multiple, 56–59
   and paper quality, 168
   planning, 268
   removing, 54, 58
Masking fluid, 30–31, 54–56, 168–169,
   216–217
Meadow, 256
Media, mixed, 197
Memories, 140
Memory, working from, 122–123
Mental blocks, overcoming, 132
Monochromatic color scheme, 100
Mood, 45, 178, 185
   creating, wet-in-wet, 52
   fixing, 135
   and value, 85, 185
Moon, 232
Morning Dance One, 206
Morning Dance Two, 206
Mountains, snowy, 280–281
Movement, 68, 83, 178, 189, 203

Narrows, The, 42
Nearing Banff, 281
Negative painting, 73–77, 166–167, 240
   closure in, 73, 77
   defined, 33
   flowers, 74–75
   hills, 77
   layering, 73, 167

pigments for, choosing, 73
   rocks, 76
   trees, 166, 219, 273
Northern lights, 193, 241
November Blues, 63

October Point, 148
On Silent Wings, 269
On the Rocks, 42
On Time Cartage, 83
Out of the Mists, 277

Paint. *See* Watercolor
Painting, 85
   evaluating a, 134–136
   a series, 124–127
   See also Creativity; Intuition
Painting sticks, 28, 39, 54
Paintings, problems with, 134–136
Palette, color
   layout, 24, 96–97, 181
   layout, fixing a, 129
Palette, high-key, 96
Palette knife, 28
   masking, 54
   painting, 38–39, 49, 170, 173
Palettes, painting, 24–27, 165
   choosing, 165
   making, 26–27
   storing, 24
   types of, 24
   well shapes, 25, 129
Pansies, 104
Paper, 21–23, 165
   stretching, 23
   texture, 22
   types of, 21
   weight, 23
   wetting, 58, 160, 231
Passage, shape, 72, 74
Pattern
   and balance, 105
   fan, 188, 266
   in a series, 127
   shape, 81
   types of, 188–189
   zigzag, 189, 201–203
Perspective, 178, 186–190
   eye level line, 186–188
   distance in, creating, 186–189
   model for, using a, 190

vanishing point, 188
   waves, 201
Photos, using, 106–109, 112–113,
   177–178
Planning, 132, 178
   See also Intuition, versus planning
Planting Time, 65
Plants, tropical, 254–255
Players of Spring, 139
Point at Ostler Lake, 109
Point of view, 126, 197
   in a series, 126
   and shapes, 78
Promises of Spring, 31

Rails End Surprise, 192
Rain, 233, 235
Realism, 133
Reducing glass, 134
References, photo, 106–109, 112–113,
   177–178
Reflections
   calm, 211, 215
   laws of, 209–210
   sky, 226–227
   tree, 215
   water, 161, 189, 208–211
Renewal, 8
Repetition, shape, 81
Research, 115
Rhythm, shape, 81
Ripple Study, 208
River Diamonds, detail, 84
Roads, 189, 266–267
Rocks, 76, 156, 159, 161, 218–219,
   245–247
   beach, 246
   light on, reflected, 184, 247
   mottled, 62
   negative painting, 76
   palette knife, 212
   spattered, 173, 245
   sponged, 42
   stenciled, 267
   underwater, 226–227, 229
Rock's Edge, 120
Rose Buds, 75
Rounding the Point, 196
Royal Visit, 55
Runback. *See* Water blossom

St. Polycarp, France, 197

Salt, using, 41, 50
Sea spray, 216–217
Seasons, 124–125
Sentries of the Heart, 199
Series, painting a, 124–127
Shades. *See* Value, dark
Shadows
    adding, 59
    brush for, 89
    cast, 86–88, 110, 247
    converging versus parallel, 89
    foliage, 92–93
    local, 86–87
    and sky light, 86–87
    warm and cool, 86–87
    wet-in-wet, 92
Shapes, 178
    background, 53
    brushstrokes for, 33
    classifying, 79
    and direction, 80
    edges of, 78
    embellishing, 118
    feelings implied by, 78
    foreground, 53, 56, 59
    grouping, 81
    hook, 118
    implications of, 79
    leading the eye with, 82
    lines of, 78
    masking out, 56–58
    and movement, 83
    negative, 72 (*see also* Negative
        painting)
    outlining, 112
    overlapping, 116, 186
    pattern of, 81
    and point of view, 78
    positive, 72
    repetitive, 81
    and rhythm, 81
    seeing, 112, 134
    shading, 118
    sponged, 30
    value, 90–91, 110
    as visual elements, 109
Sightings, 267
Sketching, 110–121, 276
    abstract to real, 114–115
    a bridge, 120
    idea exploration through, 121
    from imagination, 122–123, 195

and intuition, 110, 114–115
    lines, 118
    from memory, 122–123
    real to abstract, 112–113
    shapes, lines and shading, 116
    shapes, shading and embellishing,
        118
    value, 90–91, 112–113
    variations, 116, 118
    viewfinder, 111
    See also Composition
Skies, 230–243
    lifting color from, 240–241
    dropping paint onto, 243
    dropping water onto, 243
    dynamic, 242
    reflected, 226–227
    spraying and tilting, 242
    wash, graded, 238–240
    wet-in-wet, 63, 231–232
    See also Clouds
Sky holes, 231, 233
Skylight, 86–87, 184
Snow, 185, 215
Snow Before Its Time, 193
Snowstorm, 268–269
Solar Symphony, 193
Solitude, 275
Solitudes, 123
Southwest Homestead, 105
Space, picture, dividing, 66–67
    See also Negative painting
Splatters, fixing, 136
Sponges, 29
    elephant's ear, 135
    holding, 40
    loading, 40
    masking, 54
    negative-space, 77
    preparing, 29
    sea, natural, 29, 49
    and shapes, 30, 41
    using, 40–41, 49
Spray bottle, choosing a, 160
Spring Chorus, 138
Stamping, 54
Star Light, Star Bright, 85
Stars, 232, 272–273
Sticks, painting, 28, 39
Stream Study, 192
Strokes. *See* Brushstrokes
Style, developing a, 133

Subject matter, 72, 65–69, 196–197
    choosing, 65
    finding, 196
Sulfur, 119
Summer Apartments, 110–111
Summer Choristers, 53
Summer Dancers, 117
Summer Light, 119, 263
Summer Respite, 248
Summer's Arsenal, 66
Sun Flurries, 185
Sunlight, 86–87, 93, 183
Sunset Swells, Lake of the Woods, 192
Sunspots, 42, 62, 266–267
Superior, North Shore, 225
Supper's Ready, 271
Supplies. *See* Tools
Surf Rider, 222

Tape, masking with, 30–31, 60,
    168–169
Technique, wet-in-wet, 48–53, 160,
    227, 232, 235
    adding paint, 49
    adding salt, 50
    ethereal effects, 52
    examples of, 52–53, 63
    for mood, 52
    mottled effect, 231
    for removing color, 50–51
    shadows, 92
    shapes, 53
    wetting the paper for, 48
Techniques, 152, 172–173
    color, lifting, 173, 223
    color, pouring, 59
    drybrush, 213–214, 218, 239
    fading out, 46–47, 161–163, 172,
        233–234
    glazing, 44–45, 153, 164
    masking, 54–61, 168–169
    painting stick, 39
    palette knife, 38–39, 170, 173, 253
    sanding, 216
    scraping, 170
    spattering, 49, 173, 217, 245
    sponge, 40–42, 171–173, 253
    tilting the surface, 172, 231
    water, dropping, 172
    wet-in-wet, 48–53, 172, 212, 220
    wet-on-damp, 160, 231–232
    wet-on-dry, 160, 213, 231

See also Negative painting; Texture; Washes; *and under specific technique*
Techniques, brush, 33–37, 158–159, 253
  butt end, using the, 55
  contouring, 33
  dragging, 37
  drybrush, 37, 159, 213–214, 218, 239
  flat, 18, 36–37, 49, 89, 156–159
  leaf strokes, 35–36
  line width, 34–37
  lines, close, 36
  paint application, 49
  paper wetting, 48
  practicing, 33
  rigger, 34–35
  round, 34
  script, 35
  scrubbing, 47
  spattering, 49, 54, 245
  texturing, 37
  twisting, 35–36
  zigzagging, 37
Texture, 37, 159, 218
  paper, 22
  salt, 41
  in a series, 127
  sponge, 171
  variety in, 127
Time of day
  dusk to dawn, 196, 270–273
  night, 232, 272–273
  See also Light
Tints, 84
  See also Value
Tools, 10, 152
  buying, 10, 165
  spray bottle, 160
  See also under specific tool
Trees, 63, 100, 159, 173, 248–255
  birch, 55
  branching, 34–35, 249, 251
  coniferous, 252–253, 259–260, 274–276
  deciduous, 249–252
  foliage, 250, 253
  forest of, 259–265
  line of, 259–260
  masking, 55
  negative painting, 166, 219, 273

palette knife, 38–39, 63, 170, 173
palm, 254–255
reflections of, 215
sponged, 41–42, 240
trunks, 249, 258
Triads, color, 102–103, 182
  mixing, 205, 270
Trout Stream, 62

Under the Stars, 273

Vacancy, 256
Value, 178, 180
  and color selection, 94
  contrast, 84, 193–194
  dark, 84, 90–91
  defined, 84
  dominance, 85
  fixing, 135
  identifying, 90
  incorrect or ineffective, 135
  light, 84, 90–91
  medium, 90–91
  and mood, 135, 185
  reversing or rearranging, 91
  seeing, 90–91, 110, 112, 134
  sketching, 90–91, 112–113
  as visual elements, 109
Vantage Point, 188
Viewfinder, using a, 111, 204

Washes, 19–20, 44–45, 164
  drybrush on, 239
  graded, 238–240
  hot-in-cold, 239
  partial, 214–215
Water, 63, 100, 200–229
  big, 220–221
  calm, 202, 204
  choppy, 202
  foamy, 156, 159, 222
  moving, 192, 212–215
  moving, interrupted, 204
  rapids, 212–213, 218–219
  reflections on, 208–211
  rippling, 207–208
  sea spray, 216–217, 220–221
  seeing into, 226–227
  sparkling, 62, 67, 109, 204–205, 232
  spraying, 49
  turbulent, 204

under-, negative painting, 77
under-, seeing, 116, 194, 197, 228–229
whitecap, 223–225
See also Waves
Water blossom, 43, 135, 160
Water Music, 244
Watercolor, 11–17, 153–155
  to avoid, 16–17, 154
  buying, 153–154
  characteristics, 13–15, 153
  choosing, 12
  differences, 14
  flow, 12
  fugitive, 12
  hydrodynamics, 43, 161
  labeling, 16, 154
  names, 15–17, 154
  numbers, 16–17, 153–154
  opaque, 12, 153
  permanency, 12
  pouring, 49
  quality, 13–15, 153–155
  reliability, 16–17, 153–154
  saturation, 12
  semitransparent, 12, 153
  staining, 12, 34, 153, 170
  transparent, 153
  types of, 153
  values, 94
  See also Color
Waterfalls, 212, 215, 218
  negative painting, 76
Waves, 158, 192, 201–206, 220–221
  breaking, 224–225
  crashing, 213
  direction of, 203
  flowing, 213
  light on, 225
  surface patterns, 203–204
  swelling, 192, 202
  whitecap, 223–225
Weathered palette, 96
Wet-in-wet. *See* Technique, wet-in-wet
Wild Flags, 108
Winter Closing, 174
Winter Rays, 123

The material in this compilation appeared in the following previously published North Light Books, and appears here by permission of the author. (The initial page numbers given refer to pages in the original work; pages numbers in parentheses refer to pages in this book.)

MacKenzie, Gordon, *The Watercolorist's Essential Notebook* ©1999, 2–141 (2–141)

MacKenzie, Gordon, *The Watercolorist's Essential Notebook: Landscapes* ©2006, 2–141 (142– 281)

ISBN-13: 978-1-4403-0905-2

 Other fine North Light Books are available from your local bookstore, art supply store or online supplier. Visit our website at www.fwmedia.com.

20 19 18 17   13 12 11 10

DISTRIBUTED IN CANADA BY FRASER DIRECT
100 Armstrong Avenue
Georgetown, ON, Canada L7G 5S4
Tel: (905) 877-4411

DISTRIBUTED IN THE U.K. AND EUROPE BY F+W MEDIA INTERNATIONAL
Brunel House, Newton Abbot, Devon, TQ12 4PU, England
Tel: (+44) 1626 323200, Fax: (+44) 1626 323319
Email: postmaster@davidandcharles.co.uk

DISTRIBUTED IN AUSTRALIA BY CAPRICORN LINK
P.O. Box 704, S. Windsor NSW, 2756 Australia
Tel: (02) 4577-3555

Ideas. Instruction. Inspiration.

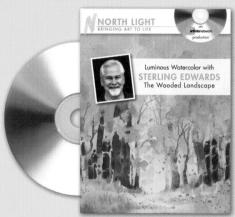
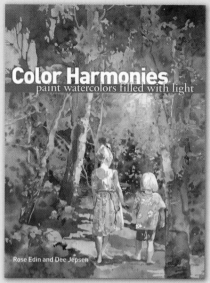
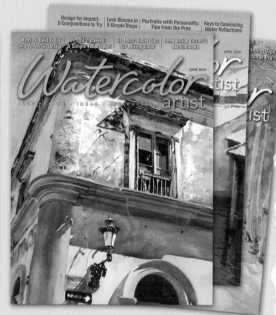
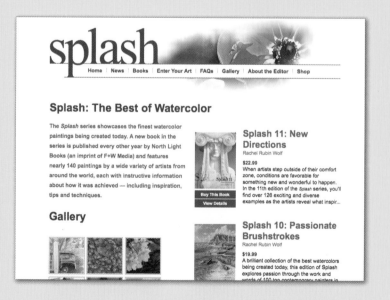